THE
SKETCHUP
WORKFLOW
FOR ARCHITECTURE

For my mom, Becky Yovich, in appreciation of her infinite love, support, and encouragement.

For my loyal dog, Kodiak, whose daily companionship and late night camaraderie are sincerely missed.

And for my wonderful and loving wife, Marisa, who keeps a smile on my face.

THE
SketchUp
WORKFLOW
FOR ARCHITECTURE

Modeling Buildings, Visualizing Design, and Creating Construction Documents with SketchUp Pro and LayOut

Second Edition

MICHAEL BRIGHTMAN

WILEY

Library of Congress Cataloging-in-Publication Data:

Names: Brightman, Michael, 1980- author.
Title: The SketchUp workflow for architecture : modeling buildings,
    visualizing design, and creating construction documents with SketchUp Pro
    and LayOut / by Michael Brightman.
Description: Second edition. | Hoboken, New Jersey : Wiley, 2018. | Includes
    index. |
Identifiers: LCCN 2018011134 (print) | LCCN 2018011521 (ebook) | ISBN 9781119383635 (paperback) |
ISBN 9781119383659 (epdf) | ISBN 9781119383642 (epub) | ISBN 9781119410171 (oBook)
Subjects: LCSH: Architectural drawing—Computer-aided design. | Architectural
    Design—Data processing. | SketchUp. | BISAC: ARCHITECTURE / Design,
    Drafting, Drawing & Presentation.
Classification: LCC NA2728 (ebook) | LCC NA2728 .B75 2018 (print) | DDC
    720.28/40285668—dc23
LC record available at https://lccn.loc.gov/2018011134

Printed in the United States of America

V10002635_071918

Contents

Visit **brightmandesigns.com/TSWFA** for access to companion tutorial videos and other resources related to the book.

Visit **brightmandesigns.com/TSWFA** for access to companion tutorial videos and other resources related to the book.

PART I

Starting the Flow

Get ready to elevate your SketchUp skills and design workflow to the highest radical extremes of efficiency. *The SketchUp Workflow for Architecture* contains tips, tricks, and strategies for modeling in SketchUp as well as methods to leverage SketchUp and LayOut during every step of the design process. Let's start with a few tips on how to get the most out of this book, how building information modeling (BIM) plays a part in the SketchUp workflow, how to select a computer for three-dimensional (3D) modeling and design, and how to effectively manage a PROJECT folder.

The big idea is that this book shows the big picture, fills in some details, and directs you to fill in other details on your own. Tech changes fast, so it's better to understand the big picture. Be armed with the tools to figure it out on your own. Always know you can find the latest on the Brightman Designs blog and "The SketchUp Workflow for Architecture" page at brightmandesigns.com/TSWFA.

Chapter 1
Introduction

This book is the missing set of standards for SketchUp and LayOut. *The SketchUp Workflow for Architecture* provides a flexible, clear set of rules for organizing any type of building project in SketchUp: renovation, new construction, residential, commercial, high-rise, low-rise, industrial. It is up to the user to process these techniques and strategies and then apply them to projects. In this chapter, you will pick up a few tips on how to best absorb the information and get the most out of this book.

This book covers advanced concepts performed with advanced operations. These are not work-arounds; rather, they are clever ways to use SketchUp to expedite the design process. With *The SketchUp Workflow for Architecture* and some practice, you will be able to:

- ☑ Speak knowledgeably about BIM
- ☑ Select the right computer for 3D modeling and design
- ☑ Speak confidently about computer components, hardware, and specs
- ☑ Organize and manage PROJECT folders in an efficient manner
- ☑ Effectively use the modeling tools and organization containers in SketchUp
- ☑ Create and customize a time-saving SketchUp template
- ☑ Tailor the SketchUp modeling environment to fit your professional needs
- ☑ Create and organize collections for materials, components, styles, and templates
- ☑ Find, install, and utilize valuable extensions
- ☑ Fully understand the value of LayOut and its dynamic links to SketchUp and other insertable content
- ☑ Tailor the LayOut drafting environment to fit your professional needs

- ☑ Find or create building context models around a specific site
- ☑ Efficiently document existing buildings and create accurate as-built drawings using SketchUp Pro and LayOut
- ☑ Transition a design model into an accurate 3D model
- ☑ Create inspiring LayOut presentations that accurately represent your designs
- ☑ Accurately model and organize various types of buildings in SketchUp Pro
- ☑ Prepare a model for photorealistic renderings and virtual reality presentations
- ☑ Extract information from SketchUp and LayOut in useful formats for use in other computer-aided design (CAD) programs, for yourself and consultants
- ☑ Create and organize collections for scrapbooks and title blocks
- ☑ Compile and draft construction documents using SketchUp Pro and LayOut

THE UPDATED WORKFLOW

The term *"workflow"* loosely describes the collection of tools designers use and the order in which they use those tools to produce a final design. Designers use many different tools and software to produce their final products, which are typically new, built environments; some of many initial products are construction documents.

Many different workflows can be used to design and create construction documents; however, the best workflows minimize the use of several different programs because something always gets lost during translation between programs.

The workflow explained in this book uses SketchUp and LayOut as the primary tool for every phase of the design process. You can use other programs to supplement SketchUp, but SketchUp Pro and LayOut are at the core of this process. For example, you could use an image editor to postprocess exports and modify textures, but you will simply be using the image editor to complement SketchUp. As another example, you could use a spreadsheet program for schedules, but keep all your drafting in SketchUp and LayOut.

There are also peripheral programs such as Lumion for photorealistic rendering and extensions such as ConDoc that will drastically increase efficiency when using this system.

TIP ConDoc was created after the first edition was published. This extension simplifies and automates the entire SketchUp Workflow for Architecture and is highly recommended for professionals.

This workflow is not a regimented design process; you can adapt all or part of it and use the organizational and design tips. The process of moving from sketches to construction documents is expedited by the SketchUp Workflow for Architecture (Figure 1.1).

The evolution of a client's vision to an actual building involves many small steps and phases. There is no right or wrong way to produce a design, but there are critics out there who will judge your designs. The

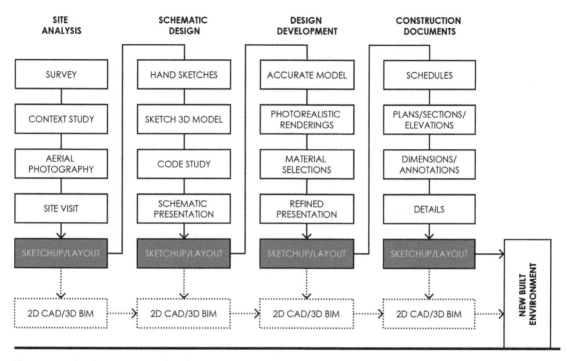

SITE ANALYSIS	SCHEMATIC DESIGN	DESIGN DEVELOPMENT	CONSTRUCTION DOCUMENTS
SURVEY	HAND SKETCHES	ACCURATE MODEL	SCHEDULES
CONTEXT STUDY	SKETCH 3D MODEL	PHOTOREALISTIC RENDERINGS	PLANS/SECTIONS/ ELEVATIONS
AERIAL PHOTOGRAPHY	CODE STUDY	MATERIAL SELECTIONS	DIMENSIONS/ ANNOTATIONS
SITE VISIT	SCHEMATIC PRESENTATION	REFINED PRESENTATION	DETAILS
SKETCHUP/LAYOUT	SKETCHUP/LAYOUT	SKETCHUP/LAYOUT	SKETCHUP/LAYOUT
2D CAD/3D BIM	2D CAD/3D BIM	2D CAD/3D BIM	2D CAD/3D BIM

NEW BUILT ENVIRONMENT

Figure 1.1 The SketchUp Workflow for Architecture.

most important audiences, however, are your clients. The more time you spend on the design, the better. The SketchUp Workflow for Architecture is focused on design and will ultimately provide more time for you to explore real designs in three dimensions.

WHO SHOULD READ THIS BOOK?

Anyone interested in mastering SketchUp will benefit greatly from this book—architects, landscape architects, designers, interior designers, contractors. Large firms, one-man shows, and every office size in between can benefit. If you are using SketchUp to design a built space, you should practice the SketchUp Workflow for Architecture. Most sizable firms already have a design workflow with 3D BIM software and standards in place. BIM is excellent for huge projects with extensive scheduling and square footage, but does it really help on the smaller projects? For large firms, the SketchUp Workflow for Architecture will fit in where a bloated, overfeatured software suite is not necessary. Also, large firms will benefit from the standards, which will get the entire team on the same page. The techniques in this book give you the freedom to simplify your model by including only the building information you need to get the project done on time.

On the other end of the spectrum is the one-man show looking to cut overhead costs. When compared to other popular design and documentation programs available on the market, this workflow is very inexpensive. By adding a few plugins to SketchUp Pro, you'll have full capability to efficiently design, draft, render, analyze, and document any project.

This book speaks directly to professionals, someone who works for fees and has the ability to invest time and money to increase workflow efficiency. A professional sees a benefit in charging fixed fees and finding tools that reduce hours, realizing higher hourly rates. This book will make you faster, more organized and efficient, resulting in faster turnarounds and increased profits.

Anyone who reads this book will take away excellent organization and problem-solving strategies for SketchUp. The techniques presented will help any designer create more engaging and accurate 3D models that are easily shared across several platforms.

WHAT'S IN THIS BOOK?

The advanced concepts and operations covered in this book are organized into five separate and distinct parts.

Part I: Starting the Flow

Part I takes care of some administrative tasks and disclaimers common in an instructional software book. In Part I, you will learn the benefits of using SketchUp Pro and LayOut, and you will be introduced to the power of this system. Also, you will be exposed to a new way of thinking about BIM. The intimidating task of selecting a computer is demystified. Part I wraps up by explaining folder and file organization techniques that will help keep your projects running smoothly.

Part II: SketchUp

In Part II, you will learn the basic, intermediate, and advanced SketchUp skills necessary to complete the exercises in this book. You will also tune your SketchUp environment for professional use. You will learn to create utility styles and scenes, custom layers, and ultimately your own custom default template. Even if you are an experienced SketchUp user, you will benefit from the refresher and most likely will develop a new understanding of the old features.

Figure 1.2 The SketchUp logo.

Part III: LayOut

Part III is an "everything you need to know" guide for LayOut. At times, this section may read more like a manual than a tutorial because it explains every menu, dialog, and setting you will come across in SketchUp's two-dimensional (2D) counterpart. Study this part closely even if you have used LayOut previously. The skills you learn in Part III will make you a fast and effective draftsman.

Figure 1.3 The LayOut logo.

Part IV: Model Organization

Part IV is everything you need to know about putting your model together, an overview map of nesting groups and layering. This part includes a detailed description of each layer and the contents that belong in the group it is assigned. In this part, you will also see a full illustration of a renovation and new construction timeline. When you start a new project, you will likely visit this chapter when you kick off. This is a reference chapter that will keep you on track for many years to come.

Part V: Visualization

Part V is a crash course in visualization, which is used to communicate design in different media. Each presentation type, stills, animations, virtual tours, and virtual reality all have respective strengths and weaknesses and appropriate times to be used. You will learn about preparing a model for rendering in SketchUp and LayOut and open your workflow to endless professional visual capabilities with external rendering programs and internal extensions. Although you won't get a lot of step-by-step instructions, you will learn where to look for more information and how to prepare your models for any visualization program.

Part VI: Construction Documents

Part VI brings everything together for the final dance. Meticulous model organization pays off big when you are building construction documents. You will now dissect your model to stack viewports into descriptive construction diagrams including multiple types of plans, sections, elevations, and details. Included in this part are more than a dozen recipes for mixing styles, layers, and line weights into beautiful construction documents. This part also covers creating title blocks, compiling scrapbook collections, and adding annotations to clarify your drawings. Part VI closes with exporting for print, sharing work with consultants, and migrating to other CAD programs.

WHAT ARE THE PREREQUISITES?

This is an extremely advanced book. It assumes that you are already familiar with many of the tools and basic functions in SketchUp, including groups, components, edges, surfaces, dividing surfaces, styles, layers, and scenes. You also need to know and understand basic computer terms and concepts such as right-click, left-click, windows, files, folders, drop-down menus, zipped, unzip, extract, etc.

To make the most of this book, you should have some experience with SketchUp, but even if you don't, you can still benefit. You don't have to have any experience with LayOut. Parts II and III cover the essential skills you'll need to complete the advanced exercises in Parts IV, V, and VI.

The following resources will help you make the most of this book:

☑ SketchUp for Professionals is an excellent class to help you get over the initial SketchUp learning curve; it is offered for free at **brightmandesigns.com/learn**. The topics covered in SketchUp for Professionals

Figure 1.4 The SketchUp for Professionals logo.

include creating geometry, modifying geometry, ConDoc tools, LayOut, inference locking, and ultimately building and rendering a master suite. It includes several building exercises that pull everything together and extended content that is commercially available.

☑ SketchUp for Professionals Advanced is a commercially available class that covers the next level of intermediate concepts; it is available at **brightmandesigns.com/learn**. The topics covered include groups, components, layers, scenes, styles, LayOut, geo-modeling, and effective model organization. Complex modeling operations to create geometry show you how to build the models that you will use in this book from the very beginning.

☑ LayOut for Professionals is a commercially available class that covers LayOut, step by step, from the beginning. It is offered at **brightmandesigns.com/learn**.

☑ File Management for Professionals is a commercially available class that covers the basics of managing and organizing your projects, resources, and computer. Avoid losing work and save time with these strategies. This course is offered at **brightmandesigns.com/learn**.

These classes are a tremendous help before absorbing everything in this book and provide a solid foundation, but they are not required to utilize the SketchUp Workflow for Architecture. Everything you need to organize your models is included in this book.

SKETCHUP MAKE OR SKETCHUP PRO?

SketchUp Make and my.SketchUp are for hobbyists—they are intended for the weekend warrior designing a deck or a doghouse. These free versions have been stripped of many capabilities that are needed to create professional presentations; they lack exporters for 3D models and can't create high-resolution images or animations, features that professionals need.

SketchUp Pro contains everything professionals need to create engaging and precise presentations that accurately represent their designs. Using the Pro version, you can present and explain 3D designs in LayOut (2D page-creation software included with SketchUp Pro), use several export options to share work (including .dwg format), and create high-definition (HD) animations and high-resolution renderings. Figure 1.5 compares the features of SketchUp and SketchUp Pro.

TIP Read the end-user licensed agreement—you have agreed to not use the free version for commercial projects. If you are making money in any way using SketchUp for work, you should pay for a pro license.

SketchUp Features	Make	Pro
Build 3D models	✓	✓
Geo-locate Models	✓	✓
Import CAD files	✗	✓
Export CAD and PDF files	✗	✓
Create multipage presentation sets	✗	✓
Produce construction drawings	✗	✓
Export animation videos of any size	✗	✓
Present files and full-screen presentations	✗	✓
Add custom attributes and behaviors	✗	✓
Generate lists and reports	✗	✓
Use solid modeling tools	✗	✓
Make hand-drawn rendering styles	✗	✓
Work with simulated film cameras	✗	✓
Email technical support	✗	✓
Licensed for commercial use	✗	✓
Import, export, and create IFC files	✗	✓
Use terrain and satellite imagery with geo-located models	✗	✓

Figure 1.5 Features of SketchUp and SketchUp Pro

ONLINE CONTENT

Many of the exercises in this book require digital files to illustrate certain points in the tutorials. You can download all of the class files for the entire book at **brightmandesigns.com/TSWFA**. Once you have downloaded the files, extract the folder and all contents to your desktop or an appropriate project folder (or to the TEMP folder, see Chapter 4, File and Folder Management).

Additional video tutorial explanations, models, case studies, title blocks, scrapbooks, and project models are available at **brightmandesigns.com/TSWFA**. This site complements this book and expands on advanced topics. Any updates to the workflow, news, and extra content will always be easily accessible from this page.

MENTAL PREPARATION

SketchUp is fast, fun, and intuitive—but only after a lot of practice! SketchUp is not easy. SketchUp marketing has focused on the simple use of the program, despite its professional capabilities. It is extremely approachable in that you can open the program, click on the Line tool, and start drawing. Shortly after you create your first surface, the Push/Pull tool will enable you to quickly generate massive amounts of 3D geometry. However, once you start modeling with these simple tools, you'll quickly have more questions than answers. This lack of knowledge coupled with the desire to perform advanced operations can cause frustration.

Mentally prepare yourself to learn this software and the workflow presented in this book. Push aside any preconceived notions of "3D for everyone." Ignore your colleague's comments about SketchUp being easy to learn, simple to use, and not nearly as powerful as other 3D programs. SketchUp is similar to other CAD, BIM, and modeling programs in that you need to spend a significant amount of time learning to use it in order to fully leverage it. Accept the fact that any program is easy to open and play with, but to fully understand any 3D application, including SketchUp, you'll need to fully invest your time, patience, and effort.

PORTFOLIO

The examples in Figures 1.6 through 1.12 are just some of the types of models and documents you can create using the SketchUp Workflow for Architecture. See the latest and greatest of Brightman Design's portfolio at **brightmandesigns.com/portfolio**. We rarely show our SketchUp models as final output. With the progression of Lumion, why would you? The following is our portfolio of SketchUp models rendered in Lumion and ConDoc construction documents drafted in LayOut.

Figure 1.6 One of the projects used later in this book to describe a new construction project is a hip new coffee shop in the River North district in Denver. Design, Lumion renderings, and SketchUp model by Brightman Designs.

Figure 1.6 (continued)

Figure 1.7 The 3655 Milwaukee Renovation is used later in this book to describe a renovation project. Design, SketchUp model, and Lumion renderings by Brightman Designs.

Figure 1.8 SketchUp models rendered in Lumion make a much more refined and polished presentation. Here, Bay Club Sofi. Design by others; model and renderings by Brightman Designs.

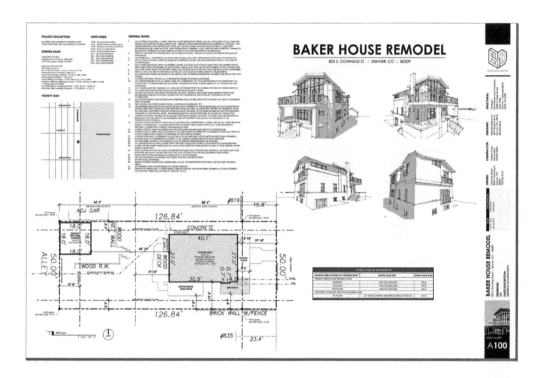

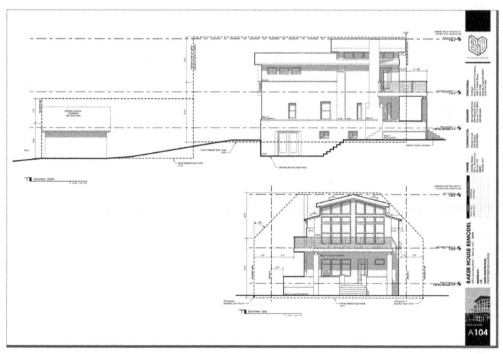

Figure 1.9 SketchUp Pro and LayOut have the full capability to produce large sets of construction documents. Here, Washington Park Home remodel in Denver. Design, SketchUp model, and drawings by Brightman Designs.

Figure 1.10 Create a winter scene by lightening and desaturating texture images. Here, Timber Creek at Okemo house. Design by Bensonwood Homes; model by Brightman Designs.

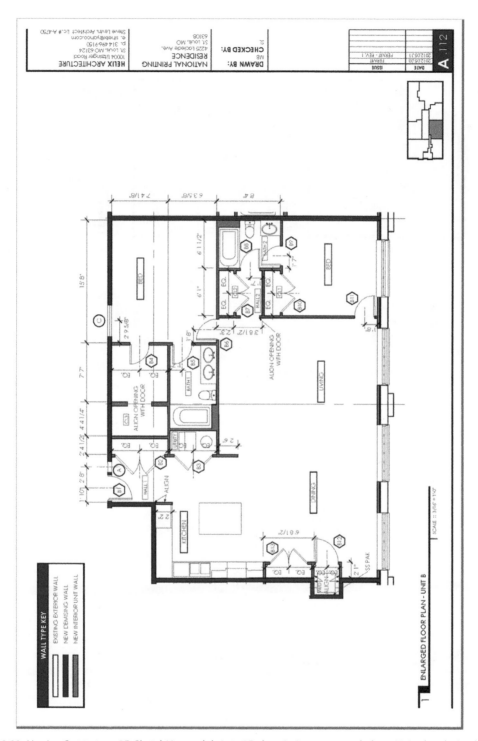

Figure 1.11 Use LayOut to turn 3D SketchUp models into 2D descriptive annotated plans. Unit plan design by Stephen Levin, Helix Architecture; SketchUp model and drawings by Brightman Designs.

Figure 1.12 By combining geo-modeling techniques and accurate modeling strategies, you can quickly and accurately communicate realistic design possibilities. Proposed Lowry House addition. Design and model by Brightman Designs.

CHAPTER POINTS

☑ Download all book resource files at **brightmandesigns.com/TSWFA**.

☑ SketchUp for Professionals is a comprehensive course, a highly recommended prerequisite for this book. It and additional online content can be found at **brightmandesigns.com/learn**.

☑ Mentally prepare yourself for a rewarding challenge while completing the exercises in this book.

☑ The workflow presented in this book centers around SketchUp Pro and LayOut but it also recognizes that many other software packages complement the design process.

☑ The SketchUp Workflow for Architecture is not a rigid system. It can be changed or abandoned at any stage of the design process. This workflow can be used in part or in its entirety.

☑ Many of the tedious tasks in this book can be automated and expedited by the ConDoc Tools extension for SketchUp.

Chapter 2
Building Information Modeling

Building information modeling (BIM) is a continued buzz in architectural design and drafting. Is BIM a revolution or just the way the industry works these days? In this chapter, you will be encouraged to contemplate and challenge the popular assumptions and standard definition of BIM. By doing so, you should realize that integrating the benefits of BIM into your workflow is easier and cheaper than you ever thought.

WHAT IS BIM?

"BIM is a digital representation of physical and functional characteristics of a facility . . . a shared knowledge resource for information about a facility forming a reliable basis for decisions during its life cycle," which is defined as existing from earliest conception to demolition (National BIM Standard-United States). A BIM is an intelligent model that integrates design, visualization, simulation, and collaboration into one process. The model is a physical representation that can also be informative. The model not only shows a client what a building will look like but it also gives the client and designer a better understanding of how the building will function. A BIM is essentially a shared, digital building prototype that helps everyone on the design team make better decisions.

Stages and Uses

A BIM is intended to be used during every phase of the design process and by every member on the team.

Architects typically create the main model and then share it with consultants who use the BIM to ensure that their trades don't interfere with the building's function or other trades. For instance, a duct physically can't run through a beam. It is better to catch issues like this on the computer rather than in the field. This BIM feature is commonly referred to as *clash detection*.

Building owners and facility managers can also use the BIM after the building is complete. For example, a BIM could help them track down the source of a stained ceiling by locating plumbing lines or by indicating possible weaknesses in the roof membrane.

TIP In reality, most building owners and facility managers won't use the BIM to solve problems—but they could. If they were to use a program, however, they'd find that the SketchUp viewer is free and approachable.

Features

BIM is a concept, not a software program. However, there are software programs that use that concept to execute the design process. There is no official BIM features list, but here are a few popular features that most people expect to find in a BIM program:

- ☑ Three-dimensional (3D) modeling
- ☑ Model life cycle use with the building, from predesign to demolition
- ☑ Interoperability with consultants and their computer-aided design (CAD) platforms
- ☑ Dynamic links between the 3D model and the construction documents (when a change is made in a plan, that change is reflected in all other drawings, sections, elevations, and reflected ceiling plans)
- ☑ Photorealistic rendering and raytracing
- ☑ Parametric modeling, both input and output
- ☑ Clash detection
- ☑ Energy analysis
- ☑ Cost analysis
- ☑ Four-dimensional (4D) construction phasing and schedule management

SKETCHUP AND LAYOUT AS BIM

It may come as a surprise that SketchUp and LayOut contain many of the most popular BIM software features. With the workflow presented in this book, SketchUp and LayOut pull the best features from each of the most popular drafting platforms (two-dimensional [2D] CAD and 3D BIM). Using this workflow, you can incorporate BIM's fundamental features into your projects. This section outlines what makes SketchUp and LayOut such powerful design and documentation tools and explains why they are a unique design and documentation method.

Advantages

Some of the advantages of using SketchUp and LayOut as a design and documentation method are:

☑ SketchUp is a *surface modeler*, which means that all objects created in SketchUp are composed of lines and surfaces. The process of drawing lines in SketchUp is very similar to the familiar process used to draw lines in 2D CAD. SketchUp could be described as a 2D CAD program that operates in a 3D environment.

☑ When you build a 3D model in SketchUp using the SketchUp Workflow for Architecture, you are simultaneously creating the construction documents. All 2D plans, sections, and elevations are dynamically linked to the 3D model. SketchUp allows you to think and design in 3D, which is the way your brain is wired to work. This is in sharp contrast to using other popular BIM software where you draft the construction documents, which in turn creates the 3D model. In SketchUp, you think and design in 3D; the presentation and construction documents are products of the design process. (See Figure 2.1 and Figure 2.2.)

☑ The lack of some features in SketchUp is a blessing in disguise. Because the rules for modeling and organizing are simple, there are fewer questions for the program to ask and, therefore, fewer questions for you to answer. The simplicity of SketchUp and LayOut lets you create and organize the model quickly, without interruptions. For example, to add a wall in some BIM software packages, you would

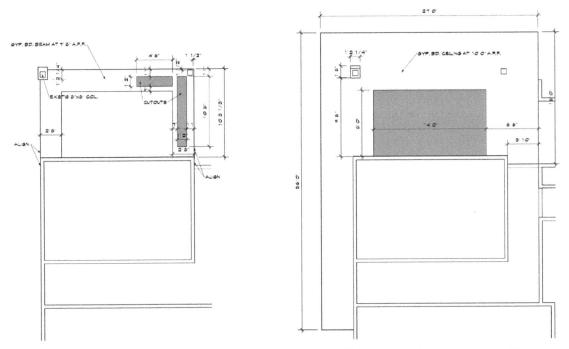

Figure 2.1 Office remodel. Enlarged ceiling plans describe the two soffit levels of the lounge area. These 2D drawings were pulled dynamically from the 3D model. All of the drafting and modeling were completed using SketchUp Pro, LayOut, ConDoc Tools extension, and the SketchUp Workflow for Architecture.

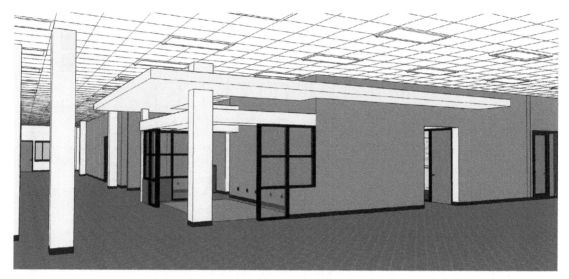

Figure 2.2 Office remodel. All 2D drawings describing this unique ceiling condition are dynamically linked to this 3D model.

have to assign several properties, such as height, thickness, material, color, and insulation. To add a wall in SketchUp, you simply draw a rectangle and pull it up—no questions asked. (In Figure 2.3 through Figure 2.5, the drafting and modeling were completed using SketchUp Pro, LayOut, ConDoc Tools extension, and the SketchUp Workflow for Architecture.)

☑ SketchUp offers real-time rendering, which provides infinitely better information so you can make better design decisions than you can with other software. In SketchUp, a house looks like a house, siding looks like siding, and concrete looks like concrete. In 2D CAD, a house looks like a flat collection of cyan and magenta lines. The graphical representations of most textures leave disconnects between the drawings and real-world applications of the materials. The better the 3D information is that you have during the design process, the better your design decisions will be. Figure 2.6 shows the same project in 2D CAD and in SketchUp.

Disadvantages

Some of the disadvantages of using SketchUp and LayOut as a design and documentation method include:

☑ SketchUp lacks parametric modeling features. Dynamic components can be used to compensate for some of this, but they are fairly difficult to master. Ultimately, parametric modeling attributes can be exported and viewed in spreadsheets as reports; however, changing the spreadsheet will not be reflected in the model.

☑ Scheduling is done the old-fashioned way. The door and window tags are not connected to the door and window schedules. The tags and schedules must be coordinated manually.

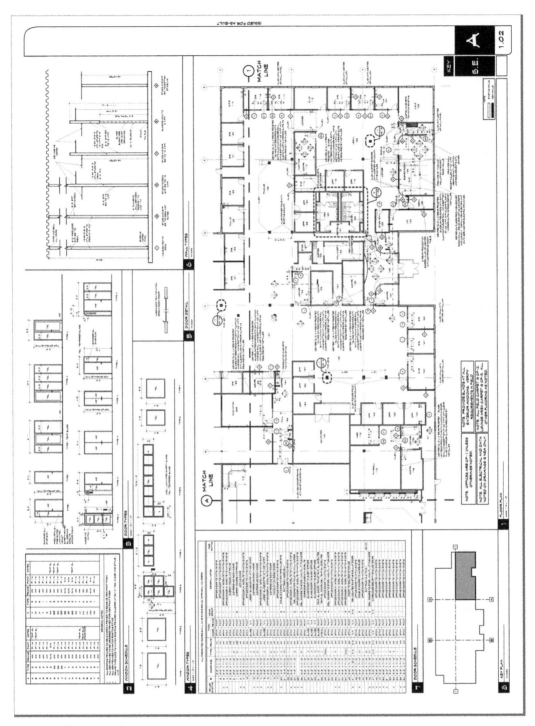

Figure 2.3 Office remodel. Sheet A1.02 contains a partial floor plan, a door schedule, door types, a window schedule, window types, wall types, and a key plan.

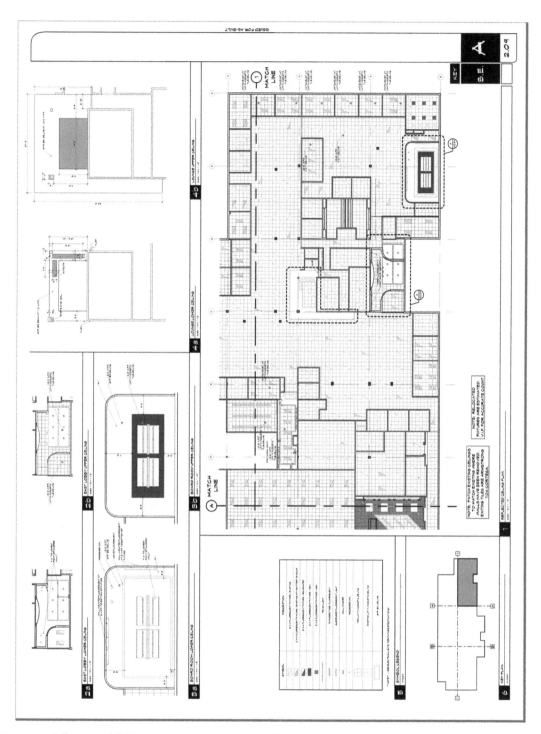

Figure 2.4 Office remodel. Sheet A2.09 contains a partial reflected ceiling plan, enlarged reflected ceiling plans, details, and a key plan. A reflected ceiling plan is created by cutting the model similar to a plan but looking up at the ceiling.

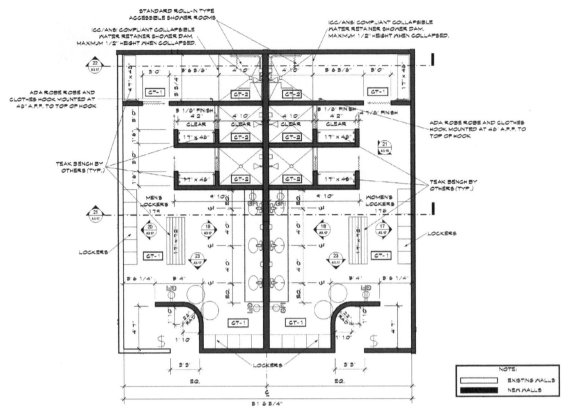

Figure 2.5 Office remodel. These enlarged plans show detailed locations of fixtures and other information that will not fit on a building plan.

☑ Sheets are coordinated the old-fashioned way as well. There is no information exchange between sheets, drawings, tags, and callouts. The drawings must be coordinated manually, with a little help from the auto-text feature in LayOut.

☑ Entities do not attach to one another. For instance, windows and doors do not attach to walls. So if you move the wall, you also need to move the doors and windows separately.

FILLING IN THE BIM BLANKS

You can use extensions to extend SketchUp's BIM features. Third parties are creating extensions that expand the SketchUp universe and provide features that fill the BIM voids. Although many of the extensions listed in this section are not officially endorsed by or included in the SketchUp Workflow for Architecture, they provide a great place to begin your search to expand BIM capabilities.

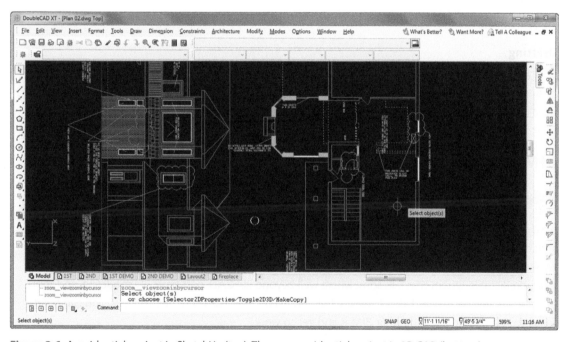

Figure 2.6 A residential project in SketchUp (top). The same residential project in 2D CAD (bottom).

Cost Analysis

☑ Estimator for SketchUp: **estimatorforsketchup.com**

Energy Analysis

☑ Sefaira: **sefaira.com**

Parametric Modeling

☑ Viz Pro: **fluidinteractive.com/products/sketchup-extensions/viz/**

☑ Instant Architecture: **valiarchitects.com/sketchup_scripts**

☑ Dynamic Components: **sketchup.com/intl/en/product/dcs.html**

4D Timeline

☑ 4D Virtual Builder for SketchUp: **4dvirtualbuilder.com**

Rendering

☑ Lumion: **lumion3d.com**

☑ SketchFX: **fluidinteractive.com/products/sketchup-extensions/sketchfx/**

☑ Twilight Render: **twilightrender.com**

☑ Shaderlight: **artvps.com**

☑ SU Podium: **suplugins.com**

Drafting

☑ ConDoc Tools: **condoctools.com**

In Figure 2.7 and Figure 2.8, the drafting and modeling were completed using SketchUp Pro, LayOut, the ConDoc Tools, and the SketchUp Workflow for Architecture.

BIM BURNOUT

How sick are you of hearing about BIM? There is nothing wrong with using a BIM program, but do you wonder whether you really need all that functionality? Is it worth paying for? Do you need lines on paper now, or do you need a complex model for pricing and coordination? My guess is most architects just need lines on paper today with a few added BIMefits.

SketchUp, LayOut, ConDoc, and the SketchUp Workflow for Architecture provide an affordable, efficient, predictable system that falls somewhere well beyond 2D CAD, past basic 3D modeling, and short of complex, features-bloated BIM. It's just what you need to get lines on paper today so you can build tomorrow. Let's stop debating what BIM is and get to work.

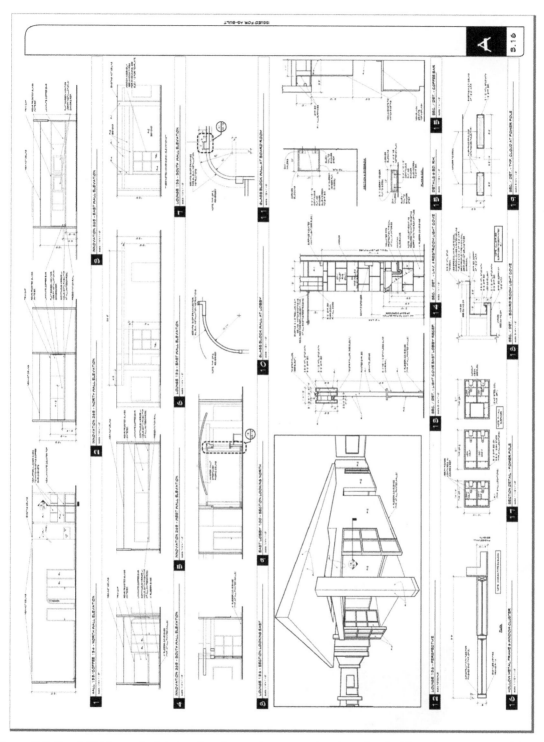

Figure 2.7 Sheet A3.16 contains interior elevations and a perspective view, all pulled from the same 3D model.

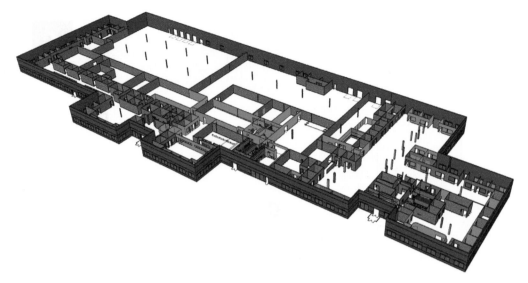

Figure 2.8 Utility styles display additional layers of information contained in a 3D model. This image represents a scope diagram, where all existing objects are shown in gray and all new objects are shown in green.

THE SKETCHUP OUTLOOK

SketchUp's focus has emerged as a platform for 3D modeling and design. More focus on the online products (Figure 2.9) rather than the core SketchUp offering. In recent years, they have released my.SketchUp online, updated the 3D warehouse, and released the extension warehouse, HoloLens app, tablet apps, etc. It appears to me that the goal is to keep the main SketchUp platform stable but not develop new tools within the program. Leave that up to the third-party extension developers.

SketchUp's tagline is "3D for everyone," but in this approach, there is true value for no one. Maybe hobbyists who have time to invent obscure standards for their own needs or, more likely, don't even realize they need them. As a professional, it is of the utmost importance that you have a clear path to success, an

Figure 2.9 SketchUp's current focus is on the supporting cast.

organized system for using this software. It is unlikely that SketchUp will release "SketchUp Architectural Desktop" with all of the tools included for architects. For this reason, we need to compile our own. It is up to professionals like me to push content and up to users to seek out the way.

The good news is we already have a base of great SketchUp tools in the native program plus a healthy community of third-party extensions and stand-alone programs that complement the SketchUp Workflow for Architecture. Read this book, get the ConDoc Tools, and start building your own SketchUp Architectural Desktop based on your specific project type and documentation needs.

CHAPTER POINTS

☑ BIM is a loose concept open to interpretation.

☑ BIM is not a software program; it is a concept used by design and documentation software programs.

☑ There is no absolute set of features that defines BIM software.

☑ SketchUp is not marketed as BIM software, but it does offer several popular BIM features.

☑ Plugins can be used to fill in the BIM blanks.

☑ Most facilities managers won't touch BIM. However, if they do, they would be likely to use SketchUp.

☑ BIM is a catchphrase that has worn off. Let's just use the best tool for the job rather than force a solution.

Chapter 3
Hardware

There are certain topics you should not discuss openly, those taboos that are just not polite conversation: politics, religion, money, operating system. Gasp! But let's discuss computers.

Technology changes constantly and rapidly, so much so that it is hard to make a recommendation today that will be valid tomorrow. The goal of this chapter is to provide benchmarks and tools for understanding and comparing so you can make informed decisions about complex and often misunderstood buying choices. All suggestions in this chapter are assuming you are fully vested in the SketchUp Workflow for Architecture using SketchUp Pro, LayOut, ConDoc, and Lumion. Time to nerd out.

MAC VERSUS PC

Have you ever heard a colleague say, "Macs are good for design"? I have, and I cringe every time. Macs are popular in less taxing creative fields—two-dimensional (2D) graphic design, film editing, or music production—but when it comes to heavy three-dimensional (3D) modeling and rendering for architects, Macs are simply underpowered.

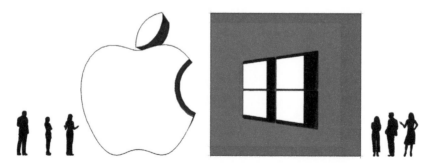

Figure 3.1 The Apple and Windows logos.

You see, no brand is "good for design"; only the guts of a machine, the specs, can make it that way. An underpowered PC is not good for 3D modeling and design either.

For the most part, an operating system is a vehicle to see applications. SketchUp on a Mac is very similar to SketchUp on a PC. Terminology between the platforms may be different, but they ultimately accomplish the same goal—organizing files in folders and providing access to applications to get work done.

It is prudent to not let the tail wag the dog. In regard to your hardware solution, don't let an allegiance to an operating system determine your hardware specs; let the hardware specs determine your operating system. In the following sections, we will lay out the numbers so you can make the right choice for a machine for 3D modeling and design.

SPECS

Setting brand loyalties and opinions developed from years of marketing aside, let's take an objective look at choosing the right computer, with the right specs, specifically for 3D modeling and design. It's easy to get lost in the details when selecting a machine, so in this section, we will focus only on what really matters.

TIP Review a detailed parts list of my current machines at brightmandesigns.com/blog/myrig.

Minimum and recommended specs are on SketchUp's website at help.sketchup.com/en/article/36208. You can completely disregard minimum specs; we are professionals and will need far more than what it takes to open the program. I pulled specs from the website then combined the SketchUp-recommended specs for Mac and PC together into the most stringent case (Figure 3.2). This way, we have one control set to compare different recommended machines and setups to.

> **Combined recommended hardware for Windows and Mac:**
>
> - 2.1+ GHz Intel processor
> - 8+ GB RAM
> - 700 MB of available hard disk space
> - 3D class video card with 1 GB of memory or higher and supports hardware acceleration. Please ensure that the video card driver supports OpenGL version 3.0 or higher and is up to date
> - Three button scroll-wheel mouse

Figure 3.2 Combined recommended specs for Windows and Mac, representing the more stringent case.

TIP SketchUp Checkup (Figure 3.3) diagnoses your computer for compatibility issues with SketchUp 2017 and identifies problems your computer might encounter when running SketchUp. Checkup also creates a report so you can easily communicate issues to technical support. Download it at help .sketchup.com/en/article/3000318.

Computer Components

A graphics card, processor, memory, and peripherals are the critical ingredients of an effective computer for use with the SketchUp Workflow for Architecture. Many pieces play a part, but these are the most important. Network cards, USB connection speeds, and Bluetooth specs improve the overall experience—and ideally are top-of-the-line and fast—but they are not critical for making SketchUp, LayOut, and Lumion ripping fast. Juice up your graphics card, processor, RAM, and peripherals for a machine that will be the envy of your colleagues.

Each of the mentioned components plugs into the motherboard (Figure 3.4). Peripherals are externally connected through the USB plugs in the back of the computer, which are part of the motherboard. The graphics card, processor, and memory are all internally connected to the motherboard.

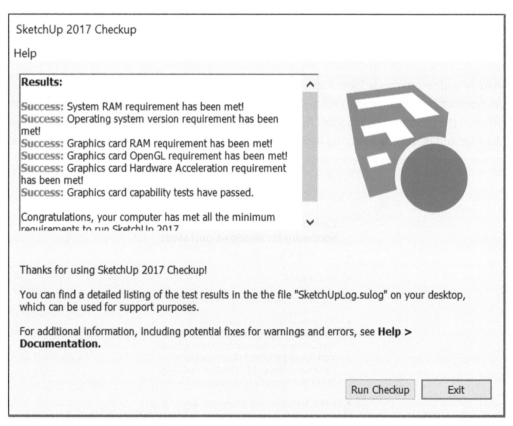

Figure 3.3 The SketchUp Checkup application will call out deficiencies in your hardware.

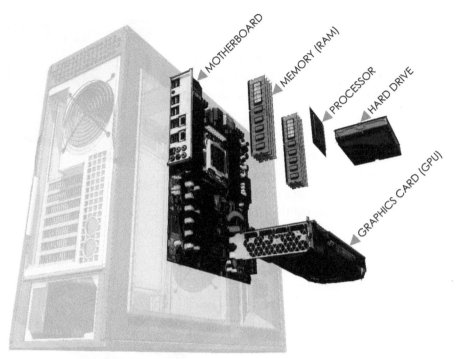

Figure 3.4 The main components of a computer are the graphics card, RAM, hard drive, and processor. All components are connected to the motherboard.

Graphics Card

The graphics card is by far the most important component for working in 3D. The graphics card handles the heavy lifting, instant rendering, and processing that put crisp, beautiful, high-resolution images on your monitor (Figure 3.5).

The graphics card is accessible from the back of the machine through HDMI and display plugs to connect your monitor(s) to the computer.

Nvidia GTX cards are the most cost-effective and productive when leveraging the software I recommend for the SketchUp Workflow for Architecture. Make sure that your graphics card is 100 percent Open Graphics Library (OpenGL) compatible so it can take advantage of Sketch-

Figure 3.5 The graphics card has HDMI and display outputs that connect to a monitor.

Up's hardware acceleration. Check out this article for more information on SketchUp and Open GL compatibility, **https://help.sketchup.com/en/article/114278**.

Processor

A fast central processing unit (CPU) is important, but it's possible to go too far (Figure 3.6). These days, all processors are pretty good, and most of the rendering happens on the graphics processing unit (GPU). Furthermore, most of the programs we run don't max out the processor, and most processors offer plenty of power.

Figure 3.6 You will find the processor buried in the motherboard, usually under a fan and cooling system.

SketchUp will run on multiple processor machines but use only one processor. Hyperthreading or multithreading is not supported at this time, so multiple cores do not necessarily speed up SketchUp, but they will allow your computer to run more applications at the same time, including several instances of SketchUp.

Memory

There is a significant difference between random access memory (RAM) and storage memory. The amount of memory a computer's hard drive comes with—that is, storage—has nothing to do with the RAM, which affects performance of the machine.

Figure 3.7 Hard drives are buried in the case, out of sight and often unnoticed.

A hard drive holds files and folders (Figure 3.7). This is where you store your .skp, .layout, and .lumion files. A hard drive is like a bigger trunk—it holds more stuff—but it has nothing to do with performance. So when you see a huge number, such as a 5 TB hard drive, know that it has nothing to do with being faster; it only offers room to hold files. Solid state drives (SSD) access information faster, booting up and opening programs and files faster.

RAM (Figure 3.8), on the other hand, is on-demand storage, allowing you to open more large files and run more programs concurrently without

Figure 3.8 Adding RAM is an easy do-it-yourself upgrade. The amount of RAM your computer can hold is limited only by your motherboard.

compromising performance. More is better—and the good news is it's cheap. Get as much RAM as you can—at least 16 GB minimum, ideally more.

Peripherals

Most of the other components increase performance, but peripherals enhance the tactile user experience of the machine. The monitors offer the look of your rig, and the mouse and keyboard offer the feel. If it doesn't look and feel good, it's no fun! Don't skimp here—this is the actual interface that you will touch and hold day in and day out.

The most critical piece of hardware is the three-button scroll wheel mouse. Buy a good gaming mouse; fewer buttons are usually better. Also, wireless mice tend to lag and can run out of batteries quickly. I prefer a wired mouse.

TIP The Apple Mighty Mouse is simple and intuitive but horrible for jamming out on a 3D model. Same with any trackpad. You will double your speed by simply buying a three-button scroll wheel gaming mouse.

If the mouse is your right-hand man, the keyboard is your left-hand man. A comfortable keyboard with just the right click is pure joy. It's all about personal preference here, but again, stick with the gaming keyboards and find something comfortable and stylish.

Monitors are the face of your machine. All the hardware in the world is for naught if you don't have a monitor to properly display those beautiful 3D graphics. These days, it is best to stick with a 4K resolution. Multiple monitors make multitasking easier. I like the ultra-wide monitors because I can have multiple programs open and visible at the same time. See Figure 3.9.

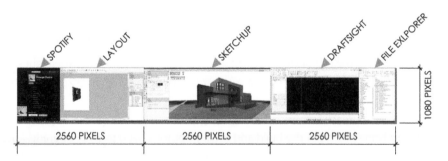

Figure 3.9 Three widescreen monitors offer up more information with less switching between applications.

COMPARISON SHOPPING

Before you swipe away, be sure that you are buying the right machine, with the right hardware, and spending money where it is most impactful. Videocardbenchmark.net (Figure 3.10) keeps a running list of the latest and greatest computer components. Use this site to choose computer components, check pricing against performance, and keep an eye on the latest specs. The format makes it easy to understand the critical point of diminishing returns for graphics cards and processors.

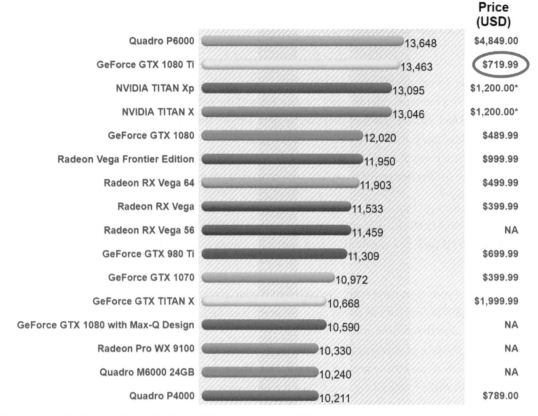

		Price (USD)
Quadro P6000	13,648	$4,849.00
GeForce GTX 1080 Ti	13,463	$719.99
NVIDIA TITAN Xp	13,095	$1,200.00*
NVIDIA TITAN X	13,046	$1,200.00*
GeForce GTX 1080	12,020	$489.99
Radeon Vega Frontier Edition	11,950	$999.99
Radeon RX Vega 64	11,903	$499.99
Radeon RX Vega	11,533	$399.99
Radeon RX Vega 56	11,459	NA
GeForce GTX 980 Ti	11,309	$699.99
GeForce GTX 1070	10,972	$399.99
GeForce GTX TITAN X	10,668	$1,999.99
GeForce GTX 1080 with Max-Q Design	10,590	NA
Radeon Pro WX 9100	10,330	NA
Quadro M6000 24GB	10,240	NA
Quadro P4000	10,211	$789.00

Figure 3.10 The best choice at the time of this book being published.

For graphics cards, go to the top of the high-end graphics card list and look for the highest GTX card on the list that's around $400 to $900. Of course you can spend more, but in my experience, this is the point of diminishing returns.

You can use a similar approach for processors. Although I don't usually seek out a specific processor, I do look at what I am being offered in the build and usually opt for a $200 to $400 upgrade. I use the high-end CPU list on cpubenchmark.net to make sure I am toward the top of the list and paying the right price.

Custom-Build

Windows desktops and laptops are infinitely configurable—there is a whole world of components out there. The PC free market inspires competition, lower prices, and better specs. Picking and choosing can be difficult, so consider hiring someone to do it for you.

Oftentimes, a local shop can custom specify, order, build, and warranty a machine for several hundred dollars less than if you did it yourself. Just call your local shop and have them read this chapter. In short, you need a "gaming rig with a high-end GTX card for 3D modeling and rendering."

SYSTEMS

Now that we understand the required specs, how to compare hardware, and how they all function together to render polygons, let's compare some Apple and Windows systems pound for pound within their respective classes. For all you Mac users out there, keep an open mind—the numbers don't lie.

Netbooks

Netbooks are the new class of lighter, smaller computers designed primarily for accessing Internet-based applications (Figure 3.11).

Figure 3.11 Netbooks have a slim form factor, no room for high-performance components.

These are great for e-mail and cloud-based Web apps but not for image processing and video editing, and they are far from the required power for 3D modeling and design. They are small and portable at the cost of graphics and computing performance.

Analysis

☑ These machines are drastically underpowered, so don't expect anything out of these machines (Figure 3.12).

☑ Most have onboard chip graphics to conserve space; there is literally no graphics card.

☑ Outside the minimum specs, you might be able to run SketchUp but not well.

☑ These machines are best suited for surfing the Internet and writing papers.

☑ They will even choke with 2D applications such as Photoshop, so they are definitely not the right choice for an architect working with 3D.

☑ There is a viewer for SketchUp that runs on Apple and Android tablets and phones, but keep in mind that a big model will still choke the viewer.

TIP The MacBook Air and Microsoft Surface are in this netbook category. This category is included only to make clear how underpowered these machines are for 3D modeling and design.

NETBOOK

MODEL	MacBook Air	BENCHMARK		Microsoft Surface
		-	-	
PRICE	$1,349.00	-	-	$1,599.00
PROCESSOR	2.2GHz Intel i7 processor	4190	6145	2.5GHz Intel i7 Processor
STORAGE	256GB SSD	-	-	256GB SSD
MEMORY	8GB	-	-	8GB
GRAPHICS	Intel HD Graphics 6000	830	1465	Intel Irid Plus Graphics 640
SCREEN RES	3840 x 2160	-	-	2736 x 1824

Figure 3.12 Comparison between the MacBook Air and Microsoft Surface.

Laptops

Laptops are likely the first on the list of machines to buy (Figure 3.13). They are portable and now powerful enough to replace your desktop. Go big—spend the right amount here. When it comes to 3D modeling and design, it's all about the graphics card; if you are buying a desktop replacement, look for a machine with a desktop card.

Figure 3.13 The right laptop can be your only machine, used as a desktop when docked.

Analysis

☑ Laptops are very capable of replacing desktops. Many can fit a full-sized graphics card (Figure 3.14).

☑ If you can afford only one machine, spend money on a laptop. Macs are limited on selection for 3D computing power and fall short of specs offered by a similarly priced PC.

All-in-Ones

An all-in-one computer is a compact, stylish desktop solution that sacrifices function over form (Figure 3.15). These machines push for space saving and portability from a machine that is static. They make for a cool workspace but at the price of cost and performance.

Analysis

☑ Burying all the components of a computer inside a monitor is a good strategy for a portable laptop, but it doesn't make sense for a desktop (Figure 3.16).

☑ I wouldn't recommend buying this as a desktop; I would rather have the performance than the form factor.

Figure 3.15 All-in-ones sacrifice power for a sleek form.

LAPTOP			
		BENCHMARK	
MODEL	Macbook Pro	-	-	Razer Blade
PRICE	$3,499	-	-	$2,499
PROCESSOR	2.9GHz Intel i7 Processor	9687	8973	2.8GHz Intel i7 Processor
STORAGE	1TB	-	-	1TB
MEMORY	16GB	-	-	16GB
GRAPHICS	Radeon Pro 460	3492	8719	NVIDIA GeForce GTX 1060
SCREEN RES	15", 2880 x 1800	-	-	15", 3840 x 2160

Figure 3.14 MacBook Pro versus Razer Blade.

ALL IN ONE				
		BENCHMARK		
MODEL	iMac	-	-	Digital Storm Aura
PRICE	$2,699.00	-	-	$2,971.00
PROCESSOR	4.2GHz Intel i7 processor	**12133**	**12133**	4.2GHz Intel i7 processor
STORAGE	2TB Fusion Drive	-	-	480GB SSD, 1TB
MEMORY	16GB	-	-	16GB
GRAPHICS	Radeon Pro 580	**8060**	**12001**	GeForce GTX 1080 8GB
SCREEN RES	27", 5120 x 2880	-	-	34", 3440 x 1440

Figure 3.16 iMac versus Digital Storm Aura. Microsoft Studio and Dell all-in-ones were also considered.

☑ A big bulky desktop replacement laptop with a monitor is a better solution.

☑ If you are going to buy a Mac, an iMac offers the most comparable specs.

Desktop

A desktop computer is a fixed asset—a tower with monitors and multiple peripherals attached (Figure 3.17). This is your home base, your daily driver, the machine that can render anything you throw at it.

Figure 3.17 A desktop is the most powerful and least costly solution. You get the most bang for your buck.

Analysis

☑ When comparing costs, keep in mind that you will need to buy monitors, a keyboard, and a mouse (Figure 3.18).

☑ A Windows desktop can easily be upgraded over the years and kept up-to-date as hardware evolves so that it still meets the required specs. Macs cannot.

DESKTOP				
		BENCHMARK		
MODEL	Mac Pro	-	-	Custom Windows Build
PRICE	$3,999.00	-	-	$2,235
PROCESSOR	3.5GHz Intel Xeon Processor	**10,281**	**11,191**	4.00GHz Intel i7 Processor
STORAGE	1TB SSD	-	-	1TB SSD (OS, Programs), 3TB (Data)
MEMORY	32GB	-	-	32GB
GRAPHICS	AMD FirePro D500	**10303**	**11,309**	GeForce GTX 980 Ti
SCREEN RES	N/A	-	-	N/A

Figure 3.18 Mac Pro versus a custom Windows build.

☑ Lumion leverages only one GPU. SketchUp leverages only one CPU. There's no need to waste money on multiple underpowered cards/chips. The Mac Pro has multiple graphics cards that will go unused in this workflow.

TIP If you have never opened up your existing desktop, these LED lights (available at goo.gl/X919ds) are a fun DIY project, and although not proven, I am convinced they increase performance.

Conclusions/Recommendations

Now it's up to you to make the right decision for yourself. Here are a few tips to help you do just that:

☑ A custom build doesn't cost as much as you would think; talk to your local guys. This is the best, easiest, and most cost-effective option.

☑ Upgrading your existing Windows machine is not as hard or expensive as you might think.

☑ If you can afford only a laptop, go big. If you can afford a laptop and a desktop, go big on both. You will never stare at a frozen rendering machine and think, "I sure am glad I saved a few hundred dollars on this underpowered machine." You will likely see the extra few hundred dollars at work in performance and appreciate it every day that you sit at your desk.

☑ Don't buy an all-in-one. These machines are better suited for home use, not for everyday professional computing and rendering. However, if you have to have a Mac, it appears the iMac all-in-one is the best option.

☑ You will never regret the investment for a fast machine that you use every day of your professional career.

☑ Many software companies don't develop for Mac, including Lumion. Parallels and Bootcamp are unsupported environments for running just about any program and getting support.

☑ Talk to any gamer who values 3D performance. They run a Windows machine.

☑ Are you VR-ready? Macs will not be supported simply because they don't have the graphics cards that come close even to the lowest spec. It is possible that they will work with an external GPU, but this is a significant additional cost.

☑ Macs look good. Beautiful cases. Machined aluminum. The glowing apple is synonymous with sophistication and intelligence. But this is marketing! These machines are primarily designed to sell, not perform for 3D modeling and design. You are paying for the name and style, not necessarily the performance.

☑ Don't be offended if my opinion differs from yours. I completely understand brand loyalty; just know that when your Mac crashes, or spins the wheel of death, you will then understand why. It is underpowered for this type of work. While waiting, make sure you turn it around to admire that glowing apple on the back.

CHAPTER POINTS

☑ Always remember, leverage technique over hardware and you will prolong your hardware's life cycle. At this point, my hardware does everything I need it to with my lightweight, well-organized models.

☑ Macs are not suited to professional 3D modeling and design. You pay a lot more for far less (when it comes to performance).

☑ Tablets might claim to run 3D programs, but they won't run them well. Don't bother.

☑ All-in-ones are neat but not suitable for professional work. You are paying for form rather than performance.

☑ Apple's high-end desktop is simply not configured for 3D work with SketchUp and Lumion.

☑ A custom-built Windows machine is far cheaper and blows away performance.

☑ A no-brainer laptop choice is the latest Razer Blade or Razer Blade Pro. They are not cheap, but you will recover your investment in reliability, speed, and longevity.

☑ A no-brainer desktop choice is to pay a local computer shop to build a custom gaming computer. Pick your graphics card from videocardbenchmark.net, then tell them to give you the most bang for your buck on everything else. Expect to spend around $2,000 for the tower alone.

Chapter 4
File and Folder Management

Unwavering, relentless organization is essential to a successful project. Just like a messy desk, a messy PROJECT folder can cause miscommunication and lost work, and it can ultimately cost you time and money. The techniques illustrated in this chapter will help you organize your design projects. Keep in mind that this is not a rigid system; the suggested workflow is flexible and can be tweaked to meet your specific needs. In other words, you are encouraged to modify this method any way you see fit to meet your project type and office standards.

FOLDERS AND FILES

Approaching folders and files the same way every time will help your team collaborate efficiently. First, you need to understand some standard ground rules regarding how to organize and manage the contents of your PROJECT folders. Then you can apply the logic of this system to your PROJECT folders and further develop your own standards.

TIP File Management for Professionals is a commercially available comprehensive course of step-by-step tutorials on how to manage and organize files at **sketchupforprofessionals.com**.

Naming Standards

Take a moment to invent an identifying acronym. This shouldn't be too hard; architects and designers do it all the time—common examples are HOK, RNL, and SOM. Your identifying acronym will be used to name files and many other things that you create in the digital world. This is important—not necessarily from a marketing point of view but from an organizational one so that everyone knows who made the file. The acronym used for the examples in this book is BD, which stands for Brightman Designs. Anticipate replacing BD with your own identifying acronym as you complete the exercises in this book.

Folders

Folders contain files and other folders, and they have a strong tendency to become a complete mess. Read the next sentence several times so it is etched into your memory. *The contents of a folder should present the fewest number of choices, and all choices should be self-explanatory.* That sentence thoroughly describes folder organization logic, and it is the keystone of an organized project.

All PROJECT folder names should be in all capital letters to clearly and concisely describe the folder—for example, OFFICE REMODEL. Ideally, all subfolder names within the project folder will be one word in all caps; frequently, subfolder names are abbreviated. For instance, administrative files such as contracts and correspondence will be stored in a folder named ADMIN. Pictures, sketches, and diagrams will be kept in a folder named IMAGES. By capitalizing the file folder names, you are visually separating those folder names from the filenames residing in the same folder.

Files

An efficient filename gives the user as much information as possible without ever looking at the file properties (Figure 4.1).

For example, examine the filename `BD_Office Remodel - Existing Conditions.skp`. This file was created by Brightman Designs, is part of the Office Remodel project, illustrates the existing conditions, and opens in SketchUp. By providing this information in the filename, you answer many questions about the file before anyone even tries to open it. Any consultant or member of your team who opens your files will immediately know where the files came from and how to use them.

Only one current version of each file should be stored in the main PROJECT folder. Avoid giving files confusing names that will make sense only at the moment you name it. Do not name files with the words `current`, `best`, `use this`, or `delete`. These types of filenames do not make it clear which file in the main PROJECT folder is actually the current file. Vague filenames provide users with ambiguous information, cause confusion, and ultimately lead to duplicated work and lost time. See Figure 4.2.

Standard Folders

By placing your folders in logical places, you help your team keep track of active projects and their associated files. To start organizing your projects, you need only four folders: a TEMP folder, an ACTIVE PROJECTS folder, an ARCHIVE folder, and a RESOURCES folder. Again, this is not a rigid system; you can customize it to a system that works for you.

TEMP Folder

One way to keep junk files from accumulating on your machine is to create a place to dump them. Create a TEMP folder on your desktop.

AUTHOR_Project - File Description.extension

Figure 4.1 A clear, concise, and informative filename.

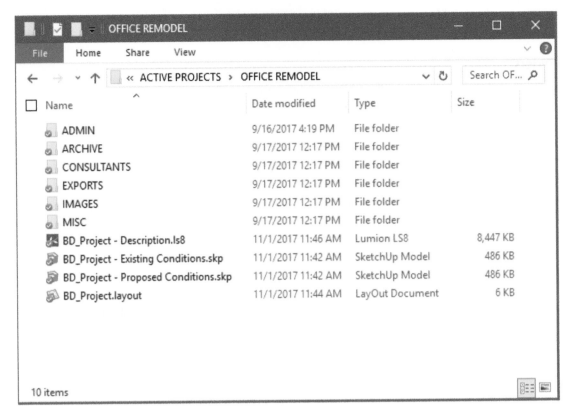

Figure 4.2 A typical PROJECT folder.

This folder is for anything that you don't need to keep—it is a great place to save program installers, quick sketches, and e-mail attachments. Files saved here should not be missed when the folder is emptied. Every month or so, go into the TEMP folder and delete all the contents. If you wonder whether you will need a file, you should more than likely save it in a PROJECT folder rather than the TEMP folder.

On a side note, never save anything onto your desktop. The only items that should be on your desktop are the Recycle Bin, TEMP folder, ACTIVE PROJECTS folder, ARCHIVE folder, and possibly some application shortcuts. If you just need to use a file briefly, save it in the TEMP folder. If you ignore this rule, your desktop will become a mess (Figure 4.3).

TIP Eliminate application shortcuts from your desktop by dragging them to the Start Bar menu or by dragging them to the bottom of your screen and pinning them to the taskbar.

ACTIVE PROJECTS Folder

An active project is one that you access on a daily to weekly basis. The files within the ACTIVE PROJECTS folder may change daily. Create a folder on your desktop and name it ACTIVE PROJECTS or place it on a

Figure 4.3 A clean desktop is neater and easier to use than a messy desktop.

shared server. Save all current and active projects into this folder using the folder and file naming structures previously described.

TIP If you use Dropbox, your ACTIVE PROJECTS folder should be in your Dropbox for safe-keeping in the cloud.

TIP Always be aware of exactly where you are saving your active files and projects. Never use Recent Documents to open files.

ARCHIVE Folder

An inactive project is a project that has already been invoiced and paid and probably won't be accessed again. Saving all finished work is important, just in case phase two comes around or you need to pull a piece of a model from a past project to use on a current one. Create a folder on your desktop and name it ARCHIVE. Inactive projects should be saved in the ARCHIVE folder on your desktop.

TIP For more information about adding completed projects to the ARCHIVE folder, see "Closing a Project" later in this chapter.

RESOURCES Folder

Create another folder on your desktop named RESOURCES. The RESOURCES folder holds all your components, materials, plugins, scrapbooks, styles, and templates. You can also store Windows themes, preferences.dat files, fonts, and anything else you use across all your machines in this folder. Add a folder for each category, as shown in Figure 4.4.

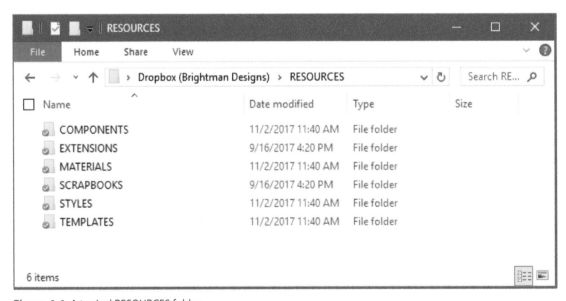

Figure 4.4 A typical RESOURCES folder.

TIP You can also add additional folders to your RESOURCES folder, such as APPLICATIONS, for sharing installers across your machines/office. Other examples include FONTS, MUSIC, or MISC. Adapt to your needs.

COMPONENTS *Folder*

The COMPONENTS folder holds all your objects. Whenever you download something new from the Podium Browser or FormFonts (see Chapter 8, SketchUp Collections), place it here. It is extremely helpful to add subfolders here that relate to ConDoc ELEMENT layers (Figure 4.5).

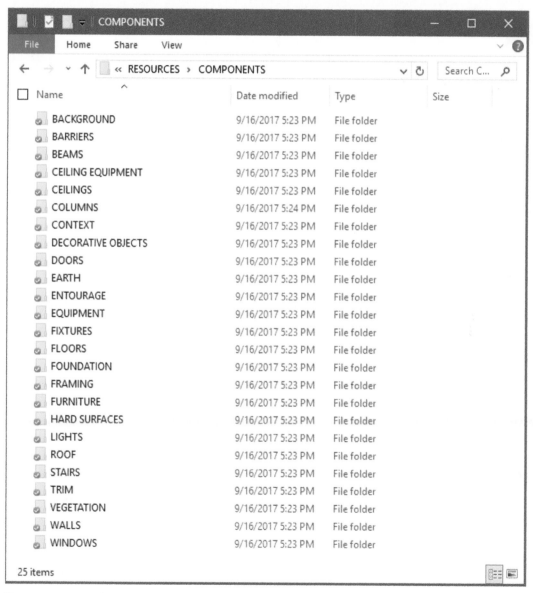

Figure 4.5 A typical COMPONENTS folder is organized with subfolders named the same as ConDoc ELEMENT Layers.

MATERIALS Folder

The BD MATERIALS folder holds all texture images downloaded from SketchUp Texture Club and Google Images (see SketchUp Collections). It is helpful to add subfolders reflecting the Lumion Material Categories. Not only does this help when working in Lumion, but it is also a system of organization that makes sense and eliminates the need to invent your own (Figure 4.6).

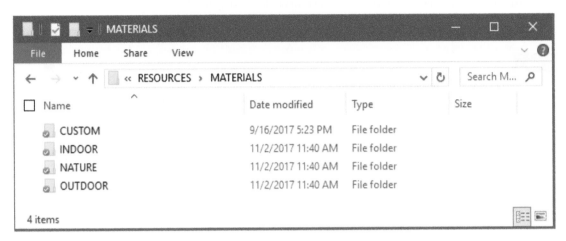

Figure 4.6 A typical MATERIALS folder organized using the same categories as Lumion.

SCRAPBOOKS Folder

The SCRAPBOOKS folder holds all .layout files that represent annotations and all palettes. It is typically not necessary to add subfolders for organization. You will path here in LayOut (Figure 4.7).

EXTENSIONS Folder

The EXTENSIONS folder holds all .rb, .rbs, and .rbz files. It is typically not necessary to add subfolders for organization. You will path here to install extensions (see Chapter 9, Extensions). No organization is necessary, and it makes transitioning to new versions of SketchUp easier to have all of these in one place (Figure 4.8).

STYLES Folder

The STYLES folder holds all .style files created in SketchUp. You will create some styles in this book, both utility and presentation (Figure 4.9).

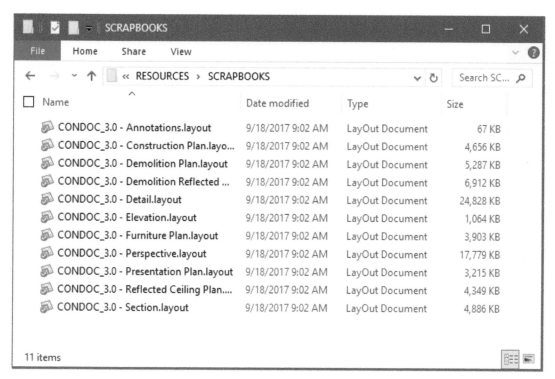

Figure 4.7 A typical SCRAPBOOKS folder.

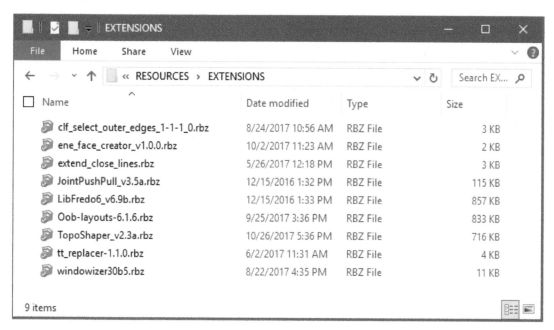

Figure 4.8 A typical EXTENSIONS folder. It makes transitioning to new versions of SketchUp easier to have all of these in one place.

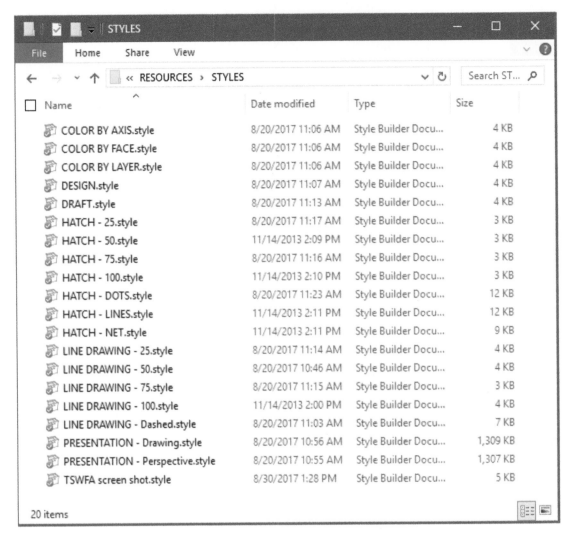

Figure 4.9 A typical STYLES folder.

TEMPLATES Folder

The templates for all programs—SketchUp, LayOut, Lumion, etc.—will be found in this folder. Common file extensions are .skp, .layout, and .ls8 (Figure 4.10).

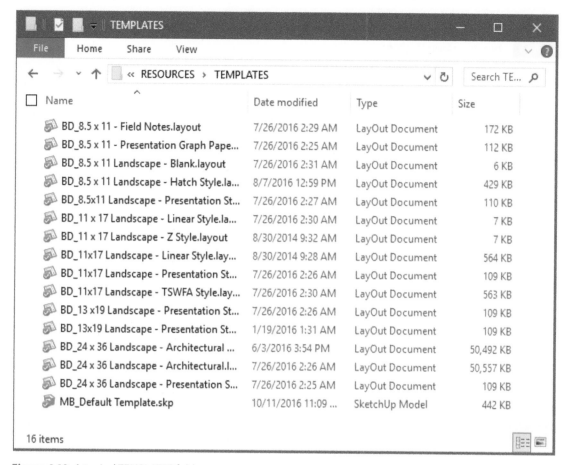

Figure 4.10 A typical TEMPLATES folder.

PROJECT Folders

This section suggests a starting point and system to help you organize your PROJECT folders. A PROJECT folder should contain the following subfolders: ADMIN, ARCHIVE, CONSULTANTS, EXPORTS, IMAGES, and MISC. Your particular projects can include other folders if needed.

The main project files, typically SketchUp and LayOut files, should be stored in the main PROJECT folder with the other project subfolders (Figure 4.11). This will provide easy access to the most frequently used files, which usually have the `.skp` and `.layout` filename extensions.

ADMIN Folder

The ADMIN folder should contain all administrative files. You should save contracts, time sheets, product specification sheets, correspondence, and memos that relate to the project in this folder (Figure 4.12). A safe rule of thumb is that if a file is not graphic in nature, it probably belongs in the ADMIN folder. Typical file extensions found in this folder are `.doc,` `.xls`, and `.pdf`.

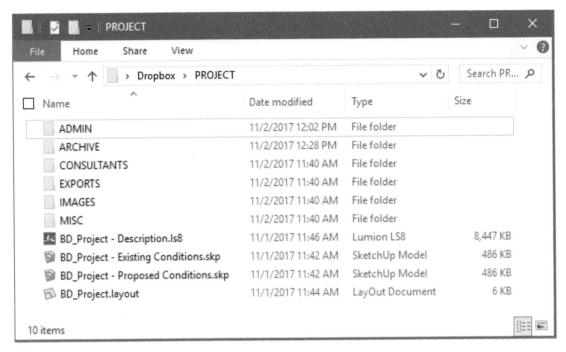

Figure 4.11 A typical PROJECT folder.

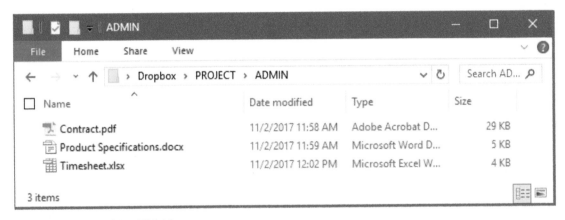

Figure 4.12 A typical ADMIN folder.

ARCHIVE Folder

The ARCHIVE folder is used to preserve past versions of all important project files. Typically, you should store only zipped files and zipped folders in the ARCHIVE folder (Figure 4.13). All files should be titled with the naming convention YYMMDD_Files.zip or YYMMDD_Exports.zip. By designating project files and exports within the .zip filename, you will be able to easily sort the archives and find any files you need. Because you will rarely access these files, they can be compressed into .zip files to save disk space.

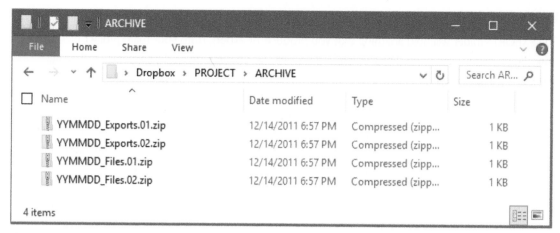

Figure 4.13 A typical ARCHIVE folder.

TIP For more information on creating .zip files and backing up your work, see "Archiving" later in this chapter.

CONSULTANTS Folder

All of the files you receive from consultants should be saved in the CONSULTANTS folder within their respective sub folders. Typical subfolders include ELECTRICAL, MECHANICAL, PLUMBING, and STRUCTURAL (Figure 4.14). Each consultant you work with should have their own folder. Typically, a consultant's folder contains not only **.dwg** files but also **.pdf** files that represent the **.dwg** files.

Within each consultant's folder, add subfolders with the naming convention YYMMDD. This will provide a record of when you received the files from each consultant.

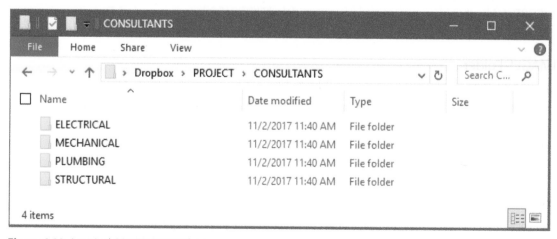

Figure 4.14 A typical CONSULTANTS folder.

EXPORTS Folder

The EXPORTS folder will hold anything that you produce, or export, from your main project files. Some examples of exports are three-dimensional (3D) models, two-dimensional (2D) .dwg files, and image exports. To keep track of your exports, use the YYMMDD naming convention for subfolders. This folder naming system will also make it easy to create archive .zip files.

Because you probably will be exporting several files a day, it is convenient to have one folder that always has the current backgrounds and the entire current set of files ready to print. Create a CURRENT SET subfolder. This folder should always contain all the current .dwg backgrounds and .pdf prints associated with the project. Whenever someone needs to have a set of documents printed or computer-aided design (CAD) backgrounds updated, you can go to this folder to access the most current set. This also means that whenever you export to a YYMMDD folder, you will need to overwrite the files in the CURRENT SET folder to keep those exports up to date. See Figure 4.15.

Figure 4.15 A typical EXPORTS folder.

TIP As the project progresses, turn your EXPORTS folders into .zip files. The folders within the EXPORTS folder should be compressed when new, dated EXPORTS folders are created. Once you are confident that these exports are not needed on a daily basis, move them to your ARCHIVE folder.

IMAGES Folder

The IMAGES folder will hold any photographs, field measurements, sketches, and diagrams relating to the project. Organize the subfolders using the YYMMDD_Description naming convention. You probably will want to separate site photos from interior photos and from concept photos. The following folders will help keep them organized not only by the subject of the photographs but also by date: YYMMDD_Site Visit, YYMMDD_Interiors, YYMMDD_Concepts (Figure 4.16).

MISC Folder

The MISC folder is the TEMP folder of a project. Save whatever you want within this folder as long as it relates to the project—everyone needs a junk drawer. Subfolders of the MISC folder should be named

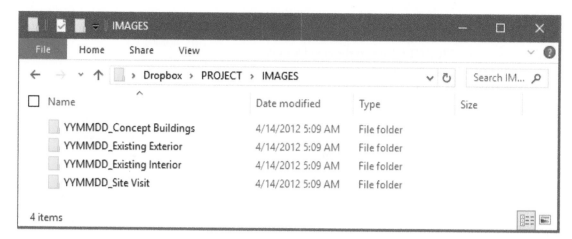

Figure 4.16 A typical IMAGES folder.

using capitalized initials so that everyone on the team has their own junk drawer (Figure 4.17). Typically, components, sketch models, and texture images will end up here. Take time every month or so to clean out the backup files and auto-save files to be sure you're not wasting space on your system.

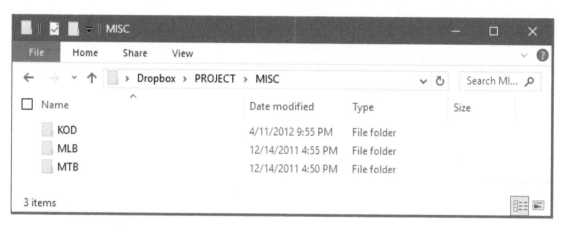

Figure 4.17 A typical MISC folder.

Refer to the chapter files to see a typical PROJECT folder that has already been created (Figure 4.18). You can copy it to your own PROJECT folder and use it as a template for new projects.

ACTIVITY

CLOUD STORAGE

Consider saving your PROJECT folders to the cloud for safekeeping, automatic archiving, and additional sharing options (Figure 4.19). Some standard features that many cloud storage solutions offer include:

☑ Automatic archiving

☑ File sharing without the need for an FTP site

☑ Access to previous versions of files and folders

☑ Seamless access to all files and folders on all your computers

☑ File access from an Internet browser or smartphone

☑ Large file sharing without the need to e-mail them

☑ Team sharing of PROJECT folders, even with team members who are not in your office

ARCHIVING

Clients change their minds. Systems crash. Data get lost. Archiving is your free insurance policy to protect your time and work. Archiving is essential to a clean PROJECT folder and successful file management.

Archiving allows you to keep a copy of your work in case of an unexpected crash, accidental deletion, or any loss of data. Archiving also helps protect you from indecisive clients because you can revert back to previous versions without recreating work. The techniques outlined in this section make it easy to keep a running record of your work for a swift recovery.

Strategy

You don't need to archive everything all the time. You need to archive only the files that are constantly changing. Typically, these will be the files saved in the main PROJECT folder—the `.skp` and `.layout` files. You don't need to constantly archive the IMAGES or the ADMIN folders because they rarely change and do not reflect your time and work.

PROJECT
  ADMIN
  ARCHIVE
    YYMMDD_Exports.01.zip
    YYMMDD_Exports.02.zip
    YYMMDD_Files.01.zip
    YYMMDD_Files.02.zip
  CONSULTANTS
    ELEC
      YYMMDD
    MECH
      YYMMDD
    PLUMB
      YYMMDD
    STRUCT
      YYMMDD
  EXPORTS
    YYMMDD
  IMAGES
    YYMMDD_Concept Buildings
    YYMMDD_Existing Exterior
    YYMMDD_Existing Interior
    YYMMDD_Site Visit
  MISC
    JLM
    MTB
    RAY

Figure 4.18 A typical PROJECT folder expanded.

Figure 4.19 Several cloud services are available, many of which have free or low-cost plans.

TIP You would be wise to archive before making any major changes. Typically, you should archive at least once a day for an active project.

Creating a Project Snapshot

Select all the current project files, right-click on the selections, select Send to, and then choose Compressed (zipped) folder. Name the `.zip` file using the file-naming convention `YYMMDD.01_Files.zip`. Use the number at the end to track snapshots throughout the day (Figure 4.20).

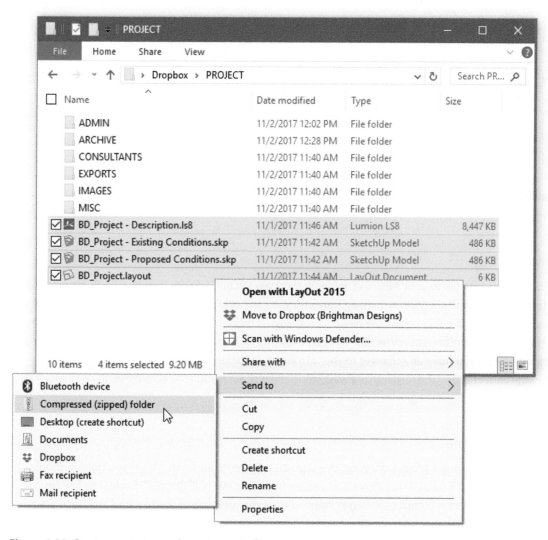

Figure 4.20 Create a project snapshot using a .zip file.

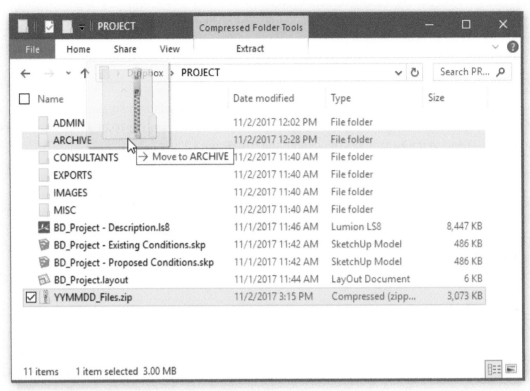

Figure 4.21 Drag the new .zip file to the ARCHIVE folder.

Organizing

Now drag the `.zip` file to your ARCHIVE folder in the main PROJECT folder (Figure 4.21). By naming the `.zip` archive files with the YYMMDD naming standard, you can easily sort by name. Just click on the Name header in your file browser to put the files in chronological order by the date they were created and also in the proper order throughout the day. You could use the Date modified tab within your file explorer as well; however, if you make any changes to the `.zip` file while looking for an old file, the files will no longer be in the correct order. The filename is always static and will allow you to keep archives in chronological order.

Closing a Project

Regardless of how long a project drags on, one day you will eventually finish. When you do, you should remove the PROJECT (i.e., OFFICE REMODEL) folder from your ACTIVE PROJECTS folder to free up disk space. Once a project is complete, it is important to close the project and create a final archive in your main ARCHIVE folder.

TIP Before you archive a project, consider deleting all past archives within the project ARCHIVE folder. This may or may not be appropriate depending on the project and its potential to resurface.

Archive the entire project folder by right-clicking on the actual PROJECT folder, selecting Send To, and then choosing Compressed (zipped) folder. This creates a separate `.zip` file that contains the files and folder structure of your project file in a compressed format. You can now delete the entire project folder and move the project `.zip` file to your ARCHIVE folder on your desktop. Here it will sit until you need to access the contents in the far and distant future.

TIP To be safe, burn these archives onto a disk, send them to the cloud, store them on a jump drive, or copy them to an external hard drive, and then store them in a safe as an additional layer of protection. You never know what can happen!

Reopening a Project

The time may come when you need to reopen a project. To do so, right-click on the project `.zip` file within the ARCHIVE folder and choose Extract All. Click on the Browse button, and choose the ACTIVE PROJECTS folder on your desktop. Click Extract. All of the files will be restored to your PROJECTS folder and maintain their original file and folder structures.

If you need only a couple of files within the archive, double-click into a zipped folder to view its contents, the same as you would a regular folder. Once in the zipped folder, drag and drop individual files into your TEMP folder for inspection. This does not actually move the file out of the `.zip` file; it makes a copy of it and leaves your archive intact.

CHAPTER POINTS

- ☑ The small amount of time you invest in organizing files will pay for itself hundreds of times over throughout the design process.
- ☑ Always know where you are opening a file from and where you are saving it. Never use Recent Documents to open files.
- ☑ Archive often, sometimes multiple times during the day. It is better to archive too much rather than too little.
- ☑ Archive with `.zip` files to save disk space.
- ☑ For added convenience and protection from data loss, send your current files to the cloud.

PART II

SketchUp

SketchUp is an excellent design tool that gives designers the flexibility they need to sketch in a three-dimensional (3D) digital world. SketchUp was once considered useful only for preliminary schematic designs; however, if you incorporate the organizational techniques taught in *The SketchUp Workflow for Architecture,* SketchUp is capable of much more. In this section, you'll learn about the SketchUp tools and environment and how to use collections and extensions. Before you get into the details, however, you need to make sure you are up to snuff on the basics and that your default SketchUp template is optimized for professional use.

Chapter 5
SketchUp Basics

In order to use the methods in this book, you must understand the concepts, tools, and commands presented in this chapter. Any additional knowledge you have is a plus. However, don't underestimate the usefulness of this chapter, even for those who consider themselves to be SketchUp experts. It has plenty of tips, tricks, and helpful theories that will come up again later.

FIVE CORE CONCEPTS

Before you even open SketchUp, you need to understand the core concepts that make it unique. First, SketchUp is a surface modeler that is unlike most 3D modeling programs. Everything in SketchUp is composed of edges and surfaces—they're the basic building blocks used in SketchUp. A surface cannot exist without a closed loop of coplanar edges, and the simplest surface possible is a triangle (Figure 5.1).

Second, because it is a surface modeler, there are no true, perfect vector curves, arcs, or circles in SketchUp. However, you can still represent circles and curves with a series of small edges (Figure 5.2).

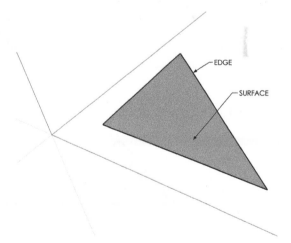

Figure 5.1 All of the endpoints (corners) of the triangle are at the same blue elevation—in other words, the edges are all on the same plane (coplanar).

Third, SketchUp geometry has a tendency to stick together, a concept known as the "stickiness of geometry." Adjoining surfaces stick together and move with one another. Connected endpoints will move with each other and stretch their corresponding lines (Figure 5.3). Even though this can be frustrating at first, once you learn to control the stickiness with containers, you will realize how much it speeds up the modeling process.

Fourth, geometry does not stack in SketchUp. Only one edge or surface can exist between the same series of points. Even when multiple edges are drawn on top of each other, the edges simply combine into one. When an edge that intersects or overlaps an existing edge is drawn, the existing edge will be broken into two pieces (Figure 5.4).

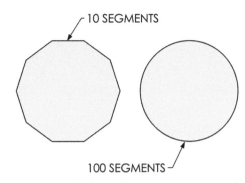

Figure 5.2 Circles and curves are represented by a series of smaller line segments. Increasing the number of segments makes a smoother circle, but that can also lead to large file sizes and decrease computer performance.

Lastly, the *inference engine* is the "brain" in SketchUp that is always working for you; it is what assumes meaningful relationships between points, edges, and surfaces. Although you can't turn off the inference engine, you can control it through the power of suggestion. There are several inferences available in SketchUp; some are shown in Figure 5.5.

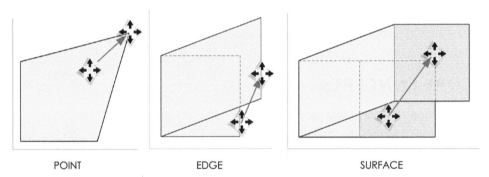

POINT   EDGE   SURFACE

Figure 5.3 Adjacent geometry sticks together in SketchUp.

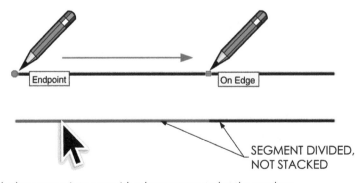

Figure 5.4 Stacked edges merge into one with edges segmented at the overlaps.

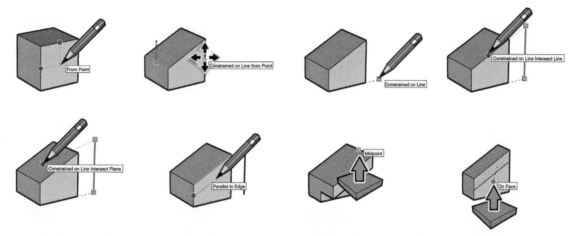

Figure 5.5 Most inferences require modifier keys or hovering on entities to "encourage" an inference.

LEVERAGING SKETCHUP

The five core concepts combine to make SketchUp a fast, fun, and unique 3D modeling program, but using it is not necessarily easy. By embracing and controlling these core concepts, you'll be able to successfully leverage SketchUp into your workflow.

Selecting a Template

When you open the SketchUp application, the first window you'll see is the Welcome to SketchUp window (Figure 5.6). You can also access it by clicking on the Help drop-down menu and choosing Welcome to SketchUp. From there, you can access learning resources, license information, and, most important for now, your default template. Within the Template tab, select the Construction Documentation–Feet and Inches template, and then click on Start using SketchUp. To start a new document with the selected template, click on the File drop-down menu and choose New.

Navigating the 3D Environment

The best way to navigate in SketchUp is to use a three-button scroll wheel mouse, even when you're working on a laptop with a touchpad. Push down on the scroll-wheel button to orbit, hold down the Shift key with the scroll wheel button to pan, and roll the scroll wheel to zoom (Figure 5.7).

You don't need to use the Camera tools icons on your screen because all the navigation tools are readily available at your fingertips (Figure 5.8). Actually, you'll be better off if you completely ignore these icons. If you use them, you'll have to search your screen outside of the work area. Every time you take your eyes off your design, you focus on the wrong thing. Furthermore, you'll give yourself a headache hunting around the screen for buttons.

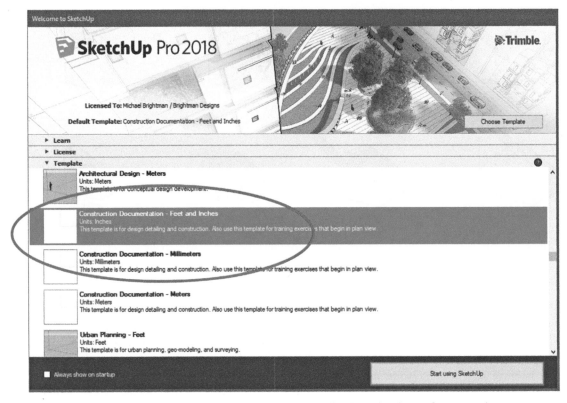

Figure 5.6 The Welcome to SketchUp window appears automatically when SketchUp is first opened.

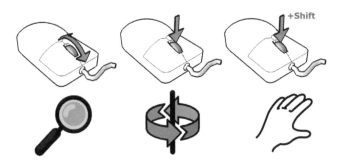

Figure 5.7 Mouse navigation diagrams.

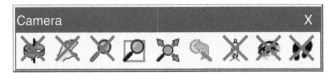

Figure 5.8 Avoid using the Camera tools icons. The most frequently used navigation tools are readily available on your three-button scroll wheel mouse.

TIP If you are using the trackpad, 3D mouse, or the Apple Mighty Mouse, you are running at a fraction of the speed possible. The biggest improvement in speed is gained by simply switching to a three-button scroll wheel mouse.

Your cursor is the focal point of all navigation. Position it on the object you want to zoom in on, pan by, or orbit around so you will have more navigational control.

When you're completing any task in SketchUp, always navigate to a view that is strategic for the task at hand. For instance, if you are trying to work on the elevation, don't look at the model from a plan view. For any operation, you should always first determine the view that will make it easiest to perform the task. Also, be sure to utilize your large LCD monitor and zoom in on the area you are working on.

Measurements

The Measurements dialog in SketchUp gives you complete control over any tool. Keep in mind that it is always ready for your input. You never need to click in the Measurements dialog to enter a precise dimension or value; you just need to start typing.

By default, the Measurements toolbar is docked at the bottom-right corner of the SketchUp interface. You can reposition this toolbar by clicking on the View drop-down menu and choosing Toolbars > Measurements. Once the Measurements toolbar is floating, it can be repositioned or docked anywhere on the screen (Figure 5.9). The screen captures used in this chapter show a floating Measurements toolbar.

MODELING STRATEGY

At this point, it should be very clear that you can be very loose and sketchy in SketchUp, or you can be accurate and precise. Just as each project type has a unique organizational strategy, each also has a unique modeling strategy. There are two schools of thought: model sketchy and then clean up, or model precisely from the beginning. There is no one right way to design in SketchUp, but some of the suggestions presented here can help you determine how SketchUp is best leveraged.

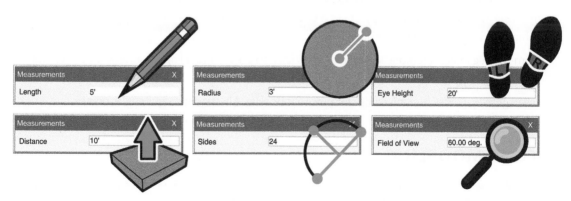

Figure 5.9 The Measurements dialog changes depending on the tool and the type of input it needs.

Sketchy Modeling

If you model without paying attention to precise dimensions, you are creating a *throw-away model*. When you create sketchy models, the amount of effort you'll need to edit the loose geometry back into precision is not worth the time it would take. Typically, it is easier to rebuild the design in a new file after you have poured your thoughts into the sketchy model. If you are going to model in this way, keep these tips in mind:

☑ Turn on length snapping in the Model Info > Units tab to make the sketchy dimensions snap to a clean, round number. This will make it a little easier to transition if you are cutting and pasting into your precise model.

☑ Group everything! Once geometry is stuck together, it becomes much more difficult (but not impossible) to sort it all out. It's easier to explode a group rather than piece one together.

☑ Assume that your sketchy model is going to be a throw-away model. Usually, it takes more effort to edit the geometry back into precise dimensions than it would to rebuild the model.

☑ During the schematic design phase, create a programming diagram, mass models, and quick plan sketches without being too hung up on precise modeling practices.

☑ A new construction project lends itself to brainstorming on a larger and freer scale, sometimes without paying close attention to precise dimensions. Because you aren't limited by the constraints of an existing building, you are free to develop any style and space plan you desire.

Precise Modeling

Modeling with exact dimensions from the beginning is the best method. Even though it is easy to push, pull, move, and scale without being precise, there is really no reason to do that. Keep your dimensions clean from the beginning by organizing your model and performing accurate operations. If you are going to model in this way, keep these tips in mind:

☑ If you have used a sketch model, or concept, then start a new file to create the precise model.

☑ Move groups, components, and entities between groups and components and even other files using the Paste in Place command. Copy or cut a selection, and once you are inside the desired model or container, click on the Edit drop-down menu and choose Paste in Place.

☑ From the beginning, a remodeling project lends itself to precise modeling because you need to work within the constraints of the existing construction.

☑ Leverage axes, guides, and inferences for precise modeling. Always draw right angles on axis.

PRECISE MODELING

It is critical to be a clean modeler when using SketchUp. Despite having the word *sketch* in the name, it is important to model with impeccable precision. When drawing lines that are parallel and perpendicular, stay on axis. Precise, accurate, pristine models composed of flawless geometry are accomplished through properly leveraging axes, guides, and inferences.

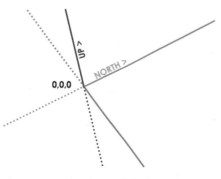

Axes

Axes are the red, green, and blue lines that represent the x, y, and z directions in three dimensions (Figure 5.10). These axes can be moved and rotated to make modeling easier. The axes control much of the inferences. Be sure to draw lines on axes.

Figure 5.10 SketchUp's default axes.

Origin

The origin is the center point where the axes converge—and the center of the SketchUp world. This is 0,0,0. You can get back to the base origin by right-clicking on any axis and choosing reset.

Move Sketching Context

Right-click on any axis and choose Move to access the Move Sketching Context dialog (Figure 5.11). You can now move the origin to a known point or rotate the axes about one axis to a precise degree. You will use the Move Origin function to create grid shift utility scenes.

Axes Tool

The Axes tool allows you to move the axes with your cursor rather than a dialog. This comes in handy when you need to align your axes to an object in your model or fix a group's or component's axes that do not align with the geometry within (Figure 5.12). Follow these steps.

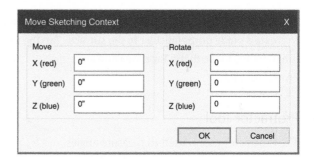

Figure 5.11 The Move Origin dialog.

1. Double-click into a group and activate the Axes tool.

2. Click to set the origin of axes.

3. Click again to set the red axis.

4. Click one more time to set the green axes.

Guides

Guides can be created with the Tape Measure tool and the Protractor tool. Guides are a special type of line that go on for infinity.

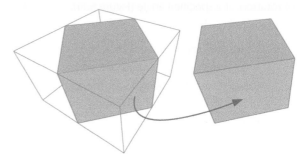

Figure 5.12 The Axes tool is used to fix groups and components that were created off-axis.

Guide visibility is a product of a style. If you adjust using the drop-downs, make sure you understand how to update your style if you want it to stick.

Delete guides as you would any other geometry, or all at once by clicking on the Edit drop-down menu and choosing Delete Guides. If you are in a group and run this command, only the guides in the current group, and deeper, will be deleted.

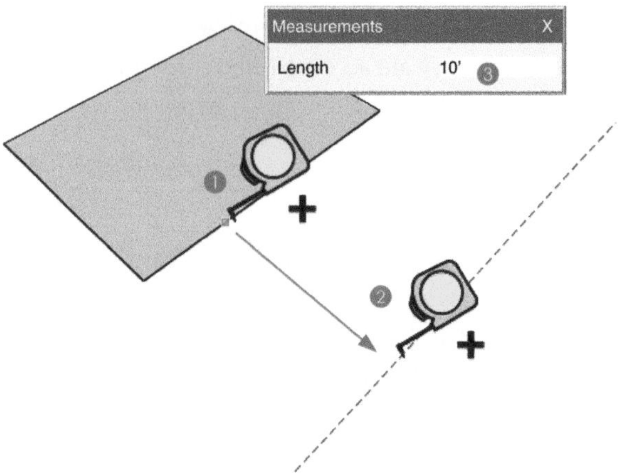

Tape Measure Tool

The Tape Measure tool (Figure 5.13) is used to measure elements within your model and to create guidelines. To do the latter, follow these steps:

Figure 5.13 The Tape Measure tool.

1. Activate the Tape Measure tool, hover on an edge, and click once to start.

2. Move your cursor away, and you will see a guideline parallel to the edge that you clicked on appear.

3. Click again to finish, then type in a precise dimension.

TIP Start the process on a point to create a guideline and guide point. Double-click on a surface to create a guide perpendicular to the surface. Tap the Control key (Option on Mac) to toggle guide functionality for both the Tape Measure and Protractor tools.

Protractor Tool

The Protractor tool is used to measure angles between entities and create a guide off a specified line, around a defined center point of rotation, at a specified angle (Figure 5.14). To use it, follow these steps:

1. Using the Protractor tool, click and hold at the desired center point of rotation, and drag away to set the axis of rotation. Look for the inference line to turn red, green, or blue.

2. Release once you have found the desired axis of rotation—for this example, rotate about the green axis.

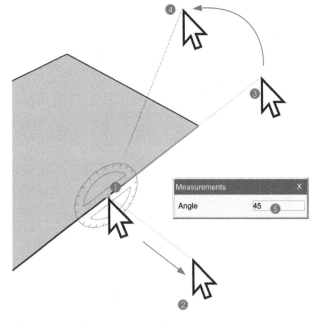

Figure 5.14 The Protractor tool.

3. Move your cursor around and notice that it is locked at the defined center point of rotation. Hover on an edge, then click to define the reference angle.

4. Move your cursor and click again to define the degree of rotation away from the reference angle.

5. You can click at a random angle, or at this point, let go of the mouse and enter a precise angle into the Measurements dialog—for example, 45. This will set the guide 45 degrees off the reference angle around the defined center point of rotation.

TIP You can also type 1:12 to set a roof pitch rather than an angle. This works for the Rotate tool as well.

Inferences

The inference engine is always running in the background and is there to help keep your geometry aligned in accurate and meaningful ways. Mastering inferences is essential to fast and efficient drafting in SketchUp. The inferences discussed in this section are advanced techniques; becoming familiar with each will make you faster at drawing in SketchUp. Try to think of ways to eliminate clicks from your own modeling process. Often, inferences can eliminate guides and clicks. Many of the following inferences work with both the Drawing tools and the Edit tools.

TIP The inference engine cannot be turned off, but why would you want it to? Once you master the available inferences, you will wonder how you ever lived without advanced inferences.

Multiple Points

You can encourage an inference from a point, a midpoint, or even two points (Figure 5.15). Follow these steps:

1. With the Line tool active, hover on an endpoint until you see the Endpoint notification. When you see it, the edge is loaded into the inference engine.

2. Hover on another endpoint until you see the Endpoint notification. When you see it, the edge is loaded into the inference engine.

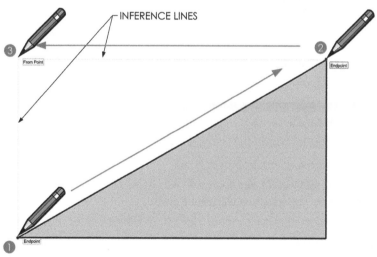

Figure 5.15 Encouraging two inference points to use a meaningful starting point.

3. Move your cursor away from the point, and you will see two dotted inference lines projecting from the two inferenced points.

4. Click to start the line. Now you can go on to encourage more inferences and click to finish.

Parallel to Edge

Draw parallel to an existing edge by encouraging a Parallel to Edge inference (Figure 5.16). Follow these steps:

1. Click once to start a line.

2. Position your cursor on the edge to which you want to draw a parallel line. Wait for the On Edge inference to appear—this lets you know that SketchUp loaded that edge into the inference engine.

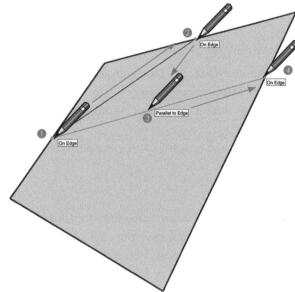

Figure 5.16 A Parallel to Edge inference.

3. Position your cursor roughly parallel to the edge. The active line will turn magenta, and you will see the Parallel to Edge notification appear. At this point, you can hold down the Shift key to lock the inference.

4. Position your cursor over a point or edge to specify the distance, and click to finish.

Constrained on Line

The Edge Constrained on Line inference allows you to either start or finish an operation along a specific edge (Figure 5.17). Follow these steps:

1. Using the Line tool, hover on a line. When you see the On Edge inference, hold down the Shift key.

2. Move your cursor until the starting point of the line is constrained along the edge, you will see a Constrained on Line inference, click to start your line.

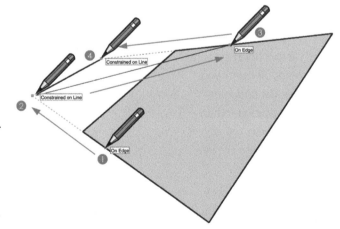

Figure 5.17 A Constrained on Line inference.

3. Hover on another edge. Once you see the On Edge inference, hold down the Shift key.

4. Move your cursor until the next point of the line is constrained along the edge.

TIP You can also constrain an operation on a surface by first hovering on the surface and then holding the Shift key. This will limit any line that you draw to be coplanar with the inferred surface. Constrained inferences, both edge and surface, are especially helpful when working out complex roofs in three dimensions.

Line Intersect

Use the Line Intersect inference to take the place of guides and project intersections between lines (Figure 5.18). Follow these steps:

1. To encourage the inference, use the Line tool to hover on an endpoint until you see the Endpoint inference notification.

2. Move your cursor down away from the endpoint on the green axis and click to set the starting point.

3. Move your cursor to the left until you find the red axis. Once the active line turns red, hold down the Shift key to lock the axis.

4. Position your cursor on the angled line. The endpoint of the line has been projected to the intersection of the locked axis that was started on the inferenced edge. Click to finish the line.

CREATING GEOMETRY

The most frequently used tools for creating geometry in SketchUp can be categorized into two groups: the Drawing tools and the Edit tools. To get started with any model, you must first create the geometry using the Drawing tools (Line, Rectangle, Circle, Arc, Polygon, and Freehand). Once you've created simple two-dimensional (2D) geometry, you can shape and change that geometry into a more complex form using the Edit tools (Move, Push/Pull, Rotate, Follow Me, Scale, and Offset). Throughout the modeling process, you will likely go back and forth between these toolsets (Figure 5.19).

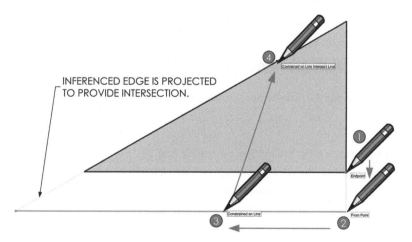

Figure 5.18 The Line Intersect inference.

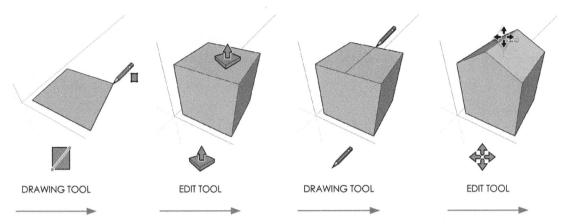

DRAWING TOOL   EDIT TOOL   DRAWING TOOL   EDIT TOOL

Figure 5.19 To efficiently model in SketchUp, you'll need to move back and forth between the Drawing and Edit tools. Use the Drawing tools to make additional edges and break surfaces to set up operations for the Edit tools.

Drawing Tools

The Drawing tools can be further broken down into two groups: the Surface Drawing tools and the Edge Drawing tools. A Surface Drawing tool creates a closed loop of coplanar edges, including a surface, in a specified shape. An Edge Drawing tool creates straight and curved edges (no surface). These tools provide infinite combinations to complete additive and subtractive modeling operations (Figure 5.20).

In this section, we will cover the most useful tools for this workflow. Don't hesitate to explore other toolbars.

Surface Drawing Tools

The Surface Drawing tools include the Rectangle, Circle, and Polygon, all of which create a closed loop of coplanar edges and a surface. It is best to start building a model using these tools (Figure 5.21).

To use the Surface Drawing tools, click once to start, move your cursor to suggest a direction, then click again to finish. Keep in mind that you can enter precise dimensions during or after the command until another command is started. The same is true for most SketchUp tools.

TIP The best way to execute most SketchUp commands is to use the click-and-release method. The click-and-drag method will get you into trouble because it is easy to accidentally perform small, unnoticeable commands with many of the tools. Typically, you should click once to start, move your cursor, click again to finish, and then enter a precise dimension.

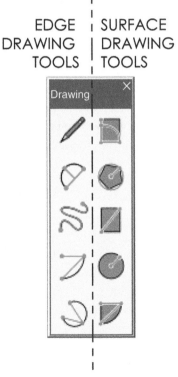

EDGE DRAWING TOOLS | SURFACE DRAWING TOOLS

Figure 5.20 The Drawing toolbar.

Rectangle Tool

The Rectangle tool is very effective for creating surfaces, and it certainly is one of the most frequently used tools in SketchUp. One of its great features is that the geometry it creates is always aligned with the axes. This means that you can create four edges and a surface, all squared up, with just two clicks (Figure 5.22).

1. Activate the Rectangle tool and click once to start.

2. Move your cursor to suggest a direction, and click again to finish.

3. At this point, you can enter precise dimensions such as 120,120 and then press Enter.

Figure 5.21 Typically, you will begin a model using one of the Surface Drawing tools.

TIP The Rectangle tool can be locked to an axis using the arrow keys. If you find the square or golden rectangle, hold the Shift key to lock the inferences.

Circle and Polygon Tools

Because SketchUp is a surface modeler—meaning that the basic building blocks are edges and surfaces—there are no true circles in SketchUp. All circles are represented by a series of connected edges. The more sides a circle has, the smoother it looks (Figure 5.23). The default number of sides for a circle is 24 sides, and this number works for just about any circle you will need to create. Keep in mind that when you extrude a circle into a 3D form, every edge will become a surface with three additional edges. As a result, the more edges you have, the more 3D surfaces you create, and ultimately the slower your model will perform, which can be problematic.

Be aware of what you are modeling and how many sides you need to achieve the quality you want. If you are creating a close-up rendering of a column, it would be appropriate to increase the number of sides before you create the circle base of the column. If you are rendering several columns for a building off in the distance, you could

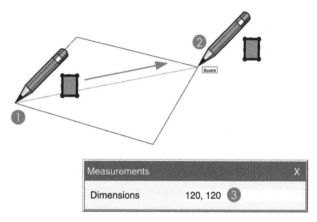

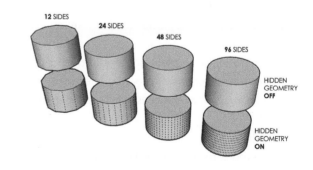

Figure 5.22 The Rectangle tool in action.

Figure 5.23 Two cylinders with different side counts. At what point are more segments unnoticeable?

decrease the number of sides used to create the circle bases of the columns. There are times when a drastically lower number of sides is not noticeable. When you activate the Circle tool, you can change the default number of sides used to represent a circle (Figure 5.24).

To create a circle, follow these steps:

1. Activate the Circle tool, then immediately type 48 and press Enter to change the default number of sides on a circle to 48 sides.

2. Click once to define the center point of the circle.

3. Move your cursor away from the center point on axis, then click again to finish.

4. At this point, you can enter a precise radius such as 120 and then press Enter.

The Polygon tool works the same way as the Circle tool. The difference between the two is that a polygon's edges are not softened when extruded (Figure 5.25).

TIP When drawing circles and polygons, it is best to keep your cursor aligned with an axis. This way, the segments of the circle are likely to merge in a more regular, symmetrical way.

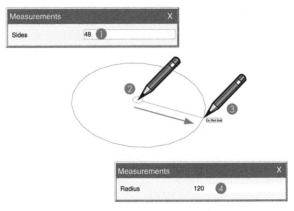

Figure 5.24 The Circle tool in action.

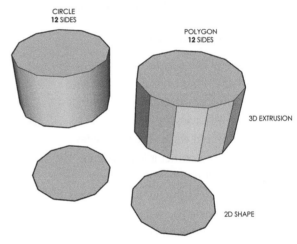

Figure 5.25 A circle and polygon in 2D; a circle and polygon extruded into 3D.

Edge Drawing Tools

The Edge Drawing tools include the Line, Arc, and Freehand (Figure 5.26). These tools create only edges, not surfaces. You can use the Edge Drawing tools to make small additive and subtractive adjustments to existing surfaces. Although they aren't the most efficient tools for creating surfaces from scratch, you can use them to actually draw the sides of a closed loop of coplanar edges.

Line Tool

The Line tool is the most basic Edge Drawing tool in SketchUp, and it is the tool with which most designers begin. Although it has many uses, surprisingly, using it is not the most effective way to create geometry. The Line tool is best used to make small adjustments and modifications.

Figure 5.26 The Edge Drawing tools.

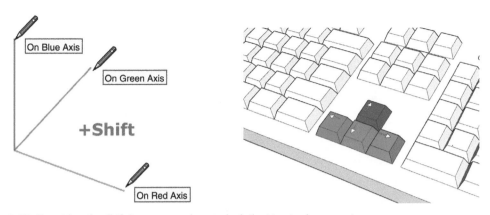

Figure 5.27 Use either the Shift key or arrow keys to lock the Line tool on an axis.

When you're drawing in 3D with the Line tool, you can draw on axis by locking the Line tool on an axis. To lock an axis, first find the axis and then hold down the Shift key to lock it. Finish the operation by clicking on a point to define the distance, then release the Shift key. You can also lock an axis by tapping an arrow key while drawing a line. The right arrow key locks the red axis, the left arrow key locks the green axis, and the up arrow key locks the blue axis. The down arrow key locks various magenta inferences.

Locking an axis eliminates two of the three dimensions, so all you need to do is define a distance along the specified locked axis (Figure 5.27). You can do this by using the inference engine to snap to a point, edge, or surface. Also, you can enter precise dimensions into the Measurements dialog.

The Line tool can also be used to heal surfaces (Figure 5.28). Right-click on an edge of a surface and choose Erase. When you erase an edge, you break the closed loop of coplanar edges and, in turn, lose the surface. Redraw the line from point to point, and you will have the edge and surface back.

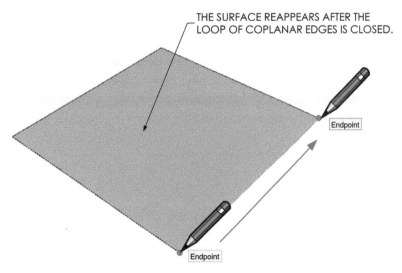

Figure 5.28 Redraw a deleted edge using the Line tool to recreate the edge and surface at the same time.

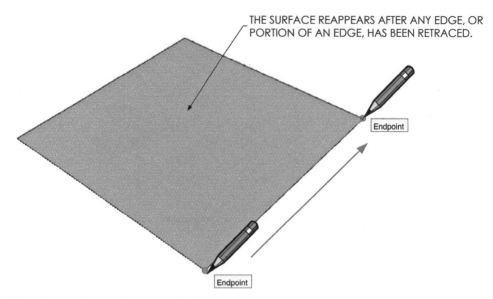

THE SURFACE REAPPEARS AFTER ANY EDGE, OR PORTION OF AN EDGE, HAS BEEN RETRACED.

Endpoint

Endpoint

Figure 5.29 Heal a deleted surface using the Line tool.

Now, right-click on the surface and choose Erase to delete only the surface. Use the Line tool to retrace any edge around the closed loop of coplanar edges. The surface is now healed (Figure 5.29). Keep in mind that because geometry does not stack in SketchUp, there is only one edge remaining where you traced the edge.

Two-Point Arc Tool

Use the Arc tool to create precise curves.

1. Click once to define the starting point of the arc.
2. Click again to define the endpoint of the arc, or enter a precise dimension into the Measurements dialog.
3. Click once more to define the bulge (Figure 5.30).
4. Using the Measurements dialog, you can also enter a specific distance for the bulge.

When you're using the Arc tool to round the corners of a rectangle, look for the magenta Equidistant and Tangent to Edge inferences (Figure 5.31). When you're continuing an arc, look for the cyan Tangent at Vertex inference to make a smooth transition between the two arcs (Figure 5.32).

TIP The Arc, Three-Point Arc, and Pie tools are pretty worthless.

Freehand Tool

The Freehand tool is one of the few tools that require you to click and drag (Figure 5.33). You can use it to draw loose, sketchy lines.

1. Click and drag to draw a line.
2. Release on the starting point to finish and create a surface.

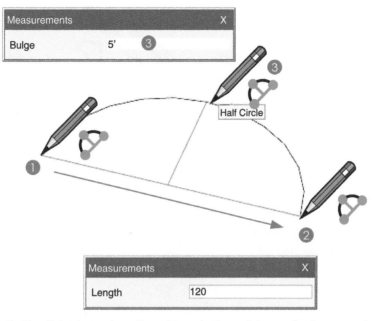

Figure 5.30 To use the Two-Point Arc tool, you'll need to make three clicks: one for the start point, one for the end-point, and one for the bulge.

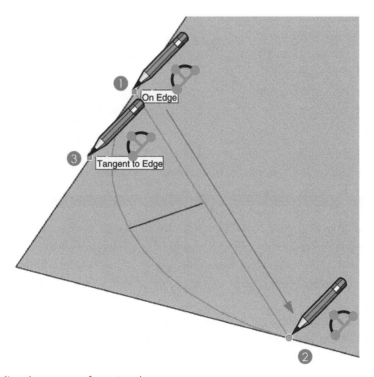

Figure 5.31 Rounding the corners of a rectangle.

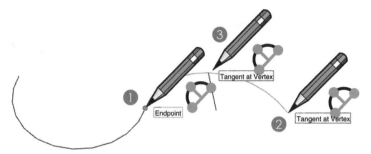

Figure 5.32 Continuing an arc.

TIP The Bezier Curve extension draws more accurate loose curves; download it from the Extension Warehouse. You will learn more about extensions in Chapter 9, Extensions.

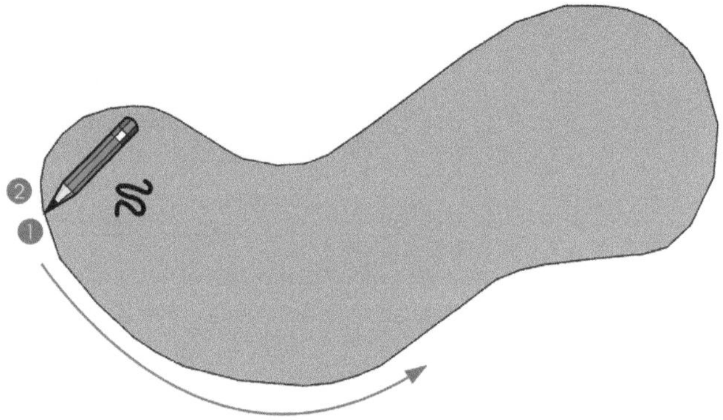

Edit Tools

Once you've created the geometry using the Drawing tools, you can change it using the Edit tools (Figure 5.34). These tools can quickly transform 2D geometry into 3D objects and create complex geometry by scaling, stretching, moving, and copying.

Figure 5.33 When using the Freehand tool, be sure to finish on the starting point to create a surface.

The Select Tool

The Select tool is included in the Principal tools, but it is critical for using the Edit tools. Of all the tools you need to master, this one is by far the most underestimated and the most important. You will use the Select tool before

Figure 5.34 The Edit tools are available in the Edit toolbar.

you use most of the other SketchUp tools. Typically, you will default back to the Select tool after issuing a command. All Edit operations are complemented by the Select tool. It is best to preselect an entity before you use the Edit tools. Some have a hot spot that autoselects entities, but you will find that you can obtain complete control by first preselecting an entity with the Select tool.

TIP Navigate to a view that is strategic for what you are selecting. Try Parallel Projection Plan and Elevation views. Right-click on a surface and choose Align View to get to a perpendicular elevation view fast.

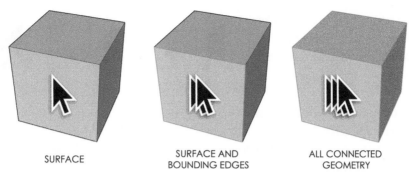

| SURFACE | SURFACE AND BOUNDING EDGES | ALL CONNECTED GEOMETRY |

Figure 5.35 Single-click, double-click, or triple-click to quickly select individual or multiple entities.

Click once on an edge or surface to select it. Double-click on a surface to select the surface as well as the bounding edges. Triple-click on a surface to select all the connected geometry (Figure 5.35).

To perform a window selection, click and drag from left to right over the entities you want to select (Figure 5.36). Only the entities that are completely in the selection window will be selected. A window selection is represented by a solid selection window.

To perform a crossing selection, click and drag right to left over the entities you want to select. A crossing selection will select the entities that are completely within the selection window as well as any entity that the selection window touches. A crossing selection is represented by a dashed selection window.

Hold down the Ctrl key (Option on a Mac) while you are using the Select tool to add entities to the selection. Hold down the Ctrl (Option on Mac) and Shift keys while you are using the Select tool to remove

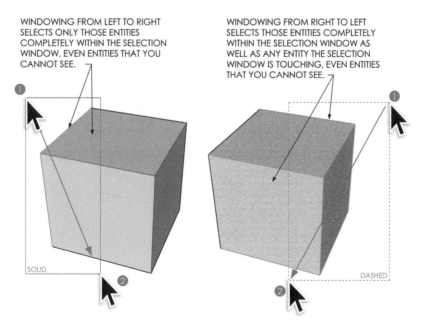

WINDOWING FROM LEFT TO RIGHT SELECTS ONLY THOSE ENTITIES COMPLETELY WITHIN THE SELECTION WINDOW, EVEN ENTITIES THAT YOU CANNOT SEE.

WINDOWING FROM RIGHT TO LEFT SELECTS THOSE ENTITIES COMPLETELY WITHIN THE SELECTION WINDOW AS WELL AS ANY ENTITY THE SELECTION WINDOW IS TOUCHING, EVEN ENTITIES THAT YOU CANNOT SEE.

SOLID

DASHED

Figure 5.36 Click and drag with the Select tool to create selection windows.

entities from the selection. Hold the Shift key while you are using the Select tool to inverse the selection. All of these modifier keys work with selection windows, too (Figure 5.37).

ADD (CTRL)   SUBTRACT (CTRL + SHIFT)   INVERSE (SHIFT)

TIP Before starting any command, it is best to clear all selections. You can deselect all of

Figure 5.37 You can alter a selection by using modifier keys.

the entities in a model by clicking on the Edit drop-down menu and choosing Deselect All or by right-clicking on the model background.

To see additional selection options, right-click on an edge or surface (Figure 5.38). From this menu, you can select Bounding Edges, Connected Faces, All Connected, All on same Layer, or All with same Material. These unique selection options can help you make complex selections faster.

If you find yourself tediously picking through a model, keep in mind that there is always a fast and easy way to make the selection you need. Use a combination of all the selection techniques to select only what you need in the most effective manner. Approach the selection process just as you do the modeling process; the process can be additive or subtractive. Before starting the selection, ask yourself whether it would be easier to select several entities and then deselect what you don't need or whether it would be better to add each piece individually. Perhaps using a combination of the two techniques would be most effective. Every selection is different, so be sure to keep your approach flexible.

TIP The Selection Toys extension opens up many new ways to make clever, helpful selections and can be found at **extensions.sketchup.com/en/content/selection-toys.**

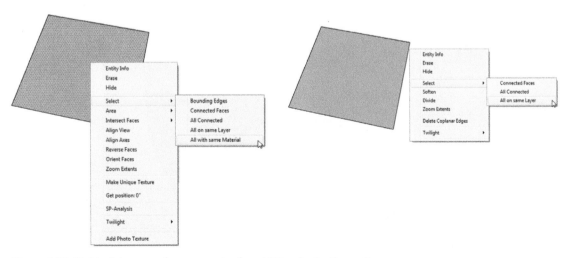

Figure 5.38 Right-click on a surface or an edge for additional selection options.

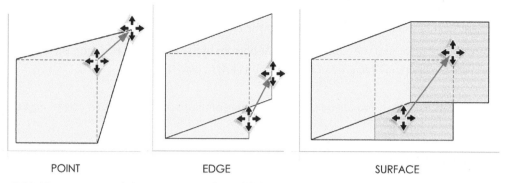

POINT   EDGE   SURFACE

Figure 5.39 Move a point, and the connecting edge will follow. Move an edge, and the connecting edges will follow. Move a surface, and all the bounding edges of the surface will move as well.

The Move Tool

The Move tool's efficiency relies heavily on the stickiness of the geometry. You can move points, edges, and surfaces using the tool. Doing so has a different effect on the entity, as well as the adjacent, connected entities (Figure 5.39). The Move tool's hot spot is right in the middle of the icon. Place your cursor on an edge or a surface, and note that the Move tool will autoselect entities. Click once to pick an entity up, then click again to put it down.

TIP Beware! The Move tool is the number one destroyer of models. Be careful about what you are selecting and what is beyond your selection. You can select entities that are visibly blocked by other geometry, which makes it easy to move entities accidentally and "blow out" the back of a model.

Precise Move

A *precise move* is executed by preselecting entities and then moving the selection from a specific spot on the selection to another in the model (Figure 5.40). A precise move can be started and ended on an edge, endpoint, midpoint, or surface, depending on the desired final location.

To make a precise move, follow these steps:

1. Using the Select tool, preselect the entity you want to move.

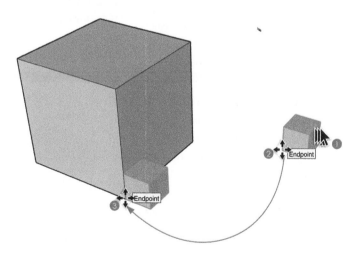

Figure 5.40 A precise move.

2. Activate the Move tool. Hover on the front-bottom corner of the cube until you see the Endpoint inference notification. Click once to pick up the cube.

3. Move your cursor, and the cube, to the front-bottom of the large cube. Hover on the corner until you see the Endpoint inference notification and click to place the cube.

TIP Don't "eyeball it" when you can be precise. When performing a precise move, be sure to snap to other entities in your model.

Linear Copy and Array

The Move tool is also the "Copy" tool. To toggle the Copy command on and off, tap the Ctrl key (Option on a Mac). As you are moving any entity, tap the Ctrl key (Option on a Mac) to leave a copy of it behind.

To make a copy, follow these steps (Figure 5.41):

1. Using the Select tool, preselect the entity that you want to copy.

2. Activate the Move tool, and click once on the entity (you can start the copy from anywhere in the model).

3. Tap the Ctrl key (Option on a Mac) to toggle on the Copy command while you move the cursor along an axis, then click again to finish.

4. At this point, enter a precise distance into the Measurements dialog, such as 20', then press Enter.

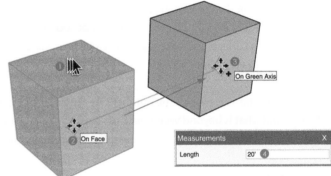

Figure 5.41 To create a copy of any entity, use the Move tool and the Copy toggle.

5. To create multiple copies at a specified distance immediately after you complete the Move/ Copy command, enter the number of copies you want to make—for example, type 4x, then press Enter. This will create four copies of the selection in addition to the original, just as a copy machine would (Figure 5.42).

Another way to array using the Move tool is to divide the distance between the copies (Figure 5.43). After you complete a copy, specify the number of divisions between the two copies within the Measurements dialog, as follows:

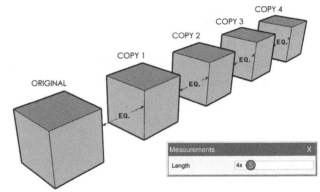

Figure 5.42 Create multiple copies at set intervals using the multiply array.

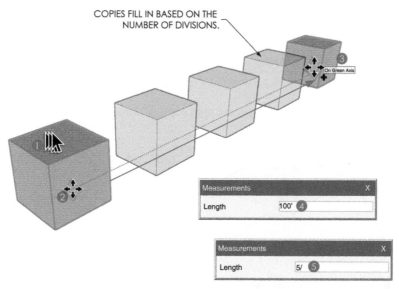

COPIES FILL IN BASED ON THE
NUMBER OF DIVISIONS.

On Green Axis

Measurements   X
Length   100'

Measurements   X
Length   5/

Figure 5.43 Use the divide array to create multiple copies at set intervals.

1. Using the Select tool, preselect the entity that you want to copy.

2. Activate the Move tool, and click once on the entity (you could start the copy from anywhere in the model).

3. Tap the Ctrl key (Option on a Mac) to toggle on the Copy command while you move the cursor along an axis, then click again to finish.

4. At this point, enter a precise distance into the Measurements dialog—for example, type 100'—and then press Enter.

5. Immediately after entering the distance, enter the desired number of divisions between the two copies—for instance, type 5/—and then press Enter.

You can continue to modify the copy and array until you start another command. Try entering different numbers of copies and different distances, and switch between using multiply and divide arrays. Once you click on another tool, you will lose the ability to modify the array (Figure 5.44). At that point, the new geometry will be just that—geometry. You will need to delete or reposition geometry to change the array.

Autofold

If a surface does not have the proper lines, or breaks, to fold the surface, SketchUp will not allow the selection to move on all axes. The Autofold command automatically draws all the lines needed to break a surface and allow the selected surface to move in any direction (Figure 5.45). While performing a move, tap the Alt key (Command key on a Mac) to toggle the Autofold command on.

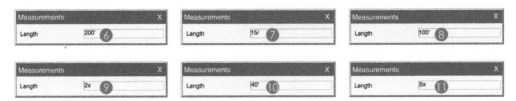

Figure 5.44 You can continue to modify the copy and array until you invoke another command.

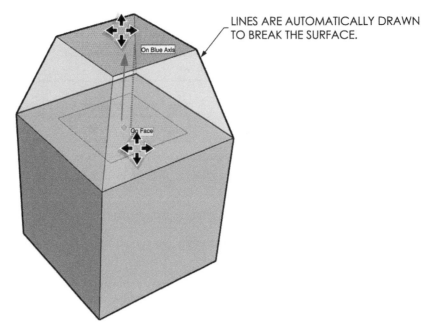

LINES ARE AUTOMATICALLY DRAWN TO BREAK THE SURFACE.

Figure 5.45 Autofold in action.

TIP Don't use the Autofold command as a crutch. Although it can appear to help make an entity move where you want it to sometimes, it can actually create off-axis geometry that will be problematic later.

TIP Master the Move tool through repetition. Develop muscle memory with the Move Tool Obstacle Course in SketchUp for Professionals.

Push/Pull Tool

The Push/Pull tool is one of the fastest and easiest ways to generate large amounts of geometry. This tool extrudes 2D surfaces into 3D forms, perpendicular to the starting face. This means that geometry is typically on-axis or at least perfectly square with the starting surface. The Push/Pull tool affects only surfaces. Follow these steps:

1. Position the Push/Pull tool on a surface; it will autoselect the surface. The hot spot of the Push/Pull tool is at the tip of the red arrow on the icon. Click on the surface to start the operation.

2. Move your cursor to push or pull the surface. The surface will extrude perpendicular to the starting surface (Figure 5.46). Click again to finish.

3. At this point, you can enter a precise dimension—for example, type 5'—then press Enter.

Tap the Ctrl key (Option on a Mac) before or during any Push/Pull operation to leave a copy of the starting face (Figure 5.47). This is a toggle, so tap the Ctrl key (Option on a Mac) again, and the starting face will disappear. In Chapter 17, Renovation, you will see how valuable this function is for creating floorplans.

TIP The Push/Pull tool has a memory. Once you have completed a Push/Pull operation, you can double-click on another surface to reproduce the last push/pull.

Follow Me Tool

The Follow Me tool generates massive amounts of complex geometry with very few clicks. This tool works by extruding a 2D profile along a path (Figure 5.48). A path can be a series of connected edges or a surface that defines the path with its bounding edges. Follow these steps:

1. Using the Select tool, preselect the path—in this example, a surface.

2. Activate the Follow Me tool.

3. Click on the profile to finish.

TIP The profile does not have to touch the path for the Follow Me tool to work, though the operation and results make more sense and are easier to predict if it does.

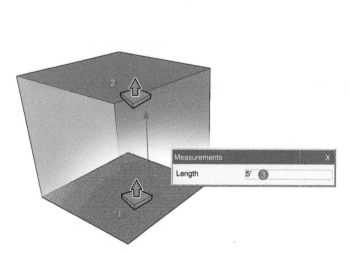

Figure 5.46 The Push/Pull tool in action.

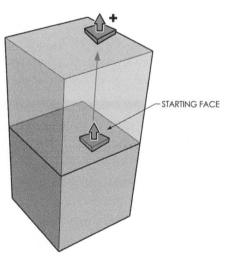

STARTING FACE

Figure 5.47 The Push/Pull tool can leave a copy of the starting face behind if desired.

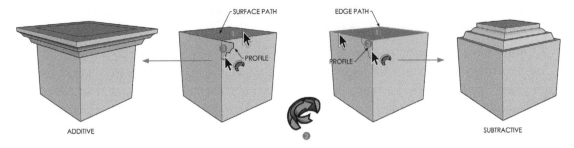

Figure 5.48 The Follow Me tool in action.

TIP Try the Follow Me Tool Obstacle Course in SketchUp for Professionals Extended.

Rotate Tool

The Rotate tool spins entities around a defined center point of rotation at a specified angle (Figure 5.49). To use it, follow these steps:

1. Using the Select tool, preselect the entity you want to rotate.

2. Activate the Rotate tool. Click and hold at the desired center point of rotation, and drag away to set the axis of rotation. Look for the inference line to turn red, green, or blue. Release once you have found the desired axis of rotation—for this example, rotate about the red axis.

TIP Use guides or encourage an inference to specify a meaningful center point of rotation. Also, the arrow keys will lock an axis of rotation.

3. Move your cursor around and notice that it is locked at the defined center point of rotation. Click to define the reference angle. The reference angle can be arbitrary for most rotations, unless you are trying to align one object with another.

4. Move your cursor and click again to define the degree of rotation away from the reference angle.

5. You can click at a random angle, or at this point, let go of the mouse and enter a precise angle into the Measurements dialog—for example, type 90.0—then press Enter. This will rotate the object 90 degrees off the reference angle around the defined center point of rotation.

Similar to the Move tool, during any rotation, tap the Ctrl key (Option on a Mac) to toggle on the Copy command. This will leave a copy of the selected object behind (Figure 5.50). To perform a polar copy and array, follow these steps:

1. Preselect the entity you wish to rotate and copy. Activate the Rotate tool, hover on a point to encourage an inference, and choose a meaningful starting point.

2. Click and drag and release on the blue axis.

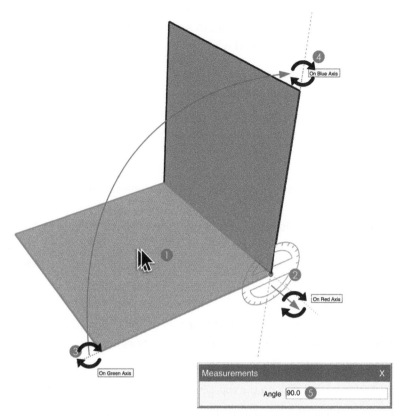

On Blue Axis

On Red Axis

Measurements X

Angle 90.0 5

On Green Axis

Figure 5.49 Use the Rotate tool to spin entities around a specified axis.

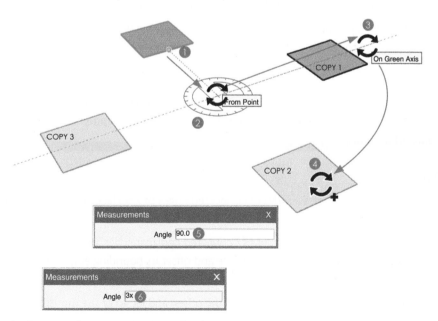

On Green Axis

COPY 1

From Point

COPY 3

COPY 2

Measurements X

Angle 90.0 5

Measurements X

Angle 3x 6

Figure 5.50 The Rotate tool can create copies and polar arrays.

3. Move your cursor to the right, and click once to set the reference line. Tap the Ctrl key (Option on a Mac) to toggle on the Copy command while you move your cursor down the screen.

4. Click to place the copy.

5. Immediately type a precise degree of rotation, such as 90.0, then press Enter.

6. To make three copies, for example, immediately type the number of copies as 3x, then press Enter. You can continue to change both the degree of rotation and the number of copies until you invoke another command.

TIP Try the Rotate Tool Obstacle Course in SketchUp for Professionals Extended.

TIP Similar to the way you use the Move tool, you can also enter the overall copy rotation and specify divisions. For example, after making a copy, type 180, press Enter, immediately type 5′, then press Enter again. This will make the original copy at 180 degrees and fill the space in between with five divisions.

Scale Tool

The Scale tool distorts entities based on a scale factor or a "hard" dimension. The hot spot of the Scale tool is at the tip of the red arrow, but it usually is best to preselect entities before scaling. Follow these steps:

1. Using the Select tool, preselect the entity you want to scale.

2. Activate the Scale tool and click on the top-center grip.

3. Move your cursor to scale the object, and click to finish the command.

4. Immediately enter a scale value—such as 1.50—then press Enter.

5. You can also type a precise dimension into the Measurements dialog—for example, 20′—then press Enter. Be sure to specify feet or inches because the Scale tool defaults to a scale value rather than the model's default units (Figure 5.51).

TIP The Scale tool also has modifier keys to help you achieve the desired scaling effect. Hold the Shift key to toggle between a uniform and nonuniform scale. Hold the Ctrl key (Option on a Mac) to scale about the center of the entity.

Offset Tool

The Offset tool concentrically copies a series of connected edges or a surface's bounding edges (Figure 5.52). Follow these steps:

1. Use the Select tool to preselect a series of connected coplanar edges, or use the tool's hot spot at the tip of the red arrow to autoselect a surface and offset its bounding edges. Hover on an edge and click to set the starting point.

2. Move your cursor to suggest the direction of the offset, and let go of the mouse.

3. At this point, you can type a precise dimension—such as 2′—then press Enter.

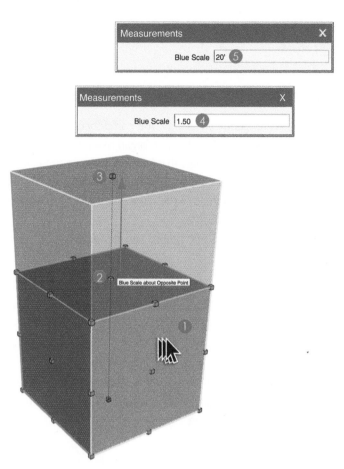

Figure 5.51 The Scale tool distorts entities based on a scale factor or set dimension.

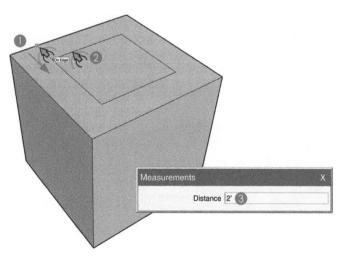

Figure 5.52 The Offset tool in action.

TIP The Offset tool also has a memory. You can double-click on another surface or series of coplanar lines to reproduce the last offset.

ORGANIZING GEOMETRY WITH CONTAINERS

SketchUp has two basic containers for geometry: groups and components (Figure 5.53). These containers not only separate edges to control stickiness, but they also organize entities and geometry to make more efficient models. Groups are unintelligent containers that have no connection between copies. Groups simply hold geometry. Components, on the other hand, are intelligent in that each instance is connected. If any instance of a component is modified, all instances of the same component will reflect those changes as well.

TIP In this book, the term *container* refers to both groups and components.

Groups

Groups are unintelligent containers that simply hold geometry (Figure 5.54). If you make a copy of a group, there will be no connection between the original and the new copy. Almost every object should be made part of a group. It is almost impossible to make too many groups. Groups are mainly used to contain entities, form a hierarchy of layers, and control the stickiness of geometry.

The organization techniques utilized during the SketchUp Workflow for Architecture require advanced layering and organization of groups. Model organization diagrams (Figure 5.55) are used to complement the text and further explain layering and grouping.

Creating a Group

To create a group, follow these steps:

1. Using the Select tool, select at least two entities (edges, surfaces, groups, or components).

2. Right-click on the selection and choose Make Group, or click on the Edit drop-down menu and choose Make Group.

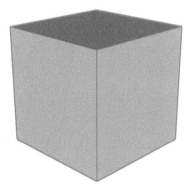

Figure 5.54 Groups can hold any entity created in SketchUp. When selected, both groups and components highlight with a green bounding box when using the ConDoc default template.

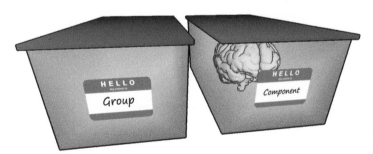

Figure 5.53 Components are intelligent; groups are not.

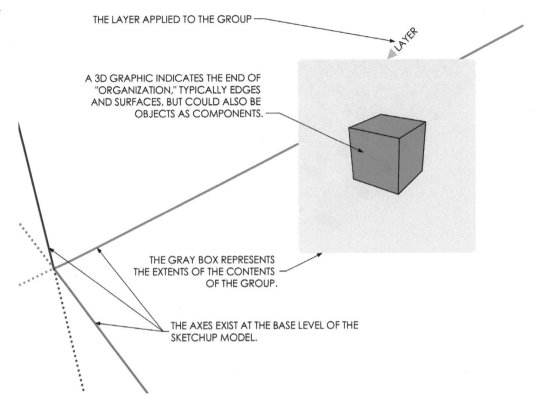

THE LAYER APPLIED TO THE GROUP

LAYER

A 3D GRAPHIC INDICATES THE END OF
"ORGANIZATION," TYPICALLY EDGES
AND SURFACES, BUT COULD ALSO BE
OBJECTS AS COMPONENTS.

THE GRAY BOX REPRESENTS
THE EXTENTS OF THE CONTENTS
OF THE GROUP.

THE AXES EXIST AT THE BASE LEVEL OF THE
SKETCHUP MODEL.

Figure 5.55 A simple group model organization diagram.

Components

Unlike groups, components are intelligent containers. They hold geometry just as groups do, but there is a link between all copies of a component. Suppose you make a component and then copy it several times throughout a model. If you edit any one instance of a component, all instances of that component will update simultaneously to reflect those changes (Figure 5.56).

Components are used to make extremely efficient models. When you see repeating elements, similar elements, and lines of symmetry, you should think component.

TIP A component's behavior is similar to a block in computer-aided design (CAD) or a smart object in Adobe Photoshop.

Creating a Component

To create a component, follow these steps (Figure 5.57):

1. Using the Select tool, select at least two entities.

2. Right-click on the selection, and choose Make Component.

3. In the Create Component dialog, assign the desired properties and choose Create.

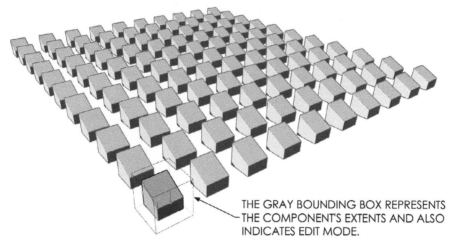

THE GRAY BOUNDING BOX REPRESENTS
THE COMPONENT'S EXTENTS AND ALSO
INDICATES EDIT MODE.

Figure 5.56 Any changes to the contents of a component are reflected in all instances of that component.

TIP If you are making a copy of a group, it should most likely be made into a component first. To change a group into a component, right-click on the group and choose Make Component.

Making Unique Components

The Make Unique command is used for similar elements. It is similar to a Save Copy As command in other programs. The original component instance(s) are left connected and intact, and a new component instance is created based on the selected component (Figure 5.58). To make a component, or multiple components, unique, select them, then right-click on the selection and choose Make Unique.

Navigating Containers

The ability to quickly move in and out of containers is essential to fast and efficient modeling in SketchUp. The first way to navigate containers is slow and methodical. Use this method when you're initially learning to navigate containers; it is easy to understand which container level of the model you are in. Follow these steps:

1. Right-click on a container, and choose Edit Group or Edit Component, depending on which type of container you are editing.

2. To close the container, right-click outside of the container bounding box, and choose Close Group or Close Component.

Figure 5.57 The Create Component dialog.

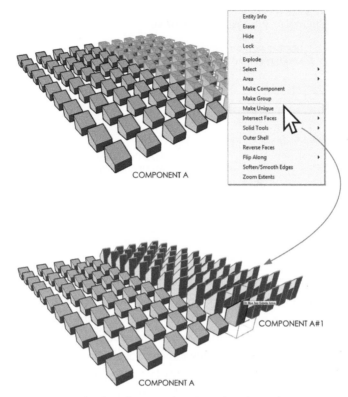

Entity Info	
Erase	
Hide	
Lock	
Explode	
Select	▶
Area	▶
Make Component	
Make Group	
Make Unique	
Intersect Faces	▶
Solid Tools	▶
Outer Shell	
Reverse Faces	
Flip Along	▶
Soften/Smooth Edges	
Zoom Extents	

COMPONENT A

COMPONENT A#1

COMPONENT A

Figure 5.58 Once a component or selection of components is made unique, the components are independent of the original instance and are connected only to each other.

A much faster method for navigating containers utilizes the Select tool. Use this method after you have a solid understanding of which container level you are in. Follow these steps:

1. Using the Select tool, double-click on a container to move in one level (Figure 5.59).

2. To close the container, press the Esc key to back out while the Select tool is active. You can also click outside the bounding box of the container to back out one level.

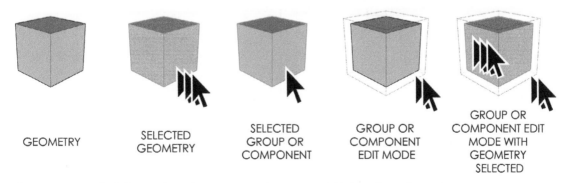

GEOMETRY   SELECTED GEOMETRY   SELECTED GROUP OR COMPONENT   GROUP OR COMPONENT EDIT MODE   GROUP OR COMPONENT EDIT MODE WITH GEOMETRY SELECTED

Figure 5.59 Use the Select tool to select entities and navigate quickly in and out of containers.

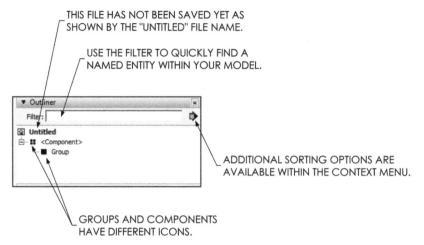

THIS FILE HAS NOT BEEN SAVED YET AS SHOWN BY THE "UNTITLED" FILE NAME.

USE THE FILTER TO QUICKLY FIND A NAMED ENTITY WITHIN YOUR MODEL.

ADDITIONAL SORTING OPTIONS ARE AVAILABLE WITHIN THE CONTEXT MENU.

GROUPS AND COMPONENTS HAVE DIFFERENT ICONS.

Figure 5.60 The Outliner.

The Outliner shows a file-structure-type diagram of the contents of your model to help you find your way through the various container levels (Figure 5.60). To open the Outliner, click on the Window drop-down menu and choose Outliner. Click on entity names in the Outliner to select them. Double-click or right-click on containers within the Outliner to navigate in and out of the container.

The Outliner is very helpful when all the groups and components in your model are accurately named. Groups and components can be named using the Entity Info dialog. To open this dialog, click on the Window drop-down menu and select Entity Info (Figure 5.61). Then, use the Select tool to select an entity; its

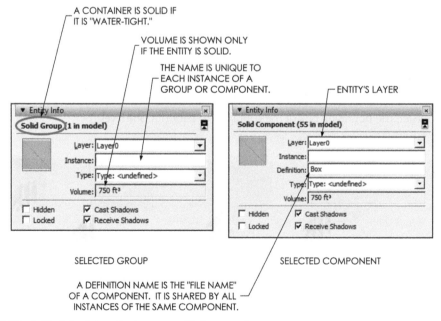

A CONTAINER IS SOLID IF IT IS "WATER-TIGHT."

VOLUME IS SHOWN ONLY IF THE ENTITY IS SOLID.

THE NAME IS UNIQUE TO EACH INSTANCE OF A GROUP OR COMPONENT.

ENTITY'S LAYER

SELECTED GROUP

SELECTED COMPONENT

A DEFINITION NAME IS THE "FILE NAME" OF A COMPONENT. IT IS SHARED BY ALL INSTANCES OF THE SAME COMPONENT.

Figure 5.61 The Entity Info dialog displays any entity's properties.

properties will be displayed in the Entity Info dialog, where they can also be edited. Make sure to assign logical names. For instance, if a group contains walls, name the group WALLS.

Modifying Containers

Containers in SketchUp, including groups and more important components, can be modified without affecting the contents of the container. For instance, you can move and rotate a container without affecting its contents. Remember, if you were to move or rotate the contents of a component, all instances would reflect that change. Rotating and moving are fairly easy concepts to grasp, but there are also more abstract ideas related to modifying containers covered in this section. You will learn to make components (and groups) different without affecting the contents of the component.

Move Tool

Use the Move tool to reposition containers exactly the same way you would reposition edges and surfaces. The Move tool also autoselects entire containers and offers a rotate option (Figure 5.62). Just follow these steps:

1. Deselect all entities by right-clicking on the background, activate the Move tool, and hover over a container. The Move tool autoselects the container and displays red crosses on each side that you hover on.

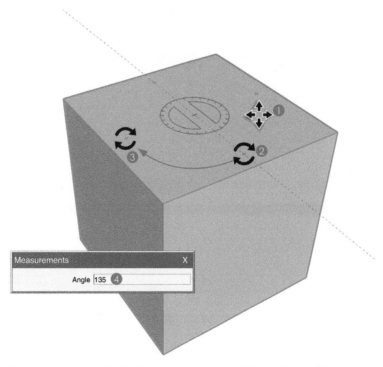

Figure 5.62 Autoselect a component with the Move tool, and rotate. The contents of the container will not be modified.

2. Hover on one of the red crosses, and you will see the Rotate tool positioned at the center of the container. Click once to start the rotation.

3. Move your cursor to rotate the container, then click again to define the actual rotation of the container.

4. At this point, you can enter a precise degree of rotation—for example, 135—and then press Enter.

Scale Tool

The Scale tool allows you to stretch and distort geometry as well as containers. Scaling a container does not affect the contents of the container, so these changes will not be reflected in all instances of the component (Figure 5.63).

To create a line of symmetry, use the Scale tool and assign a scale factor of −1 to mirror the component (Figure 5.64).

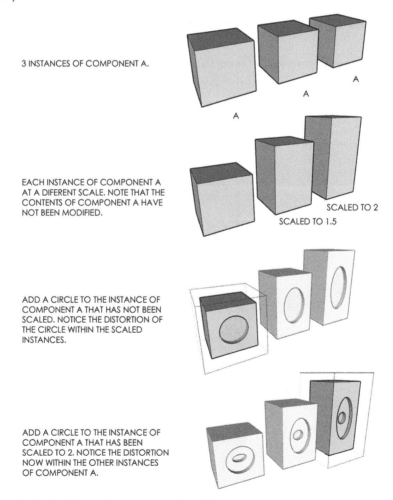

3 INSTANCES OF COMPONENT A.

A

A

A

EACH INSTANCE OF COMPONENT A AT A DIFERENT SCALE. NOTE THAT THE CONTENTS OF COMPONENT A HAVE NOT BEEN MODIFIED.

SCALED TO 2

SCALED TO 1.5

ADD A CIRCLE TO THE INSTANCE OF COMPONENT A THAT HAS NOT BEEN SCALED. NOTICE THE DISTORTION OF THE CIRCLE WITHIN THE SCALED INSTANCES.

ADD A CIRCLE TO THE INSTANCE OF COMPONENT A THAT HAS BEEN SCALED TO 2. NOTICE THE DISTORTION NOW WITHIN THE OTHER INSTANCES OF COMPONENT A.

Figure 5.63 The effects of scaling on the component container.

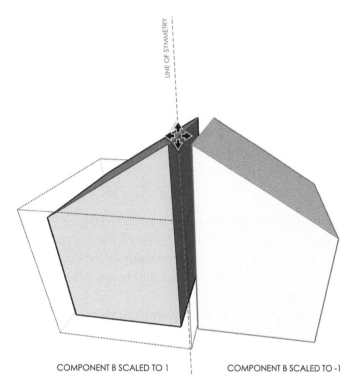

LINE OF SYMMETRY

COMPONENT B SCALED TO 1   COMPONENT B SCALED TO -1

Figure 5.64 Copying and mirroring a component creates a line of symmetry but does not modify the contents of the container.

TIP Scaling to –1 does the same thing as the Flip Along command; however, the Scale tool is more visual and therefore easier to use. If you choose to use the Flip Along command, you can access it by right-clicking on an entity and choosing Flip Along. You will then have to define the axis along which you want to flip.

Default Material

Any surface in a container that has the default material applied to it will take on the material of its parent (Figure 5.65). In other words, suppose there is a cube (six surfaces) in a container that has the default material applied to each surface. If you paint the outside of the group with a material, all the surfaces in the group will take on that material. This default material can be overridden by applying a different material to the actual surface in the group.

By leveraging the default material behaviors, you can have components that have efficiently

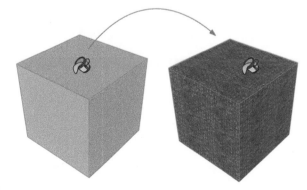

Figure 5.65 The default material is applied to every edge and surface that is created. Any surfaces in a container with the default material applied to them will take on the material applied to the "outside" of the container.

linked geometry but display different materials. This characteristic can come into play when you use repeating elements that need to be slightly different. For example, you could have a chair component that is efficiently linked but has a different colored cushion.

TIP At some point, you may try to right-click on a surface with a material applied to it and not see the Texture menu. If this happens, you are probably actually clicking on a surface that has the default material applied to it within a group that has a texture image material applied to the outside of it. You can fix this by applying the desired texture image material directly to the surface.

Nested Containers

Nested containers are containers within containers within containers (Figure 5.66). There is virtually no limit to the number of levels deep your model can be. Mastering the concept of nested containers is essential to organizing for the SketchUp Workflow for Architecture and ConDoc.

Select any two containers, right-click on the selection and choose Make Group or Make Component, depending on the desired container.

The need for nested containers depends on layering, repeating elements, and lines of symmetry. The organization techniques utilized during the SketchUp Workflow for Architecture require advanced layering and organization of nested containers, groups, and components. Model organization diagrams (Figure 5.67) are used to complement the text and further explain these layering and grouping strategies.

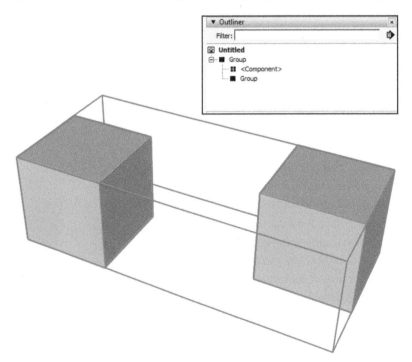

Figure 5.66 A group and a component are shown nested within a group.

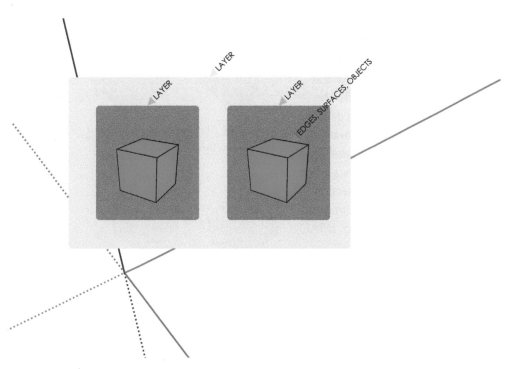

Figure 5.67 Nested containers and the layers applied to them are graphically displayed in this book using this diagram.

Explode

The Explode command could also be called the "Un-Container" tool. Right-click on a group or component and choose Explode to remove the container. Keep in mind that when a container is exploded, all entities previously within the container on layer0 take on the layer previously applied to the exploded container.

SECTION PLANES

The best way to open up a model and look inside is to use section planes. A section in SketchUp does not delete or modify geometry in any way; it simply hides geometry in front of the section plane. Follow these steps:

1. Activate the Section Plane tool.

2. Position the section plane on a face that is parallel to the desired section's cut direction (Figure 5.68).

3. Once you find the proper section orientation, hold the Shift key to constrain it. The arrow keys will constrain a section plane to an axis.

4. Continue holding the Shift key until you click again to place the section cut. You will now see the section plane hiding all geometry in front of it (Figure 5.69).

Once a section cut is placed, it can be reversed, moved, rotated, copied, deleted, activated, and deactivated. Right-click on a section plane to access a helpful context menu. The Reverse command will flip the section plane to point the opposite direction. Check Active Cut on and off to activate and deactivate the section plane. Select Create Group from Slice to generate a group containing the 2D linework of the section cut; this is great for jumpstarting your detail drafting by creating lines for ConDoc DRAFT mode.

Only one section plane can be active at a time in each level of a model. If you want to have multiple section cuts, you must separate them into containers (Figure 5.70 and Figure 5.71).

Figure 5.68 The section plane orients itself parallel to the face you are hovering on.

Figure 5.69 An active section plane hides all entities behind it.

LAYERS, STYLES, AND SCENES

Layers, styles, and scenes are all related. Layers control the visibility of entities within SketchUp. Styles control the way in which entities are displayed in SketchUp. Layers and styles attach to scenes. So by clicking on a scene, you can jump to a preset state for layers and styles, as well as several other properties that can be attached to scenes.

By mastering all three, you will gain full control over any drawing you want to create and become a faster modeler. In this section, you will learn the basic functions and operations of these features and how they relate to each other. Later in this book, you will flex these features and leverage them to make more efficient models, presentations, and construction documents.

Layers

SketchUp *layers* are different than layers in many other 3D and 2D programs—but in a good way.

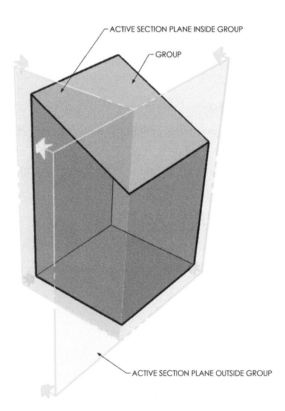

Figure 5.70 You can have more than one active section plane by separating them into containers.

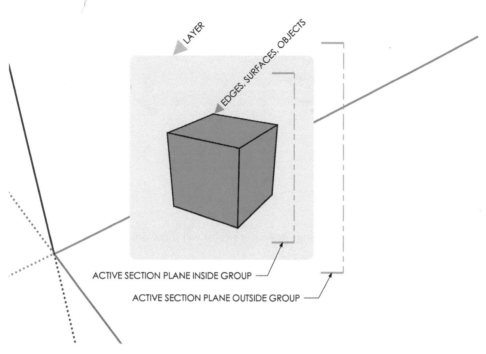

Figure 5.71 A model organization diagram representing two active section planes separated by a container.

SketchUp layers are simple. There is no stacking of layers, so the order in which layers are displayed in the Layers dialog has nothing to do with the way in which geometry is displayed in your model. Layers can be assigned to any entity in SketchUp, including edges, surfaces, groups, and components. You are able to control only whether a layer is visible and the color of the layer when on a color-by-layer style. That's it!

Click on the Window drop-down menu and choose Layers. The Layers dialog is where you set the current layer, visible layers, and layer colors; it is also where you add, delete, and rename layers (Figure 5.72).

The current layer, defined by the dot to the left of the layer name, should always be set to Layer0. Layer0 cannot be deleted or renamed. Any entity created within or added to the model will be assigned to the current layer, Layer0. It is possible to change the current layer, but doing so is not advisable. The workflow presented in this book requires that all edges and surfaces be drawn on Layer0. To work with layers, follow these simple guidelines:

☑ To add a layer, click on the plus sign (+) in the top-left corner of the Layers dialog. Once a new layer is created, you can immediately rename the layer by typing over the blue highlighted text and pressing Enter to finish.

☑ To rename a layer, double-click on the layer name and type over the blue highlighted text, then press Enter to finish.

☑ To delete a layer, first click on the layer name to select it. Then click on the minus sign (−) in the top-left corner of the Layers window to delete it. If there are entities on the layer you are deleting, you will be asked what to do with the entities.

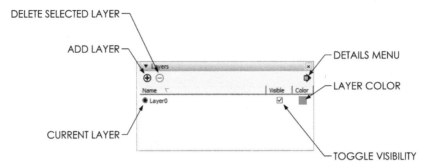

Figure 5.72 The Layers dialog.

☑ Click on a layer's color swatch to change it. A layer's color will show only when on a color-by-layer style.

☑ Click on the check box next to a layer in the Visible column to toggle the layer's visibility on and off.

☑ To organize the list of layers by name, visibility, or color, click on the headings at the top of the columns.

☑ To assign an entity to a layer, right-click on the entity and choose Entity Info. Within the Entity Info dialog box (Figure 5.73), click on the Layers drop-down menu and choose a different layer.

☑ A Layers toolbar is available by clicking on the View drop-down menu and choosing Toolbars and then Layers.

TIP When an entity is selected, the Layers toolbar works the same way as the Layer drop-down menu in the Entity Info dialog. Beware, when an entity is not selected, the Layers tool bar sets the current layer.

Once the Entity Info dialog and the Layers toolbar are open, you can simply select an entity and adjust its layer in one of these dialogs. There is no need to right-click on the entity every time.

Styles

Styles provide a different way to look at your model. Styles do not affect geometry, so you won't affect any edges or surfaces when you make the model edges sketchy, change the color of the sky, make all faces render as the same color, or use any of the other attractive visual settings, for example.

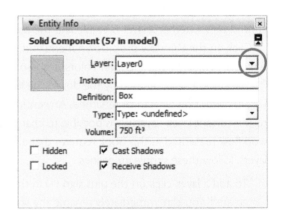

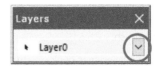

Figure 5.73 Entity Info dialog and the Layers toolbar.

To open the Styles browser, click on the Window drop-down menu and choose default tray > Styles. Within the Styles browser, you can select from preloaded styles by clicking on the Libraries drop-down menu (Figure 5.74). Once you find a style you like, click on it.

To change the properties of a style, click on the Edit tab. Five boxes in the Edit tab represent the Edge, Face, Background, Watermark, and Modeling settings (Figure 5.75). Try changing a few of the settings and see how the display properties of the geometry in your model are affected.

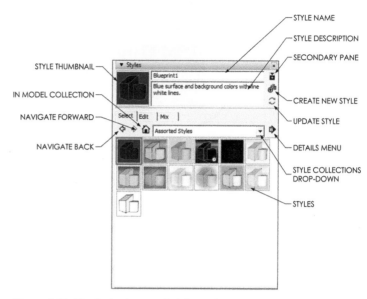

Figure 5.74 The Styles browser's Select tab.

Changing any of the Style properties means that the style is now out of date. A recycle watermark will appear on the active style's thumbnail image. In order to save any changes you've made, you must update the style by clicking on the Style thumbnail or on the Refresh button in the Style browser (Figure 5.76). If any property of a style is changed, the style must be updated to save the changes.

Use the Mix tab to make your own unique Style creations. See Chapter 8, SketchUp Collections, for more information on using the Mix tab.

TIP It is possible to change many of the Style settings using drop-down menus. For instance, if you click on View and then Axes to turn off the axes, that is a Style setting. You must be aware and update the style within the Styles browser if you want to save that change.

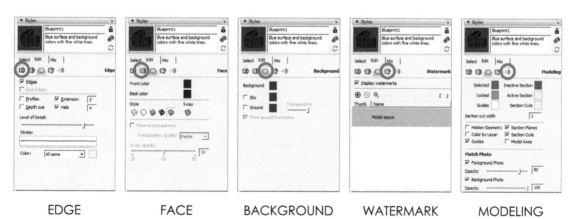

EDGE   FACE   BACKGROUND   WATERMARK   MODELING

Figure 5.75 The Styles browser's Edit tab with all five views.

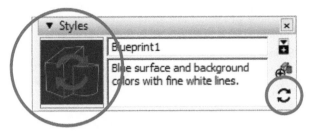

Figure 5.76 Update a style by clicking on the active style's thumbnail or by clicking on the Update Style button.

Scenes

Scenes are most often associated with a camera. In other words, most people assume that a scene is just like a bookmark for a specific view of your model. This is true, but scenes also save many other additional properties, such as hidden geometry, visible layers, active section planes, style and fog, shadow settings, and axes locations. By creating complex scenes, you can create any rendering, drawing, or diagram that you need.

Take a look at the Scenes browser by clicking on the Window drop-down menu and selecting default tray > Scenes. The Scenes browser is where you will add, name, delete, and update the scenes in your model (Figure 5.77).

In the Scenes browser, you can see that scenes have a name, description, and properties to save. The name of a scene will appear in the Scene browser as well as on the corresponding Scene tab at the top of the screen. The description of a scene, which is usually unnecessary, is displayed in the Scene browser and also when you hover your cursor over a Scene tab. The properties to save are the critical attributes of scenes (Figure 5.78). The check boxes control whether the selected scene holds onto the named settings. For example, if the Camera Location property is not checked on to be saved, there will be no camera location information associated with that scene.

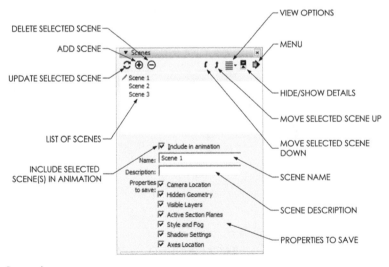

Figure 5.77 The Scenes browser.

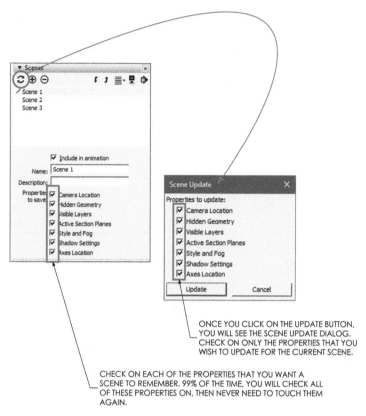

CHECK ON EACH OF THE PROPERTIES THAT YOU WANT A
SCENE TO REMEMBER. 99% OF THE TIME, YOU WILL CHECK ALL
OF THESE PROPERTIES ON, THEN NEVER NEED TO TOUCH THEM
AGAIN.

ONCE YOU CLICK ON THE UPDATE BUTTON,
YOU WILL SEE THE SCENE UPDATE DIALOG.
CHECK ON ONLY THE PROPERTIES THAT YOU
WISH TO UPDATE FOR THE CURRENT SCENE.

Figure 5.78 The properties to save and properties to update are easily confused. Make sure you understand the function of each.

Frequently, the properties to save are confused with the properties to update. Remember, 99 percent of the time, you will want all of the properties to save checked on, and you will never need to touch them again once the scene is created. When you want to modify the scene, click on the Refresh button and check and uncheck the desired properties to update.

Similar to styles, scenes also need to be updated if you want to save any changes to the scene. The tricky thing about scenes is that there is no visual cue that tells you the scene needs to be updated.

Typically, the only time you would uncheck certain properties within the Scene Update dialog is when you are applying aspects of one scene to another. For instance, to match the camera view, go to the scene with the desired camera view by clicking on its Scene tab. Then click on the scene you want to have the same camera view within the Scenes dialog. Click on the Update Scene button, and uncheck everything but the Camera Location in the Scene Update dialog. Click on Update, and the two scenes will have the same camera location.

Combining Layers, Styles, and Scenes

By combining layers, styles, and scenes, you can completely control a model. Experiment with all of the settings shown in the following diagrams until you have fully mastered them (Figure 5.79).

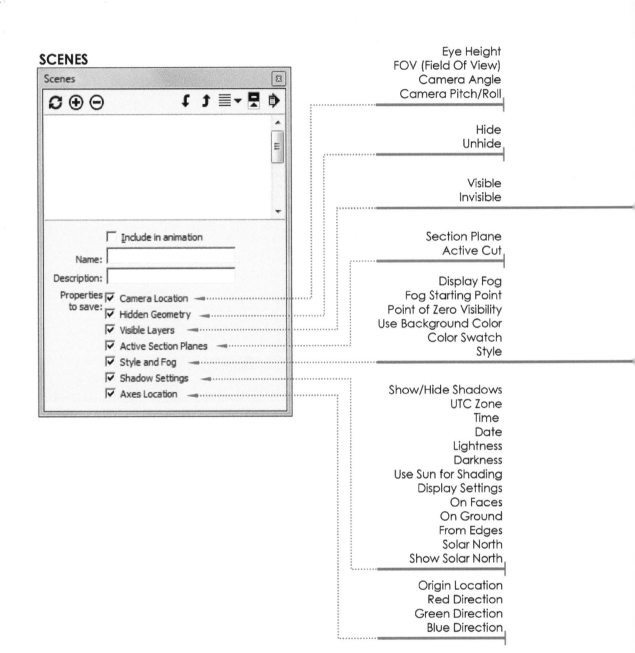

Figure 5.79 A scene's properties are stored with the scene. To save any changes you make to the listed properties, you must update the scene. Styles have several properties that are controlled through the Styles browser. If a property of a style is changed, the style must be updated.

LAYERS

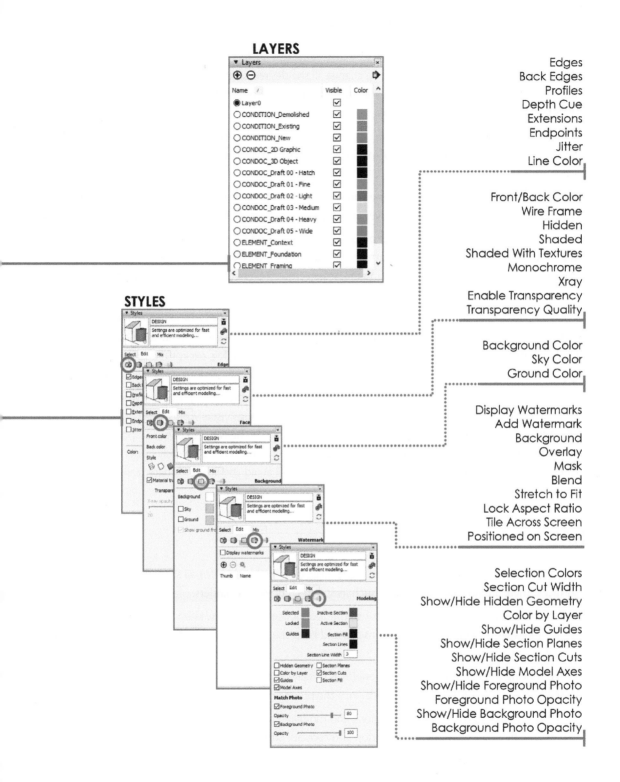

Edges
Back Edges
Profiles
Depth Cue
Extensions
Endpoints
Jitter
Line Color

Front/Back Color
Wire Frame
Hidden
Shaded
Shaded With Textures
Monochrome
Xray
Enable Transparency
Transparency Quality

STYLES

Background Color
Sky Color
Ground Color

Display Watermarks
Add Watermark
Background
Overlay
Mask
Blend
Stretch to Fit
Lock Aspect Ratio
Tile Across Screen
Positioned on Screen

Selection Colors
Section Cut Width
Show/Hide Hidden Geometry
Color by Layer
Show/Hide Guides
Show/Hide Section Planes
Show/Hide Section Cuts
Show/Hide Model Axes
Show/Hide Foreground Photo
Foreground Photo Opacity
Show/Hide Background Photo
Background Photo Opacity

Keep these tips in mind when you're working with layers, styles, and scenes:

☑ When creating scenes, it is usually best to change all the desired settings so that your screen looks the way you want the scene to look. Then you can add the scene to take a digital "snapshot" of the settings that make the screen look that way.

☑ If you decide to change a property that is saved within a style, you will need to update the style. You do not need to update the scene after making changes to a style if the style is already attached to the scene.

☑ When creating a scene, most of the time you will want to have all the properties to save checked on. After doing so once, there is almost never any reason to go back and uncheck them.

☑ If a property to save is unchecked, that property won't be saved with the scene. For instance, if Camera Location is unchecked, then no matter how many times you click on that scene or update it, it will not take you back to a camera view. Camera Location must be checked on under properties to save if the scene is to remember it.

☑ If you decide to change a property that is saved by a scene, and you want the scene to reflect those changes, you will need to update the scene. Typically, it is safest to make the adjustments, click the Update button, then uncheck all properties in the Scene Update dialog, except the properties that you have changed.

☑ If you need to modify the properties of a scene, you'll be better able to keep track of what you're doing if you first click on the Scene tab to see all the Scene settings visually presented on your screen. Make only the changes that you want, then right-click on the Scene tab and choose Update to update all the properties at the same time. This can be dangerous if you don't completely understand how to use scenes, but it will ultimately save time because you'll avoid the Scene Update dialog and all the checking and unchecking.

CHAPTER POINTS

☑ SketchUp is a surface modeler, which means its basic building blocks—for all shapes—are edges and surfaces. There are no true solid shapes such as spheres, cubes, or cylinders.

☑ While you're brainstorming in SketchUp, use the tools loosely and freely. Keep in mind that there are built-in ways to tighten up the dimensions and keep the geometry organized, even in a concept model.

☑ When moving a concept to a precise model, it is usually best to start a fresh model. Use Paste in Place to pull useful pieces of the concept model into the precise model.

☑ Typically, it is best to use precise dimensions and modeling techniques right from the beginning. Once you get the hang of the model organization and tool operations, it takes just as much effort to create a sketchy model as it does a precise model.

☑ Inferencing and axis locking allow you to interact with the 3D SketchUp environment effectively through your 2D computer screen.

☑ Typically, you should start with a Drawing tool that adds surfaces, such as the Rectangle, Polygon, or Circle tools.

☑ Use Drawing tools that only add edges to set up slight additive and subtractive adjustments.

☑ Use the Edit tools to turn simple forms into complex geometry.

☑ When you're creating components, look for repeating elements. If you need a similar element, use the Make Unique command. Mirror a component container using the Scale tool or Flip Along command to create lines of symmetry.

☑ Layers, styles, and scenes are absolutely necessary for creating a useful SketchUp model. To avoid frustration in later chapters, you should explore these combined concepts until you completely understand how they work before you proceed.

☑ The best way to learn about layers, styles, and scenes is to review this chapter while playing around with their settings. Don't be afraid to make a copy of a model and mess it up while experimenting.

Chapter 6
The Professional's SketchUp Template

S ketchUp provides several default templates that are excellent to use for learning but ultimately not fit for professional use. Your default template in SketchUp should do more than just paint a pretty picture; it should also make modeling easier and reveal deeper levels of information stored within your model. You can customize your own SketchUp template by optimizing the model settings, creating utility scenes and styles, and adding default layers that will fit any design project.

BASE TEMPLATE

Start by opening SketchUp. You should see the Welcome to SketchUp window. If you don't, click on the Help drop-down and choose Welcome to SketchUp. Uncheck the Always Show on Startup box in the bottom-left corner of the window (Figure 6.1). The Welcome to SketchUp window is designed to intro-duce first-time users to SketchUp and is not necessary for a professional.

To select a template, click on the template tab and select the Construction Documentation – Feet and Inches template from the list. To close the Welcome to SketchUp window, click on the Start using SketchUp button.

Click on the File drop-down menu and choose New to start a new model using the Construction Documentation – Feet and Inches template. To see the new template, you always need to start a new file. This template starts off with a white background and inches as the default unit. Once you have selected a stock default template, you can customize it and save it as your own default template. Click on the File

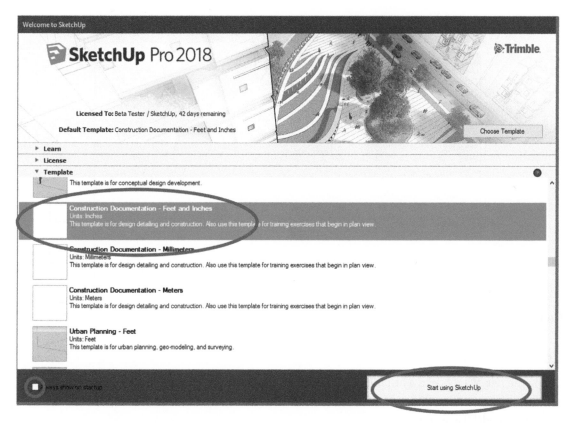

Figure 6.1 The Welcome to SketchUp Window offers links to learning resources, licensing information, and the default templates. All of this information and more is available in the Help menu and at SketchUp.com.

drop-down menu and choose Save, navigate to your RESOURCES/TEMPLATES folder, and name the file BD_Default Template.skp. Replace the BD with your own acronym or initials.

MODEL INFO

The Model Info settings travel with your model. In this section, you will modify only the settings that will help make your modeling faster and more efficient. Keep in mind that all the Model Info settings can be changed once a new model is started. To get started, click on the Window drop-down menu and choose Model Info.

Animation

Unless you are creating an animation, you won't need to see scene transitions while you're designing in SketchUp. Sure, they look cool, but they also kill a couple of seconds every time you change to a different scene. As a professional, you need instant information, so go to the Animation tab and uncheck the Enable scene transitions check box (Figure 6.2).

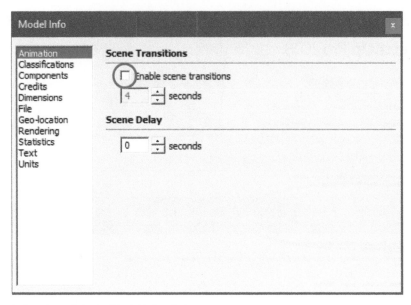

Figure 6.2 The Animation tab in the Model Info window.

Components

Hiding the rest of a model is a helpful trick for isolating the contents of a container so you see only the geometry that you are able to work on. Check the Hide boxes next to Fade similar components and Fade the rest of model (Figure 6.3).

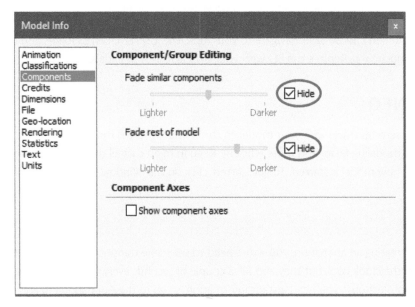

Figure 6.3 The Components tab.

Dimensions

Dimensions are best shown in LayOut, where you have full control of placement, size, scale, font, and style. In some instances, you may find it helpful to add dimensions to a quick sketch in SketchUp. When you're adding dimensions, make sure to apply your own style to set your presentations apart from other SketchUp users. Choose your font style and size from the Dimensions tab (Figure 6.4). You can also choose your favorite arrow type and alignment.

When there is not enough room to clearly display the dimensions, you can use the Expert Dimension settings to control whether to display them. Typically, there is no "best" default setting for this, so you should modify the settings on a case-by-case basis.

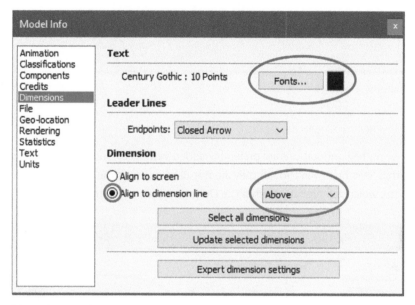

Figure 6.4 The Dimensions settings.

Rendering

Enabling anti-aliased textures may speed up SketchUp's performance (Figure 6.5).

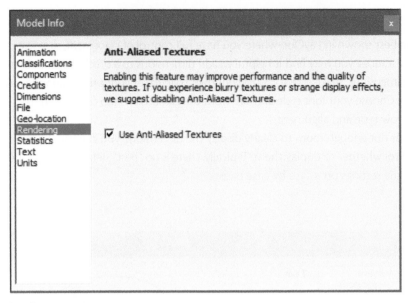

Figure 6.5 The Rendering settings.

Text

Similar to dimensions, text annotations are preferably added within LayOut though you can still customize the text style within Sketchup even though they are not used nearly as much there. Set your favorite font within the Text tab, which will probably match the Dimensions Text settings (Figure 6.6).

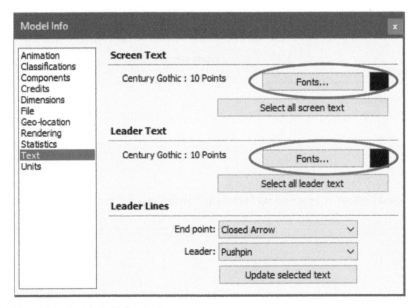

Figure 6.6 The Text tab in the Model Info window.

Units

The default units are set to inches in the Construction Documentation – Feet and Inches template. By thinking in terms of inches, you can save time while you are modeling. For example, to draw a line at five-feet, six-inches long, rather than typing 5'6" and pressing the Enter key, you can just type 66 and press Enter; there's no need for the inch marks because the default unit is inches. In this case, by thinking in inches, you cut the number of keystrokes in half. Saving three keystrokes may not seem significant, but think of the hundreds of commands you perform in an hour when you are using SketchUp.

The model's precision setting indicates the number of units that will display in the Measurements dialog box. This setting can be overridden by entering a precise dimension into the Measurements dialog box during an operation. For example, if the model's accuracy is set to 1/8" and you enter a dimension that ends in 1/64", that line will actually be drawn to the 64". However, when measured, it will be rounded to the nearest 1/8" because of the precision setting. Typically, a model's precision is set to the most accurate setting of 1/64".

TIP Professionals should always have the model accuracy set to the highest tolerance of 1/64" (Figure 6.7). It is important that the model itself have the most precise dimensions possible. Then, if necessary, you can use less precise dimensions in LayOut to clean up fractional dimensions for schematic presentations. Once you begin a model, do not change the precision setting.

Length snapping limits the dimensions of an object drawn in SketchUp to predefined intervals. Enabling length snapping is the best way to keep your dimensions clean. For example, when designing a loose preliminary sketch of a site plan or building footprint, you might set the length snapping to 6" or 12" to

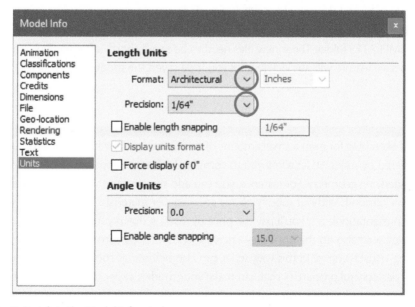

Figure 6.7 The Units tab in the Model Info window.

keep the dimensions round and clean. If you are designing with masonry block, set the length snapping to 8" to design within the limitations of the material. By entering precise dimensions in the Measurements dialog box, you can override length snapping during any operation.

STANDARD LAYERS

A logical set of layers will help you keep a model organized, which will prove helpful when you are exporting backgrounds for consultants, moving to other computer-aided design (CAD) programs, rendering with a photorealistic plugin, and creating construction documents in LayOut. Figure 6.8 displays a list of standard layers used to create SketchUp models with these tasks in mind. These are the official layers of *The SketchUp Workflow for Architecture* and the ConDoc Tools. Note that the layers are organized into five categories: LEVEL, ELEMENT, LOCATION, CONDITION, and CONDOC. LEVEL layers specifically describe the floors, or stories, of a building. ELEMENT layers are nouns, often named after actual physical objects and building elements. LOCATION layers are adjectives that describe the ELEMENT layers as being interior or exterior. CONDITION layers are adjectives that describe the ELEMENT layers as being existing, demolished, or new. CONDOC layers are more abstract and intangible but are needed to make the whole system tick.

Add these layers to your model, or access the latest ConDoc template from the class files at **brightmandesigns.com/TSWFA**, or in the trial at **condoctools.com**.

You'll learn more about how and where to apply these layers later in this book. Right now, it is important to create your customized default template and workspace so that later everything will flow easily. Add the layers shown in Figure 6.8 to your template now. Assign green to the CONDITION_New layer, orange to the CONDITION_Demolished layer, and assign gray to the CONDITION_Existing layer. All other layers can be assigned the color black or disregarded.

A SketchUp template is nothing more than a SketchUp model; save your SketchUp model into the RESOURCES/TEMPLATES folder. These new files need to be saved shortly after you first start them. SketchUp's auto-save feature will not kick in until you have saved the model once yourself.

STYLES

If you have used SketchUp for even a small amount of time, you probably have explored the enticing visual effects offered by styles. Styles allow you to completely alter the appearance of your model without affecting the underlying geometry. For instance, you can add sketchy lines, X-ray faces, watermarks, and different color backgrounds without modifying any geometry or materials. These are all great visual effects you can use for presentations, but you'll pay the price by slowing down your computer.

What if a style could also do the opposite—increase computer performance by turning off the resource-hogging visual features? In this way, styles can also be used as tools rather than just attractive visual effects. Styles control properties that can make your models easier to work on, optimize your system's performance, and visually communicate deeper levels of information stored within the model

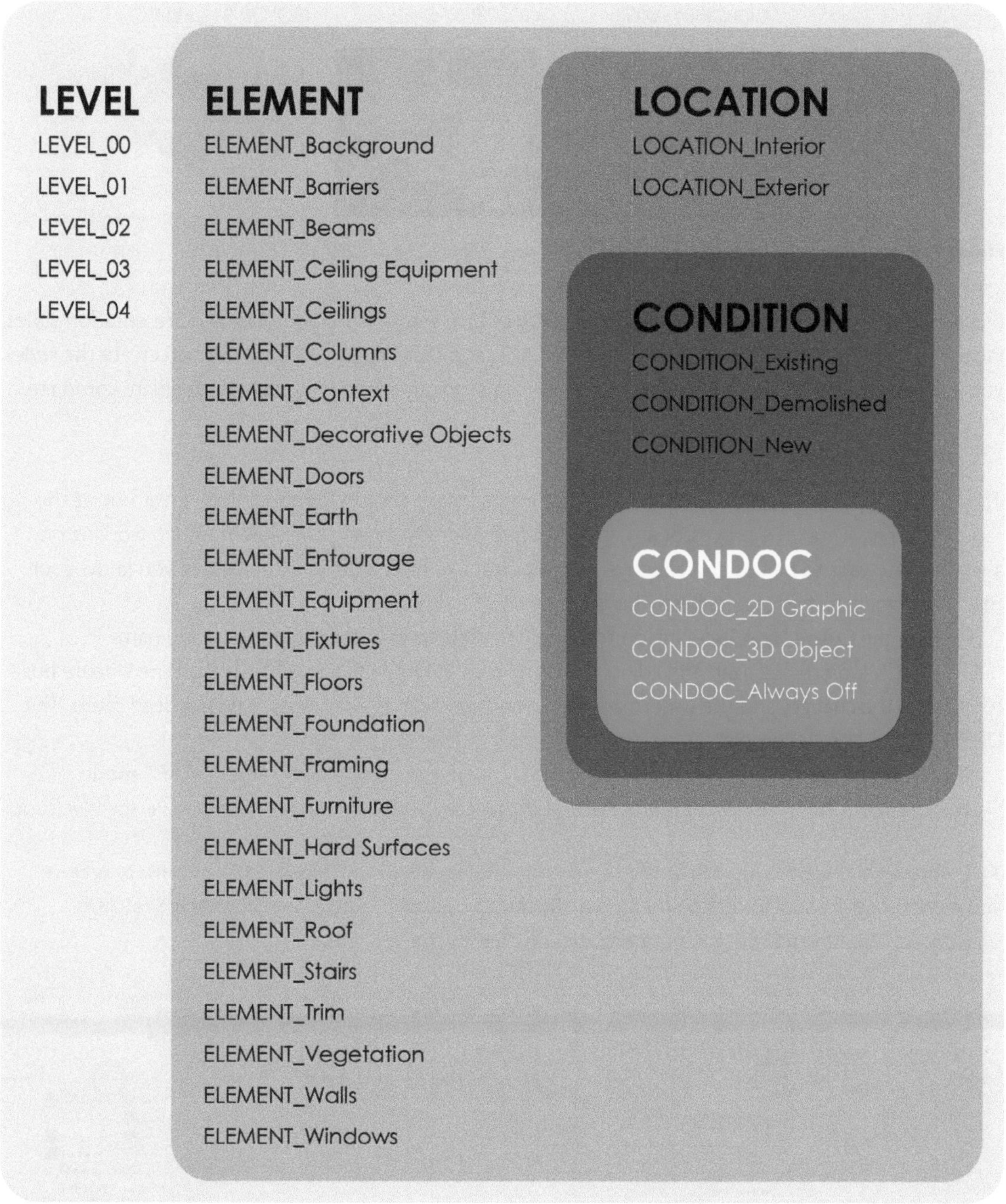

LEVEL	ELEMENT	LOCATION
LEVEL_00	ELEMENT_Background	LOCATION_Interior
LEVEL_01	ELEMENT_Barriers	LOCATION_Exterior
LEVEL_02	ELEMENT_Beams	
LEVEL_03	ELEMENT_Ceiling Equipment	
LEVEL_04	ELEMENT_Ceilings	**CONDITION**
	ELEMENT_Columns	CONDITION_Existing
	ELEMENT_Context	CONDITION_Demolished
	ELEMENT_Decorative Objects	CONDITION_New
	ELEMENT_Doors	
	ELEMENT_Earth	
	ELEMENT_Entourage	**CONDOC**
	ELEMENT_Equipment	CONDOC_2D Graphic
	ELEMENT_Fixtures	CONDOC_3D Object
	ELEMENT_Floors	CONDOC_Always Off
	ELEMENT_Foundation	
	ELEMENT_Framing	
	ELEMENT_Furniture	
	ELEMENT_Hard Surfaces	
	ELEMENT_Lights	
	ELEMENT_Roof	
	ELEMENT_Stairs	
	ELEMENT_Trim	
	ELEMENT_Vegetation	
	ELEMENT_Walls	
	ELEMENT_Windows	

Figure 6.8 The SketchUp Workflow for Architecture and ConDoc standard SketchUp layers.

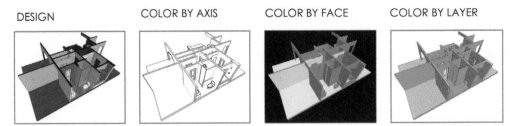

DESIGN   COLOR BY AXIS   COLOR BY FACE   COLOR BY LAYER

Figure 6.9 Styles being used as modeling and presentation tools.

(Figure 6.9). In the next section, you will explore styles by creating the core utility and presentation styles, including DESIGN, COLOR BY AXIS, COLOR BY FACE, and COLOR BY LAYER. After you create the styles, you will combine them with the power of scenes to make your time-saving default template complete.

DESIGN Style

The DESIGN style turns off all the bells and whistles that make SketchUp models look great but, at the same time, heavily tax the processor and graphics card, thereby slowing the system. When working on a model, you want to be fast and effective. It is important to have a default state where you know your machine is going to perform its best. This is the DESIGN utility style.

Click on the Create New Style button to add a new style to your template model and name it "DESIGN." Click on the Edit tab and adjust the settings as shown in Figure 6.10. Click on the Update button to save the changes and the watermark will go away, indicating that everything has been saved. The DESIGN utility style is complete.

The DRAFT style is automatically added by the ConDoc system when you enter DRAFT mode.

The LINE DRAWING – Presentation style is automatically added by the free ConDoc Perspective tool.

TIP You can also use the Mix tab to drag and drop your favorite properties into the current style. Once you are satisfied, be sure to click on the Update button to update the style. See Chapter 8, SketchUp Collections, "Creating a Style" for more information on using the Mix tab.

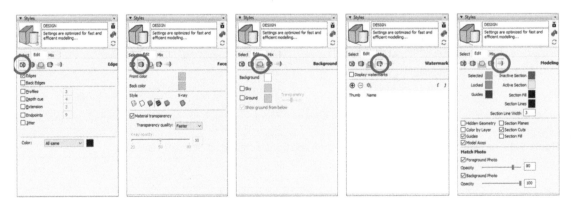

Figure 6.10 The DESIGN style settings.

COLOR BY AXIS Style

The COLOR BY AXIS style can help you troubleshoot a problematic model. If you are tracing lines and a surface will not reheal, the problem is often an edge that is off axis. By switching to the COLOR BY AXIS utility style, all the edges will be the same color as the axis they are parallel to, and all surfaces will be white. It will become immediately clear which lines are causing the problem because any off-axis edge will be black.

Click on the Create New Style button to add a new style to your template model and name it COLOR BY AXIS. Click on the Edit tab and adjust the settings as shown in Figure 6.11. Click the Update button to save the changes and the watermark will go away, indicating that everything has been saved. The COLOR BY AXIS utility style is complete.

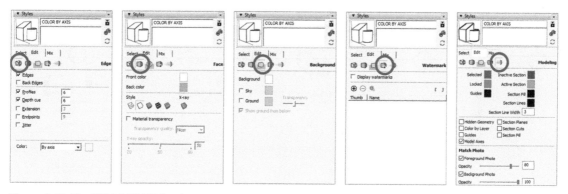

Figure 6.11 The COLOR BY AXIS style settings.

COLOR BY FACE Style

The COLOR BY FACE utility style displays the geometry of the side of the surface that is showing—the front or the back. Viewing geometry in this way will help you prepare a model for photorealistic rendering.

Click on the Create New Style button to add a new style to your template model and name it COLOR BY FACE. Click on the Edit tab and adjust the settings as shown in Figure 6.12. Click on the Update button to save the changes and the watermark will go away, indicating that everything has been saved. The COLOR BY FACE utility style is complete.

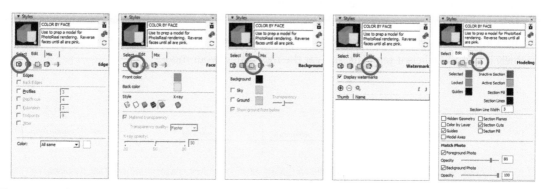

Figure 6.12 The COLOR BY FACE style settings.

COLOR BY LAYER Style

The COLOR BY LAYER utility style displays geometry according to the color assigned to the geometry's layer. This view will visually show deeper levels of information stored in the model's layers, such as new, existing, and demolished conditions.

Click on the Create New Style button to add a new style to your template model and name it COLOR BY LAYER. Click on the Edit tab and adjust the settings as shown in Figure 6.13. Click on the Update button to save the changes and the watermark will go away, indicating that everything has been saved. The COLOR BY LAYER utility style is complete.

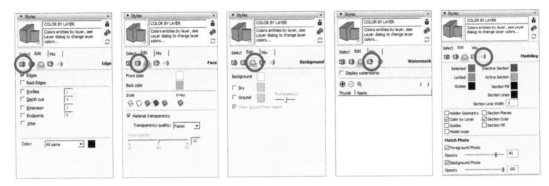

Figure 6.13 The COLOR BY LAYER style settings.

UTILITY SCENES

Styles are helpful by themselves, but the ability to attach a style—along with layer states and many other settings—to a scene means all the settings are readily available through the Scene tabs at the top of your screen. Utility scenes are the core of a professional's template. They are included in a template and used as tools, not just a visually attractive presentation view (Figure 6.14).

The ConDoc System heads-up display consolidates all utility scenes into one place, eliminating the need for actual utility scenes in your template. Using scenes, you have the ability to control properties such as camera location, hidden geometry, visible layers, active section planes, fog, shadow settings, axes locations, and, most important, styles. You can combine the best features of both scenes and styles to make an extremely useful and efficient template and get the most out of your model.

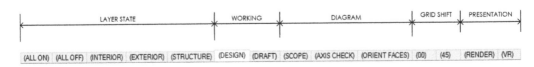

Figure 6.14 The utility scenes.

TIP In the Scenes window, you can determine whether to use thumbnail images. Click on the context arrow at the top-right corner of the Scenes window and uncheck Use Scene Thumbnails. Scene thumbnails can be helpful at times, but generating them requires extra rendering time and computer resources and you do not need them.

Layer State Scenes

Layer state scenes save only the visible layers within a scene's properties. They are the switches that turn the information you want to view on and off. Click on the Add Scene button in the Scenes dialog, then adjust the settings for each of the utility scenes.

The ALL ON utility scene makes all layers visible (Figure 6.15).

The ALL OFF utility scene makes all layers invisible (Figure 6.16).

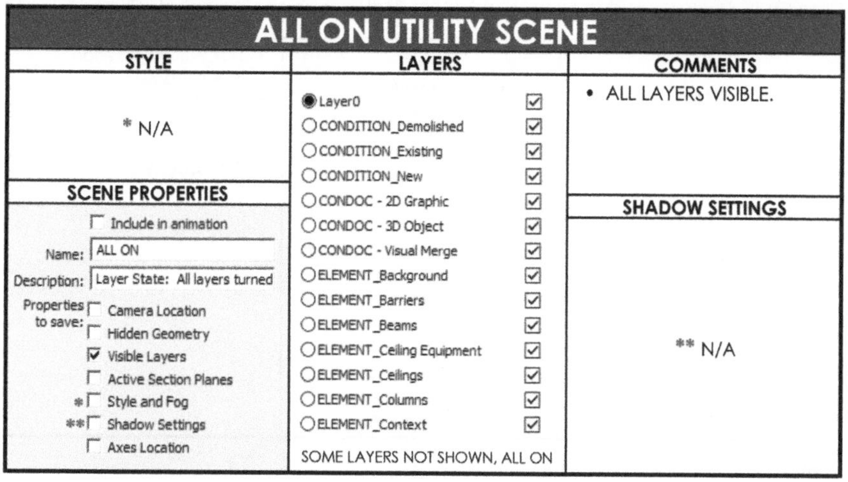

Figure 6.15 The ALL ON utility scene properties and layers.

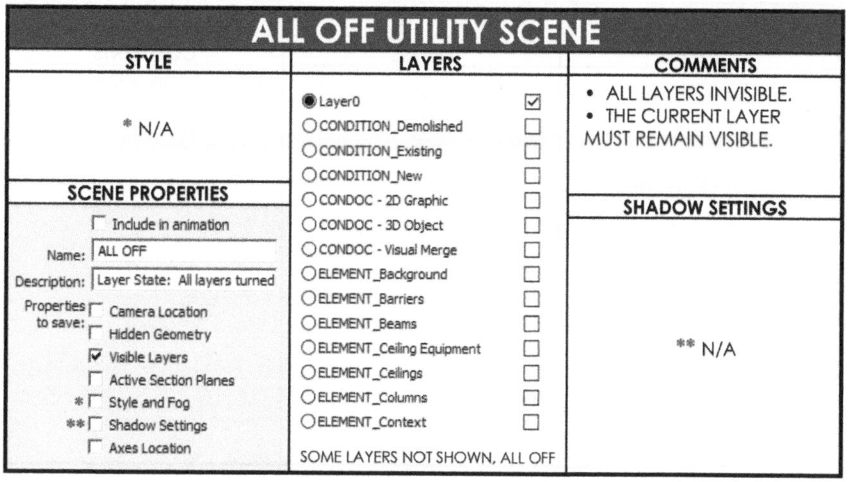

Figure 6.16 The ALL OFF utility scene properties and layers.

The INTERIOR utility scene turns on the layers and, in turn, the geometry that relates to the inside of a building (Figure 6.17). This is helpful for working on the plan without having exterior walls blocking your view of the interior.

The EXTERIOR utility scene turns on the layers and, in turn, the geometry that relates to the outside of a building (Figure 6.18). This is helpful for designing the exterior elevations without having the interior elements of the model turned on, which slows your computer.

The STRUCTURE utility scene turns on the layers and, in turn, the geometry that relates to the structure of the building (Figure 6.19). This is helpful for sorting out the columns, beams, and framing that will hold up your design.

INTERIOR UTILITY SCENE

STYLE	LAYERS	COMMENTS
* N/A	○ CONDOC - 2D Graphic ☐ ○ CONDOC - Visual Merge ☐ ○ LOCATION_Exterior ☐	• LOCATION_Exterior LAYER INVISIBLE • ALL ELEMENT LAYERS VISIBLE
SCENE PROPERTIES		**SHADOW SETTINGS**
☐ Include in animation Name: INTERIOR Description: Layer State: Interior of mode Properties to save: ☐ Camera Location ☐ Hidden Geometry ☑ Visible Layers ☐ Active Section Planes * ☐ Style and Fog ** ☐ Shadow Settings ☐ Axes Location	ALL ON, EXCEPT...	** N/A

Figure 6.17 The INTERIOR utility scene properties and layers.

EXTERIOR UTILITY SCENE

STYLE	LAYERS	COMMENTS
* N/A	○ CONDOC - 2D Graphic ☐ ○ CONDOC - Visual Merge ☐ ○ LOCATION_Interior ☐	• LOCATION_Interior LAYER INVISIBLE • ALL ELEMENT LAYERS VISIBLE
SCENE PROPERTIES		**SHADOW SETTINGS**
☐ Include in animation Name: EXTERIOR Description: Layer State: Exterior of mode Properties to save: ☐ Camera Location ☐ Hidden Geometry ☑ Visible Layers ☐ Active Section Planes * ☐ Style and Fog ** ☐ Shadow Settings ☐ Axes Location	ALL ON, EXCEPT...	** N/A

Figure 6.18 The EXTERIOR utility scene properties and layers.

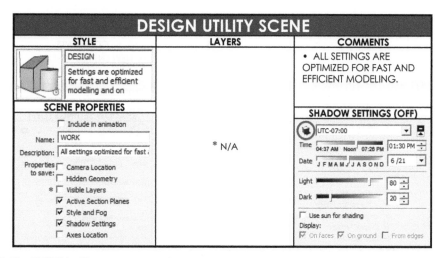

STRUCTURE UTILITY SCENE		
STYLE	**LAYERS**	**COMMENTS**
* N/A	● Layer0 ☑ ○ CONDITION_Existing ☑ ○ CONDITION_New ☑ ○ CONDOC - 3D Object ☑ ○ ELEMENT_Beams ☑ ○ ELEMENT_Columns ☑ ○ ELEMENT_Foundation ☑ ○ ELEMENT_Framing ☑ ○ LOCATION_Exterior ☑ ○ LOCATION_Interior ☑	• ALL LOCATION AND CONDTION LAYERS ON • ONLY STRUCTURAL ELEMENT LAYERS VISIBLE
SCENE PROPERTIES		**SHADOW SETTINGS**
☐ Include in animation Name: EXTERIOR Description: Layer State: Exterior of mode Properties to save: ☐ Camera Location ☐ Hidden Geometry ☑ Visible Layers ☐ Active Section Planes *☐ Style and Fog **☐ Shadow Settings ☐ Axes Location		** N/A

Figure 6.19 The STRUCTURE utility scene properties and layers.

Working Scenes

Working scenes are used to display the model in a final format, either in print or on-screen. Typically, you will use these scenes before you create additional scenes to send to LayOut.

The DESIGN utility scene combines the settings of the DESIGN utility style with additional performance-enhancing settings of scenes (Figure 6.20). Use this utility scene when you're working on the model and navigating a model in real time for on-screen presentations.

The ConDoc system extension automatically adds the necessary CONDOC_Draft layers, styles, and scenes needed for DRAFT MODE. For this reason, it is not necessary to include them in this default template. If you are not using ConDoc Tools, DRAFT mode is not possible.

DESIGN UTILITY SCENE		
STYLE	**LAYERS**	**COMMENTS**
DESIGN Settings are optimized for fast and efficient modelling and on		• ALL SETTINGS ARE OPTIMIZED FOR FAST AND EFFICIENT MODELING.
SCENE PROPERTIES	* N/A	**SHADOW SETTINGS (OFF)**
☐ Include in animation Name: WORK Description: All settings optimized for fast Properties to save: ☐ Camera Location ☐ Hidden Geometry *☐ Visible Layers ☑ Active Section Planes ☑ Style and Fog ☑ Shadow Settings ☐ Axes Location		UTC-07:00 Time 04:37 AM Noon 07:28 PM 01:30 PM Date J F M A M J J A S O N D 6 /21 Light 80 Dark 20 ☐ Use sun for shading Display: ☑ On faces ☑ On ground ☐ From edges

Figure 6.20 The DESIGN utility scene properties.

Diagrammatic Scenes

Diagrammatic scenes display the model in ways that visually communicate more information.

The AXIS CHECK utility scene can help you troubleshoot a problematic model (Figure 6.21). If you are tracing lines and a surface will not reheal, the problem is frequently an edge that is off-axis. When you switch to the AXIS CHECK utility scene, all the edges will be colored by axis and all the surfaces will be white. It will become immediately apparent which lines are causing the problem because they will be black.

The SCOPE utility scene displays the model colored by new and existing objects based on the CONDITION_New, CONDITION_Demolished, and CONDITION_Existing layers' assigned colors (Figure 6.22). The type of diagram that is generated is perfect for explaining the scope of a project to

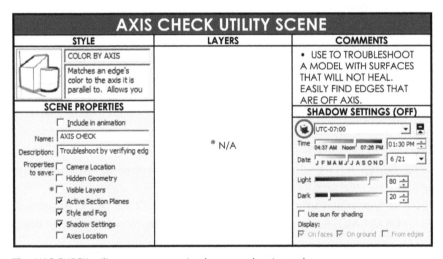

Figure 6.21 The AXIS CHECK utility scene properties, layers, and active style.

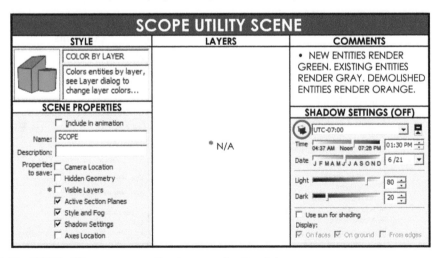

Figure 6.22 The SCOPE utility scene properties, layers, and active style.

a new team member. It gives an overall snapshot of the amount of demolition and construction to be completed.

The ORIENT FACES utility scene displays the model colored by faces (Figure 6.23). Using the diagram, you can easily right-click on the faces and reverse them until all the fronts are facing out. Your entire model should be pink, which means that all fronts are facing out—this is best for photorealistic rendering.

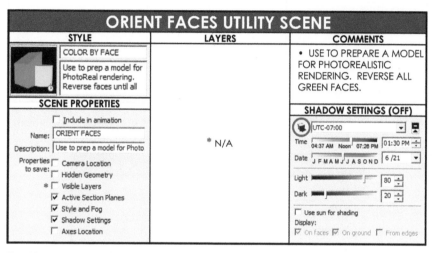

Figure 6.23 The ORIENT FACES utility scene properties, layers, and active style.

TIP The Smustard ReverseFaces extension is free and makes reversing faces quicker and easier. Download it at **smustard.com/script/ReverseFaces.**

The 00 and 45 utility scenes make it easier for you to create plans that follow two or more grids (Figure 6.24 and Figure 6.26). These axis scenes will make a grid shift easy. Also, if you geo-locate a model, you might have to work off the SketchUp original, and this will help. These types of scenes save the location and rotation of the axes. Keep in mind that in this example you are switching the grid to 45 degrees, but you could use any angle of grid shift.

Now create the 45-degree scene. First, right-click on any axis and select Move. Go to the Move Sketching Context dialog box (Figure 6.25) and change the Z rotation to 45. This will rotate the axes around the blue axis to a 45-degree angle. Update the 45 Utility Scene with the new axis orientation.

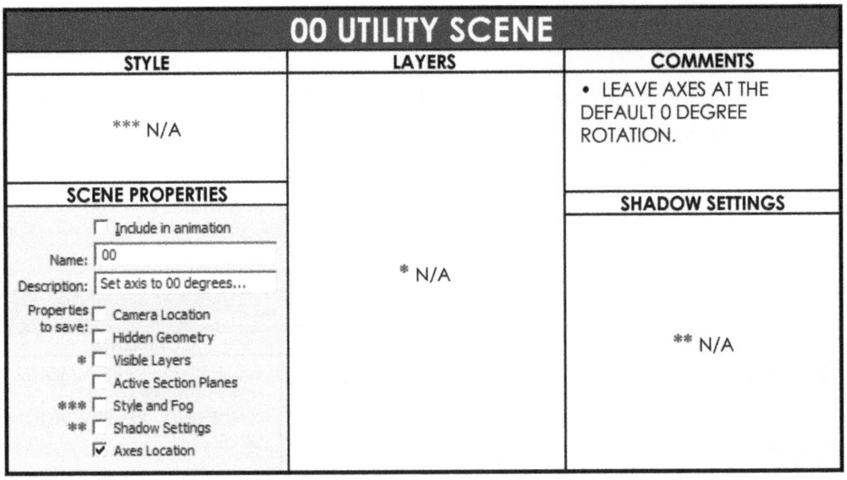

00 UTILITY SCENE		
STYLE	**LAYERS**	**COMMENTS**
*** N/A		• LEAVE AXES AT THE DEFAULT 0 DEGREE ROTATION.
SCENE PROPERTIES		**SHADOW SETTINGS**
☐ Include in animation Name: 00 Description: Set axis to 00 degrees... Properties ☐ Camera Location to save: ☐ Hidden Geometry * ☐ Visible Layers ☐ Active Section Planes *** ☐ Style and Fog ** ☐ Shadow Settings ☑ Axes Location	* N/A	** N/A

Figure 6.24 The 90 utility scene properties, layers, and active style.

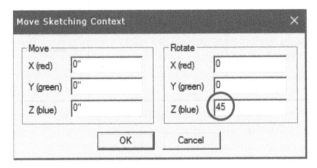

Figure 6.25 Use the Move Sketching Context dialog box to accurately modify the drawing axes.

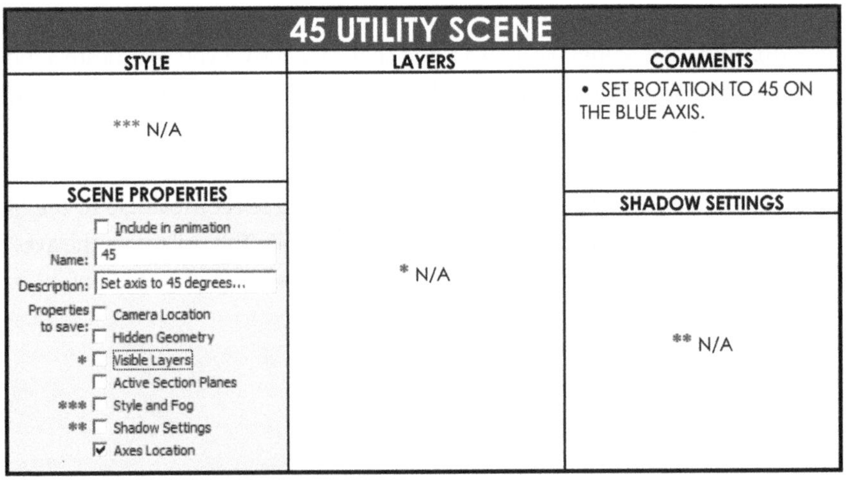

45 UTILITY SCENE		
STYLE	**LAYERS**	**COMMENTS**
*** N/A		• SET ROTATION TO 45 ON THE BLUE AXIS.
SCENE PROPERTIES		**SHADOW SETTINGS**
☐ Include in animation Name: 45 Description: Set axis to 45 degrees... Properties ☐ Camera Location to save: ☐ Hidden Geometry * ☐ Visible Layers ☐ Active Section Planes *** ☐ Style and Fog ** ☐ Shadow Settings ☑ Axes Location	* N/A	** N/A

Figure 6.26 The 45 utility scene properties, layers, and active style.

Presentation Utility Scenes

Presentation utility scenes prepare your model for photorealistic rendering in outside programs, such as Lumion, and for exploring in real time virtual reality.

The RENDER utility scene (Figure 6.27) is optimized for rendering outside of SketchUp, in Lumion, or in photo-real extensions. Entourage and vegetation are turned off because those types of objects are better represented with Lumion objects. Click this scene before you save and reload in Lumion.

The VR utility scene (Figure 6.28) is optimized for viewing in real-time virtual reality. This scene has entourage and vegetation turned on in SketchUp.

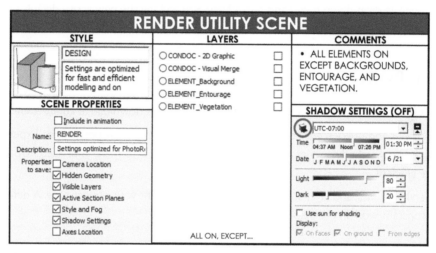

Figure 6.27 The RENDER utility scene properties, layers, and active style.

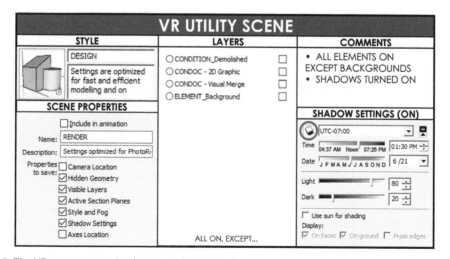

Figure 6.28 The VR scene properties, layers, and active style.

Saving as a Template

Now that you have added utility scenes, styles, and default layers to the base template, save it as your own custom template. Before saving, click on the ALL ON utility scene, then click on the DESIGN utility scene to prepare your template. Click on the File drop-down menu and select Save to update the saved version in your RESOURCES/TEMPLATES folder. Now click on the File drop-down and choose Save As Template. Name the Template with your file naming structure, BD_Default Template, and press the Tab key to move to description. This fills in the file name. No need to add a description; just save. This will save your template to the SketchUp program files set in the SketchUp Preferences window.

When you choose a new template, you must always start a new document to see the template activate. Click on the File drop-down menu and select New. You will see the new active default template with all its custom layers, styles, and scenes.

CHAPTER POINTS

☑ The ConDoc Tools trial and free default template is available for download at **condoctools.com**.

☑ The utility styles and utility scenes created in this chapter are only a few possibilities. Experiment with other properties attached to styles and scenes to determine how to make your SketchUp workflow even more efficient.

☑ All utility styles, scenes, and layer states should be modified to fit your project type. A default template is a constant work in progress.

Chapter 7

The Professional's SketchUp Environment

A professional's work environment is streamlined, logical, and organized. SketchUp provides a default environment that is great for learning but ultimately not fit for professional use. Customize the SketchUp environment to make it work best for you. Optimize system resources, remove visual clutter, and access all commands with a keystroke by adding your own set of shortcuts to enhance your SketchUp experience.

TOOLBARS

Toolbars generally clutter screen space with static icons taking up space that should be used for exciting three-dimensional (3D) graphics (Figure 7.1 and Figure 7.2). Using toolbars and icons takes your eyes off the design. It's like texting while driving: It's very distracting and can be disastrous. That might be an exaggeration, but you really should keep your eyes on the road—and model—at all times by minimizing your use of toolbars. Instead of having all those buttons and icons, it is better to have an extensive collection of keyboard shortcuts. If you can't completely eliminate toolbars and go full-screen full-time, try to limit yourself to the following settings:

☑ A pixel is a valuable commodity. Maximize your 3D workspace by minimizing your toolbar footprint. Select View > Toolbars, then click on the Options tab, and check on Large Buttons to toggle the large icons on and off.

☑ Monitors are enormous these days, so it is reasonable to allow yourself one row of toolbars across the top of your screen. Select View > Toolbars (Tool Palettes on a Mac), and open the Large Toolset

Figure 7.1 Excessive toolbars are distracting and take attention away from the task at hand, which is designing.

Figure 7.2 Utilize a sleek toolset by limiting yourself to one row of toolbars. This will encourage the use of keyboard shortcuts.

(Figure 7.3). These tools are worth keeping open all the time. When you're performing specific tasks, you'll need to open other toolbars briefly, but you don't need to have them open at all times. Once you start working with your favorite tools, you'll be able to determine which toolbars you prefer to have open and accessible at all times.

Figure 7.3 Suggested toolbars.

☑ Dock the toolbars to organize your workspace. Click and drag an undocked toolbar to the top, bottom, or side of the screen, or double-click on a toolbar name. The toolbar will lock itself to the SketchUp window. To undock a toolbar, click and drag the dotted line at the left of the toolbar, move it away from the perimeter of the SketchUp workspace, and release to place it where you want.

TRAYS AND DIALOGS

All dialog boxes and windows are available from the Window > Default tray drop-down menu. You can collapse a dialog by clicking on the window heading. Typically, it is best to keep open only the dialogs that you need regularly, such as Entity Info, Materials, Components, Styles, Layers, Scenes, and Shadows. The other dialogs are not used as often, so it is fine to open them on an as-needed basis.

You can hide all the dialogs at once by clicking on the Window > Default Tray drop-down menu and choosing Hide Tray. Unhide them by going to the same menu and choosing Show Tray. See Figure 7.4 and Figure 7.5.

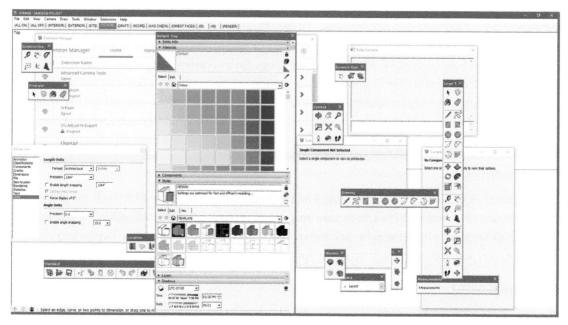

Figure 7.4 A cluttered screen is distracting and takes attention away from the task at hand, which is designing.

Figure 7.5 All the same tools and dialogs are docked in the tray and organized. A clean workspace leads to productivity.

TIP You can create, delete, and customize trays by clicking on the window drop-down and choosing Manage Trays. The stock default tray seems to suit my needs.

SYSTEM PREFERENCES

SketchUp has additional settings you can use to tweak your system and make it more streamlined and efficient. Use the Preferences dialog to adjust these settings. System preferences do not travel with the model; they are local SketchUp settings that are the same for every model you open. You will need to adjust these settings on every computer you work on. To access system preferences, click on the Window (SketchUp on a Mac) drop-down menu and choose Preferences. The only preferences covered in this chapter are the ones that make a difference in your modeling experience by increasing efficiency.

Applications

Set the default program used for editing images on the Applications tab (Figure 7.6). This is the program that will launch when you click the Edit texture image in an external editor button within the Edit tab of the Materials browser or from the right-click menu. Click on the Choose button, then navigate to your program folders and find the photoshop.exe or your image editor of choice.

Drawing

The easiest way to draw in SketchUp is to use a three-button, scroll wheel mouse utilizing click-move-click. SketchUp's default settings provide both the click-drag-release and click-move-click style of drawing.

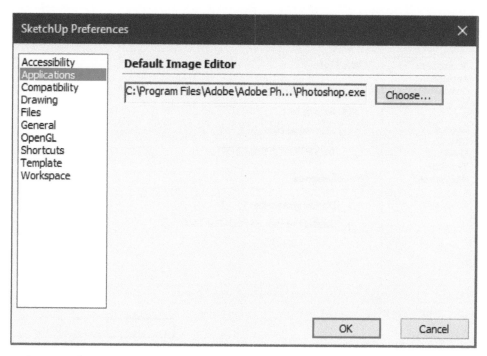

Figure 7.6 System preferences – Applications.

Change the Drawing settings to allow only Click-move-click and Continue line drawing (Figure 7.7). This will prevent you from clicking and dragging, which makes it easy to accidentally move objects by tiny increments or accidentally draw tiny, almost unnoticeable unwanted geometry. Also, if you are a SketchUp purist, disable pre-pick on the Push/Pull tool to maintain the old-school push/pull functionality. Drawing style is a personal preference, so feel free to adjust to the one that works for you.

Files

By specifying file locations, you can save time because you won't have to navigate through multiple folders to perform common SketchUp tasks (Figure 7.8). When you import, export, and open collections, SketchUp will already know where you want to look first. Select Window > Preferences and then select the Files menu at the left. Set your default file locations as follows:

☑ In the Models field, define the starting point for all open and save operations. Designate the directory path as `\Desktop\ACTIVE PROJECTS\` or your office's shared network drive.

☑ In the Components field, set the default location to use when you open or create a collection in the Components browser. Set the directory path to `\Desktop\RESOURCES\COMPONENTS\`.

☑ In the Materials field, set the default location to use when you open or create a collection in the Materials browser. Set the directory path to `\Desktop\RESOURCES\MATERIALS\`.

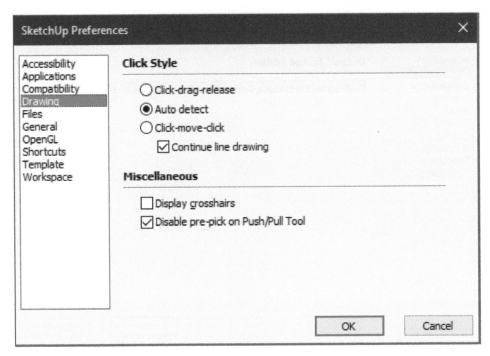

Figure 7.7 System preferences – Drawing.

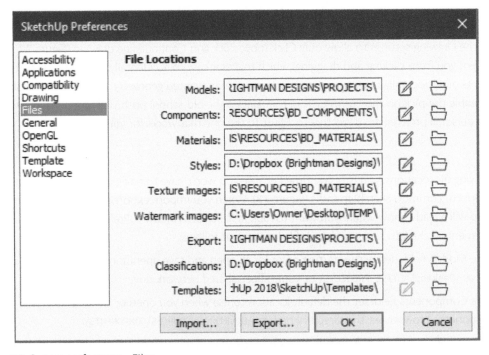

Figure 7.8 System preferences – Files.

☑ In the Styles field, set the default location to use when you open or create a collection in the Styles browser. Set the directory path to **\Desktop\RESOURCES\STYLES**.

☑ The Texture Images field is where you can set the default location for all images that can be used as textures. SketchUp will use this location as the starting point for all File > Insert > Image as Texture operations. Set the directory path to **\Desktop\RESOURCES\MATERIALS**.

☑ In the Watermark Images field, set the default location for all images that can be used as a watermark. Set the directory path to **\Desktop\TEMP**.

☑ In the Export field, set the default location for all models that are to be exported out of SketchUp. SketchUp will use this location as the starting point for all File > Export > 3D model operations. Set the directory path to **\Desktop\ACTIVE PROJECTS**.

☑ In the Classifications field, set the default location for all classifications that can be imported. Set the directory path to **\Desktop\RESOURCES\MISC**. I don't use classifications.

☑ The Templates field is not configurable. This is where templates are saved when you hit File > Save As Template.

Once you set the folders, you can easily get to the file location by clicking on the folder next to the field.

General

Within the General settings, make sure the Auto-save box is checked, and allow SketchUp to automatically save your model every 5 minutes (Figure 7.9). Auto-saving can take a long time if your model is large; however, by applying the model lightening techniques explained in this book, you will minimize that problem. Remember, SketchUp will not auto-save a new model until you have first saved it yourself.

Creating a backup file is pretty much a necessity—just in case! A backup file is saved in the same folder as the original **.skp** file and given the extension **.skb**. In the rare event that a model becomes unusable, change the file extension of the backup from **.skb** to **.skp**, and you will be able to open the file in SketchUp.

TIP Dropbox gives you access to nearly unlimited file version history, eliminating the need to save a duplicate .skb.

OpenGL

Open Graphics Library (OpenGL) settings can be used to troubleshoot your graphics card if strange things happen in your model (Figure 7.10).

Anti-aliasing smooths out the jagged edges that result from a diagonal line of pixels. Pick a setting with the highest amount of anti-aliasing your monitor can handle so your model will look its best on your screen. Dial this setting down if you are experiencing slow performance.

The Use fast feedback option is necessary; leave it turned on. Fast feedback improves SketchUp's performance, especially if you're working on a large model. SketchUp typically controls this setting on its own. If your graphics card supports this feature, SketchUp will use it.

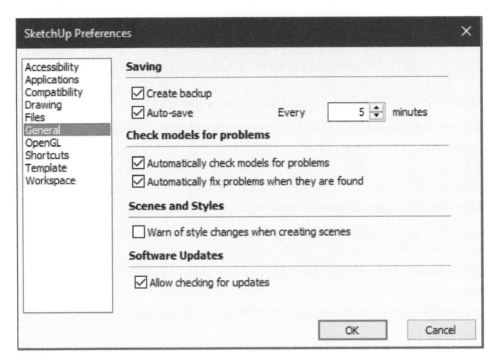

Figure 7.9 System preferences – General.

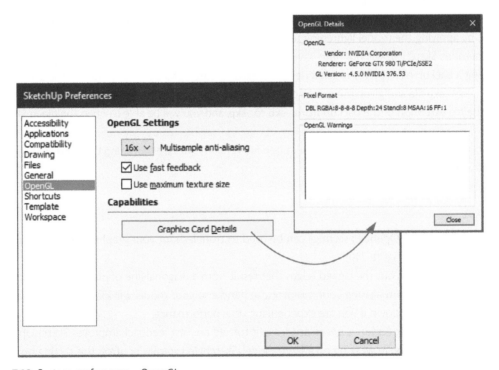

Figure 7.10 System preferences – OpenGL.

Use maximum texture size is usually not necessary and will actually slow down your computer's performance; leave this option unchecked. The maximum texture size improves the appearance of image imports and textures you see on your screen but at the cost of system performance. This setting will not improve printing or exporting resolution. It makes image imports clearer.

In the Capabilities section, click on the Graphics Card Details button to see more information on your drivers and any possible OpenGL warnings.

Shortcuts

Keyboard shortcuts allow you to access any SketchUp command with the press of a key. Use shortcuts to help you work faster and relieve a huge amount of strain on your eyes and mouse hand. Every time you take your eyes off your design, you slow down. Take the time to focus on your keyboarding technique and set up your own custom keyboard shortcuts.

Adding Shortcuts

Modify your keyboard shortcuts in the Preferences dialog box by clicking on the Window (SketchUp on a Mac) drop-down menu and choosing Preferences > Shortcuts (Figure 7.11).

1. Type a command, such as Hide, into the Filter window to parse through all the options and quickly find a command.

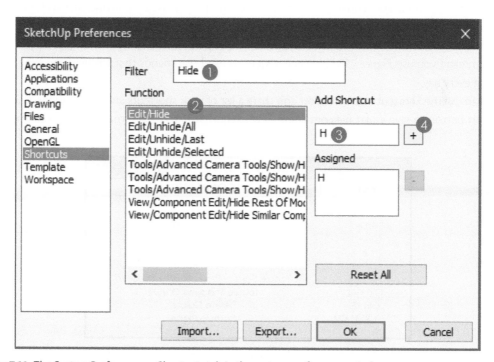

Figure 7.11 The System Preferences – Shortcuts tab in the system preferences window.

2. Click on a command in the Function box—for example, Edit/Hide.

3. Click in the Add Shortcut box and press the H key.

4. Click on the plus sign (+) to lock in the assigned keyboard shortcut.

If you try to assign a key that is already associated with another command, you will be prompted to reassign the key to the new command. Don't worry. You can always use the Reset All button to restore the keyboard shortcuts to the default state.

TIP By using shortcuts to interact with the Windows operating system, you will be able to work faster and more efficiently in any program. Hold down the Alt key and tap the Tab key to scroll through all the open applications. Once you are in an application, hold down the Ctrl key and tap the Tab key to scroll through the open files within that application.

Now that you've assigned the keyboard shortcut H to the command Hide Geometry, the H key is taken; however, several helpful hide commands are left unassigned. You may have trouble remembering them if they don't have an "H" associated with them. Fortunately, you can use combinations of modifier keys—Ctrl, Shift, and Alt—to add more shortcut options in the Add Shortcut text box. To assign a modifier key to a shortcut command, simply press and hold the modifier key while you enter the desired key in the text box. For example, to hide the rest of the model when you're editing a group or component, assign the keyboard shortcut Ctrl+H. To unhide all, assign the keyboard shortcut Shift+H. Assign the shortcut Alt+H to show/hide hidden geometry. For a less frequently used command such as Hide Similar Components, try to assign a combination of the modifier keys such as Ctrl+Shift+H.

In addition to the common commands and tools, it is helpful to have shortcuts assigned to just about every command you use. Figure 7.12 lists some frequently used commands that will help you expedite modeling every day.

You can use the Shortcuts tab to export and share a list of your shortcuts and file locations. Click on the Export button to save a **.dat** file containing all your shortcuts. You can e-mail this file to colleagues

HELPFUL SHORTCUTS	
KEY	**COMMAND**
Ctrl + D	Show/Hide Dialogs
Shift + E	Zoom Extents
Ctrl + 1	Top View
Z	Zoom Window
Ctrl +R	Reverse Faces
F9	Toggle Parallel Projection/Perspective
Ctrl + Q	Toggle Shadows On/Off
Ctrl +E	Delete Guides
Ctrl + Shift + V	Paste in Place

Figure 7.12 Take the time to add additional shortcuts. If you constantly access a command using an icon or a drop-down menu, take the time to assign a keyboard shortcut to that command.

and even use this file to set up standard shortcuts and file locations on your other machines. Simply click the Import button and select the `preferences.dat` file.

Ready Stance

To stay nimble, keep your left hand in the standard typing position with your thumb on the spacebar. This is an excellent default three-point stance for tackling SketchUp. If you already have a comfortable stance, stick with it—but at the same time, don't be afraid to try something new. Just be sure to always use the keyboard shortcuts and practice using keys without looking, even if it seems slower at first. Keyboard shortcuts will make you faster.

CHAPTER POINTS

- ☑ A clean screen will encourage efficiency and ultimately increase productivity.
- ☑ Keep your eyes on the model by using keystrokes without looking at the keyboard. Even if this technique takes longer at first, it will make you much faster in the long run.
- ☑ Customize your keyboard shortcuts in a way that makes sense to you.
- ☑ Try using keyboard shortcuts in other programs, too.

Chapter 8
SketchUp Collections

When using SketchUp, people frequently miss the opportunity to fully organize and even use collections. That is a big mistake. Collections are notoriously messy. Whether you're working with a collection of components, styles, or textures, it is easy to be lazy and not keep the collections clean and organized—but now there is no excuse. This section will show you all the rules and resources you need to build extensive, high-resolution, organized collections. Adhering to these standards will ensure that you always have the files you need right when you need them.

MATERIAL COLLECTION

You may have noticed that almost every amateur SketchUp model has the same shingles, bricks, and grass. Avoid using the materials that are preloaded in SketchUp. They are easily recognizable and will make your models look elementary. Diligently search for texture images to find ones that best represent the materials you have chosen for your design. This section contains several strategies for finding, creating, and organizing your professional material collection.

The Materials Browser

Before you begin in earnest, take a moment to explore the Materials browser. Launch it by activating the Paint Bucket tool or by clicking on the Window > Default Tray drop-down menu and choosing Materials. The Materials browser has two separate tabs: Select and Edit (Figure 8.1). The Select tab displays preloaded collections, favorite collections, and the materials in your model. This is where you find materials to apply to surfaces within your model. The Edit tab is where you can change the many properties of a material already added to your model (Figure 8.2). Use the Edit tab to change the color, scale, texture image, and opacity of the active material.

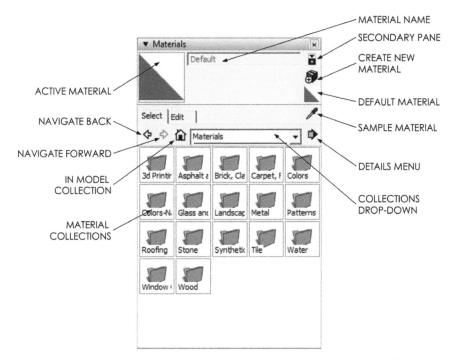

Figure 8.1 The Materials browser's Select tab allows you to choose materials from preloaded collections and see the materials already in your model.

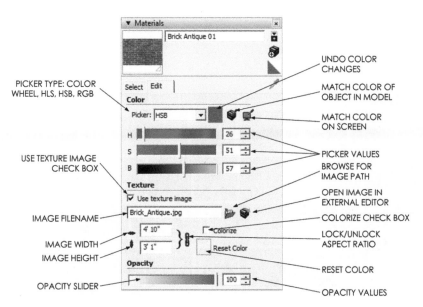

Figure 8.2 The Materials browser's Edit tab allows you to modify the properties of a material.

TIP The Materials browser is very different on a Mac, but the underlying concepts are the same. This book does not contain Mac screenshots, but it is not hard to apply the directions from Windows to Mac.

Creating a Material

Texture images are relatively small, optimized images that can repeat infinitely without seams. They are essential for creating professional-quality SketchUp materials, which you can then use to create convincing three-dimensional (3D) models to accurately represent your design.

An enormous number of texture images are available online for free. To begin collecting textures, perform a Google Images search for "tileable grass." You can sort the results from a Google Images search by many filters—most importantly, by size. For this exercise, click Medium to view images that are at a high enough resolution to look great yet still maintain a reasonable file size. When searching for images, you can find the most valuable images by adding the words "tileable," "texture," or "material" to the query (Figure 8.3).

Click on an image thumbnail to navigate to the site that hosts the image. From there, you can right-click on the image and choose Save Image As. Save the image to your TEMP folder. Raw texture images should be saved there because you won't need the original image once it is imported into SketchUp as a material.

Now, add the texture image to a new material in SketchUp. To do that, follow these steps:

1. In the Materials browser, click the Create Material button to add a new material (see Figure 8.4). When you create a new material, the Create Material dialog opens and creates a copy of the active material.

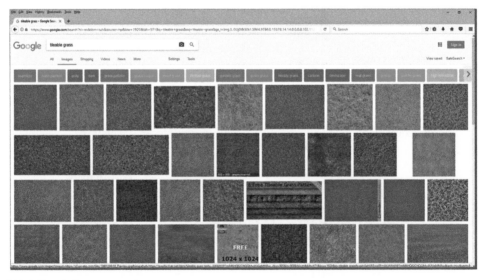

Figure 8.3 A Google Images search.

2. Name the material Grass 01.

3. Click on the folder icon to add a texture image. Navigate to your TEMP folder and select the grass texture material. Click the Open button.

4. Click OK to finish creating the material.

Once a texture is created, it resides in the current model only. You will need to add the new material to a collection to access it while working on other models. To do that, follow these steps:

1. Click on the In Model Collection (house icon) to see the materials that are in your model.

2. Right-click the Grass 01 material thumbnail and choose Save As.

3. Navigate to the RESOURCES/MATERIALS/ NATURE/GRASS folder and save the material in the appropriate material folder. If you set your default folders as described in Chapter 7, The Professional's SketchUp Environment, you will be taken there immediately.

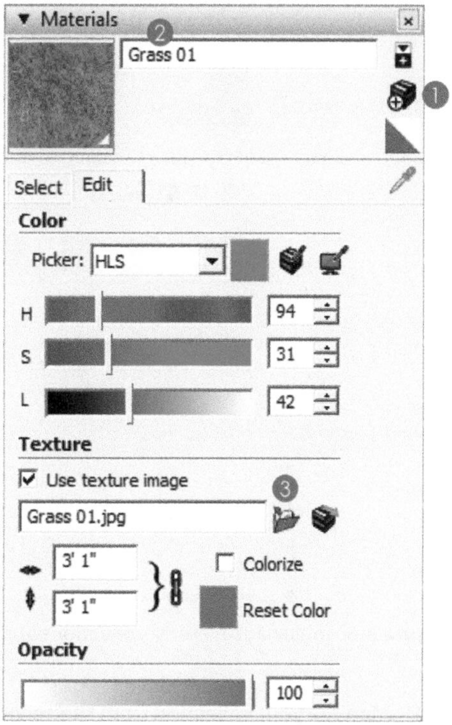

Other excellent free and commercial sources for textures are available. Try searching Google for "free textures" and see what you can find. When you use an image search and find an image you like, the site hosting it will usually have other collections and textures available. Click on the website for this image link to view more offerings from the site hosting the image.

Figure 8.4 Use the Create Material dialog to modify the properties of a new material.

Lastly, FormFonts.com, sketchuptextureclub.com, and textures.com all have extensive libraries of texture images available at very reasonable prices and are licensed for commercial work. Regardless of where you get your textures, just be sure that you keep them organized.

Adding a Collection to Favorites

Now that you have added a material to your collection, you need to add that collection to your favorites within the Materials browser. This will give you access every time you open SketchUp.

1. In the Materials browser, click the Details menu and choose Add collection to favorites (Figure 8.5).

2. Navigate to the RESOURCES/MATERIALS folder and select OK.

3. Click the Material Collections drop-down menu and select the MATERIALS folder. The new material collection will be at the bottom of the list. Once a collection is added to your favorites, you can always access it from the Collections drop-down menu in the Materials browser.

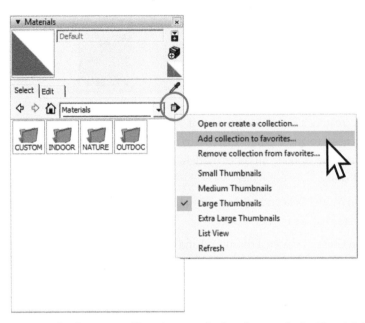

Figure 8.5 To manage material collections and favorites, use the Details menu in the Materials browser.

TIP Manage your collection from the secondary pane or from a file browser such as Windows Explorer. Within the RESOURCES/MATERIALS folder, add logical subfolders such as Nature, Indoor, Outdoor, and Custom. These are the same subfolders Lumion uses for its material library and is covered in detail in Chapter 4, File and Folder Management.

COMPONENT COLLECTIONS

Components have several useful applications, one being prebuilt SketchUp models of common objects that will save you an immense amount of time. Everyone can use objects such as lamps, plants, cars, and furniture, but no one wants to build these complex objects from scratch every time they are needed. Fortunately, component collections allow you to save and organize all these objects for easy access and reuse.

The Components Browser

The Components browser is where you can view component collections, access the Trimble 3D Warehouse, and see which components are in your model. To access the Components browser, click on the Window drop-down menu and choose Default Tray > Components (Figure 8.6).

Finding Components

Hundreds of thousands, if not millions, of components are immediately available for free within the 3D Warehouse. This is a huge repository of user-created, user-submitted, and user-rated models. Buyer beware

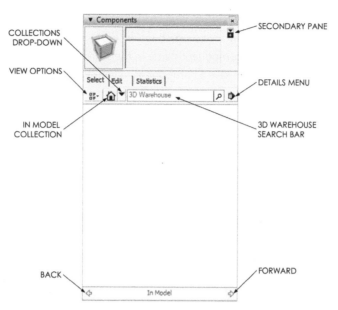

Figure 8.6 Use the Components browser to find components and organize them into collections.

though. You get what you pay for, so when you pay nothing, you should not expect much. Many of the models on the 3D Warehouse need to be optimized, correctly scaled, or even completed. Keep in mind that most of the models there are not plug-and-play; they will require some work to make them usable.

To search the 3D Warehouse, enter your query directly into the search box in the Components browser. You can search for object titles, such as chair, table, car, and people. You can also search for brand names, such as West Elm, Pella, and Mercedes; brand searches typically return more favorable results. Once your search is complete, use the arrows at the bottom left and right to navigate through the search results (Figure 8.7).

At this point, you can click on a model thumbnail in the Components browser and then click again in your model to place the component. The selected component will be copied into your model.

Searching within the Components browser is a quick way to grab models from a minimalist interface. You can also access the 3D Warehouse through the Web, which provides significantly more model information and search options. Click the Details menu, and select View in Trimble 3D Warehouse. This will launch the Web version of the Trimble 3D Warehouse, which

Figure 8.7 The results of a West Elm search.

will be larger and easier to view; most important, it will be sortable by ratings and popularity to help you filter the best models to the top. You can access search results in the 3D Warehouse Web interface from the Details menu or by clicking on the component name in the search results (Figure 8.8).

Click the Download Model button to save a component to your RESOURCES/COMPONENTS collection.

A better solution for building a component collection is to pay for the models. FormFonts.com offers an extensive collection of excellent professionally built, commercially available models. All the models there are properly scaled, textured, and optimized, making them easy to use "right out of the box." For professionals, paying for models is worth the small monetary investment to have perfect models in seconds.

Figure 8.8 To get more options and information than the Components browser provides, view the 3D Warehouse search results in a Web browser.

Adding a Collection to Favorites

Once you have created a collection, you will want to access it every time you open SketchUp. To do that, follow these steps:

1. Click the Details menu and choose Open or create a local collection (Figure 8.9).

2. Navigate to your RESOURCES folder, select the COMPONENTS folder, and then click OK.

3. Click the context arrow again and choose Add to favorites. The component collection will be available every time you open SketchUp under the Component Collections drop-down menu.

TIP Manage your collection from a file browser such as Windows Explorer. Add logical subfolders to the Components folder—for example, Landscape, Furniture, Entourage, Doors, Windows, etc. These subfolders match the ELEMENT layers and are covered in detail in Chapter 4, File and Folder Management.

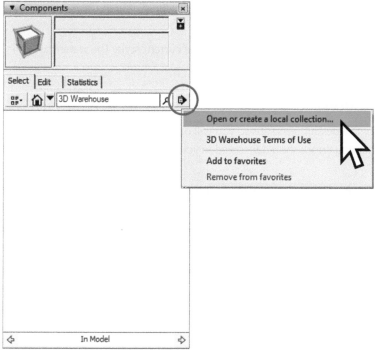

Figure 8.9 In the Components browser, use the Details menu to manage component collections and favorites.

STYLES COLLECTION

Currently, styles are not as widely available as materials and components are; this is probably because the preloaded libraries are more than enough to get you started.

Creating a Style

Use the Mix tab in the Styles browser (Figure 8.10) to combine your favorite styles into new creations. To do that, follow these steps:

1. In the Styles browser, click on the Mix tab. This automatically launches the secondary pane.

2. In the secondary pane, choose your favorite collection.

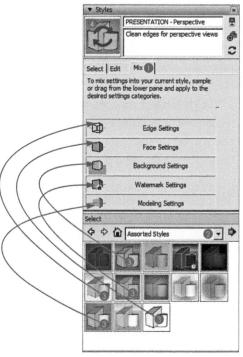

Figure 8.10 The Mix tab in the Styles browser gives you creative license to take your favorite styles and blend them.

3. Drag a style to one of the properties in the Mix tab. The current style will inherit the specified properties from the style that you dragged up.

4. Click the Style icon to update and save the changes made to the current style. The watermark will disappear upon updating.

Adding a Style to a Collection

Not every style needs to be a part of the default template, so you will need a style collection to hold additional useful styles. Any style that you create should be saved in your Styles collection. To save a style, follow these steps:

1. Click the In Model Collection (house icon) to see which styles are in your model; you will see the styles that you created in Chapter 6, The Professional's SketchUp Template.

2. Right-click on a style and choose Save As.

3. Navigate to your RESOURCES/STYLES folder, select it, and click Save. If you set your default folders as described in Chapter 7, The Professional's SketchUp Environment, you will be taken there immediately.

Adding a Collection to Favorites

So that this collection is always available when you need it, click on the Details menu and select Add to favorites. Navigate to and select the RESOURCES/STYLES folder and choose OK. The collection will be available every time you open SketchUp under the Style Collections drop-down menu (Figure 8.11).

TIP In addition to any new styles you create, add all the styles from the default template to your Styles collection.

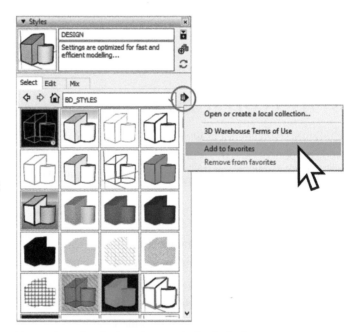

Required Styles

Now make the styles that you will need later when you create scenes for construction documents. You can also download all the styles, and many more, at **brightmandesigns.com/TSWFA**.

Figure 8.11 Use the Details menu in the Styles browser to manage style collections and favorites.

LINE DRAWING – Presentation Style

The LINE DRAWING – Presentation style is used for colorful presentation plans, sections, and elevations with sketchy lines. You will need the watermark .png included with the resource files.

Click on the Create new style button to add a new style to your template model, and name it LINE DRAWING – Presentation. Click on the Edit tab, and adjust the settings as shown in Figure 8.12 and Figure 8.13. Click on the Update button to save the changes and the watermark will go away, indicating that everything has been saved. The LINE DRAWING – Presentation style is complete.

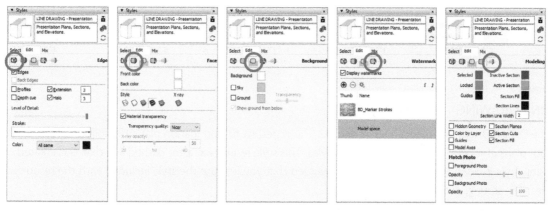

Figure 8.12 The PRESENTATION style settings.

LINE DRAWING – 00 Style

The LINE DRAWING style presents all geometry in simple black lines on a white background. This style is ideal for creating computer-aided design (CAD)-type two-dimensional (2D) output as typically seen in construction documents.

Click on the Create new style button to add a new style to your template model, and name it LINE DRAWING. Click on the Edit tab, and adjust the settings as shown in Figure 8.14. Click on the Update button to save the changes and the watermark will go away, indicating that everything has been saved. The LINE DRAWING style is complete.

Make LINE DRAWING 25, 50, and 75 styles. The number in the style name determines the brightness setting on the line color settings. This opens up the possibility of gray scale lines for your construction documents.

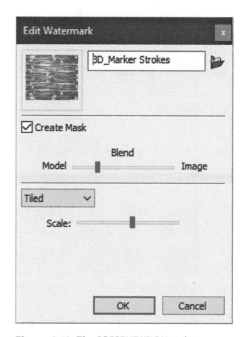

Figure 8.13 The PRESENTATION style watermark settings.

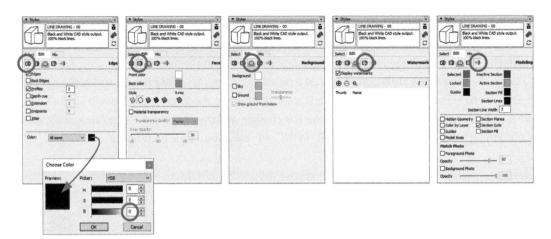

Figure 8.14 The LINE DRAWING style settings.

LINE DRAWING – Dashed Style

The DASHED style represents lines as dashed. This is perfect for foundation plans, demolition plans, and roof plans as it opens up a world of visual styles. This style requires a raster dashed line that was created using Style Builder (Figure 8.15). It is recommended that you just use the style included with the resource files. The settings are shown in Figure 8.16.

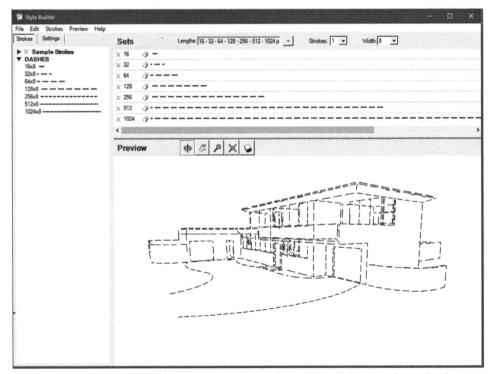

Figure 8.15 The DASHED style stroke settings created using Style Builder, which are rarely used and not covered in this book.

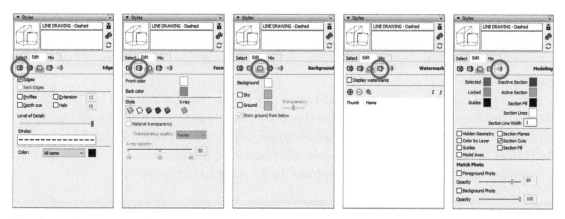

Figure 8.16 The DASHED style settings.

HATCH – 00

The HATCH – 00 styles eliminate all lines and allow you to fill in your 2D LayOut line work with dynamic solid fill hatching. (The numbers refer to the lightness slider of the front and back faces to create different shades of gray.)

Click on the Create new style button to add a new style to your template model, and name it HATCH 00. Click on the Edit tab, and adjust the settings as shown in Figure 8.17. Click the Update button to save the changes and the watermark will go away, indicating that everything has been saved. The HATCH 00 utility style is complete. Now make the 25, 50, and 75 styles.

TIP If you are using section fills, make sure the color matches the face settings color.

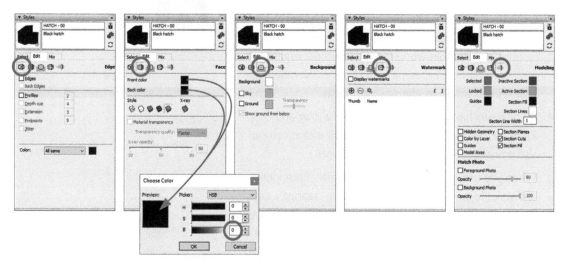

Figure 8.17 The HATCH – 00 style settings.

HATCH – Lines

The HATCH – Lines style allows you to fill in your 2D LayOut line work with dynamic hatch pattern fills. If you are using this style when you modify your design, your hatch will follow the walls. There is no need to manually fill them in.

Click on the Create new style button to add a new style to your model, and name it HATCH – Lines. Click on the Edit tab, and adjust the settings as shown in Figure 8.18 and Figure 8.19. Click the Update button to save the changes and the watermark will go away, indicating that everything has been saved. The HATCH – Lines style is complete. Now make other patterns in Photoshop.

Download more at **brightmandesigns.com**. Make the hatch dot and net styles.

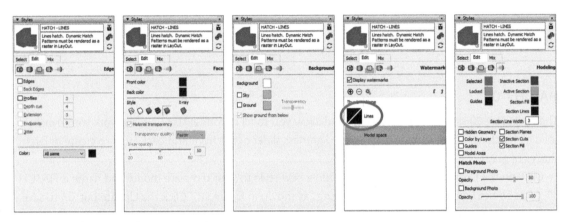

Figure 8.18 The HATCH – Lines style settings.

CHAPTER POINTS

☑ Collections are most valuable when they are kept current and organized. Organize material and component collections in a way that works for you. Consider organizing your collections by types, project, client, or even design style—for example, modern or traditional.

☑ All browsers have a secondary pane and a drag-and-drop interface that make managing collections easier. You can also manage collections from a file browser.

☑ When you use a collection to add materials, components, and styles to your current model, you are creating a copy of the original from the collection and placing that copy in the model. When you edit the materials, components, or styles, you are editing only the copy in the model, not the original in the collection.

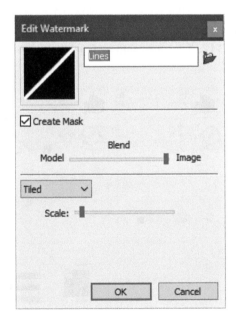

Figure 8.19 The HATCH – Lines watermark settings.

Chapter 9
Extensions

Extensions are the original apps. Before apps were extreme fajitas and potato poppers, and even before apps allowed you to digitally chug a beer on your phone, there were extensions. These little pieces of code expedite the tedious and repetitive tasks in SketchUp that drive you crazy. If you find that a certain task is taking entirely too long, take a step back and start looking for an extension. There's an app for that. In this section, you will review several useful extensions and learn how to find and install others.

FIND EXTENSIONS

Some extensions are free, and some aren't. Just as with the Trimble 3D Warehouse, you get what you pay for. When you purchase an extension, typically you can expect to receive support and clear instructions. If you grab a free extension, you should probably expect to put in a little extra effort figuring out how to use it.

A great place to buy extensions and grab a few freebies is **smustard.com**. Huge collections of free extensions are available at the Ruby Library Depot, **www.crai.archi.fr/rld/plugins_list_az.php** (or Google it), **sketchucation.com**, and **extensions.sketchup.com (Extension Warehouse)**.

The Extension Warehouse is an online repository of vetted and approved extensions. It is nice because it installs for you, is searchable, and ties in with everything. Open the Extension Warehouse in SketchUp (Figure 9.1) by clicking on the Window drop-down and choosing Extension Warehouse. You can search for specific extensions, tasks, categories, industries, and developers, or you can just browse the collections.

Figure 9.1 The Extension Warehouse.

INSTALLING EXTENSIONS

TIP Send an old .rb or .rbs to a compressed file, then rename it with the .rbz file extension, rather than .zip. Now it can be installed through the Extension Manager in SketchUp.

Extension Manager

Newer extensions that are written specifically for SketchUp 2018 are packaged as .rbz files. The compressed one-file format makes them much easier to install. The extension manager (Figure 9.2) allows you to install extensions, and also manage them. Access it from the Window drop-down, then click on Extension Manager.

To install an extension using the Extension Manager, follow these steps:

1. Click on the Install Extension button at the bottom-left corner.

2. Navigate to a folder containing an .rbz, click on the .rbz, and choose Open.

Figure 9.2 The Extension Manager's home tab.

3. To disable an extension, or prevent it from loading, click on the Enabled/Disabled button next to the extension name. This limits the number of plugins that are loaded when SketchUp starts and is helpful for keeping your system light.

4. To manage extensions, click on the Manage tab. From here, you can update and uninstall extensions. See Figure 9.3.

TIP If plugins are not working properly, it is possible that there is a conflict between two of them. Disable all plugins, then turn them back on one by one while testing to troubleshoot.

Manually Install

The truth is the Extension Manager and Extension Warehouse can be buggy and unpredictable. Although these tools work most of the time, it is best to have a full understanding of extensions and how to manage them manually.

Once you have downloaded your extension, save it to the PLUGINS folder for safe-keeping, now copy it to the system Plugins folder (for example, on a Windows machine, `C:\Users\Owner\AppData\Roaming\SketchUp\SketchUp 2017\SketchUp\Plugins`).

Figure 9.3 The Extension Manager's Manage tab.

Keep in mind that the path could vary, depending on your drive name and operating system. If an extension is zipped, you must extract the contents to this location. After the `.rb` file is saved in the system Plugins folder, you will need to close SketchUp and reopen it in order to load the new extension.

TIP For an advanced method for finding your PLUGINS folder, open the Ruby Console by clicking on the Window drop-down and choosing Ruby Console (Figure 9.4). Type, "Sketchup.find_support_file('Plugins')", and press enter. The Ruby console will return the location of your plugins folder, now it's on you to get there!

TIP Sometimes one extension depends on another to operate properly. Read through any instructions and documentation thoroughly before you try to use an extension. For example, many extensions will not work without the sketchup.rb and progressbar.rb extensions installed in the system plugins folder.

USING EXTENSIONS

You'll frequently encounter extensions that don't have any directions or documentation explaining exactly how to use them. Once an extension is installed, you may have to access it from different locations, depending on how the author designed the user experience. The first place to look is in the drop-down menus (such as Draw, Tools, and Extensions) at the top of the screen. If you still can't find it, open the extension script in a text editor to gather some clues. Authors frequently include a few notes about how to get started (Figure 9.5).

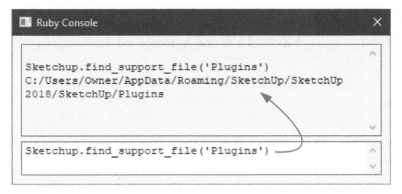

Figure 9.4 The Ruby Console.

```
# Copyright 2004, @Last Software, Inc.

# This software is provided as an example of using the Ruby interface
# to SketchUp.

# Permission to use, copy, modify, and distribute this software for
# any purpose and without fee is hereby granted, provided that the above
# copyright notice appear in all copies.

# THIS SOFTWARE IS PROVIDED "AS IS" AND WITHOUT ANY EXPRESS OR
# IMPLIED WARRANTIES, INCLUDING, WITHOUT LIMITATION, THE IMPLIED
# WARRANTIES OF MERCHANTABILITY AND FITNESS FOR A PARTICULAR PURPOSE.
#-----------------------------------------------------------------------
# Name         :    Bezier Curve Tool 1.0
# Description  :    A tool to create Bezier curves.
# Menu Item    :    Draw->Bezier Curves
# Context Menu:     Edit Bezier Curve
# Usage        :    Select 4 points-
#              :    1. Start point of the curve
#              :    2. Endpoint of the curve
#              :    3. Second control point.  It determines the tangency at the start
#              :    4. Next to last control point.  It determines the tangency at the end
# Date         :    8/26/2004
# Type         :    Tool
#-----------------------------------------------------------------------

# Ruby implementation of Bezier curves
require 'sketchup.rb'

module Bezier

# Evaluate a Bezier curve at a parameter.
# The curve is defined by an array of its control points.
# The parameter ranges from 0 to 1
# This is based on the technique described in "CAGD  A Practical Guide, 4th Editoin"
# by Gerald Farin. page 60

def Bezier.eval(pts, t)

    degree = pts.length - 1
    if degree < 1
        return nil
    end

    t1 = 1.0 - t
    fact = 1.0
    n_choose_i = 1

    x = pts[0].x * t1
```

Figure 9.5 Sometimes you will find instructions in the code.

CONDOC TOOLS
for SketchUp Pro

Figure 9.6 ConDoc Tools is a suite of tools, strategies, and templates derived from the first edition of this book. Now, they are married and work perfectly together. This book is the manual for ConDoc Tools.

general. Don't stop here—there are infinitely more extensions out there! Access our latest list and suggestions at **brightmandesigns.com/resources**.

ConDoc Tools

ConDoc Tools (Figure 9.6) was created shortly after the first edition of this book was published. It automates the most difficult tasks in SketchUp: layers, styles, and scenes. It also comes with the ConDoc System, a heads-up display that keeps you on track and your models organized.

This is by far the most valuable extension you can purchase if you are using the SketchUp Workflow for Architecture system. There are three parts: the ConDoc System, ConDoc Tools, and ConDoc Drawings.

ConDoc System

The ConDoc System (Figure 9.7) is SketchUp standards—a series of templates, layers, and model organization strategies that provide a clear path for SketchUp success. The ConDoc System is built to achieve specific results for designers—expanded arrays of line weights, dynamic hatches, the ability to draft two-dimensional (2D) details, communication with consultants, and a way to share work with a team.

Organizing your model using the ConDoc System creates lightweight, editable models. Included in your ConDoc Pro subscription are all the tutorials needed to go from beginner to pro.

The ConDoc System Extension is a heads-up display that provides real-time feedback to keep the designer informed, on track, and in line with the ConDoc Standards.

- ☑ The indicator icon will correct your layer when you get off track and also allow you to quickly toggle line weights in DRAFT mode.
- ☑ The Model Level Navigator keeps you informed on where you are in the model by combining group nesting and layering information into one concise string of text.
- ☑ The Model Complexity Meter keeps you aware of excessive geometry.
- ☑ DRAFT mode provides a 2D computer-aided design (CAD)-like drafting platform inside SketchUp!

ConDoc Tools

Automate and simplify the most difficult tasks in SketchUp. The plan generator is the keystone of the entire ConDoc System. Answer a few questions regarding project type, levels, finished floor heights, and which drawings to include in your set and a multitude of tedious plan scenes are instantly added to your model.

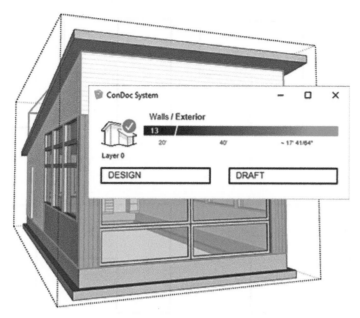

Figure 9.7 The ConDoc System.

Figure 9.8 The ConDoc Tools.

Managing layers, styles, and scenes is difficult. To mix in shadows, camera settings, and section planes, you need to be a pro. By automating these complex commands, the ConDoc Tools (Figure 9.8) give the designer more time to focus on design rather than mastering and perfecting every aspect of SketchUp required to produce construction documents.

ConDoc Drawings

ConDoc Drawings (Figure 9.9) are easily linked to the drawing scenes created by the ConDoc Tools, which forever connects these drawings to the design model. Move a wall in SketchUp, and the lines and hatch move in LayOut. This ensures you 100 percent connectivity between your three-dimensional (3D) model and your 2D construction document with no exploding needed.

Producing illustrative design packets and crystal-clear sets of construction documents has never been easier—just drag and drop. These drawings are completely optimized with a wide array of line weights and dynamic hatches beyond what is possible in the standard version of SketchUp Pro.

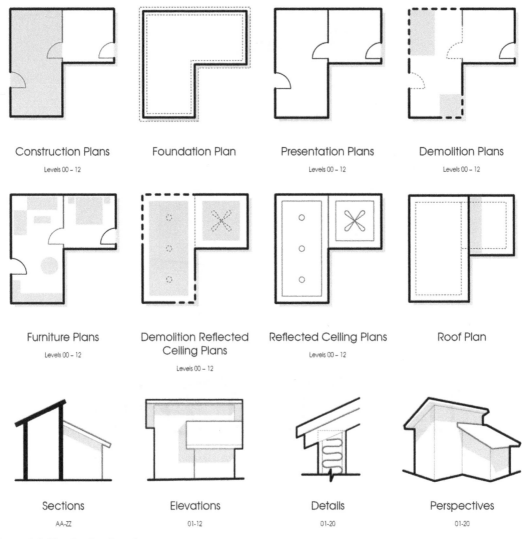

Construction Plans
Levels 00 – 12

Foundation Plan

Presentation Plans
Levels 00 – 12

Demolition Plans
Levels 00 – 12

Furniture Plans
Levels 00 – 12

Demolition Reflected
Ceiling Plans
Levels 00 – 12

Reflected Ceiling Plans
Levels 00 – 12

Roof Plan

Sections
AA-ZZ

Elevations
01-12

Details
01-20

Perspectives
01-20

Figure 9.9 The ConDoc Drawings.

Estimator

Estimator for SketchUp can estimate anything you can model in SketchUp. This extension can count and price components, materials, and lengths. You can even add quotes for labor and other intangible costs to account for all costs associated with your project inside of SketchUp. The garage model included with the ConDoc trial is already priced out using Estimator. You can download it at **estimatorforsketchup.com**.

Instant Architecture

The Instant Architecture plugins are a full suite of extremely useful tools. They expedite the creation of realistic roads in SketchUp. Clean up sites where the Sandbox tool falls short. Instant Railing is worth the cost of all the tools on its own. You can download them all at **valiarchitects.com/sketchup_scripts/ instant-road**.

Profile Builder

Profile Builder expands the Follow Me tool into an amazing modeling tool. It allows the ability to extrude profiles along paths in a more intuitive way and to create assemblies that copy along the way. This makes stairs, railings, and moldings much easier. You can download Profile Builder at **profilebuilder4sketchup.com**.

Artisan

Artisan tools make organic modeling in SketchUp a breeze. Sculpt, smooth, and pinch your terrain in a way that the default tools in SketchUp just won't let you. You can download Artisan at **artisan4sketchup.com**.

PlaceMaker

Recently, Trimble SketchUp lost the license to access Google Earth imagery and terrain. They switched over to Open Street Maps, but the imports are very low resolution.

The Match Photo tool replaces the lost street-view imagery option in SketchUp. It also brings in building masses, roads, paths, and trees. It's a great tool for jump-starting a project and investigating context.

This extension fills in the void left by the Google imagery data being pulled from SketchUp. PlaceMaker pulls in roads, paths, imagery, and even 3D building heights from open street maps and perfectly organizes everything. You can download PlaceMaker at **suplacemaker.com**.

DashedLines

The DashedLines extension will segment a selected line into several different line types. It is great for creating dashed lines to represent 2D graphics and for creating rare annotations in SketchUp (for example, center lines and column lines). You can find DashedLines at **smustard.com/script/DashedLines**.

Zorro

The Zorro tool is helpful when transitioning a sketch model to a refined design or when breaking a model into levels. With the Zorro tool, you draw a line across geometry that slices through all the geometry, even the groups and components. Typically, a head-on parallel projection view is the best view to use for full control of this extension. You can download it at **extensions.sketchup.com/en/content/zorro2**.

Shape Bender

Shape Bender takes an object and bends it along a path. It is hard to describe just how valuable this tool is until you need it. It works great for complex ramps, curved stairs, and complex organic objects. You can download Shape Bender at **extensions.sketchup.com/en/content/clf-shape-bender**.

FredoScale

FredoScale allows you to twist, shear, taper, scale, and stretch in ways that SketchUp just can't. As with Shape Bender, you won't realize just how valuable this plugin is until you need it. It requires LibFredo6 to function properly. You can download it at **sketchucation.com/plugin/1169-fredoscale**.

CHAPTER POINTS

- ☑ I created ConDoc Tools to simplify and expedite the most difficult tasks in this book. This is highly recommended to not only get the most out of this book but also to automate all the processes outlined in it.
- ☑ If you are performing a task that is repetitive, tedious, and taking entirely too long, stop immediately and look for an extension script.
- ☑ Paying for extensions is worth it. They are usually inexpensive and will save you hours of labor working on mind-numbing, repetitious tasks and searching for freebies.

PART III

LayOut

Like Kevin from *Home Alone,* LayOut is easily overlooked and very much underestimated. More often than not, LayOut is an afterthought—if it is even considered at all—yet this program is the keystone of an effective SketchUp workflow. LayOut turns three-dimensional (3D) SketchUp models into stylized print and screen presentations—presentations that ultimately sell your ideas and produce the instructions to build the spaces you envision in SketchUp. In Part III, you will receive a complete education in all that is LayOut, from theory to the toolset.

Chapter 10
Introduction to LayOut

Sketchup Pro is a software suite that includes the unrestricted version of SketchUp, as well as the invaluable presentation application LayOut. Although SketchUp Pro is undeniably excellent by itself, SketchUp Pro becomes truly radical when paired with LayOut (Figure 10.1).

Figure 10.1 The free version of SketchUp is for hobbyists; SketchUp Pro is for professionals.

WHAT IS LAYOUT?

In short, LayOut is a multifaceted presentation tool. It is a page-creation program that has 3D presentation capabilities coupled with two-dimensional (2D) crafting tools (Figure 10.2 and 10.3). In LayOut, you arrange 3D perspective views and scaled 2D orthographic views on a sheet of paper to graphically explain a design. When you're done, you can use LayOut's sleek drawing toolset to add informative annotations on top of those views and provide an additional layer of information for your audience. With LayOut's tools, you can quickly and easily add dimensions, text, leader text, callouts, and custom line types.

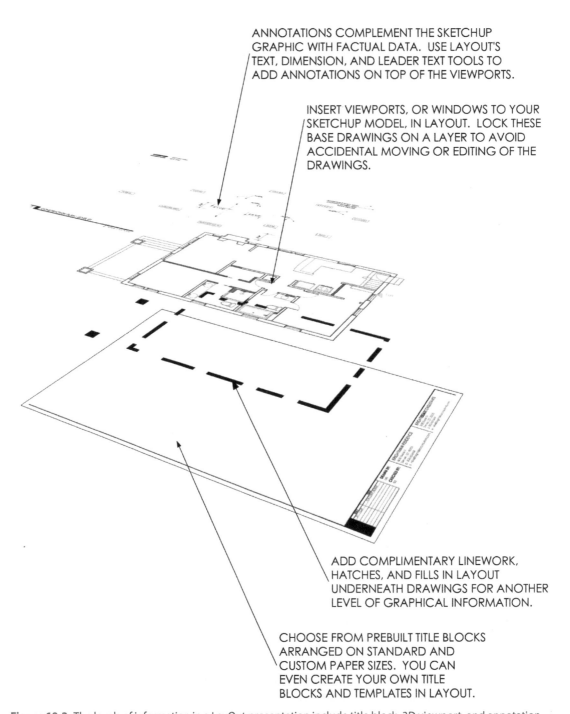

ANNOTATIONS COMPLEMENT THE SKETCHUP
GRAPHIC WITH FACTUAL DATA. USE LAYOUT'S
TEXT, DIMENSION, AND LEADER TEXT TOOLS TO
ADD ANNOTATIONS ON TOP OF THE VIEWPORTS.

INSERT VIEWPORTS, OR WINDOWS TO YOUR
SKETCHUP MODEL, IN LAYOUT. LOCK THESE
BASE DRAWINGS ON A LAYER TO AVOID
ACCIDENTAL MOVING OR EDITING OF THE
DRAWINGS.

ADD COMPLIMENTARY LINEWORK,
HATCHES, AND FILLS IN LAYOUT
UNDERNEATH DRAWINGS FOR ANOTHER
LEVEL OF GRAPHICAL INFORMATION.

CHOOSE FROM PREBUILT TITLE BLOCKS
ARRANGED ON STANDARD AND
CUSTOM PAPER SIZES. YOU CAN
EVEN CREATE YOUR OWN TITLE
BLOCKS AND TEMPLATES IN LAYOUT.

Figure 10.2 The levels of information in a LayOut presentation include title block, 3D viewport, and annotation.

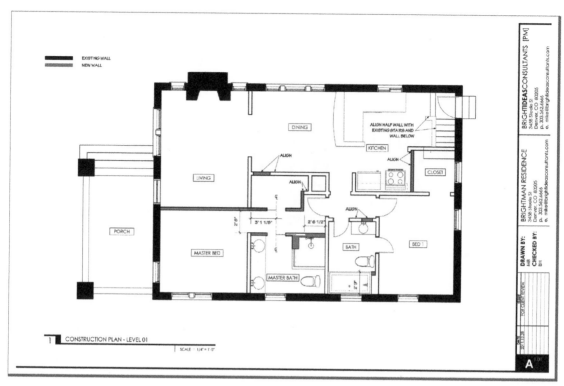

Figure 10.3 When all the graphics and annotations are flattened, you have an architectural drawing.

Design in SketchUp. Present in LayOut. That is the basic concept. For a more in-depth explanation, read on to learn about paper space, model space, and the dynamic link between the two that makes LayOut such a valuable tool.

Paper Space and Model Space

Now for the longer, technical answer: LayOut is SketchUp's equivalent to computer-aided design (CAD) paper space. Take a moment to fully grasp the concept of designing in model space and presenting in paper space.

Model Space

SketchUp's *model space* is where your design comes to life. Everything built in SketchUp 3D is drawn at a 1:1 real-world scale. This means that if a wall is to be built 10 feet tall in the real world, you draw the wall 10 feet tall in your SketchUp model. You don't need to crunch the numbers into an architectural scale while working in model space. Everything in SketchUp is built to the size it is intended to be built to in the real world (Figure 10.4).

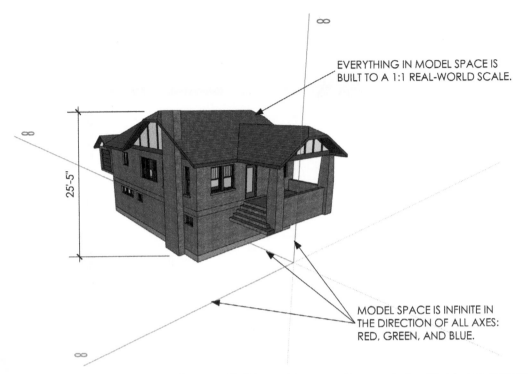

∞

EVERYTHING IN MODEL SPACE IS
BUILT TO A 1:1 REAL-WORLD SCALE.

∞

25'-5"

MODEL SPACE IS INFINITE IN
THE DIRECTION OF ALL AXES:
RED, GREEN, AND BLUE.

∞

Figure 10.4 Model space is where you design and build a model representing your design. Model space contains mostly 3D objects rather than graphics and annotations.

Paper Space

LayOut's *paper space* is where your presentation comes to life (Figure 10.5). Place the *viewports* (windows looking into your SketchUp model) on a standard paper size. Arrange the viewports on the sheet and set the orthographic views to architectural scales. In other words, LayOut will very quickly do the math so you can present your life-sized designs at a reduced architectural scale. This is where you will determine what sheet size you need to present your design at a specific architectural scale.

Dynamic Link

The 3D SketchUp model space and the 2D LayOut paper space are connected. The dynamic link between them is critical to the efficiency of the SketchUp Workflow for Architecture. After you modify and save the SketchUp model, LayOut will let you know that the link needs to be updated. When you update or refresh the model within LayOut, all the linked 2D drawings in your presentation will reflect the most current design (Figure 10.6). This dynamic link eliminates the need to re-export every time you make a presentation. This feature also gives you the freedom to make last-minute design changes in 3D and then simply update your presentation before a meeting. This dynamic link gives you the power to progressively build your presentation in small, one-at-a-time pieces leading up to the final presentation and

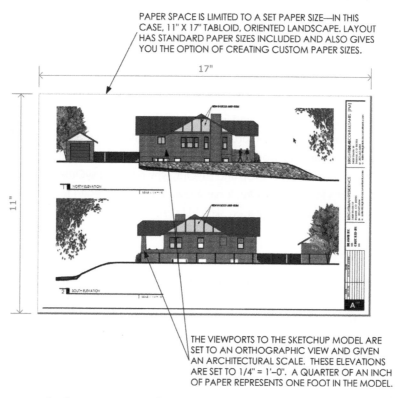

PAPER SPACE IS LIMITED TO A SET PAPER SIZE—IN THIS CASE, 11" X 17" TABLOID, ORIENTED LANDSCAPE. LAYOUT HAS STANDARD PAPER SIZES INCLUDED AND ALSO GIVES YOU THE OPTION OF CREATING CUSTOM PAPER SIZES.

17"

11"

THE VIEWPORTS TO THE SKETCHUP MODEL ARE SET TO AN ORTHOGRAPHIC VIEW AND GIVEN AN ARCHITECTURAL SCALE. THESE ELEVATIONS ARE SET TO 1/4" = 1'–0". A QUARTER OF AN INCH OF PAPER REPRESENTS ONE FOOT IN THE MODEL.

Figure 10.5 Paper space is where you create and organize the pages of your presentation based on a specific paper size. Paper space contains only 2D annotations and text overlayed on static 2D views of the 3D SketchUp model.

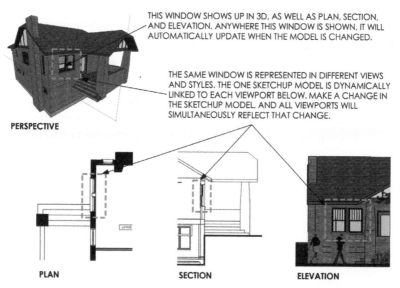

THIS WINDOW SHOWS UP IN 3D, AS WELL AS PLAN, SECTION, AND ELEVATION. ANYWHERE THIS WINDOW IS SHOWN, IT WILL AUTOMATICALLY UPDATE WHEN THE MODEL IS CHANGED.

THE SAME WINDOW IS REPRESENTED IN DIFFERENT VIEWS AND STYLES. THE ONE SKETCHUP MODEL IS DYNAMICALLY LINKED TO EACH VIEWPORT BELOW. MAKE A CHANGE IN THE SKETCHUP MODEL, AND ALL VIEWPORTS WILL SIMULTANEOUSLY REFLECT THAT CHANGE.

PERSPECTIVE

PLAN   SECTION   ELEVATION

Figure 10.6 When a SketchUp model is dynamically linked to a LayOut presentation, all drawings are derived from one model and updated simultaneously.

construction documents. This type of process is much more manageable than tackling a large presentation or an entire set of construction documents all at once.

WHY LAYOUT?

After you've worked in SketchUp, you may find it difficult to go back to the cyan and magenta world of 2D CAD or the tedious world of building information modeling (BIM). SketchUp and LayOut are much faster, more fun, and more colorful to work with than other drafting programs. If you can accomplish the same goals and so much more with SketchUp and LayOut, why not use LayOut? In addition, there are a few purely utilitarian reasons for using LayOut. It has a few professional design features that should convince you—or your boss—to pull the trigger on SketchUp Pro.

Expanded Export Options

SketchUp Pro and LayOut offer several export options for presenting, sharing with consultants, and moving the project into other software packages. You can export a **.pdf** from LayOut to produce large format prints and deliverables to pass out at a meeting. You can also export the LayOut presentation paper space or SketchUp model space as a CAD file in **.dwg** or **.dxf** format. To finish the job, you can then open the LayOut file in your familiar 2D drafting program. Finally, you can export all pages as **.jpg** files or **.png** files from LayOut. This option replaces the need for exporter plugins within SketchUp, and it expedites the entire export process.

Professional Renderings

If you are a professional designer building a SketchUp model, you probably want others to see it. Because it is limited to your screen resolution, the free version of SketchUp does not have the export capabilities required by professionals. SketchUp Pro—mainly LayOut—gives you all the tools and rendering settings you'll need to maximize your SketchUp model for presentation and sharing.

Exporting from SketchUp Pro allows you to create extremely high-resolution raster images and crisp vector drawings (Figure 10.7). Exporting from LayOut, you can even combine the best of raster and vector into one hybrid view. This concept will be covered in detail later in Chapter 11, The LayOut Interface.

EXPORTING FROM SKETCHUP (FREE) LIMITS YOU ON SCREEN RESOLUTION. LINES ARE PIXELATED, BULKY, AND BLURRY. THIS IS THE BEST YOU WILL EVER GET WITH SKETCHUP (FREE).

EXPORTING FROM SKETCHUP PRO GIVES YOU NEARLY UNLIMITED RESOLUTION FOR EXPORTS. THIS IS GOOD, BUT THE LINES START TO FADE OUT AT HIGHER RESOLUTIONS.

EXPORTING FROM LAYOUT GIVES THE OPTION FOR HYBRID RENDERING. THIS SETTING COMBINES A HIGH-RESOLUTION RASTER IMAGE WITH VECTOR LINEWORK LAID ON TOP. WHEN PRINTING AT A HIGH-RESOLUTION OR LARGE FORMAT, YOU WILL GET EXPONENTIALLY BETTER RESULTS.

Figure 10.7 SketchUp Pro can create much better images to use for large-scale presentations.

Software Replacement

When you render and export images from your 3D model, you have to insert those images into page-creation software to create the deliverables. Then if you want to make a slideshow, you need to insert those same images into slideshow software to create the presentation. Then you have to use another application to create a completely separate set of construction documents. If you need to make any changes, you need to re-export, reinsert, re-export, reinsert, and so on. LayOut gives you the ability to link one 3D model to a program that can create all these drawings and presentation materials at the same time and simultaneously update all the drawings and renderings. For example, with LayOut, you don't need to export from SketchUp and use programs such as InDesign, Photoshop, and Illustrator to arrange those images on a sheet. LayOut can do all of this—and it can do it better—with the dynamic link to SketchUp and the expanded rendering settings optimized for SketchUp models.

SketchUp Pro, LayOut, and ConDoc DRAFT mode together can replace all your CAD drafting software. The techniques provided in this book pull the best strategies and features from BIM and 2D drafting into one efficient workflow centered around SketchUp Pro. SketchUp Pro, LayOut, and the ConDoc Tools can also replace Architectural Desktop, Revit, and Vectorworks, as well as any other 2D or 3D BIM vector drafting programs.

LayOut replaces slideshow software such as PowerPoint. When it's time for you to present at a meeting, you can use LayOut's presentation mode to display your 2D LayOut presentation on a projection screen. This mode enables you to present each page as a slide, and it has a red Line tool you can use to mark up a set of drawings while you're giving your presentation in front of an audience (Figure 10.8). The red lines are conveniently added to a time-stamped layer for easy review, revision, and deletion later. LayOut doesn't offer any transitions or sound effects, but animated page curls and swoosh noises really don't do much to sell a design.

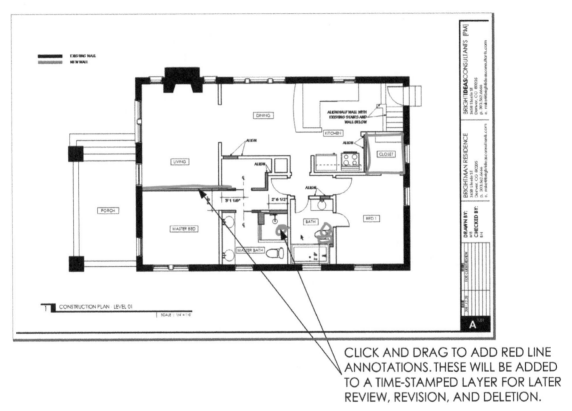

CLICK AND DRAG TO ADD RED LINE ANNOTATIONS. THESE WILL BE ADDED TO A TIME-STAMPED LAYER FOR LATER REVIEW, REVISION, AND DELETION.

Figure 10.8 Red lines in LayOut's presentation mode allow you to mark up a set in front of an audience.

Line Control

SketchUp's Profiles, Depth Cue, and Section Cuts settings give you some ability to control line weights. They offer everything you need to make compelling 3D views and animations. LayOut gives you full control over line weights even when you're working with scaled 2D drawings that require several line weights to align with industry graphic standards.

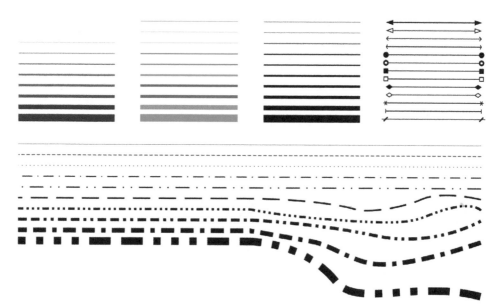

Figure 10.9 Line weights, line types, and arrows are abundant in LayOut.

Each viewport within LayOut can be set to a specific line weight independent of other viewports. This flexibility allows you to thicken large detail drawings and thin out smaller scaled plans.

The annotation lines and shapes you add in LayOut can be set to any line weight. You can assign several different line types and arrowheads to any line you draw in LayOut (Figure 10.9), and you can adjust their color as well. The combination of these settings gives you the ability to create any symbol or annotation in the graphic style you choose.

CHAPTER POINTS

- ☑ SketchUp Pro is a necessity for professional designers. SketchUp (free) offers just enough of the program for hobbyists to learn how to build 3D models.

- ☑ SketchUp Pro can replace many popular software packages, which will save you money and make creating all-inclusive presentations easier.

- ☑ Design, think, and explore in 3D SketchUp's model space.

- ☑ Present, annotate, and explain in 2D LayOut's paper space.

Chapter 11
The LayOut Interface

This chapter explains the intricacies of the LayOut interface and introduces all the settings, toolbars, and features you'll need to use LayOut. Use it now as a roadmap while you tour LayOut and become familiar with the interface. Even after you've mastered the concepts explained here, you'll be able to use this chapter as a helpful resource to answer any questions you have about individual menus, settings, and dialogs.

GETTING STARTED

To open LayOut, click the icon on your desktop. The Getting Started window will appear, allowing you to access new templates, recent files, and recovered presentations.

New Tab

Initially, you will be taken to the New tab by default (Figure 11.1). Preloaded templates that you can use to create new presentations will appear in the right pane. From the Default Templates library, select either a title block or a plain piece of paper. To select a default template (a template you will always start with), check the Always Use Selected Template box. Typically, you won't need to use this feature because you use different sizes of paper and title blocks for each presentation you create.

Recent Tab

The Recent tab displays all the documents you have worked on in the not-so-distant past. When you use this tab, be careful because it is similar to Recent Documents. Even though a file is shown there today, it

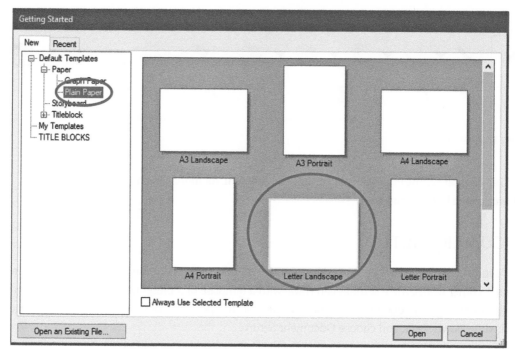

Figure 11.1 The New tab in the Getting Started window.

might not be tomorrow if you open other LayOut presentations. If you are using the Recent tab, you may not be aware of where you are saving the actual file.

The best way to open a file that you have already created is to click the Open an Existing File button at the bottom-left corner of the Getting Started window. Make sure you know where you are saving files so you can navigate to the appropriate project folder when you need them. To open a file, you can either double-click on its thumbnail or select the thumbnail and choose Open.

Recovered Tab

The Recovered tab at the top of the Getting Started window appears when files need to be recovered; you can use the recovery feature to help you get back work that was lost during a crash. LayOut does crash at times if you overload it, but it also does a great job of recovering files. Don't worry, though; the techniques you'll learn in this book will drastically reduce the number of crashes you experience. If LayOut does crash, reopen LayOut and look for your recovered document in the Recovered tab.

MAIN TOOLBAR

The Main toolbar in LayOut contains the most commonly used and basic tools (Figure 11.2). Undock a LayOut toolbar by clicking and dragging on the line at its far left. Dock a toolbar by dragging the header to the top, bottom, or side of the screen.

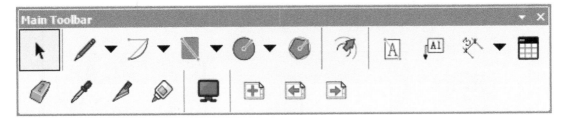

Figure 11.2 The Main toolbar.

TIP See Chapter 12, The Professional's LayOut Environment, for more information on creating and customizing the LayOut toolbars.

DOCUMENT SETUP

The Document Setup settings apply to the currently open document; they are not global settings for LayOut. In other words, these settings can travel with a template or a presentation file, but they will not change globally for every document you open in LayOut. To open the Document Setup dialog, click on the File drop-down menu and choose Document Setup.

Auto-Text Tab

Auto-text is a simple internal reference system within LayOut (Figure 11.3). This allows you to swap a simple tag with more complex text, eliminating the need to comb through a document repetitively replacing text. With Auto-text you can easily change one piece of text that propagates through the entire presentation.

1. Double-click on an auto-text tag to modify the identifying tag.
2. Click on the plus sign to add a new auto-text tag. You can choose from Custom Text, Page Number, Page Name, File Name, Current Date, Date Created, Date Modified, and Date Published.
3. Click on the duplicate button to make a copy of the current auto-text tag.
4. Click on the minus sign to delete an auto-text tag.
5. When a tag is selected above, you can modify the text that will be swapped in the presentation area.

TIP Auto-text works within the Text, Label, and Dimension tools, as well as within tables. This can be a very powerful, time-saving tool when set up properly.

Grid Tab

The Grid tab is where you can adjust the size and visual properties of the grid (Figure 11.4).

TIP The numerals in the diagrams refer to the keyed notes and do not represent any order of operation.

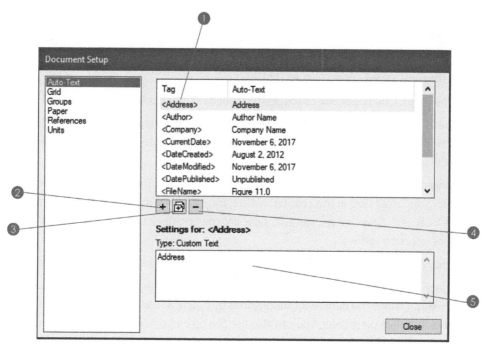

Figure 11.3 The Auto-Text tab.

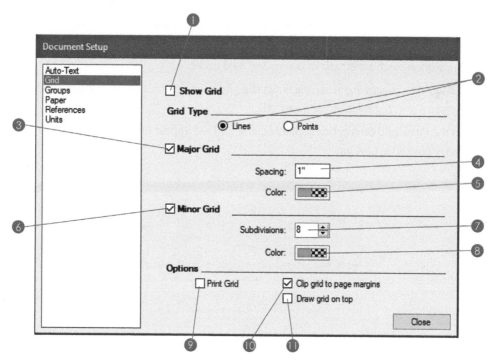

Figure 11.4 The Grid tab.

1. You can check and uncheck the Show Grid check box to toggle between making the grid visible and invisible.

2. You can use the radio buttons to set the grid type to lines or points. Typically, a traditional line grid is the most useful option (Figure 11.5).

3. Click the Major Grid check box to toggle the visibility of the thicker grid lines on and off.

4. To adjust the major grid spacing, click in the Spacing text field, enter the grid spacing you want, and then press Enter. You can use decimal format, or you can use a space to separate inches (the default units) from fractions.

5. To change the color of the major grid, click on the color block. This automatically opens the Colors inspector (discussed later in this chapter), where you can select a color from several different tabs: Wheel, RGB, HSB, Grays, Image, and List. Typically, the first three tabs offer the easiest way to make the color selection you want.

6. Click the Minor Grid check box to toggle the visibility of the thinner grid lines on and off.

7. The minor grid is composed of thinner lines and fills in the major grid by the specified number of subdivisions. Change the number of subdivisions by typing a new number into the Subdivisions text field, and then press Enter. You can also use the up and down arrows to the right of the Subdivisions field to adjust the number of subdivisions.

8. To change the color of the minor grid, click on the color block. This automatically opens the Colors Inspector where you can select a color from several different tabs: Wheel, RGB, HSB, Grays, Image, and List. Typically, the first three tabs offer the easiest way to make the color selection you desire.

9. When the Print Grid box is checked, the grid will always be printed. This feature is helpful when you are working with schematic drawings and field notes.

10. The Clip grid to page margins setting limits the grid to the extents of the margins. The presentation margins are controlled in the Paper tab.

11. When the Draw grid on top box is checked, the grid will appear on top of any viewports and geometry created in LayOut.

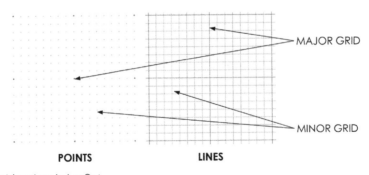

POINTS   **LINES**

MAJOR GRID

MINOR GRID

Figure 11.5 The grid options in LayOut.

TIP You can adjust how tools interact with the grid by right-clicking in the presentation background. From this right-click menu, you can turn the grid and object snap on or off, as well as toggle between grid visibility and invisibility.

Paper Tab

The paper properties are where you indicate the overall size of the sheet of paper you will use for your presentation and where you determine the quality of the renderings within your presentation (Figure 11.6).

1. Click the Paper drop-down menu to choose from preloaded standard paper sizes.

2. The Landscape and Portrait radio buttons allow you to select the orientation of the sheet.

3. You can create a custom paper size by entering the dimensions of the sheet into the Width and Height text fields. Press Enter to lock in the dimension entries.

4. Change the color of the paper, or presentation background, by clicking on the color block. This automatically opens the Colors inspector, where you can select a color from several different tabs: Wheel, RGB, HSB, Grays, Image, and List. Typically, the first three tabs provide the easiest way to make the color selection you want.

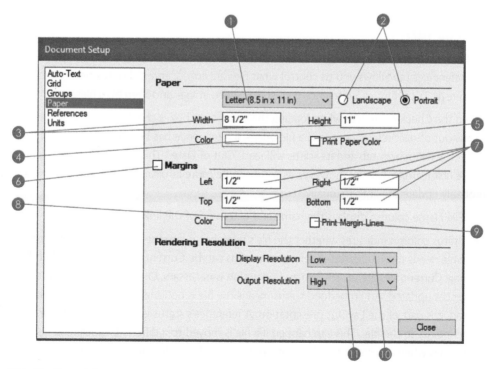

Figure 11.6 The Paper tab.

5. Check the Print Paper Color box only if you are using someone else's printer. This wastes expensive ink by reproducing the background color on the paper, which is rarely necessary.

6. Turn on the margins by clicking the Margins check box.

7. Set your margin depths by entering the dimensions in the Left, Right, Top, and Bottom fields.

8. Change the color of the margin lines by clicking on the color block. This automatically opens the Colors inspector, where you can select a color from several different tabs: Wheel, RGB, HSB, Grays, Image, and List. Typically, the first three tabs provide the easiest way to make your color selections.

9. Click the Print Margin Lines check box so that the margin lines will appear on the final prints and exports.

10. The Display Resolution setting determines the rendering quality while you're working in a LayOut presentation. In other words, it indicates the quality, or how clear the SketchUp models and images will appear on the screen while you're working in LayOut.

11. The Output Resolution setting determines the final rendering quality when the project is exported or printed. In other words, it determines how clear the SketchUp models and images will appear on the paper that comes out of the printer.

TIP Always use low-quality settings when you're editing a document. If you don't, you will waste a lot of time rendering at a high resolution you don't need.

References Tab

A *reference* is an external file that is inserted into your LayOut presentation and connected with a *link* (or path). The References tab allows you to control what files are linked, and it shows whether those files are current (Figure 11.7). LayOut can reference text, spreadsheet, image, and SketchUp files.

1. When the Check references when loading this document box is checked, LayOut will alert you to any out-of-date references when a file opens. If a reference has been modified, it will appear in red in the References tab and its status will read "Out of Date." This is a good setting to use when you're first learning LayOut; however, as you become more familiar with the program, you will probably update the links manually.

2. The File Name column displays the name and extension of the linked file.

3. The Status column indicates whether the file's reference is current—in other words, it tells you if the file needs to be updated. A reference's status can be Current, Out of Date, Embedded, or Missing. Current files are up-to-date and no action is necessary. Out-of-date files need to have the references updated. An Embedded status means the file is no longer linked to the original source; instead, it is part of the LayOut presentation. A reference's status is "Missing" when the path no longer points to the file. This can happen if a file is moved to a different folder, renamed, and sometimes when accessed on a different machine that has different drive names.

4. The Insertion Date column tells you when the file was added to the LayOut presentation.

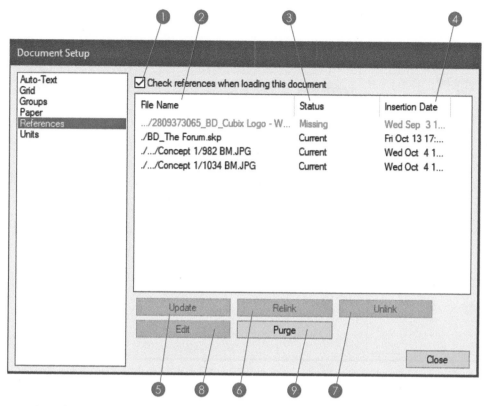

Figure 11.7 The References tab.

5. To update a link, highlight the out-of-date red filename and click the Update button at the bottom of the Document Setup window. A selected viewport will highlight the reference within the References tab and vice versa.

6. Relink a missing file by highlighting the filename and then clicking Relink. Navigate to the file you want to relink to, or swap, and choose Open. You'll need to do this if you move the original file or want to swap to a different version.

7. If you click the Unlink button at the bottom of the Document Setup window, the file will be *embedded* (become part of the LayOut presentation).

8. Click the Edit button to automatically open the reference in the associated program. You can assign preferred programs for word documents, spreadsheets, and images in the Preferences window (covered later in this chapter).

9. Click the Purge button to delete references that are no longer used in your presentation. Purging will keep the file size small and the presentation running fast.

TIP References are shown similar to the details view in a file explorer. Click on the File Name, Status, and Insertion Date headers to sort the files.

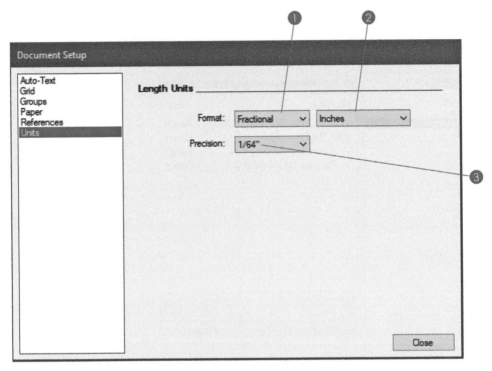

Figure 11.8 The Units tab.

Units Tab

The Units tab is where you indicate the type of measurement units to use, as well as the level of precision or accuracy (Figure 11.8).

1. Click the Format drop-down menu to choose Fractional or Decimal.

2. Click on the next drop-down menu to set the default units of the current presentation to Inches, Feet, Millimeter, Centimeter, Meter, or Points.

3. Click on the Precision drop-down menu to set the precision of the units used. Fractional units can be displayed at a precision from 1" to 1/64". Decimal units can be displayed at precisions up to .01".

PREFERENCES WINDOW

The Preferences window is where you set up your system preferences for LayOut. It contains the default settings that will be the same every time you open LayOut, regardless of which presentation you open or whether you start new. To adjust the settings, click the Edit (LayOut on a Mac) drop-down menu and choose Preferences.

Applications Tab

The Applications tab contains the settings for default programs (Figure 11.9). These programs will launch automatically when you right-click on a reference and choose Edit from the menu or from the References tab in the Document Setup window.

1. Set the Default Image Editor to your favorite image editor, such as Adobe Photoshop.
2. Set the Default Text Editor to your favorite text editor, such as Microsoft Word.
3. Set the Default Table Editor to your favorite text editor, such as Microsoft Excel.

TIP GIMP is a free and very powerful image editor available at **gimp.org.**

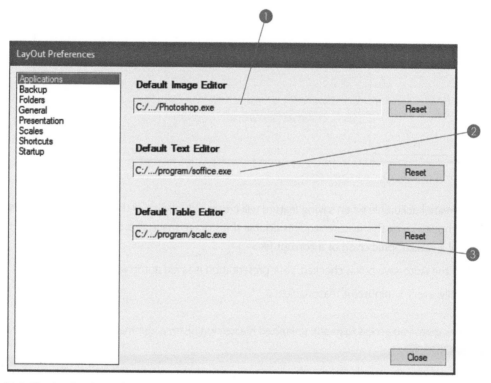

Figure 11.9 The Applications tab.

TIP OpenOffice is free and includes a very powerful word processor and spreadsheet editor, and it is available at **openoffice.org.**

Backup Tab

You can use the Backup settings to keep your work safe by creating additional files and automatically saving your work in case a file crashes or is corrupted (Figure 11.10).

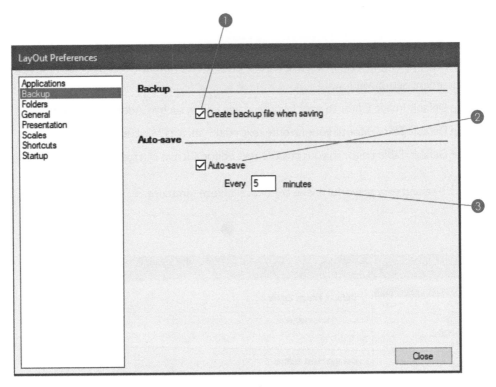

Figure 11.10 The Backup tab.

1. The Create backup file when saving feature will create a duplicate of the file prefixed with BACKUP_. Even though using this feature requires double the storage space, it provides extra peace of mind in case of a catastrophic crash or a corrupt file.

2. When the Auto-save box is checked, your presentation is saved automatically at a set interval of time.

3. Typically, every 5 minutes is reasonable.

TIP Dropbox gives you access to nearly unlimited file version history, eliminating the need to save a duplicate BACKUP_ file.

Folders Tab

Add your own Template and Scrapbook collections to be accessed in LayOut (Figure 11.11). By default, the collections folders are already *pathed* (referenced) to the program files provided by LayOut, so now you can add your own folder locations. This will give you easy access to your custom title blocks, templates, and scrapbooks.

1. Templates are displayed in the Getting Started window on the New tab. They can be title blocks, plain paper, or graph paper. You can add more locations by clicking on the plus sign (+).

2. Click on the minus sign (−) to remove a selected folder from the Templates collection.

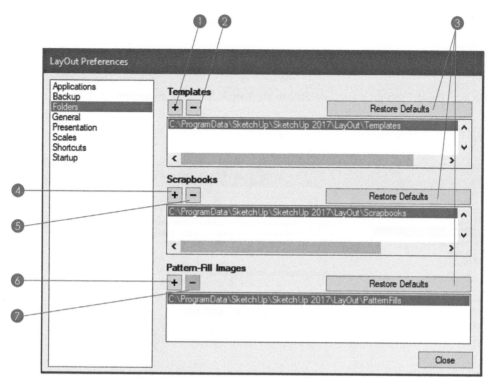

Figure 11.11 The Folders tab.

3. Click the Restore Defaults button to go back to the LayOut default folders.

4. The Scrapbooks folder contents are displayed in the Scrapbooks inspector. Scrapbooks are LayOut presentations that contain prebuilt pieces of annotation and palettes for use in other LayOut presentations. Add more locations by clicking on the plus sign (+).

5. Click on the minus sign (–) to remove a folder from the Scrapbooks collection.

6. The Pattern-Fill Images folder contents are displayed in the Pattern Fill inspector. Pattern fills are applied to LayOut geometry and are used for manual hatching. Add more locations by clicking on the plus sign (+).

7. Click on the minus sign (–) to remove a folder from the Pattern-Fill collection.

General Tab

The General settings are the catchall settings that just don't fit anywhere else (Figure 11.12).

1. When you update a model or make any settings changes that invalidate the previously rendered image, you will have to re-render your SketchUp model. The Auto Render setting, when turned on, will automatically render all viewports that need to be rendered.

2. Change the color of the tools by clicking on the color block. This automatically opens the Colors Inspector, where you can select a color from several different tabs: Wheel, RGB, HSB, Grays, Image,

and List. Typically, the first three tabs provide the easiest way to make the color selection you want.

3. Click on the Reset button to go back to the default LayOut tool color.

TIP The Auto Render setting is also available in the SketchUp Model inspector.

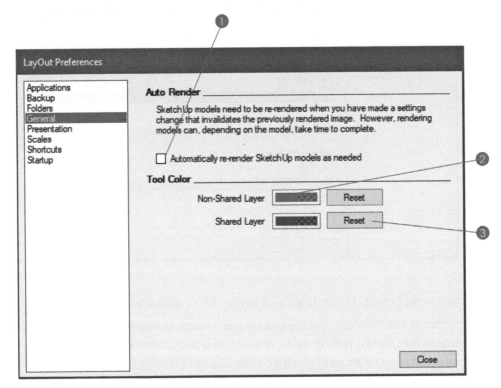

Figure 11.12 The General tab.

Presentation Tab

When you are using multiple monitors to make a presentation, you can display the presentation on the same monitor as window, the primary monitor, or the secondary monitor. You can make this selection in the Presentation tab (Figure 11.13).

Scales Tab

Under the Scales tab, you can manage the available scales at which to render your drawings (Figure 11.14).

1. The Available Model Scales section lists all the scales that are available in LayOut.

2. Check the Show All Scales By Default check box to list all the scales in the SketchUp Model dialog box. Uncheck it to filter the scales based on the LayOut document's units setting. Documents using metric units will display only metric scales, and documents using imperial units will display only imperial scales.

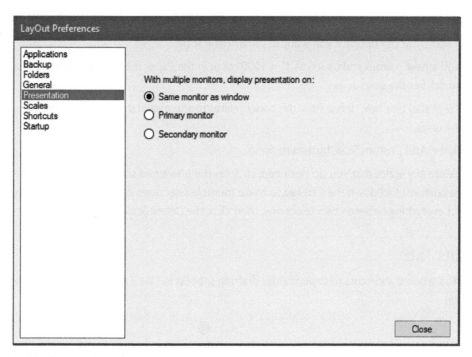

Figure 11.13 The Presentation tab.

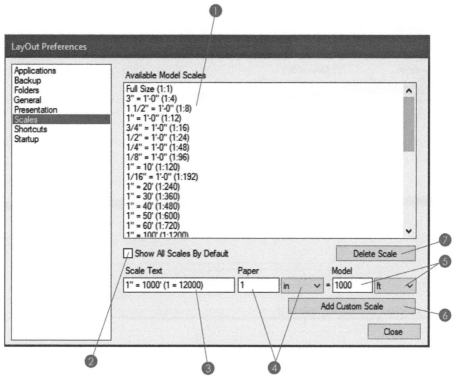

Figure 11.14 The Scales tab.

3. The Scale Text box displays the name of a scale. This box will fill in automatically when you create a new scale; you can decide if you want to rename the scale.

4. To add a new custom scale, such as 1" = 1000', click in the Paper text box and enter 1 (the paper distance). Set the units as in.

5. In the Model text box, define how the paper relates to the model space. Enter 1000, and choose ft as the units.

6. Click the Add Custom Scale button to finish.

7. To delete any scales that you do not need, click on the unwanted scale and then click the Delete Scale button. Hold down the Ctrl key to make multiple selections, or hold down the Shift key to select everything between two selections, then click the Delete Scale button.

Shortcuts Tab

You can add keyboard shortcuts to expedite the drafting process in LayOut in the Shortcuts tab (Figure 11.15).

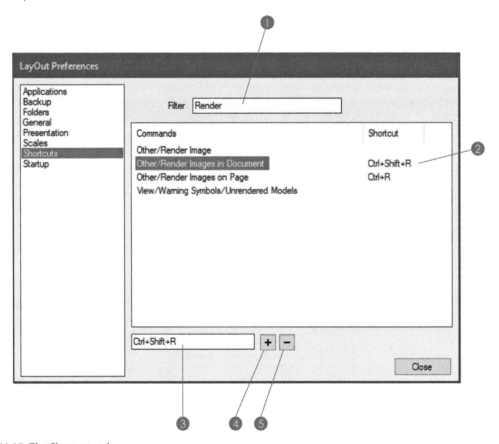

Figure 11.15 The Shortcuts tab.

1. To help locate what you are looking for, enter a command into the Filter.

2. Using the bar on the right side, scroll down to see all the commands that are eligible for a keyboard shortcut.

3. Enter the desired shortcut key into the text box. Use modifier keys such as Ctrl, Alt, and Shift to make several variations of one key.

4. Click on the plus sign (+) to add the current shortcut.

5. To remove an already assigned shortcut, select a command that already has a shortcut and then click on the minus sign (–).

TIP See Chapter 12, The Professional's LayOut Environment, for tips on adding custom keyboard shortcuts and optimizing the LayOut interface.

Startup Tab

You can tell LayOut what to do upon first being opened in the Startup tab (Figure 11.16).

1. Choose Create a new document, Re-open files from last session, or Don't do anything. This setting is based on your personal preferences.

2. The self-explanatory Allow checking for updates is a good one to turn on so your software is always current.

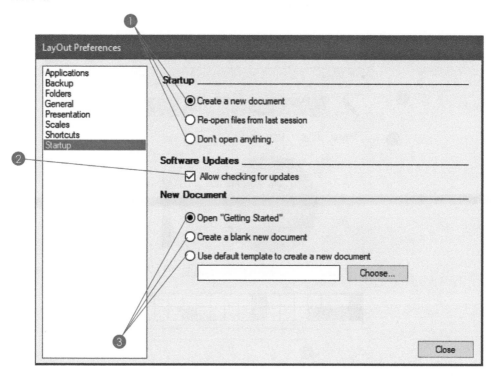

Figure 11.16 The Startup tab.

3. Once LayOut is open, you can tell LayOut what to do when you start a new document. Choose from Open "Getting Started" (opens the window), Create a blank new document, and Use default template to create a new document (selects the default you've indicated).

INSPECTORS

Inspectors give you full control over LayOut's geometry, viewports, and annotations. Take a moment to become familiar with all the LayOut inspectors, which can be accessed from the Window drop-down menu in LayOut.

Colors Inspector

The Colors inspector does not stand alone; it mainly supports the Text Style and Shape Style inspectors, along with any dialogs or menus that require a color selection (Figure 11.17). When choosing colors for strokes, fills, and text, you will use the color selection tools in the Colors inspector.

1. The sample color from screen tool allows you to match the active color to any pixel on your screen.

2. The active color selection box displays the results from the color pickers.

3. This inspector box has six tabs that accomplish the same goal of selecting a color: Wheel, RGB, HSB, Grays, Image, and List. Each tab allows you to mix and create using different properties of colors, although typically the first three are the easiest to use.

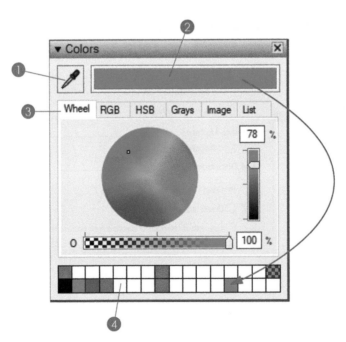

Figure 11.17 The Colors inspector.

4. Click and drag your color selection to the white squares at the bottom of the Colors inspector to create a collection of favorite colors for easy use in any LayOut presentation. These favorites are local to your machine and will be available for every LayOut presentation you open.

Pattern Fill Inspector

The Pattern Fill inspector (Figure 11.18) is similar to the Colors inspector, but you control the patterns applied to LayOut entities. Patterns are repeating images, similar to a texture image in SketchUp. This opens up a world of possibilities for graphic styles.

1 Click on the library drop-down to choose a pattern from the preloaded collections.

2. Select Import custom pattern to make your own pattern to customize your visual style.

3. Click on Add custom collection to path to a folder where you store your repeating texture images. This opens the LayOut Preferences dialog on the Folders tab, where you can path to a collection of pattern fill images, which are likely stored in your materials collection.

4. Click on the Rotation drop-down to choose from preset rotations. You can also type in your custom input.

5. Click on the Scale drop-down to choose from preset scale factors. You can also type in your custom input.

6. Click on any pattern to set it as the active pattern.

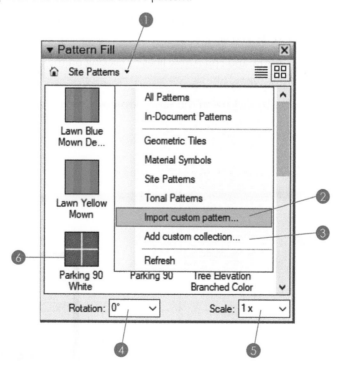

Figure 11.18 The Pattern Fill inspector.

Shape Style Inspector

The Shape Style inspector is where you change the appearance of shapes and lines (Figure 11.19). If an entity is selected, modifying the shape style will affect the selection. If no entity is selected, modifying the shape style will set the current tool's shape style defaults.

1. When an entity is selected, you can toggle on the fill, pattern, and stroke. *Fill* refers to the color within the shape. *Pattern* refers to the repeating texture image within the shape. *Stroke* refers to the line surrounding the shape as well as any single lines (see Figure 11.20). In Figure 11.19, the Fill and Pattern are toggled off and the Stroke is toggled on, indicated by the blue highlight on the button.

2. Click on the Fill or Stroke color to modify it within the Colors inspector. In Figure 11.19, the Stroke color is active in the Colors inspector, indicated by the darker box around the color swatch.

3. Change the stroke thickness by clicking on the Stroke Thickness drop-down menu. Select from the list or type in your own number, and press Enter.

4. Assign dashes to a stroke by selecting a pattern from the Dashes drop-down menu. A dash pattern must be assigned to choose a dash's scale.

5. Adjust the dash pattern's length interval with the Scale drop-down menu. Select from the list or type in your own number, and press Enter.

6. Stroke Style refers to the visual properties of the edges around the shape. Corners can be set to miter, round, or beveled. Ends can be set to flat, round, or square. Miter corners with flat ends will typically give you the most desired effects.

7. You can adjust the Start Arrow and End Arrow lines by clicking on the drop-down menus and selecting from several arrow types.

8. Adjust the size of an arrow by clicking on the Scale drop-down menus with numbers. Select from the list or type in your own number, and press Enter.

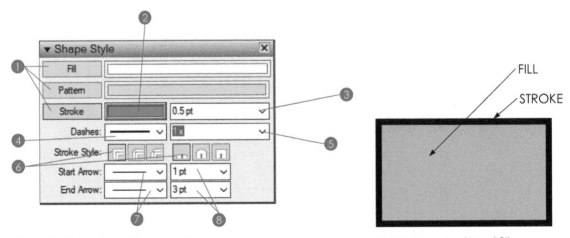

Figure 11.19 The Shape Style inspector.

Figure 11.20 Stroke and fill.

SketchUp Model Inspector

The SketchUp Model inspector provides settings that affect the manner in which SketchUp models are displayed in LayOut. There are two tabs: View and Styles.

View Tab

The View tab contains the settings to adjust what is shown in the selected viewport as well as how it is shown (Figure 11.21). The most effective workflow is to first create scenes in SketchUp that already have all the camera view, style, and shadow properties assigned. Then in LayOut, select a scene from the View tab within the SketchUp Model inspector. You must select a viewport in order to use the SketchUp Model inspector to modify a viewport's properties.

1. Use the Scenes drop-down menu to choose from scenes already created in the SketchUp model. This gives you the most control over a viewport and is by far the best method to use for this workflow.

2. Use the Standard Views drop-down menu to access Top, Bottom, Front, Back, Left, and Right views.

3. With the viewport selected, click on the Ortho button to toggle between perspective and parallel projection views.

4. Click on the Scale drop-down menu to assign an architectural scale to the selected viewport. A viewport must be selected and Ortho must be on to assign a scale.

5. The Preserve Scale on Resize button will keep your drawing at scale regardless of how you modify the viewport. When this check box is unchecked, the drawing will change scale to match the modified viewport.

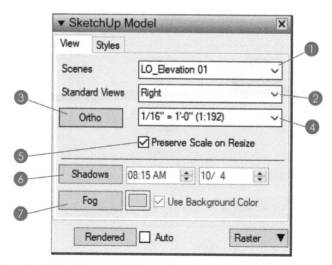

Figure 11.21 The SketchUp Model inspector's View tab.

TIP Scale a viewport about the center by holding down the Alt key (Command on a Mac) and clicking on and dragging the perimeter. Scaling about the center overrides the Preserve Scale on Resize setting.

6. Click the Shadows button to display shadows in the selected viewport. You can modify the shadows by adjusting the time of day and date.

7. Click the Fog button to display fog in the selected viewport. Click on the color swatch to change the color of the fog, or check the Use Background Color box to set the fog color to be the same as the Style's background.

TIP LayOut has limited Shadow and Fog settings. For the best results, create a scene in SketchUp with the desired view, as well as the desired Shadow and Fog settings, and then assign the scene to a viewport in LayOut.

Styles Tab

The Styles tab gives you access to any style in your model and even in your Styles library (Figure 11.22).

1. Click on the house icon to navigate through the In Model styles. Also use the drop-down menu to navigate through your entire Styles library.

2. Change the style applied to a viewport by first selecting the viewport and then clicking on a style within the Styles tab.

3. Display the Styles in list view or thumbnail view, depending on your personal preference.

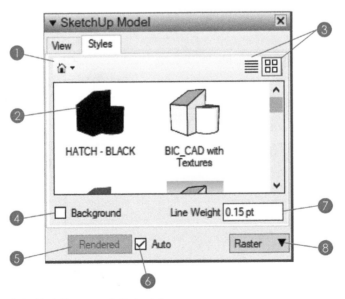

Figure 11.22 The SketchUp Model inspector's Styles tab.

4. Click on the Background check box to fill in the background of a viewport. This means that nothing behind the viewport will be visible through the images in the foreground. This setting comes into play when you are creating a collage of several views and models and do not want the sky or background to show.

5. An exclamation mark on a yellow triangle next to the Render button indicates that a viewport needs to be rendered. To do this, select the viewport and then click on the Render button in the SketchUp Model inspector. Once the viewport is rendered, the Render button will change to Rendered.

6. Check the Auto check box to automatically render all viewports when they are out of date. This setting is also available in the Preferences dialog on the General tab.

7. Change the overall line weight applied to the selected viewport by entering a new number.

8. To change the rendering settings of a selected viewport, click on the Rendering Settings drop-down menu and choose Raster, Vector, or Hybrid.

Scaled Drawing Inspector

The Scaled Drawing inspector allows you to draft two-dimensional (2D) scaled diagrams right inside of LayOut and also overlay accurate 2D accent lines on top of viewports (Figure 11.23).

1. Click on the Make Scaled Drawing button to start a new drawing. This launches the Scaled Drawing interface.

2. Select an architectural scale to apply to the new drawing. These scales are pulled from the architectural scales set up in the Preferences > Scales dialog.

3. Choose a different length to work in different units.

4. Begin drafting using the standard tools in LayOut. While drafting, enter units in full model space scale, and the scaled drawing will do the math to create the drawing at the right size on the page.

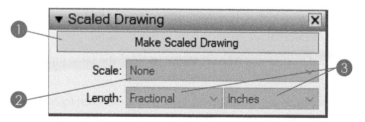

Figure 11.23 The Scaled Drawing inspector.

Dimension Style Inspector

The Dimension Style inspector gives you full control over dimensions (Figure 11.24). Use it to set the default properties for the Dimension tool. Also, you can select a dimension and modify the properties of the selection within the Dimension Style inspector.

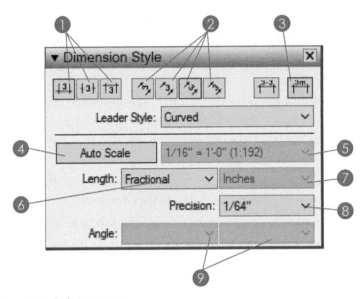

Figure 11.24 The Dimension Style inspector.

1. Adjust the placement of the dimension text as above, centered with, or below the dimension line.
2. Set the dimension text orientation to vertical, horizontal, aligned, or perpendicular. Typically, dimensions are best shown aligned.
3. Toggle whether the units are displayed at the end of the dimension text.
4. Auto Scale will automatically set the dimension scale, depending on the scale assigned to the viewport you click on with the Dimension tool.
5. When the Auto Scale feature is turned off, you can set the Dimension Scale manually.
6. Length can be displayed as Decimal, Architectural, Engineering, or Fractional.
7. The unit type can be set to Inches, Feet, Millimeters, Centimeters, Meters, or Points only when the Length value is set to Decimal.
8. The Precision of the dimensions can be set to .01" or 1/64", the same precision tolerances used in SketchUp.
9. Angular dimensions can be set to radians or degrees. The precision tolerances can be set up to .0001 radians or .01 degrees. The Angular Dimension tool must be activated to adjust these settings.

TIP The visual properties of dimension lines are set within the Shape Style inspector. Activate the Dimensions tool, then set the default stroke thickness, arrow type, arrow scale, and color within the Shape Style inspector.

Text Style Inspector

The Text Style inspector has a familiar interface that is used in most word processors and e-mail programs (Figure 11.25). Activate the Text tool and then use the Text Style inspector to set the default text properties. You can also select a piece of text within a text box and modify the properties of the selection with the Text Style inspector.

1. In LayOut, you can access any font that is loaded in your system fonts. Choose a font family, typeface, and size. Keep in mind that you can select from the Size list or manually enter a font size that is not listed.

2. You can apply an underline and/or a strikethrough to text.

3. Click on the color swatch to modify the text color. This automatically opens the Colors inspector, where you can select a color. The active swatch will have a darker box around it, as shown in Figure 11.25.

4. Justify the text to the left, center, or right of the text window.

5. Anchor the text to the top, middle, or bottom of the text window.

6. Text in LayOut can be either bounded or unbounded. *Bounded text* is contained within a window and will drop to the next line as it approaches the boundary of the text window. *Unbounded text* runs straight across the screen uninterrupted.

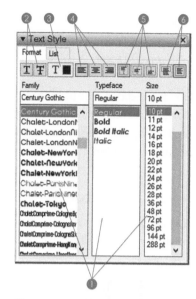

Figure 11.25 The Text Style inspector.

Pages Inspector

The Pages inspector is where you manage the pages in your presentation (Figure 11.26).

1. Click on the plus sign (+) to add a new page.

2. Click on the minus sign (–) to delete the current page.

3. Click on the Duplicate Page button to make a copy of the current page. You'll be using this button frequently to create new pages and at the same time copy annotation pieces of the title block from page to page. It is easier to just erase what you don't need on a duplicated page.

4. Display the pages in list view or thumbnail view. Typically, list view is sleeker and allows you to see more of the pages in your presentation.

5. The current page is highlighted in blue. Double-click on a page name to rename it. Click and drag a page to reposition it within your presentation.

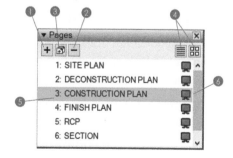

Figure 11.26 The Pages inspector.

6. Click on the monitor icon to the right of the page name to toggle whether that page is included in the screen presentation.

TIP Right-click on the page to see a context menu. This also allows you to move the page up or down, rename the page, duplicate it, and choose whether to include the page in your screen presentation.

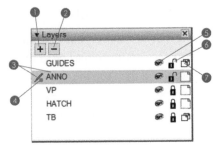

Figure 11.27 The Layers inspector.

Layers Inspector

Layers in LayOut are similar to most page-creation software in that they control what is shown on top by the layer order, as well as what layers are visible. You manage them in the Layers inspector (Figure 11.27).

1. Click on the plus sign (+) to add a new layer.

2. Click on the minus sign (–) to delete the selected layer. If you delete a layer with entities on it, you will be prompted to delete the entities completely or move them to the active layer.

3. The active layer is highlighted in blue and is also indicated by a pencil icon to the left of the layer name.

4. A selected entity's layer is represented by a small box to the left of the layer name.

5. Click on the eye icon to toggle the layer visibility on and off. Layer visibility is set on a per-page basis, meaning that if you turn a layer off on one page, it is still visible on other pages.

6. Click on the padlock icon to lock the layer. *Locking* a layer prevents the entities on it from being deleted or modified. Locking a layer applies across all pages.

7. Click on the last icon to toggle whether the layer is shared. A shared layer's contents will appear the same on every page. If the contents of a shared layer are modified, they will be modified on every page. Repeating entities, such as title blocks and guides, should be on a shared layer.

TIP To change an entity's layer, right-click on the entity or a selection of entities and choose Move to layer, then choose the desired layer.

Scrapbooks Inspector

The Scrapbooks inspector allows you to seamlessly access collections of prebuilt pieces of annotation from preloaded libraries as well as your own (Figure 11.28).

1. Select a scrapbook collection from the drop-down menu. LayOut comes with several scrapbooks that stylistically match the preloaded title blocks.

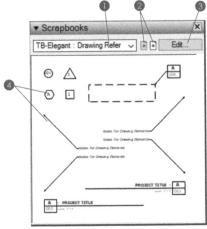

Figure 11.28 The Scrapbooks inspector.

2. Use the arrows next to the Collections drop-down menu to navigate through the pages of the scrapbook.

3. Click on the Edit button to edit the scrapbook. This automatically opens the LayOut scrapbook file. Add, edit, or delete scrapbook pieces, and then close the file and save your changes. The updated scrapbook will appear in the Scrapbook inspector.

4. Add a scrapbook by clicking on a Scrapbook symbol in the Scrapbook area, and then click in your presentation to place it.

TIP Scrapbooks aren't some magical file type buried in LayOut. A *scrapbook* is simply a LayOut file containing lines, shapes, text, and fills grouped together into meaningful symbols. You will create and organize your own custom collection of Scrapbooks in Chapter 24, Annotations.

Instructor Inspector

The Instructor inspector will help you explore LayOut and find hidden functions buried in the tools (Figure 11.29). Activate any tool and you'll see the instructions for using that tool, as well as invaluable modifier keys associated with the tool.

CHAPTER POINTS

☑ The Document Setup dialog box controls the settings that travel with a model.

☑ The Preferences dialog box controls the settings that are local to your machine and are the same every time you open LayOut.

☑ Take the time to become familiar with the settings that each menu and inspector controls, and then use this chapter as a reference.

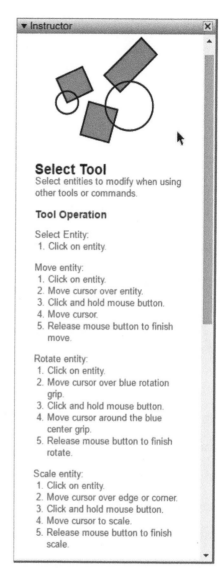

Figure 11.29 The Instructor inspector.

Chapter 12
The Professional's LayOut Environment

Aprofessional's work environment is streamlined, logical, and organized. LayOut provides a default environment that is great for getting started, but ultimately, it is not adequate for a professional. Fortunately, you can customize the LayOut environment in several different ways to make it work best for you. You can customize toolbars, optimize system resources, and remove visual clutter. By adding your own set of shortcuts, you can even access all your frequently used commands with just a few keystrokes. In this chapter, you will learn how to use all the settings needed to increase productivity, computer performance, and quality of design.

NEW PRESENTATION

To get started and create a new presentation, follow the steps detailed here (Figure 12.1).

1. Open LayOut.
2. If you see the Getting Started window, move on to the next step; otherwise, click on the File drop-down menu and choose New.
3. Select Default Templates, then Paper, then Plain Paper.
4. Select the Letter Landscape template.
5. Click the Open button to begin.

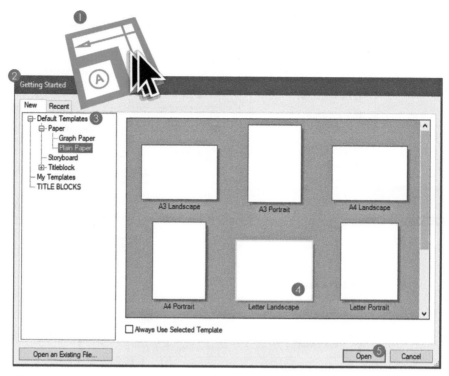

Figure 12.1 The Getting Started window.

SYSTEM PREFERENCES

System preferences do not travel with a model, but they will be the same for every LayOut presentation you create on your computer. To set your preferences, click on the Edit (LayOut on a Mac) drop-down menu and choose Preferences. Take a moment to optimize the system preferences with the following settings.

Applications

LayOut is powerful by itself, but it can also be complemented by external programs that exclusively work with text and raster graphics. You can assign external applications to handle these text and image files in the Applications tab (Figure 12.2).

1. In the Applications tab, click the Choose button for the Default Image Editor.

2. Navigate to and select the executable (**.exe**) file for your favorite image editor.

3. Click the Open button to assign the Default Image Editor.

4. Repeat steps 1 through 3 for the Default Text Editor.

5. Repeat steps 1 through 3 for the Default Table Editor.

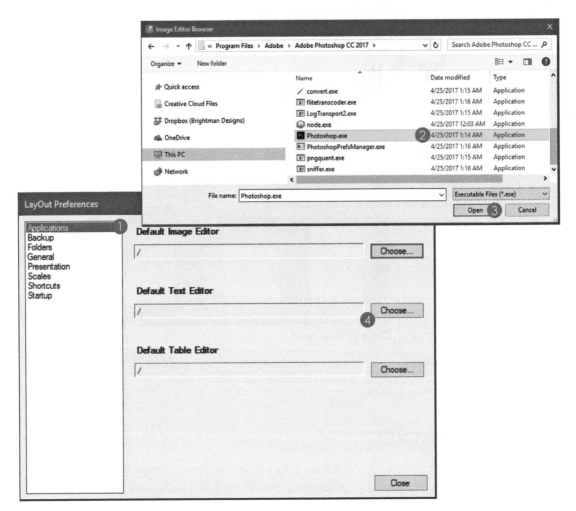

Figure 12.2 The Applications tab optimized.

TIP When you're navigating to the application shortcut or .exe file, first look on your desktop. If you can't find a shortcut there, you can find it somewhere in the **C:/program files** folder.

Folders

To access your own custom collections in LayOut, add default folders in the Folders tab by following these steps (Figure 12.3):

1. Click on the plus sign (+) next to Templates, then navigate to and select the RESOURCES/ TEMPLATES folder.

2. Click the OK button. Now any template added to the TEMPLATES folder can be accessed from the Getting Started window in LayOut.

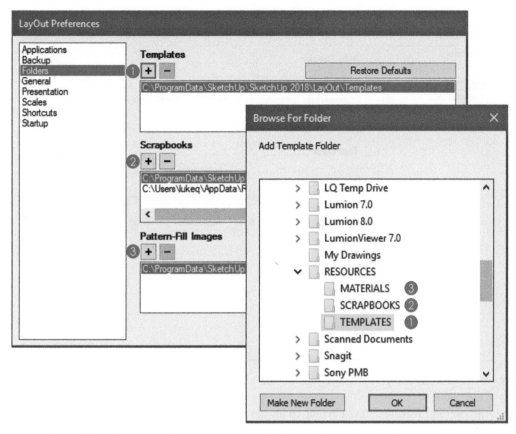

Figure 12.3 The Folders tab optimized.

3. Click on the plus sign (+) next to Scrapbooks, then navigate to and select the RESOURCES/ SCRAPBOOKS folder.

4. Click the Open button. Now any scrapbook file added to the SCRAPBOOKS folder can be accessed from the Scrapbooks Inspector.

5. Click on the plus sign (+) next to Pattern-Fill Images, then navigate to and select the RESOURCES/ MATERIALS folder.

6. Click the Open button. Now any texture image file added to the MATERIALS folder can be accessed from the Pattern Fill inspector.

Auto Render

Rendering is the number one memory hog in LayOut. Depending on the size, complexity, and organization of the model, rendering can take a significant amount of time to complete. It is important to keep in mind that a clean and organized SketchUp model is the best way to shorten rendering times. In addition, it is pertinent to render only at the necessary resolution and only when absolutely necessary.

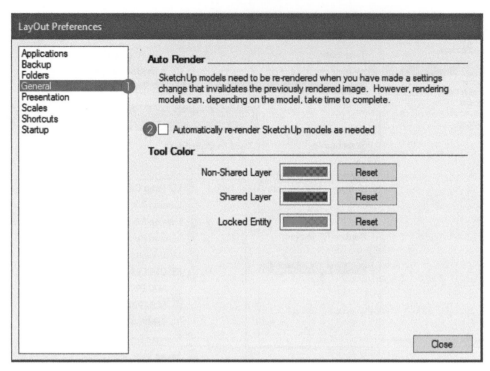

Figure 12.4 Rendering settings optimized.

The Auto Render feature allows LayOut to always render a viewport when it is updated and needs to be rendered. This is a helpful button to have turned on when you are learning to use LayOut, but as your presentations grow and your SketchUp models become more detailed, you will want to turn off this setting and manually control rendering (Figure 12.4). Consider keeping Auto Render off at all times and instead render using your keyboard commands, using the SketchUp Model inspector, or by right-clicking on the presentation background and choosing Render Images on Page.

To manually control rendering, follow these steps:

1. Navigate to the General tab.

2. Uncheck the Automatically re-render SketchUp models as needed check box.

TIP The Auto Render setting is also available in the SketchUp Model inspector, where it is called Auto. Keep in mind that this setting does not travel with the presentation; it is a global setting that applies to every presentation you open in LayOut.

Shortcuts

Just as in SketchUp, keyboard shortcuts will enable you to work faster. Try to avoid using the icons on your screen, even if it feels slower at first. Once you learn all the keyboard shortcuts, you will become amazingly faster (Figure 12.5).

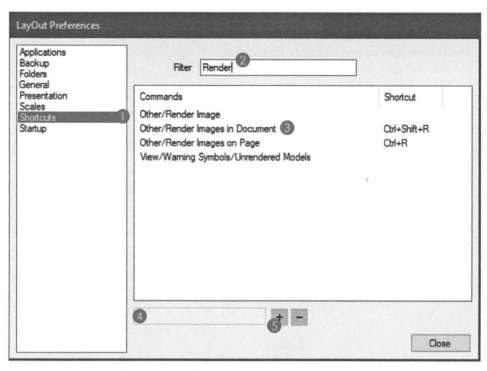

Figure 12.5 Use the Shortcuts tab to add keyboard shortcuts to your favorite and most-used commands.

1. Click on the Shortcuts tab.

2. Type, for example, Render in the Filter text box. As you are typing, the results list will get shorter.

3. Click the Other/Render Images in Document command.

4. Click in the Shortcut text box at the bottom-left corner of the dialog. Hold down the Ctrl and Shift keys, then press the R key. (The modifier keys will appear in the text box.)

5. Click on the plus sign (+) to add the shortcut.

Consider adding the helpful keyboard shortcuts in Figure 12.6.

HELPFUL SHORTCUTS	
KEY	**COMMAND**
Ctrl + R	Other/Render Images on Page
Ctrl + Shift + R	Other/Render Images in Document
Ctrl + Right	Pages/Next
Ctrl + Left	Pages/Previous
Q	Tools/Join
W	Tools/Split
Shift +E	View/Zoom to Fit
Ctrl + D	Window/Hide Tray
Ctrl + G	Edit/Group
Ctrl + Shift + G	Edit/Ungroup
Shift + D	File/Document Setup

Figure 12.6 Suggested keyboard shortcuts.

TIP You can add a simple shortcut, such as a letter, or you can add combinations of keys by holding down modifier keys, such as Alt, Ctrl, and Shift, while you press a key. The modifier keys give you almost endless possibilities for adding keyboard shortcuts.

CUSTOM TOOLBARS

The default toolbar is adequate, but it is missing a few vital buttons. Not every command has a logical keyboard shortcut; to compensate, you can keep a row of tool icons on your screen. You can optimize the LayOut workspace by building your own custom toolbars (Figure 12.7).

1. Click on the View drop-down menu and choose Toolbars, then Customize. Click the New button to add a new toolbar.

2. Name the toolbar DRAWING.

3. From the drop-down menu, select an initial location for the toolbar. The exact location doesn't really matter because you can drag the toolbar and dock and undock freely, but Floating makes it easier for you to work on the new toolbar. Click OK.

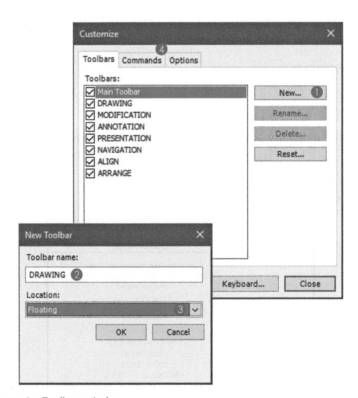

Figure 12.7 The Customize Toolbars window.

4. Click on the Commands tab (Figure 12.8).

5. Sort through the categories to narrow your search, and select the Tools/Lines category.

6. Drag the Line command from the Commands column into your new toolbar.

7. Continue adding the desired commands to the toolbar. Click the Close button when you are finished.

Consider turning off the Main toolbar and adding these custom toolbars to your professional LayOut environment (Figure 12.9):

ANNOTATION:	Text, Leader Text, Dimensions
PRESENTATION:	Next Page, Previous Page, Duplicate Page, Delete Page
ARRANGE:	Move Backward, Move to Back, Move to Front, Move Forward
DRAWING:	Line, Rectangle, Circle
MODIFICATION:	Select, Split, Join, Erase, Style
ALIGN:	Top, Bottom, Right, Left, Vertically, Horizontally
NAVIGATION:	Zoom to Fit, Actual Size

TIP Right-click on a toolbar and choose Lock the Toolbars. This will hold the toolbars in place and remove the draggable lines for docking and undocking. You can always right-click on a toolbar again to unlock it.

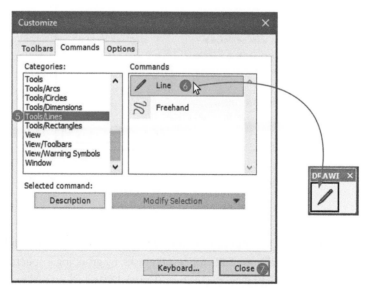

Figure 12.8 The Commands tab.

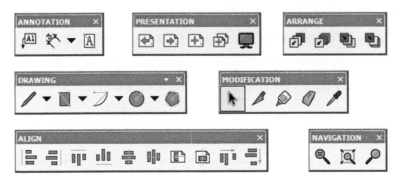

Figure 12.9 Custom toolbars.

You can personalize some of the toolbar behaviors on the Options tab. Be sure to turn off all fades and animations to optimize system performance (Figure 12.10). Activating the Show ScreenTips on toolbars option will be helpful when you're learning to use a tool. Even more valuable is to turn on the Show shortcut keys in ScreenTips option to remind you of the shortcut key.

Figure 12.10 The Customize Toolbar Options tab optimized.

TRAYS

Trays allow you to organize the LayOut inspectors in the Windows operating system only. Create custom trays to make specific inspectors readily available for certain tasks. By grouping inspectors together by task, you can streamline your workflow. Just follow these steps (Figure 12.11):

1. Click on the Window drop-down menu and choose New Tray.

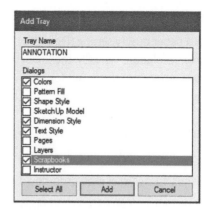

Figure 12.11 The PRESENTATION and ANNOTATION custom trays.

2. Name the new tray PRESENTATION. This will contain everything you need to navigate your LayOut presentation.

3. Check the SketchUp Model, Pages, and Layers inspectors check boxes.

4. Click the Add button to finish creating the tray.

5. Click on the Window drop-down menu and choose New Tray.

6. Name the new tray ANNOTATION. This will contain everything you need to make annotations in your presentation.

7. Check the Colors, Shape Style, Dimension Style, Text Style, and Scrapbooks inspector check boxes.

8. Click the Add button to finish creating the tray.

After you've created the tray, click the pushpin icon next to the Close button to set the tray to autohide. Now, when the tray is not in use, it will automatically close and give you more working screen space. To access the tray, simply hover on the Tray tab. Click and drag on a tray to make it floating, or dock it at the top, bottom, or sides of the LayOut application. Now that you know all the methods, you can organize your screen any way you like.

TIP If you click on the View drop-down menu and choose Restore Default Workspace, you will return to the default LayOut environment and all custom trays and toolbars will be deleted.

TIP If you don't prefer the autohide feature, use the Ctrl+D keyboard shortcut to toggle between hiding and unhiding the trays.

BASIC LAYOUT TEMPLATE

Create a basic, blank layout template to use as a starting point for any new presentations, scrapbooks, or title blocks you make in the future. All the settings that travel with the file will be optimized to ensure that LayOut is running at full speed.

Rendering Quality

Each model has a paper quality setting (Figure 12.12). Set the Display Resolution to Low, which is acceptable for the screen resolution. Typically, the low setting will render everything well enough that you can evaluate a model without having to wait for a high-quality render. Set the Output Resolution to High for exports and presentations. Rendering at a high setting is worth the wait when you're creating the final output.

To optimize the Paper settings, follow these steps:

1. Click on the File drop-down menu and choose Document Setup > Paper.

2. Click on the Display Resolution drop-down menu, and choose Low.

3. Click on the Output Resolution drop-down menu, and choose High.

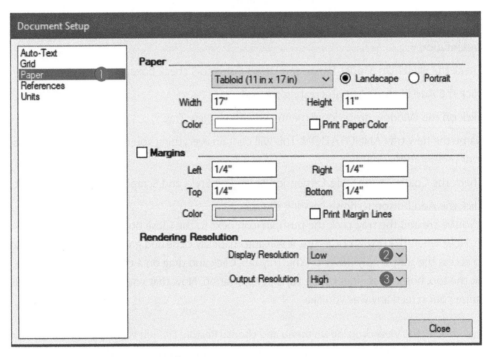

Figure 12.12 The Paper settings optimized.

Layers

Layers in LayOut work in the traditional fashion of stacking and visibility. If a layer is turned on, the contents on that layer are visible. If a layer is turned off, the contents on that layer are not visible. The stacking order of the layers will determine which entities are on top. So, if a layer is on the bottom of the stack, any object on the layers above will cover up the bottom layer entities.

There are only three layers that a professional absolutely needs in every presentation: ANNOTATIONS, DRAWINGS, and TITLE BLOCK.

At the top of the stack is the ANNOTATIONS layer. This layer contains labels, leaders, dimensions, text, and lines that further explain drawings and images. Also on the ANNOTATIONS layer is anything within the title block that does not repeat, such as page numbers and descriptions. This is typically the most-used layer in LayOut, and it is usually unlocked.

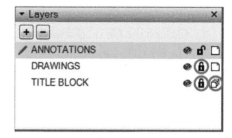

Figure 12.13 Within the Layers inspector, add the suggested default layers in LayOut.

The DRAWINGS layer contains any entity that is inserted into LayOut. This includes SketchUp models, images, maps, and photos. Basically, anything that you are going to annotate belongs on the DRAWINGS layer. Typically, you will insert several entities onto the DRAWINGS layer and then lock the layer as you annotate.

The TITLE BLOCK layer is a shared layer that contains the presentation graphics (Figure 12.13). This layer appears on every page of your presentation. Repeating graphics, watermarks, project information, logos, and page dividing lines belong on the TITLE BLOCK layer. Entities on this layer might be modified at the beginning of a project, but the layer typically remains locked most of the time.

To create the new layers, follow these steps:

1. Click on the plus sign (+) to add a new layer. Name the new layer TITLE BLOCK.

2. Click on the Share Layer toggle to share the layer.

3. To lock the layer, click on the padlock next to the layer name.

4. Click on the plus sign (+) again to add another new layer. Name the new layer DRAWINGS.

5. To lock the layer, click on the padlock next to the layer name.

6. Click on the plus sign (+) to add another new layer. Name the new layer ANNOTATIONS.

Now that you have optimized the presentation, save it at this clean, blank state to use for creating new presentations and title blocks in the future (Figure 12.14).

Figure 12.14 The Save As Template dialog.

Just follow these steps:

1. Click on the File drop-down menu and choose Save As Template . . . Name the presentation BD_8.5 x 11 - Landscape.

2. Select the RESOURCES/TEMPLATES folder.

3. Click the OK button. Now this template will be available every time you start a new presentation in LayOut.

CHAPTER POINTS

☑ Keeping your LayOut workspace clean and organized will help increase your speed and efficiency.

☑ Every professional's workspace evolves based on personal preference. It is important to know all the ways you can optimize your workspace, but you don't need to use all of them.

☑ There are also resource-heavy features you can turn off within your operating system. Personalize your Windows experience and turn off Transparencies in Windows. When you're working on a laptop, be sure that you are using the High Performance setting, rather than Balanced or Power Saver.

☑ Spend a small amount of time optimizing your work environment, and you will save an enormous amount of time on every project.

☑ The basic BD_8.5x11 - Landscape template can be used to start any new document or title block in the future with the settings and layers already optimized.

Chapter 13
LayOut Tools

Layout has a simple, sleek toolset, but don't let the simplicity fool you! With it, you can accurately create any shape you will ever need. It is deceptively simple. Every tool is described in detail in this chapter. Take a few minutes to read the description for each one, open a blank presentation, and then perform the steps following the description to practice using the tool.

NAVIGATING LAYOUT

LayOut is essentially a hybrid two-dimensional (2D) page creation and drafting software package. The best way to navigate the 2D LayOut environment is to use a three-button scroll wheel mouse (Figure 13.1). Push down on the scroll wheel to pan up, down, left, and right. Roll the scroll wheel toward the screen to zoom in, and roll away from the screen to zoom out. Just as in SketchUp, the focal point of your navigation is your cursor.

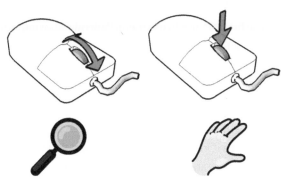

Figure 13.1 When you use a three-button scroll wheel mouse, the Navigation tools in LayOut are always at your fingertips.

DRAWING TOOLS

Use the Drawing tools to add geometry, symbols, annotations, title blocks, and decorations to your LayOut presentation. Each of the Drawing tools has additional features and options buried within it. Pay special attention to the modifier keys and specific processes required to effectively use all the functions of the tools in LayOut.

TIP: LayOut Quick Reference Cards are available at the following link: **www.sketchup.com/quick-reference-cards/sketchup-2018/en.**

Default Settings

When you activate any of the Drawing tools, the default settings are displayed in the Shape Style inspector. By adjusting the properties there, you can change those settings for any tool that draws lines and fills. Test the new default properties of the Drawing tools by switching to the Text tool and then going back to any Drawing tool.

All the Drawing tools share the same default settings. For instance, if you change the default fill for the Rectangle tool, it will also apply to the Circle, Line, and Polygon fillings.

Use the Pick Style tool to set the default settings for any tool. Follow these steps:

1. Activate any Drawing tool.

2. Hover on a scrapbook and click to match the current tool's default settings to the selected scrapbook's settings. (See Chapter 24, Annotations, for more information on using scrapbooks as time-saving palettes.)

3. To match an entity in the presentation area, press the S key, which is the default shortcut for the Pick Style tool.

4. Click on an entity to match the current tool's inspector settings to the entity that you sampled. The entity can be in the presentation space or in a scrapbook.

TIP A tool's default settings are some of those "buried" features in LayOut. It may not be quite clear how to use the default settings when you first attempt to use them. Patiently studying and practicing so you can fully understand how the default settings operate will save you a tremendous amount of time in the future.

Lines

Use the Line tools to create straight, curved, and freehand lines. Generating lines is a key component of drawing, and there is no exception in LayOut. The Line tools will help you create annotations, title blocks, schedule grids, tables, ground lines, details, and many other entities. Take a moment to explore all the methods for drawing different types of lines.

Straight Lines

The simplest type of line to create is a straight line (Figure 13.2).

1. Activate the Line tool and set the stroke width to 1. Turn on the Fill, and set the color to Gray. Click once in the presentation area to start.

2. Move your cursor to the right along the red axis, and click again to finish the segment.

3. Move your cursor up on the green axis. Note that the Line tool has Fill properties. This time, let go of the mouse and type a precise dimension, such as 4, then press Enter.

4. Move your cursor back to the left along the red axis. Note that there is an inference engine. To finish the line segment, click where the inference line meets the active line.

5. Move your cursor back down on the green axis, and click on the starting point to finish.

TIP Press the Esc key at any time to cancel the current line segment. Doing this will cancel just about any command in LayOut.

Once a segment is finished, you can click on an endpoint with the Line tool to continue the segment. You will see the previous line segments light up blue, indicating that you are continuing that segment. Follow the previous steps to continue the straight line segment.

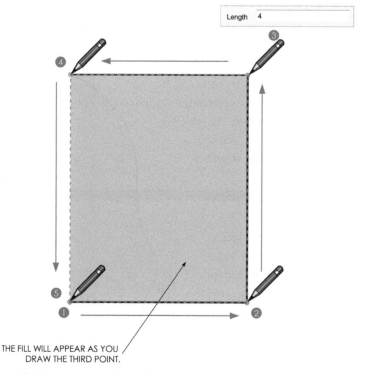

THE FILL WILL APPEAR AS YOU
DRAW THE THIRD POINT.

Figure 13.2 Create straight lines using the Line tool.

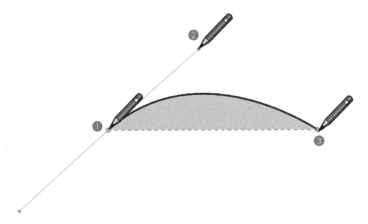

Figure 13.3 Create a curved line using the Line tool.

TIP The *inference engine* in LayOut allows you to snap to and encourage inferences from endpoints, midpoints, and edges. It is very similar to the inference engine in SketchUp.

Curved Line

You aren't limited to straight lines. Using the Line tool, you can also create curves (Figure 13.3).

1. Click and drag away from the starting point to define the tangent line.
2. Release the cursor to set the curve's tangent line relative to the starting point.
3. Double-click to finish the line segment.

TIP To add a straight line segment to a curved line, single-click to finish the curved line segment, then continue to click to add straight lines. To add a curved line segment to a straight line, you can click and drag to finish the straight line segment and add a curved line segment.

Freehand Tool

Use the Freehand tool to create sketchy, loose, and organic forms (Figure 13.4). This tool is ideal for complementing drawings, tracing topography, creating sketchy annotations, and creating unique geometry.

1. Activate the Freehand tool. Click and drag to draw a loose and sketchy line.
2. Release the click to finish the line.

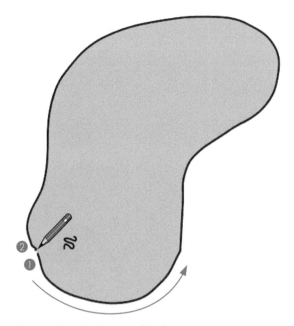

Figure 13.4 The Freehand tool.

Click and drag on an endpoint to continue the freehand line segment. The previous line segments will light up blue, indicating that you are continuing that segment.

Rectangles

LayOut's Rectangle tools enable you to draw rectangles and squares that are always on axis and in line with the paper (Figure 13.5). In addition to a traditional rectangle, LayOut has several other types: lozenged, bulged, and rounded. Each has its own tool icon, and each operates as described here.

To draw a rectangle, follow these steps:

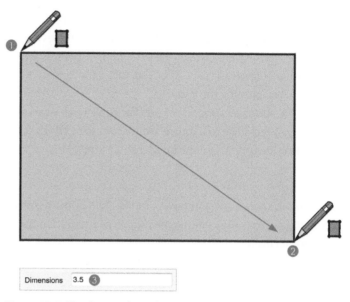

Dimensions   3.5

Figure 13.5 The Rectangle tool.

1. Activate the Rectangle tool. Click once in the presentation area to start the rectangle.

2. Move your cursor away from the starting point to suggest a direction. Click once to loosely define the dimensions of the rectangle.

3. At this point, you can enter precise dimensions, such as 3,5, then press Enter.

The other types of rectangles function the same way (Figure 13.6).

A *rounded rectangle* has radiused corners. Activate the Rounded Rectangle tool, or the Rectangle tool, and then press the up and down arrow keys to change the radius. To enter a precise radius, type in the desired radius followed with an "r"—for example, type 1/2r—then press Enter. This will set the corners to be 1/2" radius.

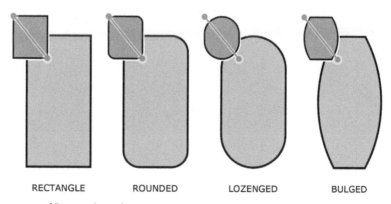

RECTANGLE   ROUNDED   LOZENGED   BULGED

Figure 13.6 Other types of Rectangle tools.

A *lozenged rectangle* has half circles at the long ends of the rectangle, so a square would actually appear as a circle. Ultimately, the Lozenged Rectangle tool creates a pill shape.

A *bulged rectangle* has arcs at the left and right sides of the rectangle. Use the up and down arrow keys to adjust the bulge of the arcs. After you adjust the bulge, you can enter precise dimensions by typing a value and then pressing the Enter key.

There are also several modifier keys that apply to all types of rectangles. Hold down the Shift key to constrain any rectangle to a square. Hold down the Ctrl key (Option on a Mac) to create the rectangle about the center point. Use the up and down arrow keys to adjust the rounded corners, lozenged sides, or bulged sides.

TIP LayOut's Measurements box is just like SketchUp's. It is always waiting for your input and constantly switches the value, depending on which tool is active and the input LayOut needs to operate effectively.

Arcs

There are several methods for drawing an arc in LayOut. The one you use depends on your personal preference and previous experience with other drafting programs. The most familiar method probably will be the Two-Point Arc tool because it is the one most similar to the Arc tool in SketchUp. Take a moment to explore all the tools for drawing arcs.

Arc Tool

Using the Arc tool, you can create the outside of a pie chart with ease (Figure 13.7).

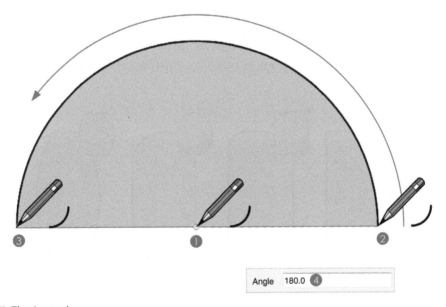

Figure 13.7 The Arc tool.

To do that, follow these steps:

1. Activate the Arc tool. Click once in the presentation area to define the center point.

2. Move your cursor to the right along the red axis to suggest a direction. Click again to define the start point of the arc.

3. Move your cursor away from the start point and click once more to loosely define the endpoint of the arc.

4. At this point, you can let go of the mouse and type a precise angle—such as 180.0—then press Enter.

Two-Point Arc Tool

The most familiar arc tool is strikingly similar to the Arc tool in SketchUp (Figure 13.8).

To create an arc with the Two-Point Arc tool, follow these steps:

1. Activate the Two-Point Arc tool. Click once in the presentation area to define the start point. Move your cursor away from the center point to suggest a direction.

2. Click again to define the endpoint of the arc, or enter a precise distance—for example, 4—and press Enter.

3. Move your cursor away from the endpoint and click once more to loosely define the bulge of the arc, or type a precise length—for example, 1—then press Enter.

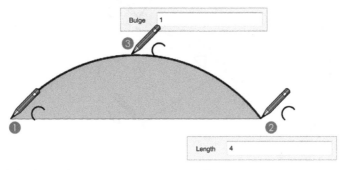

Figure 13.8 The Two-Point Arc tool.

Three-Point Arc Tool

Using the Three-Point Arc tool, you can draw arcs about a pivot point (Figure 13.9).

To do that, follow these steps:

1. Activate the Three-Point Arc tool. Click once in the presentation area to define the start point.

2. Move your cursor away from the start point to suggest a direction, and click again to define the pivot point of the arc.

3. Move your cursor away from the pivot point, and click once more to define the length of the arc.

Pie Tool

With the Pie tool, you can fill in pie charts and recreate iconic video game characters with ease (Figure 13.10).

Just follow these steps:

1. Activate the Pie tool. Click once in the presentation area to define the center point of the arc.

2. Move your cursor away from the center point, let go of the mouse, and type a precise radius—for example, 2—then press Enter.

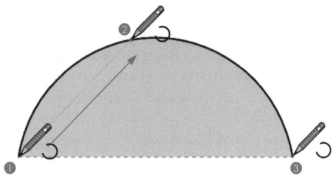

Figure 13.9 The Three-Point Arc tool.

3. Move your cursor away from the start point; you can move in either direction, clockwise or counterclockwise.

4. Either click once more to loosely define the endpoint of the arc, or let go of the mouse and type a precise angle—for example, 300—then press Enter.

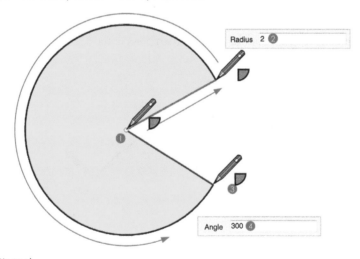

Figure 13.10 The Pie tool.

Circles

Circles, ellipses, and polygons are all created the same way. Unlike SketchUp, there are true vector circles in LayOut, so there is no need to enter the number of sides.

Circle Tool

Use the Circle tool to draw circles (Figure 13.11).

Just follow these steps:

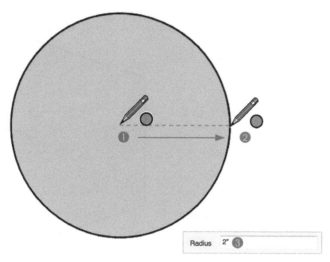

Figure 13.11 The Circle tool.

1. Activate the Circle tool. Click once to define the center point of the circle.

2. Move your cursor away from the center point to define the radius, and click to loosely define the radius of the circle.

3. At this point, you can type a precise radius, such as 2", then press Enter.

Ellipse Tool

The Ellipse tool is a variation of the Circle tool that creates ellipses (Figure 13.12). This tool operates very much like the Rectangle tool. You can also create ellipses by drawing a circle and then using the Select tool and Scale grips to distort it.

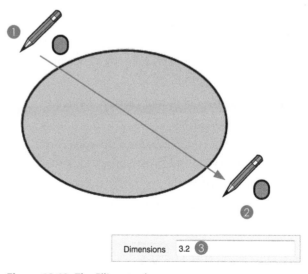

To create an ellipse, follow these steps:

1. Activate the Ellipse tool. Click once to define the start point of the ellipse.

2. Move your cursor away from the start point, and click to loosely define the dimensions of the ellipse.

3. At this point, you can type the precise dimensions—for example, 3,2—then press Enter.

The Ellipse tool also has modifier keys. Hold down the Shift key while creating an ellipse

Figure 13.12 The Ellipse tool.

to constrain it to a circle. Hold down the Ctrl key (Option on a Mac) to create the ellipse about a center point.

Polygon Tool

The Polygon tool creates geometric shapes with a defined number of sides (Figure 13.13).

1. Activate the Polygon tool. Immediately enter the desired number of sides—for example, type 5s, then press Enter.

2. Click once to define the center point of the polygon.

3. Move your cursor away from the center point, and click to loosely define the radius of the polygon.

4. At this point, you can type a precise radius—for example, type 2—then press Enter.

The Polygon tool also has modifier keys. Hold down the Shift key to lock the sides of the polygon to an axis. Hold down the Ctrl key (Option on a Mac) to create a distorted polygon, similar to what you would create with the Ellipse tool.

Offset Tool

The Offset tool (Figure 13.14) will copy a line out concentrically.

1. Activate the Offset tool, click on the shape you wish to offset.

2. Move your cursor away from the edge in the direction you would like to offset. Click to finish the offset.

3. At this point, you can type a precise distance, such as 1/2", then press Enter.

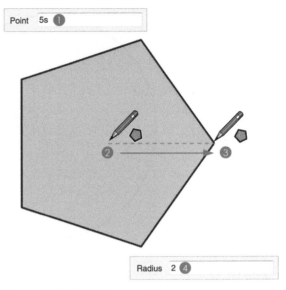

Point   5s 1

Radius   2 4

Figure 13.13 The Polygon tool.

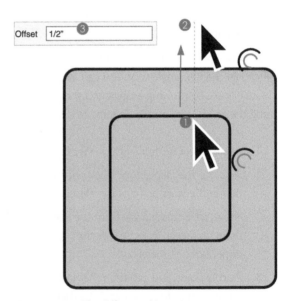

Offset   1/2"   3

Figure 13.14 The Offset tool in action.

TIP Just like in SketchUp, you can double-click on another shape to repeat the last offset distance.

ANNOTATION TOOLS

Annotation tools give you the ability to explain the graphics in your 2D presentation. Add captions, leader text, dimensions, and tables to provide another level of information.

Default Settings

When you activate any of the Annotation tools, the default settings will appear in the corresponding inspectors. The Text tool, Label tool, and Dimension tool have default settings in the Text Style inspector and the Shape Style inspector. In addition to these inspectors, the Dimension tool has default settings in the Dimension Style inspector. You can change the default settings manually by going through each setting in the Text Style, Shape Style, and Dimension Style inspectors while the corresponding tools are active.

Unlike the Drawing tools, each of the Annotation tools has its own independent default settings. For example, if you change the default font for the Text tool, the text displayed when you create labels or dimensions will not be affected.

Use the Pick Style tool to set the default settings for any tool. Just follow these steps:

1. Activate any Annotation tool.

2. To match the current tool's default settings to a specific scrapbook, hover over the scrapbook and click it. (See Chapter 24, Annotations, for more information about how scrapbooks can be used as time-saving palettes.)

3. To match an entity in the presentation area, tap the S key. This is the default shortcut for the Pick Style tool.

4. Click on an entity to match the current tool's inspector settings to the entity that you sampled. The entity can be in the presentation space or in a scrapbook.

Text Tool

LayOut has two types of text: unbounded and bounded (Figure 13.15). *Unbounded text* will just keep going across the page as you type, with no boundary or end. *Bounded text* is a constrained text window. As the text reaches the border, it will automatically drop to the next line if a word will not fit.

Typically, unbounded text is used for drawing titles, page numbers, and short bursts of text. Bounded text is better suited for larger amounts of text, such as project descriptions and notes.

The SketchUp Workflow for Architecture

UNBOUNDED TEXT

The SketchUp
Workflow for
Architecture

BOUNDED TEXT

Figure 13.15 The same text shown as unbounded and bounded.

To create unbounded text, follow these steps:

1. Activate the Text tool. Click once to create an unbounded text window.

2. Enter the desired text in the text box. It will continue across the page with no boundaries.

3. To finish, click outside the text box or press the Esc key.

4. Using the Select tool, double-click on the text to edit it.

TIP When a bounded text box is resized, the bounded text is changed to unbounded. Any text can be changed back and forth from bounded to unbounded. Right-click on the text and choose Make Unbounded or Make Bounded, depending on the setting you need.

To create bounded text, follow these steps:

1. Using the Text tool, click and drag to start the Text window (Figure 13.16).

2. Move your cursor away from the start point and release it to define the boundaries of the text window.

3. Enter the desired text. As the words you type reach the boundary, they will drop to the next line.

4. To finish, click outside the text box or press the Esc key.

5. Using the Select tool, double-click on the text to edit it.

TIP You will see a red arrow on the text box when it is not big enough. You can manually resize the text box or right-click on the text and choose Size to Fit to automatically enlarge the text box to fit the text.

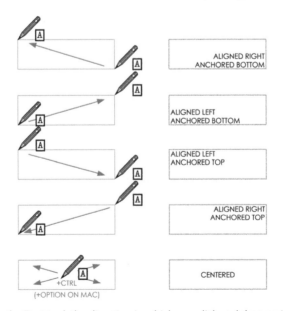

Figure 13.16 When you use the Text tool, the direction in which you click and drag assigns the justification and anchoring of the text window.

Text Properties

The Format tab within the Text Style inspector is where you can change text properties. While a text box is selected, you can adjust the font family, typeface, type size, and color. You can justify the text to the left, right, or center. You can also anchor the text to the top, bottom, or center of the text window.

All types of text can take on any property assigned in the Shape Style inspector (Figure 13.17). You can further modify the selected text's appearance by assigning a fill and stroke in the Shape Style inspector.

Label Tool

The Label tool adds a leader line and attaches text to it (Figure 13.18). Keep in mind that even though this tool creates a "label," there is no entity defined as a label in LayOut. The Label tool creates two simple entities at the same time—a piece of unbounded text and a line, each with its own shape style properties.

To create a leader line with text, follow these steps:

1. Activate the Label tool. Click once to place the arrow for the leader text.

2. Move your cursor away from the arrow and click again to place the text.

3. Enter the desired text.

4. To finish, click outside the text box or press the Esc key.

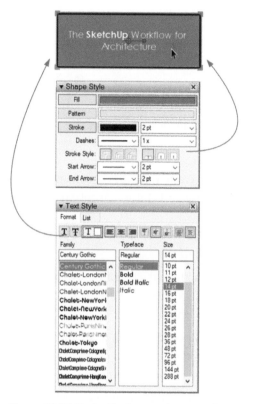

Figure 13.17 Text with shape style properties.

TIP The Label tool can also create curved leader lines—just click and drag. You can modify straight lines into curved leader lines, too. Using the Select tool, double-click on a line to edit the line's points. Holding the Alt key (Option on a Mac), click and drag on an endpoint to curve the line. See the "Select Tool" section later in this chapter for more information about editing lines.

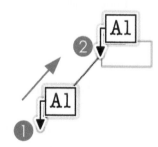

Figure 13.18 The Label tool.

Dimension Tools

Add dimensions to call out lengths and angles and further explain a design. Keep in mind that the default settings for dimensions are in several inspectors: Shape Style, Dimensions Style, and Text Style. In LayOut,

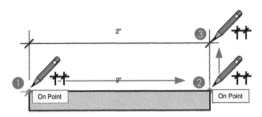

Figure 13.19 Linear dimension.

you can create two types of dimensions: Linear (Figure 13.19) and Angular (Figure 13.20).

To add linear dimensions to a presentation, follow these steps:

1. Activate the Linear Dimension tool. Click once to define the start point of the dimension.

2. Move your cursor to another point and click again to define the endpoint of the dimension.

3. Move your cursor away from the start and endpoints of the dimension line. Click to place the dimension.

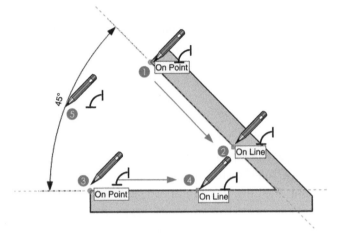

Figure 13.20 Angular dimension.

TIP Double-click on the next point to continue the string of linear dimensions.

To add angular dimensions to a presentation, follow these steps:

1. Activate the Angular Dimension tool. To define the first point of the first leg of the angle, click on the first line that you want to add dimension to.

2. Click again on the same line to finish defining the first leg.

3. To define the first point of the second leg of the angle, click on the second line that you want to add dimension to.

4. Click again on the same line to finish defining the second leg.

5. Move your cursor to adjust the arrows, and then click to position the angular dimension text.

Dimension Properties

Dimensions in LayOut utilize settings from several inspectors: Shape Style, Dimension Style, and Text Style (Figure 13.21). Select a dimension to see all its properties in the inspectors.

Editing Dimensions

Once a dimension has been created, it can be modified. Using the Select tool, double-click on a dimension to edit it (Figure 13.22).

Once in dimension edit mode, follow these steps:

1. Click and drag on the text to reposition.

2. Triple-click on the text to change the shown dimension. Although it is discouraged, you can change the text displayed to force a dimension. To revert back to the automatically measured text, erase all the forced text and press the Esc key.

3. Click and drag on the extent points to change the distance between the object being measured and the dimension line. This is called the offset.

4. To change the length of an extension line, click and drag on an offset point.

5. Click and drag on a connection point to change the points being measured and, in turn, the length of the dimension.

TIP Angular dimensions have a very similar edit mode.

TABLES

Tables in LayOut format and behave similar to a spreadsheet regarding formatting, without all the math. To add a table to a presentation, follow

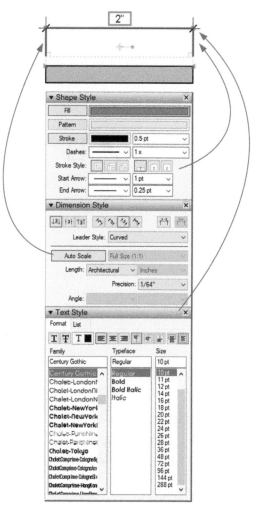

Figure 13.21 Dimensions have settings in the Shape Style, Dimension Style, and Text Style inspectors.

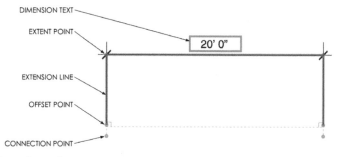

Figure 13.22 Dimension edit mode.

these steps (Figure 13.23):

1. Activate the Table tool. Click once to define the start point of the table.
2. Move your cursor to another point and click again to define the number of rows and columns.
3. Move your cursor to another point and click again to define the height and width of the table.

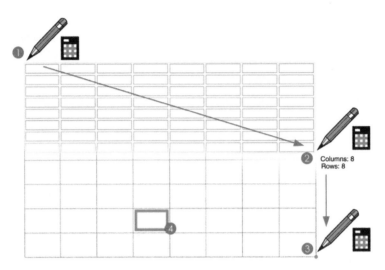

Figure 13.23 Adding a table.

Table Properties

Tables can have shape and text style properties applied to them. Just like with Drawing tools, when you activate the Table tool, the settings shown in the inspectors are the default settings that will be applied to the new table.

Once a table has been created, you can modify the visual style using the Select tool. You can apply the same fill and text properties to the table globally, or you can double-click in to assign shape and text style properties to individual cells, a selection of cells, border, and dividing edges. To edit a table into a more refined look (Figure 13.24), follow these steps:

1. Using the Select tool, double-click on a table to enter the table edit mode.
2. Click on the outer border to adjust its visual properties in the Shape Style inspector.
3. Click on an edge to adjust its properties in the Shape Style inspector.
4. Click on a cell, or click and drag to select a series of cells, to adjust its text style and shape style properties.

TIP Using the Style tool, sample one table and apply its formatting to another. The formatting is pulled based on the rows. So if you set up all of your schedules the same way, it is easy to match formatting between tables.

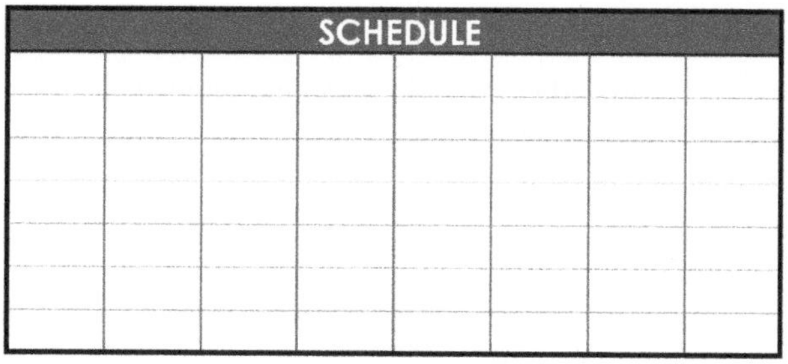

Figure 13.24 The table with different visual properties applied to cells and edges.

Once you double-click into table edit mode, expedite the formatting of cells with these tips in mind:

☑ Right-click on a cell and choose Copy style to extract its visual properties. Next, select a cell, or range of cells, right-click, and choose Paste style to apply the visual properties.

☑ The right-click menu offers a lot of spreadsheet formatting options such as insert row above or below, insert column left or right, delete columns and rows, space columns and rows to fit, and rotate text.

☑ When you are finished editing a cell, hit the Tab key to finish entering data and move across a column, or hit the Enter key to finish entering data and move down a row.

☑ Select multiple cells, then right-click Merge cells to make a series of cells into one.

☑ Hover on the border; now you can stretch the table and the cells.

☑ Click and drag from left to right to select cells. Click and drag from right to left to select the dividing lines. Single-click on any entity to isolate a selection.

☑ Click and drag on an edge to resize the row or column.

TIP See Chapter 24, Annotations, for more information on inserting, editing, and formatting tables as schedules.

MODIFICATION TOOLS

The Modification tools are used to change geometry that is already created. You can use them to move, rotate, copy, split, or join existing geometry to create new complex shapes.

Select Tool

Because it is the most frequently used tool, a safe and helpful habit is to always default to the Select tool. The default keyboard shortcut for the Select tool is the spacebar. The Select tool does much more than just select entities; it allows you to move, rotate, copy, and edit LayOut entities.

Selecting

The Select tool is used to set up many other operations within LayOut. Because it is so important, take the time to become proficient at using it to select entities. Practice these steps:

☑ Single-click on any entity in LayOut to select it. The selected entity's properties will be displayed in the relevant inspectors.

☑ Hold down the Shift key to add to, subtract from, or inverse a selection.

☑ Click and drag to select entities with a selection window (Figure 13.25).

TIP Hold the Alt key (Command on Mac) to draw selection windows without moving the objects below.

Moving/Copying

Use the Select tool to move and copy entities within LayOut. To do that, follow these steps:

1. Select an entity or multiple entities.

2. Click and drag on the selection to move the entities all at once.

3. Release the mouse button to finish the move.

4. Immediately type a precise distance, such as 5, then press Enter.

The Move feature of the Select tool also has modifier keys. Use them as follows:

☑ Click and drag while holding down the Shift key to lock an axis.

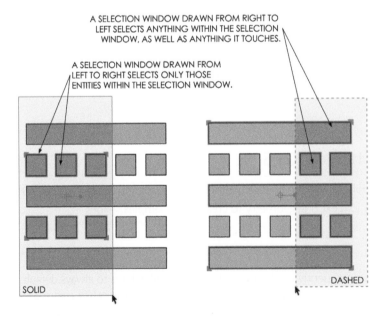

Figure 13.25 Selection windows.

☑ Click and drag while holding down the Ctrl key (Option on a Mac) to make a copy. Just like in SketchUp, you can type 5x after a copy to create five copies in addition to the original.

☑ To encourage inferences and create meaningful relationships between LayOut entities, hover endpoints, midpoints, and lines of the entity you are moving on other endpoints, midpoints, and lines of entities in your presentation.

TIP Use the arrow keys on your keyboard to nudge a selected entity 1/64" in the desired direction. Hold down the Shift key while nudging to move an entity 1/4" in the desired direction.

Precise Moving/Copying

The Precise Move grip allows you to move entities in LayOut with complete control. Use a precise move to align drawings, annotations, title blocks, and geometry to make more accurate and visually appealing presentations (Figure 13.26).

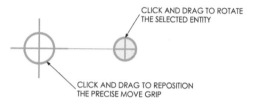

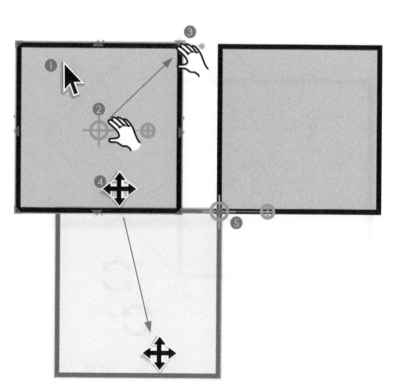

Figure 13.26 A precise move is when you move an entity from one specific point to another specific point.

Just follow these steps:

1. Select an entity and notice that the Precise Move grip appears in the middle of the selection.

2. Click and drag on the left side of the Precise Move grip to pick it up. You can encourage inferences from the Precise Move grip before placing it.

3. Release on a meaningful point to put it down.

4. Click and drag anywhere on the selection to move it.

5. Allow the Precise Move grip to snap to an inference on another entity. You can also encourage inferences from the Precise Move grip.

TIP Hold the Ctrl key (Option on a Mac) and Shift key down while performing a precise move to create a copy along an axis. Just like in SketchUp, you can create multiply and divide arrays. Simply type in 5x or 5/ after the completed copy command to create five copies or five divisions, respectively, between the copies.

Rotating/Copying

LayOut doesn't have a dedicated Rotate tool. However, you can accomplish any rotation you'll need with the Precise Move grip, which is the center of any rotation (Figure 13.27).

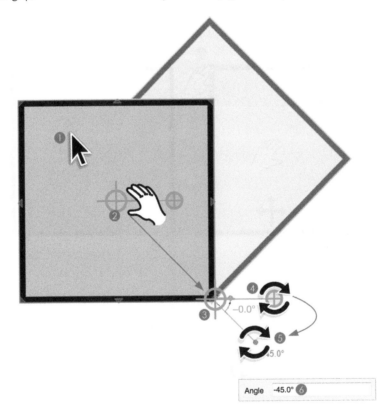

Figure 13.27 Rotate.

Follow these steps:

1. Select an entity and notice that the Precise Move grip appears in the middle of the selection.

2. Click and drag on the left side of the Precise Move grip to pick it up. You can encourage inferences from the Precise Move grip before placing it.

3. Release on a meaningful center point of rotation to put it down.

4. Click and drag on the right side of the Precise Move grip to start the rotation.

5. Release the mouse button to finish.

6. Now you can enter a precise degree of rotation—for example, type −45.0°—then press Enter.

TIP Hold the Ctrl key (Option on a Mac) down while rotating any entity to create a copy. Just like in SketchUp, you can create multiply and divide polar arrays. Simply type in 5x or 5/ after the completed copy command to create five copies or five divisions, respectively, between the copies.

Scaling

Use the Select tool to scale and distort entities in LayOut (Figure 13.28).

1. Select an entity or multiple entities.

2. Click and drag on the Perimeter grip to distort or scale the selection.

3. Move your cursor away from the Scale grip, and release it to loosely set the new scale.

4. Now you can enter a precise scale value—for example, type 2—then press Enter.

TIP There's not much space for your cursor between the Move and Scale features. Be sure to watch the cursor icon closely to determine which feature you are using.

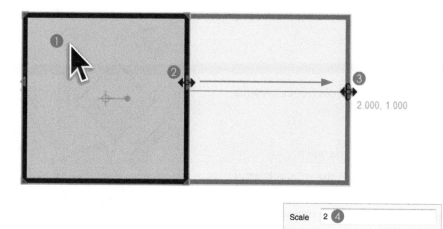

Figure 13.28 Scaling an entity in LayOut.

When you are scaling in LayOut, keeps these points in mind:

- ☑ Hold down the Ctrl key (Option on a Mac) to make a copy while scaling.
- ☑ Hold down the Shift key to constrain the selection's proportions while scaling.
- ☑ To mirror a selection, scale to –1, or right-click on an entity or selection and choose Flip, then Top to Bottom or Flip, then Left to Right.

Line Editing

Use the Select tool to edit lines and shapes in LayOut. The methods discussed here apply to all the geometry in LayOut, including lines, rectangles, circles, arcs, polygons, etc. There are several methods for modifying geometry using the Select tool. Double-click on the line or entity and then:

- ☑ Click and drag on a point to reposition it, ultimately modifying the geometry.
- ☑ Hold the Alt key (Command on a Mac), and click along the line to add control points.
- ☑ Drag a control point onto another control point to delete it.
- ☑ Hold the Alt key (Option on a Mac), and click and drag control points to curve the line. A curve can be created from any point along a line.
- ☑ Click and drag the tangent control points of a curve back to the control point to remove the curve, ultimately making the line straight.

Eraser Tool

Use the Eraser tool to delete entities from a presentation (Figure 13.29).

Follow these steps:

1. Click once on an entity to erase it.
2. Alternatively, hold down the mouse button and drag the cursor over the entities. All entities will be erased when the mouse button is released.

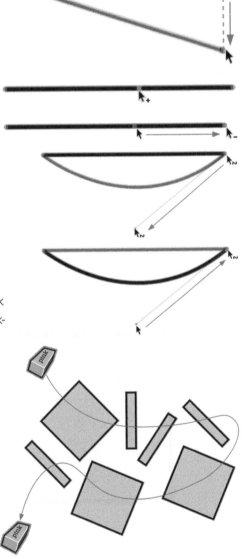

Figure 13.29 The Eraser tool.

Style Tool

The Style tool is very similar to a Match Properties tool in other programs (Figure 13.30). To use it, sample all the properties from one entity and, in one click, apply them to another entity. The Style tool can sample from and apply to any combination of shapes, edges, viewports, images, text, etc.

Follow these steps:

1. Activate the Style tool. To sample an entity's style, click on it in a scrapbook or in the document presentation area.

2. Click on the entities to which you want to apply the sampled properties.

Figure 13.30 The Style tool.

TIP Tap the Esc key to start over, or hold down the Ctrl key (Option on a Mac) to sample another entity.

Split Tool

The Split tool divides line segments and also creates breaks between overlapping shapes (Figure 13.31).

To use the Split tool to break LayOut geometry down into simpler forms, follow these steps:

1. Activate the Split tool. Click on an intersection between the two shapes.

2. Click on another intersection between the two shapes. Use the Select tool to examine the results.

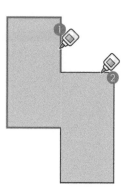

Figure 13.31 The Split tool.

Join Tool

The Join tool glues together lines that share a vertex (Figure 13.32). It is used to combine shapes to create more complex geometry.

To use it, follow these steps:

1. Activate the Join tool. Click on the first entity that you would like to join.

2. Click on the next entity that you would like to join. Use the Select tool to examine the results.

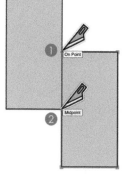

Figure 13.32 The Join tool.

CHAPTER POINTS

☑ Each group of tools has a specific function. Before you perform an operation, make a plan and think it through. Ask yourself: What is the fastest way to complete the task?

☑ Using a combination of the Drawing and Modification tools, you can create any shape, precise or sketchy, in LayOut.

☑ Instead of sorting through several dialogs, use the Pick Style tool to set the defaults for your tools.

☑ When you execute a command, most of the LayOut tools allow you to enter precise dimensions during the command. Some of the LayOut tools allow you to also modify the precise dimensions after you execute the command, until another command is started.

☑ After any copy command, you can now create a multiply or divide array.

☑ Unlike SketchUp, LayOut is mostly a click-and-drag program.

Chapter 14
Inserting Content

To move a three-dimensional (3D) design into a two-dimensional (2D) LayOut presentation, you simply insert the SketchUp model into LayOut. You can insert all sorts of content, including SketchUp models, images, text, and spreadsheets to describe your design. Any inserted content can be lightly edited in LayOut or seamlessly sent to a program more suited for editing the specific file while maintaining the dynamic link. In this chapter, you will insert and edit all of LayOut's insertable entities.

WORKING WITH SKETCHUP MODELS

Hands down, the most important file you'll insert into LayOut is the SketchUp file (.skp). The dynamic link between a SketchUp file and a LayOut presentation allows more than one person to work on a project. For example, someone could work on the design while someone else works on the presentation. By presenting your 3D model as 2D drawings and diagrams, you will be able to accurately and efficiently describe your designs and ideas.

New LayOut Presentation

To begin your new LayOut presentation, follow these steps:

1. Open LayOut and start a new presentation. Select the BD_8.5 x 11 Landscape - Presentation title block included in the book resources (you will make this title block in Chapter 22, Title Blocks), or you can choose any title block you want.

2. Within the Layers inspector, verify that the DRAWING layer is unlocked and set to the current layer. Anything that you insert into SketchUp will typically be assigned to this layer.

Inserting the File

To insert the SketchUp file, follow these steps:

1. Click on the File drop-down menu and select Insert. This launches the Open dialog box.

2. Navigate to the Class Files folder for this chapter and select the `BD_Modern Garage.skp` file.

3. Click on the Open button at the bottom-right corner of the dialog box. The SketchUp model will be inserted into a viewport in your LayOut presentation (Figure 14.1).

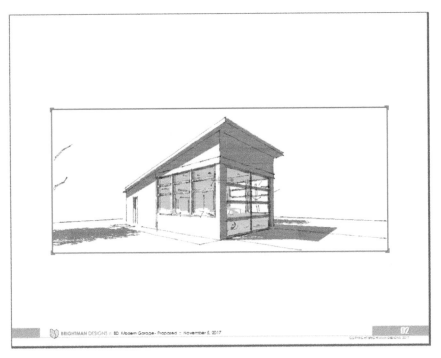

Figure 14.1 The new viewport created within LayOut.

Assigning a Scene

The new viewport will be set to the last saved scene. This is the camera view that was shown when your model was last saved. It is always best to assign a static view, or scene, to the viewport. To assign a scene in the SketchUp Model dialog, follow these steps:

1. Using the Select tool, select the viewport.

2. In the SketchUp Model Inspector, set the Viewport Scene to LO_Perspective 01 and the Rendering setting to Raster.

3. If Auto-Render is off, render the models manually by right-clicking on the presentation background and choosing Render Models on Page.

Clipping Mask

A *clipping mask* lets you control what part of an object you see. This is helpful when you're cropping viewports and images in LayOut. Clipping masks work with images and SketchUp model viewports. Just follow these steps:

1. Activate the Rectangle tool. Click once to start the rectangle in the top-left corner.

2. Move your cursor away from the start point to draw a shape covering the portion of the viewport you want to see (Figure 14.2).

3. Using the Select tool, select both the viewport and the clipping mask shape.

4. Right-click on the selection and choose Create Clipping Mask (Figure 14.3).

5. Move the clipped viewport to the top-right corner of the page, then reduce the size by about 15 percent, or a scale factor of .85 (Figure 14.4).

6. Using the Select tool, click and drag on the viewport while holding the Ctrl key (Option on a Mac) to make a copy. Also hold the Shift key to lock the axis (Figure 14.5).

7. In the SketchUp Model inspector, set the Viewport Scene to LO_Perspective 02. Because this is a copy of the Perspective 01 viewport, the rendering settings are already set to raster.

To edit a clipping mask, double-click on the masked viewport/image with the Select tool. Use the Select tool to move and scale the clipping mask shape. Tap Esc to exit edit mode. Sometimes it is easier to just right-click on the clipped object, choose Release Clipping Mask, and then edit the shape and recreate the clipping mask.

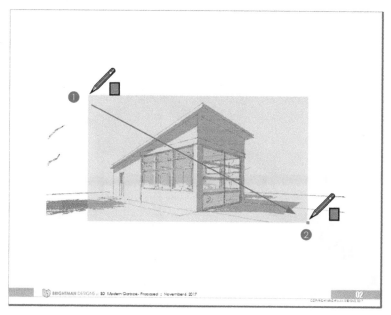

Figure 14.2 Use the clipping mask to cover the part of the object you want to be seen. The part that is covered will be the part that is visible when the clipping mask is applied.

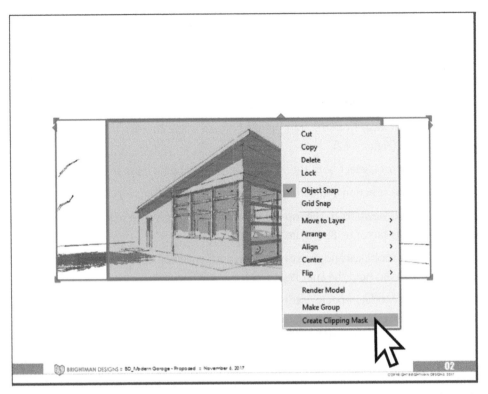

Figure 14.3 The clipping mask function is available in the right-click menu when one viewport and one shape are selected.

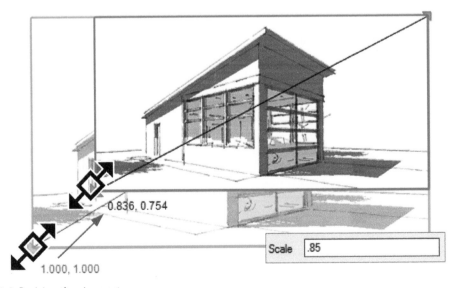

Figure 14.4 Resizing the viewport.

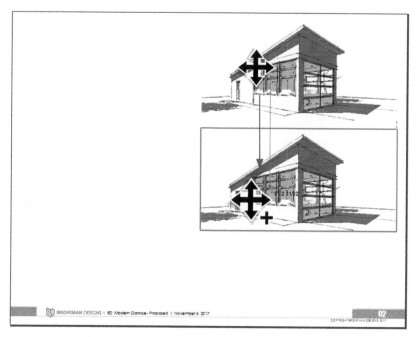

Figure 14.5 Copy the viewport.

TIP Use any of the Drawing tools to create a shape for clipping. The final clipping mask shape must be one complete shape, not a .group or collection of shapes. Use the Split and Join tools to finalize a complex clipping mask shape.

Editing the Model

A SketchUp model can be opened directly from LayOut, which will create a seamless link between SketchUp and LayOut. To enhance your design and see the results within your presentation immediately, follow these steps:

1. Right-click on the viewport and choose Open with SketchUp.

2. Make your changes to the SketchUp model.

3. Close the model and save it.

4. All the viewports linked to that model will be updated when the file is saved. If Auto-Render is off, you will need to render the viewports manually.

WORKING WITH IMAGES

Images provide another level of information and complement the style of visual information. You can insert all sorts of images, including locator maps from Google Earth or Google Maps, project photographs, watermarks, photorealistic renderings, and other diagrams.

Inserting Images

LayOut offers the option to insert images as several formats, the most used are `.jpg, .png, and .tif` files. A .jpg file is light weight and probably the most common image format. A `.png` file contains an alpha or transparency layer. This transparency gives you the ability to create watermarks without having to create elaborate clipping masks in LayOut. A .tif file holds layers for more complex editing in Photoshop. To insert an image, just follow these steps:

1. Click on the File drop-down menu and choose Insert.

2. Navigate to the Class Files folder and select the `BD_Modern Garage - Location Map.jpg` file. Click the Open button at the bottom-right corner of the dialog.

3. Using the Select tool, scale and reposition the image on the presentation area as shown in Figure 14.6. When scaling, be sure to use a corner grip and hold the Shift key to lock the aspect ratio.

Figure 14.6 The context photograph inserted, scaled, and properly positioned in the presentation.

Editing Images

The Edit Image command allows you to work seamlessly between LayOut and your favorite image editor. Use an image editor to touch up photos and crop, scale, and resize images. Just follow these steps:

1. Right-click on an image and choose Open with Adobe Photoshop or whatever image editor you assigned in Chapter 12, The Professional's LayOut Environment.

2. Modify the image within your image editor.

3. Close and save the file.

4. The image automatically updates in LayOut. If it does not update immediately, right-click on the image and choose Update Reference.

WORKING WITH TEXT

Insert text into a presentation to explain the graphics and include details such as schedules, notes, and drawing lists. The dynamic link enables the text to be edited in a word processor, which will have additional helpful features such as spell check.

Inserting Text

You can insert text as a .txt file or an .rtf file. You can't save visual text properties (such as colors, fonts, and formatting) in a .txt file, which limits its usefulness as an import. An .rtf file can store all the visual properties you apply to the text. Once you have created your text in a word processor, you can save the file as an .rtf file and insert into LayOut. Just follow these steps:

1. Click on the File drop-down menu, and choose Insert.

2. Navigate to the Class Files folder for this chapter and select the `BD_Modern Garage - Description.rtf` file.

3. Click on Open.

4. Reposition and scale the text to fit the width of the inserted image. See Figure 14.7.

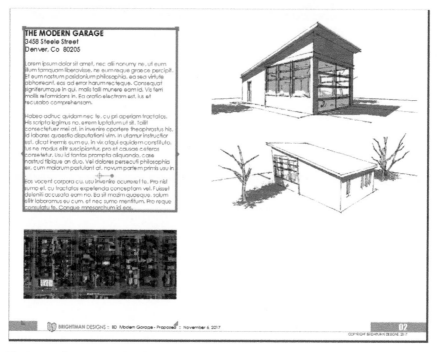

Figure 14.7 The inserted text, resized and positioned in the top-left corner.

Editing Text

The text is now part of your presentation, but you can still edit it with your favorite word processing program. To edit text outside of LayOut, follow these steps:

1. Right-click on the text, and choose Edit Text.

2. Modify the text in the default text editor.

3. Close the file and save your changes. You will see the text update within LayOut.

TIP When you double-click on text and edit in LayOut, you will break the dynamic link between the inserted file and the LayOut text. There is no way to relink edited text without reinserting the original file. It is usually best to just work with text in LayOut, rather than trying to maintain a dynamic link.

WORKING WITH TABLES

Insert tables into a presentation to create schedules. You can use Microsoft Excel or, better yet, Google Sheets (Figure 14.8) to create spreadsheets. It is possible to format within your spreadsheet program, but often it is easier to edit the data in Google Sheets then format the visual style in LayOut. However, you can still work with a visual style that will help organize the information.

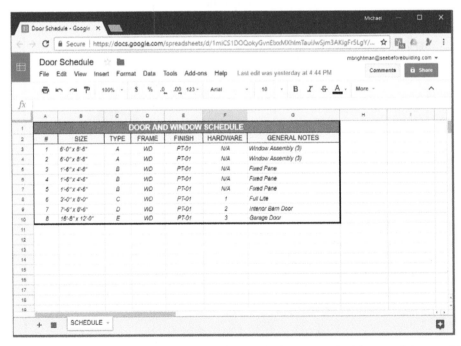

Figure 14.8 Google Sheets is free, fast, easy, and powerful. It is the best way to build compatible spreadsheets for schedules.

Inserting Tables

You can insert tables from three different formats: .csv, .tsv, and .xlsx. A .csv file will not hold formatting or sheets. The best format to use is Google Docs, which downloads as an .xlsx file and holds formatting, and sheets.

1. Click on the File drop-down menu, and choose Insert.

2. Navigate to the class files folder for this chapter and select the BD_Modern Garage - Window Schedule.xlsx file.

3. Click on Open.

4. Adjust the Excel Reference Options as needed and check on Import Excel Formatting (Figure 14.9).

5. Reposition and scale the table as shown. Select the table, then turn off the stroke in the Shape Style inspector. Also, you will likely need to double-click to resize the rows to fit (see Figure 14.10).

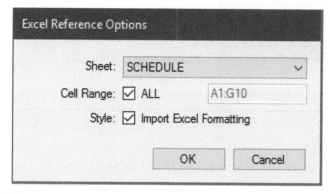

Figure 14.9 The Excel Reference Options window. Importing the Excel formatting will give you a jumpstart in LayOut.

Editing Tables

Once a table is inserted, you should avoid editing its data contents in LayOut unless you prefer to work with the table only in LayOut. The best workflow is to work in Google Sheets or Excel, redownload, then update the reference without formatting. To update a table reference in LayOut, follow these steps:

1. Adjust your data in Google Sheets.

2. Click on the File drop-down and choose Download As.

3. Overwrite the .xlsx file.

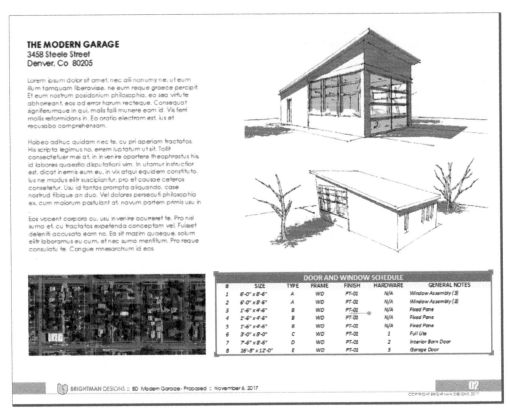

THE MODERN GARAGE
3458 Steele Street
Denver, Co 80205

Lorem ipsum dolor sit amet, nec alii nonumy ne, ut eum illum tamquam liberavisse, ne eum reque graece percipit. Et eum nostrum posidonium philosophia, eo sea virtute abhorreant, eos ad error harum recteque. Consequat signiferumque in qui, malis falli munere eam id. Vis ferri mollis reformidans in. Ea oratio electram est, ius et recusabo comprehensam.

Habeo adhuc quidam nec te, cu pri aperiam tractatos. His scripta legimus no, errem luptatum ut sit. Tollit consectetuer mei at, in venire oportere theophrastus his, id labores quaestio disputationi vim. In utamur instructior est, dicat in erris eum eu, in vix atqui equidem constituto. Ius ne modus elitr suscipiantur, pro et causae ceteros consetetur. Usu id tantas prompta aliquando, case nostrud fibique an duo. Vel dolores persecuti philosophia ex, cum maiorum postulant at, novum partem primis usu in.

Eos vocent corpora cu, usu in venire ocurreret te. Pro nisl sumo et, cu tractatos expetenda conceptam vel. Fuisset deleniti accusata eam no. Ea sit mazim quaeque, solum elitr laboramus eu cum, et nec sumo mentitum. Pro reque consulatu te. Congue mnesarchum id eos.

DOOR AND WINDOW SCHEDULE						
#	SIZE	TYPE	FRAME	FINISH	HARDWARE	GENERAL NOTES
1	6'-0" x 8'-6"	A	WD	PT-01	N/A	Window Assembly (3)
2	6'-0" x 8'-6"	A	WD	PT-01	N/A	Window Assembly (3)
3	1'-6" x 4'-6"	B	WD	PT-01	N/A	Fixed Pane
4	1'-6" x 4'-6"	B	WD	PT-01	N/A	Fixed Pane
5	1'-6" x 4'-6"	B	WD	PT-01	N/A	Fixed Pane
6	3'-0" x 8'-0"	C	WD	PT-01	1	Full Lite
7	7'-6" x 8'-6"	D	WD	PT-01	2	Interior Barn Door
8	16'-8" x 12'-0"	E	WD	PT-01	3	Garage Door

BRIGHTMAN DESIGNS :: 8D Modern Garage- Proposed :: November 6, 2017   02   COPYRIGHT BRIGHTMAN DESIGNS, 2017

Figure 14.10 Inserted table.

4. In LayOut, right-click on the table and choose Excel Reference Options. Uncheck "import excel formatting."

5. In LayOut, right-click on the table and choose Update table reference.

It is much easier to work with numbers and data in the spreadsheet interface; also you have access to cut and paste and formulas. On the other side, it is much easier to control the visual style within LayOut. Typically, you will uncheck Import Excel formatting after the initial import and handle this in LayOut.

MANAGING REFERENCES

All SketchUp, image, text, and table references can be managed from the Document Setup dialog. Click on the File drop-down, choose Document Setup, then click on the References tab (Figure 14.11).

1. Click on a reference to edit its properties.

2. Click on the Update button to refresh the link. This is the same function as right-clicking on an object in the presentation area and choosing Update reference.

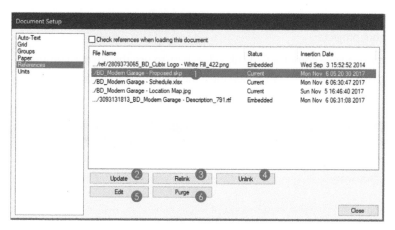

Figure 14.11 The Document Setup dialog controls all external references.

3. Click on the Relink button to choose a different file to fill the link. Keep in mind that relinking to a file that has differently named sheets, or scenes, will be filled with the last saved SketchUp view or the subsequent sheet.

4. Click on the Unlink button to embed the linked reference file within the LayOut document.

5. Click on Edit to open the reference in an external editor.

6. Click on the Purge button to remove any unused references within your layout presentation. This is important because linked files will continue to travel with the layout file until purged, increasing the file size while decreasing performance.

TIP Beware that when you select a reference here, it selects it in the LayOut presentation area. When you have stacked viewports, this is an opportunity for error in that you can select a single viewport within a group of stacked viewports from the Document Setup dialog. If you scale one stacked viewport separate from the others, the views can be skewed.

WORKING WITH CAD

You can insert computer-aided design (CAD) files into your LayOut Presentation in .dxf and .dwg formats. Importing CAD into LayOut allows you to easily incorporate consultant's work into your drawing set and revive old CAD libraries. Keep these tips in mind when working with CAD.

☑ There is no reference link or external editor. Once a CAD file is imported it becomes LayOut geometry.

☑ You can choose to import the CAD model space or paper space. Typically model space is the best choice (Figure 14.12).

☑ CAD drawings come in as a "scale drawing." Right-click on the scale drawing and choose Scale to select a new scale.

- ☑ When importing old CAD details, once optimized for LayOut consider saving them as scrapbooks for easy use in future projects.

- ☑ Beware of importing large complex CAD files. It is best to use the wblock command in your CAD program to isolate just the pieces you need into one file before importing.

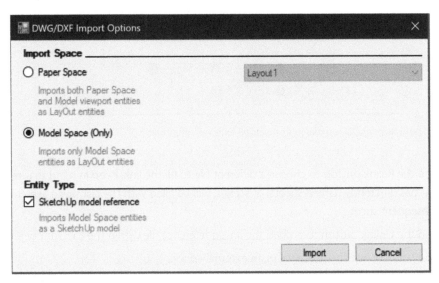

Figure 14.12 The DWG/DXF Import Options dialog.

CHAPTER POINTS

- ☑ Right-click on any linked content to open with the external editor set in Chapter 12, The Professional's LayOut Environment.

- ☑ Editing text within LayOut breaks the dynamic link. Typically, editing the bulk of your text in a word processor and then inserting that text into LayOut works best. Once it's inserted, make all your final text edits in LayOut.

- ☑ You can manage all your inserted content, or references, within the Document Setup References dialog. From there, you can relink, unlink, and edit in an assigned external program.

- ☑ The data within tables is best managed in an external editor such as Google Sheets, whereas the visual style of the table is best managed within LayOut.

- ☑ Importing CAD files can be helpful, but there is no dynamic link or external editing options.

PART IV

Model Organization

Now that you know how to create geometry, you need to organize it meticulously. Organizing your model from the beginning is the most critical piece of the SketchUp Workflow for Architecture. Without a properly organized model, nothing works. This enables you to dissect the model in several meaningful ways, create backgrounds for consultants, enable dynamic hatches and line weights, and use DRAFT mode—really everything you need depends on a properly organized model. Learn the system, then stick to it, and everything will work wonderfully. In this part you will master the dance of nested groups and layering.

Chapter 15
Model Organization Overview

Aproperly organized model can be picked apart in infinite ways to expedite design, speed up modeling, create drawings with unlimited line weights and hatches, and communicate with consultants. It is critical that you stay organized and have a plan.

TIP This portion is strongest as a reference. Check out the video on this chapter at **brightmandesigns. com/TSWFA** for a quick tutorial on model organization. This will help you absorb this chapter much quicker. Then you can look back to this area to remind yourself how it all goes together.

The system works like this: Nested groups have layers applied to each level. Group the same order every time, regardless of the project size or type: LEVEL > ELEMENT > LOCATION > CONDITION (Figure 15.1). Each part of the design model will be placed in the corresponding group. This is our baseline, our default system. Once you master it, you can expand the system into whatever you need, simplify it for your industry, and expedite it with shortcuts (at the end of this chapter) to save some time.

CORE CONCEPTS OF MODEL ORGANIZATION

☑ Layer0 is always active, all edges and surfaces are drawn on Layer0, and all groups will be assigned to Layer0 when they are created. The ConDoc System will warn you if Layer0 is not current; just click on the warning to fix it. The ConDoc System is there to keep you on track (Figure 15.2).

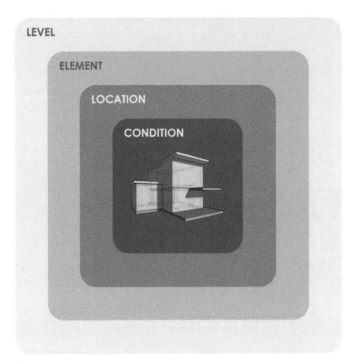

Figure 15.1 Model organization overview graphic.

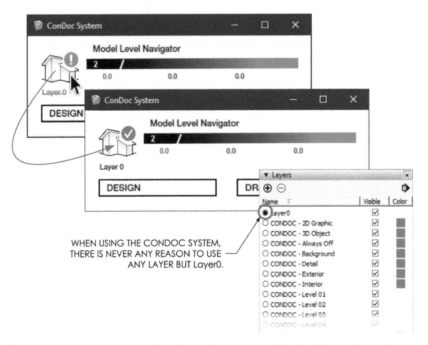

WHEN USING THE CONDOC SYSTEM, THERE IS NEVER ANY REASON TO USE ANY LAYER BUT Layer0.

Figure 15.2 The ConDoc System warns you when Layer0 is not active. Simply click on the warning to remedy the problem.

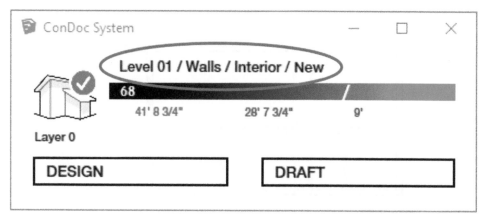

Figure 15.3 Within the SketchUp Workflow for Architecture system, the new, existing, and demolished condition is always last, or the smallest container in the nested line. The ConDoc System illustrates this in a compressed string of text.

☑ Group early and often. A model that has been grouped can be salvaged; a model that has not been grouped is unworkable. It is much easier to explode a group, or ungroup, than it is to pick through a pile of sticky geometry. When in doubt, make it a group!

☑ Group objects together by categories that the layers describe, then assign the layer to a group. Only assign layers to groups, not to edges or surfaces.

TIP One exception to this rule is the CONDOC - Always Off layer. This layer can be applied to edges to "visually merge" two groups together, making them seamless, such as first- and second-story walls on a two-story project or where new walls meet existing walls.

☑ There is a series of switches that works every time. Always assign layers to nested groups in this order: Level > Element > Location > Condition (Figure 15.3).

☑ The CONDITION groups—new, existing, and demolished layers—are always the last level of organization.

☑ Each LEVEL group gets a floor and a ceiling and everything in between. Ceilings build down off the bottom of the floor above.

☑ Interior walls go from finished floor to ceiling. Exterior walls go from finished floor to finished floor above. These are typical situations and can be broken as necessary, as shown in Figure 15.4.

☑ All door openings, interior and exterior, must be cut all the way to the bottom of the wall; otherwise, plans will not net a clean opening (Figure 15.5).

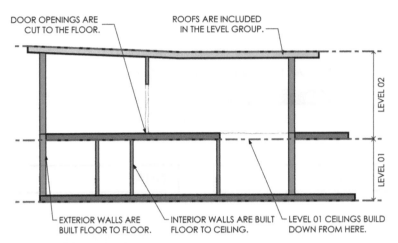

DOOR OPENINGS ARE CUT TO THE FLOOR.

ROOFS ARE INCLUDED IN THE LEVEL GROUP.

LEVEL 02

LEVEL 01

EXTERIOR WALLS ARE BUILT FLOOR TO FLOOR.

INTERIOR WALLS ARE BUILT FLOOR TO CEILING.

LEVEL 01 CEILINGS BUILD DOWN FROM HERE.

Figure 15.4 Group your model accordingly.

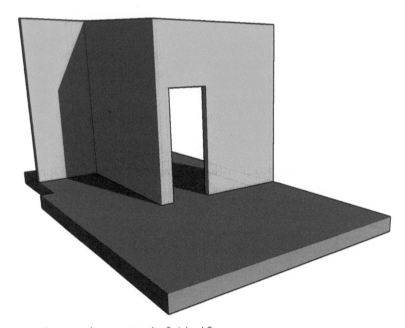

Figure 15.5 Door openings are always cut to the finished floor.

NESTING GROUPS AND LAYERS

A persistent question is why do we need nested groups? Why don't we layer per line like computer-aided design (CAD)? Once you understand the benefit, it's a no-brainer—the system presented is a foolproof, easier way of doing things. It eliminates opportunity for errors and requires less troubleshooting. Nested groups avoid having an endless layers list.

For example, if you have a two-story house with a basement, you would need hundreds, maybe thousands, of layers to accurately describe each combination of LEVEL, ELEMENT, LOCATION, and

CONDITION (Figure 15.6). Managing that many layers is hard enough; imagine applying them to all of your geometry. With nested layers, you are able to reuse layers within each LEVEL, within each ELEMENT, within each LOCATION, and within each CONDITION.

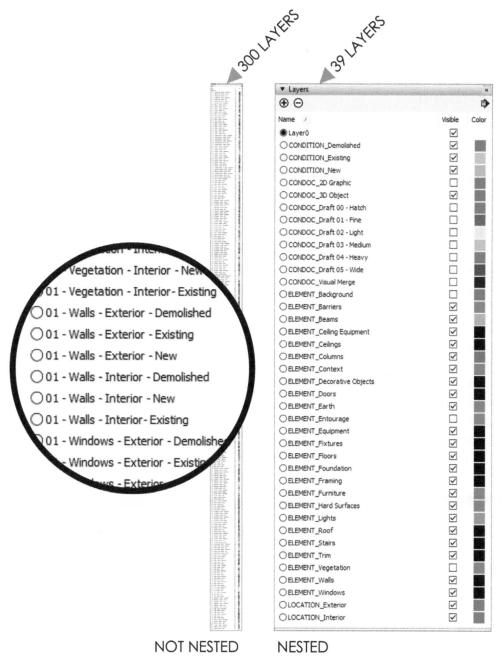

NOT NESTED   NESTED

Figure 15.6 You would need more than 300 layers to achieve the same functionality as the 39 layers used in ConDoc and this book.

The SketchUp Workflow for Architecture stock layer list is a lean 39 layers: 25 ELEMENTS, 2 LOCATIONS, 3 CONDITIONS, 9 CONDOC, plus as many LEVEL layers as you need. This drastically reduces the number of layers you need and saves time and headaches when navigating the model and creating scenes. I have done it both ways—I promise nesting is where it's at.

Nested Groups

Start with nesting groups within one another. This is the way to organize every model, for every project type, to get predictable results. This section is more theory than practice but will be a strong resource later. Just take a moment to understand the order of how the model is organized with this system; you will implement in practice for new construction and renovation projects in the following chapters. The order in which you actually group your model is likely different than the order the groups are explained in this section. What order you group doesn't matter, as long as the final organization is correct.

To start nesting groups, you first need to separate the different levels of your design into groups: one group that holds everything on the first level, another group that holds everything on the second level, and so on (Figure 15.7).

Next, double-click inside of each of the LEVEL groups; you will need to make 25 groups that hold ELEMENT entities (Figure 15.8). Select the walls, right-click, make group. Select the floors, right-click, make group. Select the roofs, right-click, make group. Do this for all 25 ELEMENT groups that correspond with the objects represented by the ELEMENT layers described later in this chapter.

Inside each of the ELEMENT groups, you will add two LOCATION groups, one to hold exterior entities, the other to hold interior entities (Figure 15.9).

Figure 15.7 The objects and geometry that represent each level of the model are first separated into LEVEL groups.

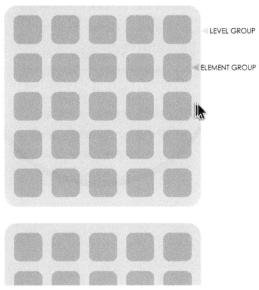

Figure 15.8 Twenty-five ELEMENT groups within each LEVEL group.

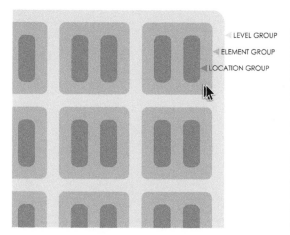

Figure 15.9 Two LOCATION groups within each of the ELEMENT groups within each of the LEVEL groups.

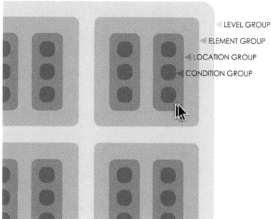

Figure 15.10 Three CONDITION groups within each of the LOCATION groups within each of the ELEMENT groups within each of the LEVEL groups.

Inside each of the LOCATION groups, you will add three CONDITION groups, one to hold new entities, one to hold existing entities, and one to hold demolished entities (Figure 15.10).

Inside CONDITION groups is where you will add edges, surfaces, and objects (Figure 15.11). Because groups are invisible containers, the best way to build a model is to get after it—that is, just start modeling. Begin by grouping objects based on the layers that you added in Chapter 6, The Professional's SketchUp Template; these layers are also further described in the next section so you know what goes in each group.

You will need to select geometry and objects in order to create the groups. Build the walls, make a group. Add doors and windows, then

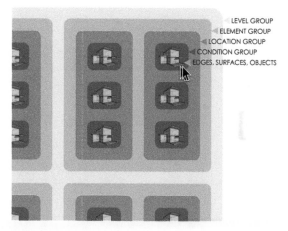

Figure 15.11 Edges, surfaces, and objects are held within each of the three CONDITION groups. This is the last level of organization for the default system.

put them each in their respective group. Add floors and ceilings, then put them each in their respective groups. Once you have a decent amount of the model built, select all the elements that make up the first level, and put them in a group. Take it from there (Figure 15.12).

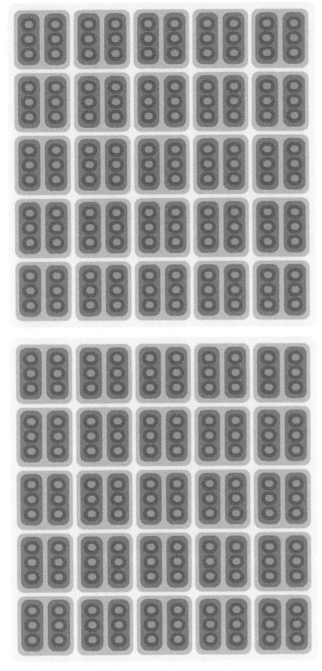

LEVEL GROUP

ELEMENT GROUP

LOCATION GROUP

CONDITION GROUP

EDGES, SURFACES, OBJECTS

Figure 15.12 The big idea.

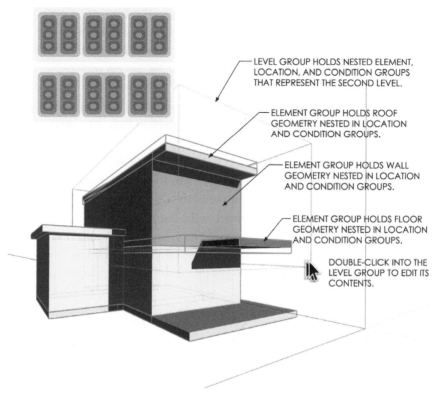

LEVEL GROUP HOLDS NESTED ELEMENT, LOCATION, AND CONDITION GROUPS THAT REPRESENT THE SECOND LEVEL.

ELEMENT GROUP HOLDS ROOF GEOMETRY NESTED IN LOCATION AND CONDITION GROUPS.

ELEMENT GROUP HOLDS WALL GEOMETRY NESTED IN LOCATION AND CONDITION GROUPS.

ELEMENT GROUP HOLDS FLOOR GEOMETRY NESTED IN LOCATION AND CONDITION GROUPS.

DOUBLE-CLICK INTO THE LEVEL GROUP TO EDIT ITS CONTENTS.

Figure 15.13 Group geometry and objects within each level based on the ELEMENT layers. For instance, roofs grouped together, walls grouped together, floors grouped together, etc. You will do this for all ELEMENT layers. Within each ELEMENT layer, the organization continues with LOCATION and CONDITION.

Let's use a simple model to illustrate the point. Figure 15.13 shows a simple two-level renovation composed of new and existing floors, walls, and a roof.

TIP You could use components just the same, but if an element is unique, not repeating, and the only one in the model, then there is no need for it to be a component. Components are better suited to objects, specifically repeating objects. Groups are better suited to overall model organization.

Layers

As you learned in Chapter 5, SketchUp Basics, layers control the visibility of entities in SketchUp; edges, surfaces, text, groups, components, section planes, and images can all have a layer applied to them. If an entity is on a layer that is not visible, the entity cannot be seen.

You can assign only one layer to each entity in SketchUp, but if the geometry is nested inside multiple groups, we can assign a layer to each of the nested groups, which ultimately controls the visibility of the geometry in the final nested group. We need nested groups primarily for the advanced layering that makes the entire SketchUp Workflow for Architecture and ConDoc System work.

TIP When I say *ELEMENT group,* I mean the group that has the ELEMENT layers applied to it. When I mention the *"LEVEL 01 group,"* I am referring to the group that has the LEVEL_01 layer applied to it.

We group entities per their LEVEL, ELEMENT, LOCATION, and CONDITION, but SketchUp doesn't know what these containers are. We need to assign layers to the nested groups (Figure 15.14). Layers are the container's nametags—they make the geometry a "roof," a "wall," or a "floor" so they will be displayed appropriately. The geometry contained in the last nested group will be visible only if all the nested layers are visible. For the following example, let's assume our model has two levels, and only the roof, walls, and floors as ELEMENTS. This will give us a simple example to test nested layer visibility.

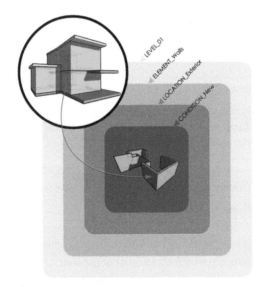

Figure 15.14 This Model Organization Diagram illustrates the new exterior walls on level 01 of the simple renovation project. If any of the layers in the chain are turned off, the walls can no longer be seen.

Let's explain what we created by assigning layers to nested groups, a series of switches to see the geometry. Like a light switch, all switches in the circuit must be on for the light to be visible (Figure 15.15). If any layer in the chain is turned off, the geometry will be invisible. Using our simplified renovation example, let's look at the walls to demonstrate the point. They are organized LEVEL_01 > ELEMENT_Walls > LOCATION_Exterior > CONDITION_New. If any one of these layers is turned off,

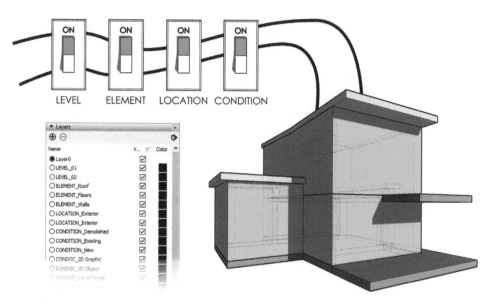

Figure 15.15 All nested layers must be visible to see the edges, surfaces, and objects within the final CONDITION group.

then the geometry that represents the walls will not be visible. If the LEVEL layer is turned off, then all other nested groups cannot be seen, regardless of whether their ELEMENT, LOCATION, or CONDITION layers are visible (Figure 15.16).

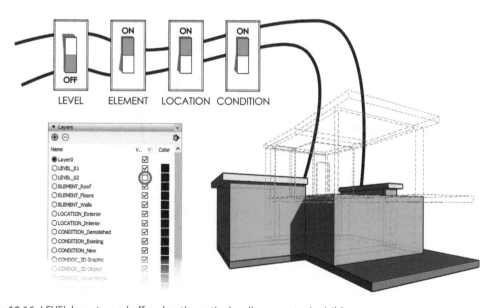

Figure 15.16 LEVEL layer turned off makes the entire level's geometry invisible.

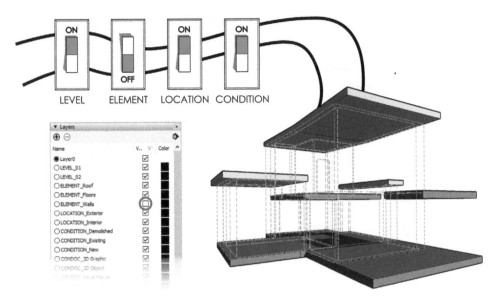

Figure 15.17 ELEMENT layer turned off makes that geometry invisible in all levels.

If an ELEMENT layer is turned off, then all groups within it will be invisible throughout each LEVEL (Figure 15.17).

If a LOCATION layer is turned off, then all groups within it will be invisible throughout each ELEMENT within each LEVEL. This is how the Interior and Exterior utility scenes peel away the exterior of a model so quickly and easily (Figure 15.18).

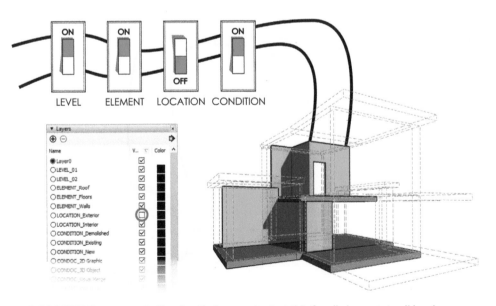

Figure 15.18 LOCATION layer turned off makes that geometry invisible for all elements in all levels.

If a CONDITION layer is turned off, then all groups within it will be invisible throughout each LOCA-TION within each ELEMENT within each LEVEL (Figure 15.19).

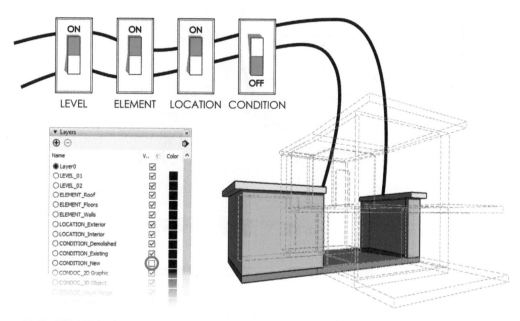

Figure 15.19 CONDITION layer turned off makes that geometry invisible in all levels.

Ultimately, if you put everything in the right place (Figure 15.20), you can use layers to control visibility with full control. This is what enables hatching, line weights, and consultant exports. The entire system runs on this concept of nesting groups with layers.

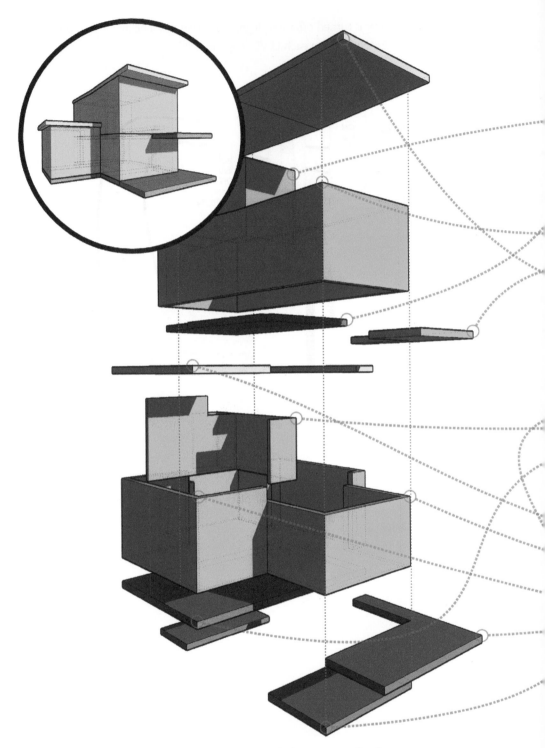

Figure 15.20 Place geometry in the correct group with the corresponding layer.

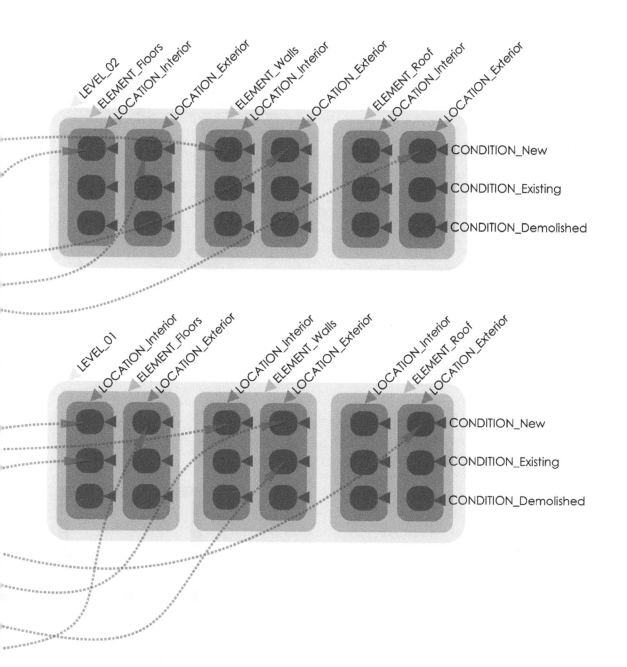

TIP Paste in place is a more powerful paste; it is used to move an entity from one group to another. Simply cut as usual, then navigate to the proper group, and choose Edit > Paste in place.

TSWFA/ConDoc Default Layers

The following section contains a detailed explanation of each of the layers included with the core system and a description of the group they are applied to and suggested contents. You will find this to be a great reference while you are in the early stages of organizing a model. These layers are the keystone of the SketchUp Workflow for Architecture, as well as the default layers used by the ConDoc Tools. There are five categories of layers: LEVEL, ELEMENT, LOCATION, CONDITION, and CONDOC.

LEVEL Layers

Level layers are simple and straightforward; they describe the stories of a building. LEVEL layers are the first level of model organization (Figure 15.21), holding all the subsequent nested groups for the respective levels: Level 01, Level 02, Level 03. These layers are automatically added by ConDoc Tools Plan Generator, but you can also create them manually (Figure 15.22). Levels are necessary to break a model apart into coherent plans.

ELEMENT Layers

ELEMENT layers are applied to the next nested group (Figure 15.23)—they can be thought of as nouns, whereas the other layers are more like adjectives. Elements are the pieces of a building that complete your design (Figure 15.24). Listed are the ELEMENT layers.

Figure 15.21 LEVEL layers are the first level of nesting.

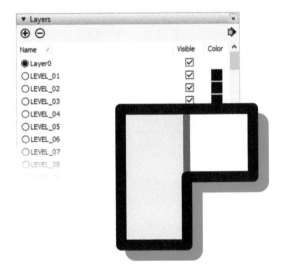

Figure 15.22 LEVEL layers can be added manually or automated for each project using the ConDoc Plan Generator.

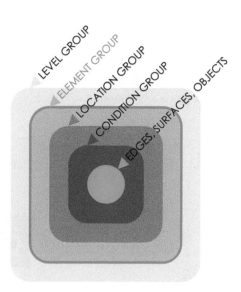

Figure 15.23 ELEMENT layers are the second level of nesting.

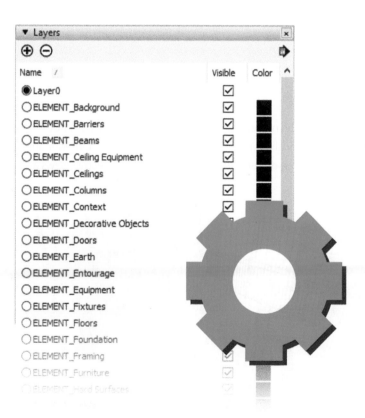

Figure 15.24 ELEMENT layers can be added manually, included in a template, or automated by the ConDoc Configurator.

ELEMENT_Background

The Background layer is applied to the nested group that holds all sketches, field measurements, and CAD imports for drawing on top of. These entities can be imported images, separate groups on Layer0, or loose geometry. Anything that drives your design is a background.

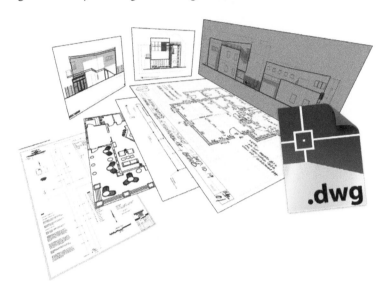

ELEMENT_Barriers

The Barriers layer is applied to the nested group that holds anything that is not necessarily a wall but that gets in the way. Think retaining walls, fences, planters, and railings, both interior and exterior. These objects are best represented using a three-dimensional (3D) object for perspective views and two-dimensional (2D) graphics for plan views.

ELEMENT_Beams

The Beams layer is applied to the group that holds components that represent the beams that hold up your design. Beams can be wood, steel, concrete—anything structural. These objects are best represented using a 3D object for perspective views and 2D graphics for plan views.

ELEMENT_Ceiling Equipment

The Ceiling Equipment layer is applied to the nested group that holds objects that are attached to the ceiling. For instance, fans, HVAC ducts, and sprinklers. These objects are best represented using a 3D object for perspective views and 2D graphics for plan views.

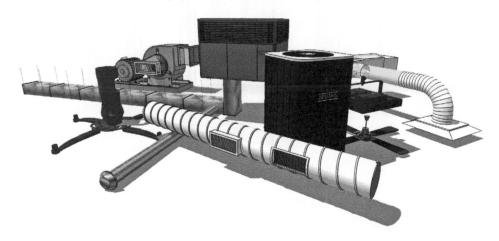

ELEMENT_Ceilings

The Ceilings layer is applied to the nested group that holds all edges and surfaces that represent ceilings. Ceilings are built down from the floor group in the level above. Even though a soffit technically has a vertical wall, it still belongs in the ceilings layer.

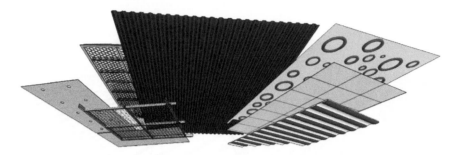

ELEMENT_Columns

The Columns layer is applied to the group that holds components that represent the columns that hold up your design—usually steel, concrete, or wood posts—sometimes exposed, sometimes buried in a wall. These objects are best represented using a 3D object for perspective views and 2D graphics for plan views.

ELEMENT_Context

The Context layer is applied to the nested group that holds all models of surrounding buildings that are worth noting. This could be detailed buildings to play off of in design or even rough block buildings to describe a cityscape. These buildings are made by geo-modeling techniques, downloaded from the 3D Warehouse or from FormFonts.

ELEMENT_Decorative Objects

The Decorative Objects layer is applied to the nested group that holds any object that breathes life into a scene. These objects will show up in perspective views and on the RENDER and VR scene tabs, but typically not in plan, section, and elevation. For instance, magazines on a coffee table, candles on the dining room table, or a bottle of wine in the kitchen. Because decorative objects are not used in plans, they do not need a 2D graphic and 3D object.

ELEMENT_Doors

The Doors layer is applied to the nested group that holds objects representing doors. Doors must be represented by a 2D graphic and 3D object in order to render properly in plan.

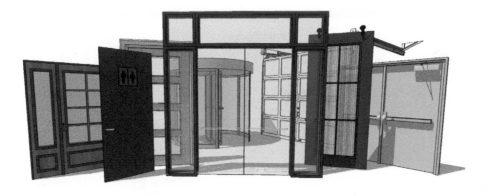

ELEMENT_Earth

The Earth layer is applied to the nested group that holds edges and surfaces representing soft ground including grass, mulch, and dirt.

ELEMENT_Entourage

The Entourage layer is applied to the nested group that holds objects representing people, animals, and action in general that bring life to a scene. This is different from decorative objects because you often want the people turned off in SketchUp but still render decorative objects in your rendering program.

ELEMENT_Equipment

The Equipment layer is applied to the nested group that holds objects that represent appliances, HVAC units, electrical boxes, and utilities. These objects are best represented using a 3D object for perspective views and 2D graphics for plan views.

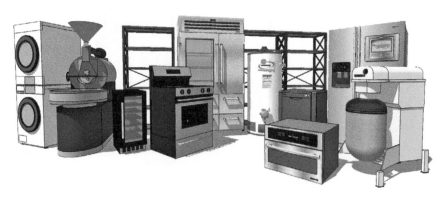

ELEMENT_Fixtures

The Fixtures layer is applied to the nested group that holds all objects that represent plumbing fixtures, millwork, sinks, vanities, cabinets, and built-ins—anything that you would have fabricated. These objects are best represented using a 3D object for perspective views and 2D graphics for plan views.

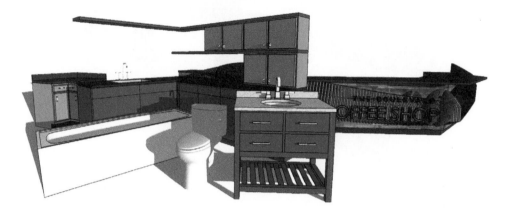

ELEMENT_Floors

The Floors layer is applied to the nested group that holds edges and surfaces that represent the floors of a building or house. You can divide the floor surface to paint different floor materials. The floor should be represented by a mass that stretches to the extents of the framing. Usually the floor framing is completely hidden by the floor ELEMENT.

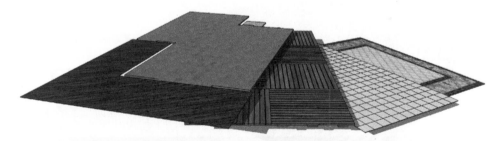

ELEMENT_Foundation

The Foundation layer is applied to the group that holds edges and surfaces that represent the footings, stem walls, and steel that support a structure. If needed, a foundation can be represented using a 3D object for perspective views and 2D graphics for plan views. Usually, a concrete slab belongs on the floor layer.

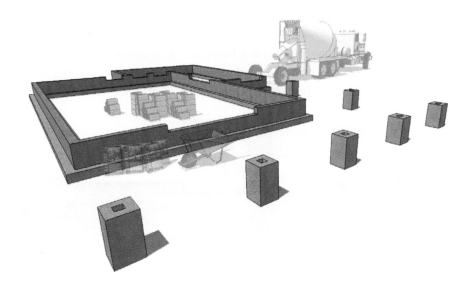

ELEMENT_Framing

The Framing layer is applied to the group that holds components that represent the minor structural framing that holds up your design. All two-bys, floor joists, and rafters belong on the framing layer. Framing is typically not seen, wrapped in drywall, buried underneath a floor, and covered by the roof ELEMENT. These objects are best represented using a 3D object for perspective views and 2D graphics for plan views.

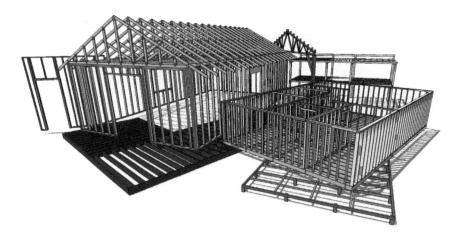

ELEMENT_Furniture

The Furniture layer is applied to the group that holds objects that represent chairs, beds, tables, and couches. These objects are best represented using a 3D object for perspective views and 2D graphics for plan views.

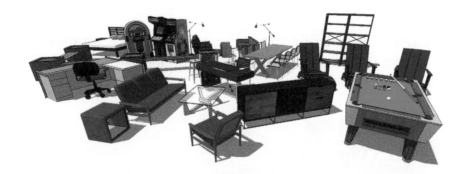

ELEMENT_Hard Surfaces

The Hard Surfaces layer is applied to the group that holds edges and surfaces that represent roads, side-walks, and patios—anything that is paved or poured outside of the house.

ELEMENT_Lights

The Lights layer is applied to the group that holds objects that represent all can lights, sconces, and chandeliers—anything that is hardwired in. A lamp typically belongs on the Decorative Objects layer, or possibly the Furniture layer if you need it to show up in the furniture plan. These objects are best represented using a 3D object for perspective views and 2D graphics for plan views.

ELEMENT_Roof

The Roof layer is applied to the group that holds edges and surfaces that represent a roof. A complex roof is best represented using a 3D object for perspective views and 2D graphics for plan views. The roof ELE-MENT usually covers the framing ELEMENTS.

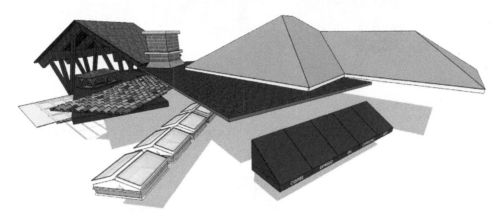

ELEMENT_Stairs

The Stairs layer is applied to the group that holds edges and surfaces that represent stairs. The stairs are usually best represented using a 3D object for perspective views and 2D graphics for plan views.

ELEMENT_Trim

The Trim layer holds geometry that represents decorative trim pieces—for instance, baseboard, fascia boards, window trim, and crown molding. Exterior trim and gutters can also be placed within this group.

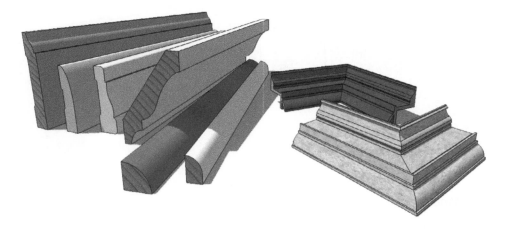

ELEMENT_Vegetation

The Vegetation layer is applied to the group that holds all objects representing trees, shrubs, and flowers. These objects are best represented using a 3D object for perspective views and 2D graphics for plan views.

ELEMENT_Walls

The Walls layer is applied to the group that holds the edges and surfaces that represent the walls in your design.

ELEMENT_Windows

The Windows layer is applied to the group that holds components that represent the windows in your design. These objects are best represented using a 3D object for perspective views and 2D graphics for plan views. The 2D graphic should cover the inside face to outside face of the wall to properly mask out wall hatches that will be stacked below.

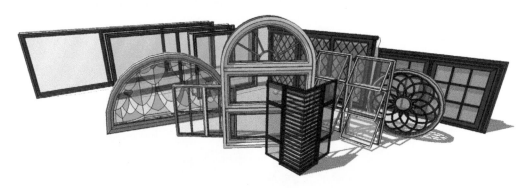

LOCATION Layers

LOCATION layers are third in line for nesting (Figure 15.25). They are used as adjectives that further explain the ELEMENT groups. These layers are assigned to the groups within groups that have ELEMENT layers. They add another switch in the chain to further control the visibility of geometry. You will make the decision whether an element is an interior element or an exterior element. If there is no clear answer, you probably don't need to assign a location (see "Simplify the System" later in this chapter).

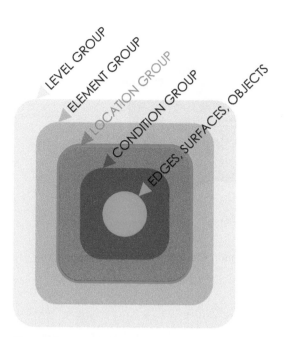

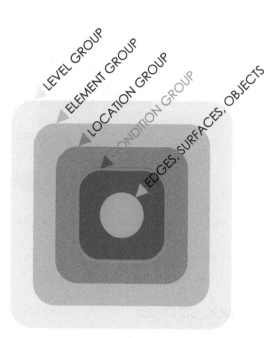

Figure 15.25 LOCATION layers are the third level of nesting.

Figure 15.26 CONDITION layers are always the last level of nesting.

CONDITION LAYERS

CONDITION layers further describe ELEMENT layers. They are always last in line for nested groups and layering (Figure 15.26). These layers are applied to a group within each of the CONDITION groups. CONDITION layers describe entities that are new or being added to the project; entities that exist in the project that are to remain; and entities that exist in the project that are to be removed, relocated, or destroyed.

CONDOC Layers

The ConDoc layers are needed to make the whole system tick and ultimately help you achieve your desired look for drawings and renderings. They are more conceptual and abstract in nature, relating more to 3D modeling than the actual built environment.

CONDOC_Always Off

The CONDOC_Always Off layer is used to visually combine two groups (Figure 15.27). This is one exception to the all-geometry-on-Layer0 rule. This layer is turned off in almost every scene. Learn more about this in Chapter 21, Crucial Concepts for Construction Documents.

CONDOC_2D Graphic

A 2D graphic is used to force a specific symbol in the final plan drawings. If you are using a 2D graphic, you must have a 3D object as well. 2D graphics will be turned on in all plan views but turned off in

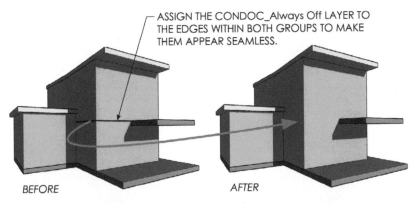

ASSIGN THE CONDOC_Always Off LAYER TO THE EDGES WITHIN BOTH GROUPS TO MAKE THEM APPEAR SEAMLESS.

BEFORE *AFTER*

Figure 15.27 Elevation where a line is removed. Use the simple diagram.

sections, elevations, and perspective views. Learn more about this in Chapter 21, Crucial Concepts for Construction Documents. See Figure 15.28.

CONDOC_3D Object

A 3D object is the real-world representation of an object. If you are using a 3D object, you must have a 2D graphic to accompany it (Figure 15.28). 3D objects will be turned off in all plan views but visible in all sections, elevations, and perspectives. Learn more about this in Chapter 21, Crucial Concepts for Construction Documents.

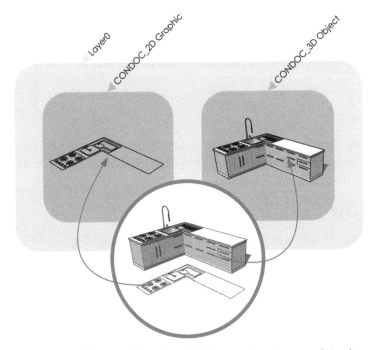

Figure 15.28 Typical grouping and layering of an object that does not render properly in plan.

CONDOC_ Draft Layers

The DRAFT layers are used specifically for ConDoc DRAFT mode, where the DRAFT layers become active. Lines are shown in a line weight–by–layer color view (Figure 15.29). This is very similar to 2D CAD.

The stock DRAFT layers give you five line weights plus one hatch layer. This is usually sufficient for drafting 2D details and diagrams. You must use the Detail tool to snapshot views. Learn more about ConDoc DRAFT mode in Chapter 23, Drawings.

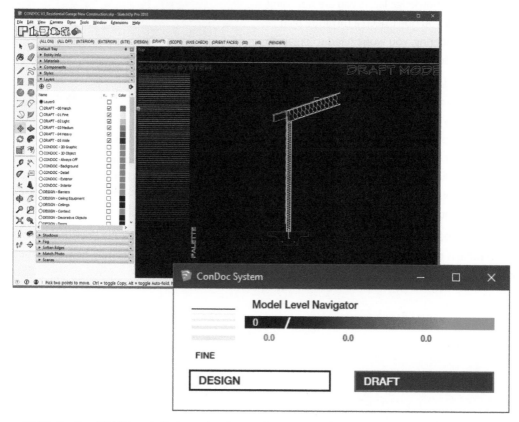

Figure 15.29 ConDoc DRAFT mode limits navigation to 2D panning and zooming. Lines are shown by layer colors, which correspond to line weights in LayOut, similar to traditional 2D CAD.

SIMPLIFY THE SYSTEM

Although there is value in predictability and doing things the same way for every project when you're learning, you can begin to cut corners once you have a full understanding of the core system. The following tips will save advanced users a lot of time and complexities in model organization:

☑ Eliminate LEVEL layers all together. For instance, if you don't have multiple levels, why bother calling out the first floor as Level 01? For single-story projects, there is no need to use LEVEL layers (Figure 15.30).

☑ Use only the ELEMENT layers that you need; simply disregard those that you don't. For example, maybe you are creating a simple, quick drawing that needs only walls, doors, and windows. Disregard everything else. You can leave them in your model just in case it develops further, but there is no need to acknowledge layers you are not using. For instance, if you don't need a furniture plan or interior rendering, you won't need to organize and layer the furniture groups.

☑ Eliminate the LOCATION layers that you don't need because there is nothing to compare them to (Figure 15.31). For instance, windows are typically all exterior, so why call them exterior if there are no interior windows to call out? This happens often with ELEMENT_Context, ELEMENT_Earth, ELEMENT_Foundation, ELEMENT_Hard Surfaces, ELEMENT_Roof, and ELEMENT_Vegetation.

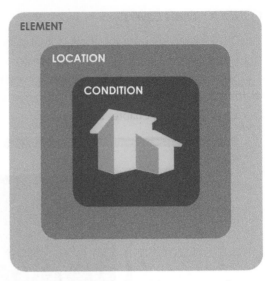

Figure 15.30 Simplified model organization for a one-level new construction project; there is no need to identify the level because there is only one and nothing else to compare it to.

☑ Eliminate CONDITION layers for new construction projects (Figure 15.32). Why call elements new when there is nothing existing or demolished to compare them to? When creating new construction projects, eliminate the CONDITION layers.

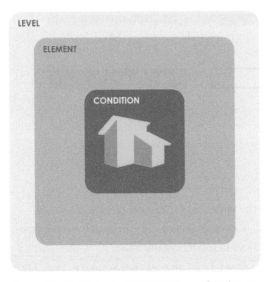

Figure 15.31 Eliminate LOCATION layers for objects that are "exterior" by default.

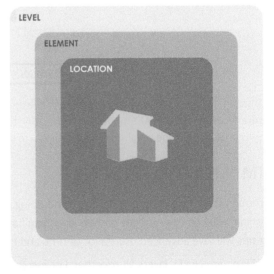

Figure 15.32 When organizing a new construction project, there is no need for new, existing, and demolished.

☑ Only model what you need. If you don't need a 3D rendering of the interior, consider just drawing simple masses or, even simpler, flat rectangles for cabinets and 2D symbols for fixtures such as toilets and sinks rather than including their more detailed 3D objects.

☑ If an object renders properly in plan, then it does not need a 3D object and 2D graphic configuration.

EXPAND THE SYSTEM

The SketchUp Workflow for Architecture can be expanded to work with any project type, level of complexity, and building typology. Stick with the same techniques for model organization and nesting, but you can add additional nested groups and additional layers to further describe your project.

For instance, you could use another descriptor to define wall types in your project. The nesting would look like Figure 15.33.

Notice that the CONDITION layers still come at the very end of the organization to ensure the scope diagram functions properly. In order to describe wall types, you will need to add corresponding TYPE layers to your model: TYPE_A, TYPE_B, TYPE_C.

Adding a wall type nested group and layer allows you to further describe the walls in your project. For instance, rather than hatching interior and exterior walls, or new and existing, you could choose to hatch wall types. This will better sync with a wall type schedule and details, and it will more clearly describe the construction.

Let's build on what we have and expand the system further to handle phased construction with wall types (Figure 15.34).

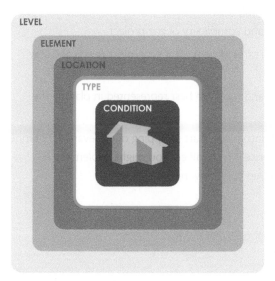

Figure 15.33 Expanding the system to include a wall type description.

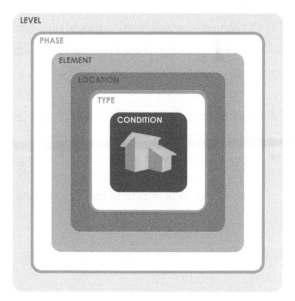

Figure 15.34 Expanding the system to include project phasing in addition to a wall type description.

In order to describe phased construction, you will need to add corresponding PHASE layers to your model: PHASE_I, PHASE_II, PHASE_III. Let's expand the system even further to handle multiple buildings with multiple units, phased construction with several options, and wall types.

In order to describe all of these additional descriptors, you will need to add corresponding BUILDING, UNIT, and OPTION layers to your model: BUILDING_01, BUILDING_02, BUILDING_03, UNIT_A, UNIT_B, UNIT_C, OPTION_1, OPTION_2, OPTION_3.

This is the most complex I could think of, though not the limit, and probably not a likely scenario. Just know that you are unlimited with this system. This scenario takes the system to the max and is unlikely to happen. If you are adding several buildings to your model, you most likely aren't concerned about granular details such as units, phases, and wall types. If you are designing multiple buildings, you likely will not be including any of the interior ELEMENT layers. Most likely you aren't pulling furniture plans out of this model—but you could.

It's endless how extremely complex you can get with your model organization. Imagine, for example, how a retail campus would break down into several buildings, each with several multilevel shops, all with their own interior and exterior spaces. Most likely you will have a one-level strip mall—that's easy! Put in the effort to understand the system as a whole and at its most extreme level. This way, the more realistic scenarios are easy—they will just flow without interruption.

CHAPTER POINTS

☑ Rigidly stick with the system and you will be less likely to mess up.

☑ Once you have mastered the beast, make it your own.

☑ Cut corners when additional organization is not necessary.

☑ Add or subtract layers based on your needs, industry, and complexity of the project.

☑ When you expand the system, ideally simplify it at the same time to fit your project needs and stay efficient.

☑ Major building elements such as walls, floors, ceilings, and roofs are best represented in plan by the geometry that makes them.

☑ Often it is best to work in 3D, then as the design falls into place, start swapping out relevant 2D graphics. For instance, you will design your roof in 3D, but once it is solidified, you might implement 2D graphics and 3D objects to further describe and clean up your drawing.

Chapter 16
New Construction

N
ow that you are armed with the skills for meticulous model organization, let's work through an entire new construction project from front to back. New construction is a little easier than a renovation project, and we are going to be working with the easiest—a single-level new construction.

Keep in mind that this chapter is best leveraged as a reference. Read it through, watch the video on the chapter 16 page at **brightmandesigns.com/TSWFA/ch16**, then go off on your own projects. When you get in a pinch, just refer to these pages.

NEW CONSTRUCTION PROCESS

It is always best to start at the drafting table, come up with an idea, then produce it on the computer. It's hard to be creative when you have to use a keyboard and mouse. Don't be quick to go straight to the computer; it's okay to figure it out with pencil and paper, then produce and refine the design on the computer, and work back and forth between the two.

A successful new construction story/scenario:

☑ Starts with a sketch, evolves to a scaled drawing of a light computer-aided design (CAD) sketch, or moves to the drafting table. Scan the drawing, or draft it in two-dimensional (2D) CAD.

☑ Is imported as a CAD drawing or as a scanned hand sketch into SketchUp.

☑ Begins to model elements of the building, as well as groups and layers. Model organization should begin early and often. See Chapter 15, Model Organization Overview.

☑ Geo-locates the site to import site imagery and topography, as well as searches for nearby buildings, shown later in this chapter.

☑ Uses Match Photo to fill in missing buildings with geo-models, shown later in this chapter.

- ☑ Runs ConDoc Plan Generator to create colorful plan for client presentations, or it makes scenes described in Chapter 23, Drawings.

- ☑ Uses the early model to create renderings and animations and explore designs in virtual reality (VR). (See Part V, Visualization.)

- ☑ Further develops design based on client feedback. Runs ConDoc Plan Generator or creates scenes as described in Chapter 23, Drawings.

- ☑ Creates a schematic design presentation or construction documents by dragging and dropping Con-Doc drawings, or stacking viewports, as described in Chapter 23, Drawings.

- ☑ Adds pre-built scrapbook annotations of text, labels, and dimensions to further describe the drawings and diagrams, as described in Chapter 24, Annotations.

- ☑ Prints drawings, sketches over, then goes back to the computer to revise, as described in Chapter 25, Exporting.

- ☑ Stamps the set, submits for permits, and starts building.

In this chapter, we are going to focus on model organization; in later chapters, you will visualize and document the design.

THE BLVD COFFEE SHOP PROJECT

The new construction project is a proposed coffee house (Figure 16.1) in Denver's RiNo district (short for River North). RiNo is in the middle of a massive transformation, with old warehouses turning into breweries and restaurants and shops popping up everywhere. There is a grittier flavor to the area. Street art is not only allowed but also encouraged. The alleys are lined with beautiful, larger-than-life murals.

We are proposing a coffee shop on the corner of 28th and Larimer Street. The coffee shop will have a bar, a roaster, and some casual interior and exterior seating. In addition to the coffee program, there will be an in-house artist space with storage and a gallery. It's a full program in a tight space—a great example of new construction.

Assume, for this project, you already have CAD drawings. The design was already completed in 2D CAD, but now it's time to make it a real three-dimensional (3D) model. This is also a common workflow for visualization projects.

Our proposed site was chosen for its location next to existing buildings and its visibility on Larimer. The focus of this chapter is to understand the process and model organization; you will create the drawings later in Part VI, Construction Documents.

TIP The proposed coffee shop is also used for SketchUp for Professionals Advanced. You will actually build the full project in SketchUp for Professionals Advanced, including advanced modeling of complex geometry, furniture, light fixtures, and the bar and sign, as well as advanced texturing.

You can download all these files and follow along at **brightmandesigns.com/TSWFA/ch16**.

Figure 16.1 The BLVD Coffee Shop.

The Project Site

A good designer will respect, or at least consider, the context surrounding their building. In this section, we will import site imagery and topography, then locate building context and make some of our own using Match Photo. Use the following techniques to import the site and building context.

To define the site, follow these steps:

1. Start a new model by opening SketchUp, or click on the File drop-down menu and select New.

2. Click on the File drop-down and choose Geo-location, Add Location to geo-locate the model.

3. Enter 28th St and Larimer St, Denver, CO, in the search bar, and zoom in several clicks to locate the site, as shown in Figure 16.2.

4. Click the Select Region button.

5. Position the pins around the site, as shown in Figure 16.3.

6. Click the Grab button to import the selected site.

7. The Location Snapshot (flat) is shown. Right-click on the imported image and choose unlock. Assign the ELEMENT_Earth layer in the Entity Info dialog, then turn off the layer visibility in the Layers dialog.

Figure 16.2 The proposed context zone and building site.

Figure 16.3 Using the Add Location dialog, select the site with pins.

8. Turn on the location terrain layer, right-click on the terrain and choose unlock, then delete the terrain. We will assume this site is flat and use only the location snapshot.

9. In the layers dialog, turn the ELEMENT_Earth layer visibility on, then delete the Location Snapshot and Location Terrain layers.

Finding Nearby Buildings

Instead of spending hours trying to measure and build your own context models, find someone else's. Geo-located models uploaded to 3D Warehouse are searchable and available for download through the Components browser. Once a location is attached to your model, you will be able to find other buildings that are close to your site in the Nearby Models collection. To do that, follow these steps:

1. To open the Components browser, click on the Window drop-down menu and choose Default Tray, Components.

2. In the Components browser, click on the Collections drop-down menu and choose Nearby Models (Figure 16.4). Remember: This collection is available only after a model has been geo-located.

3. Click on the thumbnail icon to immediately download a model directly into the current SketchUp model. Find and import the models indicated in Figure 16.5. These are the nearby models that are geo-located and modeled to an acceptable quality.

4. If needed, double-click on each of the context building models, click on the Edit drop-down menu, and choose Unhide > All. The lines you need to create a complete building elevation line drawing will appear. Also, unlock and delete the 3D terrain and aerial imagery in all the imported context models if they are included. The most current and accurate terrain is already imported into your model (Figure 16.6).

5. Select all of the imported context model, right-click on the selection and choose make group. Now, assign the ELEMENT_Context layer to the group.

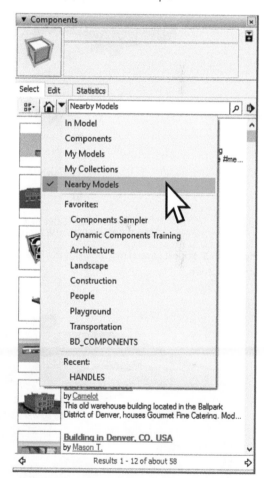

Figure 16.4 The Nearby Models collection is available in the Component Collections drop-down menu.

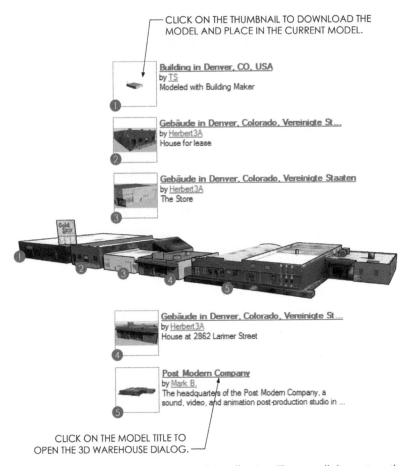

CLICK ON THE THUMBNAIL TO DOWNLOAD THE
MODEL AND PLACE IN THE CURRENT MODEL.

Building in Denver, CO, USA
by TS
Modeled with Building Maker

Gebäude in Denver, Colorado, Vereinigte St...
by Herbert 3A
House for lease

Gebäude in Denver, Colorado, Vereinigte Staaten
by Herbert 3A
The Store

Gebäude in Denver, Colorado, Vereinigte St...
by Herbert 3A
House at 2862 Larimer Street

Post Modern Company
by Mark B.
The headquarters of the Post Modern Company, a
sound, video, and animation post-production studio in ...

CLICK ON THE MODEL TITLE TO
OPEN THE 3D WAREHOUSE DIALOG.

Figure 16.5 Import several models from the Nearby Models collection. They are all shown together, not in their actual location.

Figure 16.6 The final site with context models.

PlaceMaker

Another source for gathering context is by using PlaceMaker to import the roads, trees, context building footprints, and even higher-resolution imagery. Once PlaceMaker context is imported (Figure 16.7), delete the generic buildings that overlay the more detailed buildings, move the rest into the ELEMENT_Context container, and assign Layer0 to all objects within.

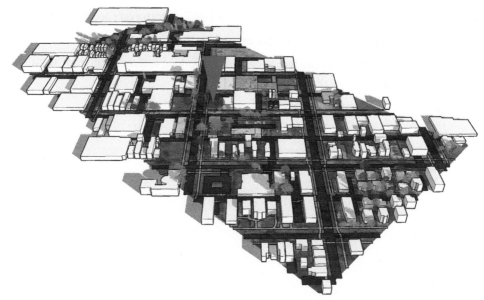

Figure 16.7 PlaceMaker will import roads, paths, buildings, and high-resolution imagery.

Geo-modeling

If you don't find everything you need in the Nearby Models collection or in PlaceMaker, you can always build models yourself.

Match Photo is a SketchUp feature that allows you to reverse engineer the perspective of a photograph to trace a 2D image and ultimately produce a 3D model. You may have completed a studio project in college where you enlarged a photograph on a copy machine, taped it to your desk, and then used a T-square to project the vanishing points onto your neighbor's desk. Then you used those points to trace the rest of the photograph and generate new designs with the same perspective. SketchUp allows you to do the same thing in a much more efficient digital interface.

The photograph is taped to your digital desk in SketchUp as an image file import. The T-square to trace the photograph and project the vanishing points is replaced with the axes bars in the Match Photo interface. Your pencil is replaced with SketchUp's Drawing and Edit tools.

Once Match Photo is set up, the process can be as easy as tracing a 2D photograph with the Drawing tools to create a 3D model. In the following exercise, you will leverage Match Photo by combining a properly scaled building footprint imported from Open Street Maps with a perspective photograph to create an accurate and detailed 3D SketchUp model.

Photographing a Building

When you're taking photographs to use in Match Photo, keep the following tips in mind:

- ☑ Do not use any special lenses on your camera. A typical, inexpensive camera or even a phone camera will work just fine.

- ☑ Walk around the entire site, and photograph the entire building from every angle possible (Figure 16.8).

- ☑ Photograph the building's details up close—for example, signs, materials, entries, windows, and doors.

- ☑ Too many pictures are better than too few. When you're working at 2 a.m., you don't want to be wishing you had shot more.

- ☑ Do not crop or resize the images before you import them into SketchUp.

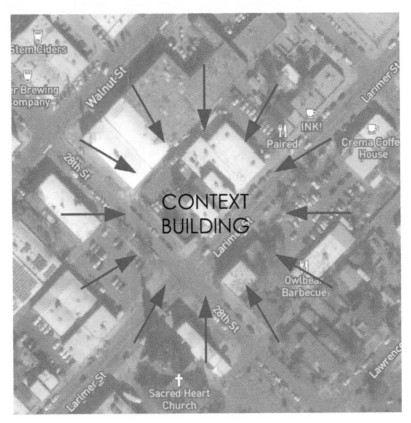

Figure 16.8 Photograph from every angle.

Figure 16.9 Opening view of the demo model.

Open Demonstration Model

Open the provided demonstration model now with the site all buttoned up so that you are closely aligned with what you see in the text. All the context is in place, except the building next door (Figure 16.9).

Creating a Mass Model

To create a building mass model, follow these steps:

1. For now, hide the other context models. To do this, right-click on the Context container and choose Hide. You could also uncheck the layer visibility for the ELEMENT_Context layer.

2. We need to shift our axes using our 45 utility scene because this part of town is shifted off the north/south grid.

3. Activate the Rectangle tool, and click once on the bottom-left corner of the building footprint.

4. Move your cursor away from the start point, and click again on the top-right corner of the building footprint to finish the rectangle (Figure 16.10). There is no need for precise dimensions on this geo-model.

5. Use the Push/Pull tool to extrude the rectangle up to an exaggerated height as shown in Figure 16.11.

6. Set the origin at an appropriate starting point for sketching. For this model, and most

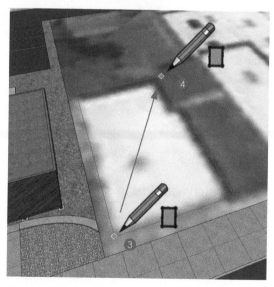

Figure 16.10 Use the Rectangle tool to trace the building footprint.

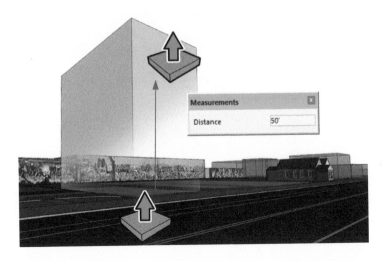

Figure 16.11 The photograph and the SketchUp model shown in similar views.

others, set the axes at the front-bottom corner of the model when viewing the model from a vantage point similar to the Match Photo photograph.

7. Within SketchUp, position yourself in a view similar to the photograph you are using for Match Photo. The Position Camera tool is helpful for this (Figure 16.12).

Using Match New Photo

To use the Match Photo interface, follow these steps:

1. Click on the Camera drop-down menu, and choose Match New Photo.

2. Navigate to your Project Files folder and select the Match Photo image: `BD_BLVD Coffee Shop - Context 01.jpg`. Click on Open to return to SketchUp; an admittedly intimidating grid will appear over the photograph. Take a moment to study the image in Figure 16.13.

Figure 16.12 Set the origin at the front-bottom corner of the building based on the photograph you are using for Match Photo.

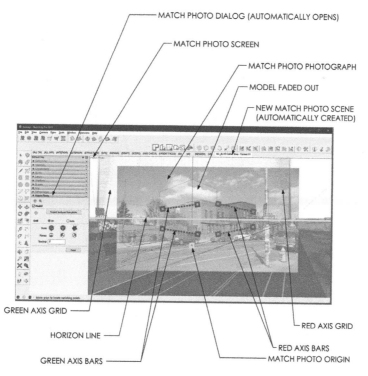

Figure 16.13 The Match Photo interface.Match Photo.

3. Navigate the Match Photo interface using familiar mouse navigation techniques. Push down and hold the scroll wheel button to pan the screen up, down, left, and right. Roll the scroll wheel toward the screen to zoom in and away from the screen to zoom out. Click outside of the Match Photo photograph to exit Match Photo mode.

TIP To get back to Match Photo mode, right-click on the automatically created Match Photo Scene tab and choose **Edit matched photo.**

4. In the Match Photo dialog box, uncheck the Model check box to turn off the model and clarify the Match Photo screen, which will make working with the Match Photo interface much easier.

5. Align the axis bars with parallel elements on the building, such as window headers and mullions, ledges, and roof lines. The green axis bars should be aligned with parallel elements on the west side of the building, and the red axis bars should be aligned with parallel elements on the south side of the building (Figure 16.14).

TIP Avoid using the ground plane as a parallel element because it will never be perfectly parallel with the building.

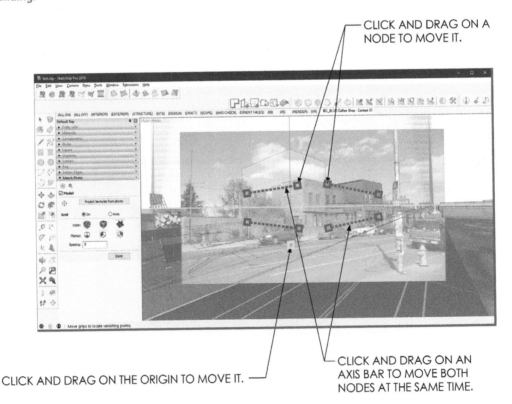

CLICK AND DRAG ON A NODE TO MOVE IT.

CLICK AND DRAG ON THE ORIGIN TO MOVE IT.

CLICK AND DRAG ON AN AXIS BAR TO MOVE BOTH NODES AT THE SAME TIME.

Figure 16.14 Manipulate the Match Photo axis bars and origin.

6. Position the Match Photo origin at an appropriate starting point for sketching (Figure 16.15). This will be at the same front-bottom corner you positioned the axes at in the beginning of the exercise.

7. In the Match Photo dialog, turn on the model visibility.

8. Zoom the Match Photo photograph to match the model by clicking and dragging on an axis until the vertical walls of the SketchUp model match the walls of the Match Photo photograph (Figure 16.16). The footprint is correct, which means the horizontal placement of the vertical walls is correct. The building height is not yet correct and should be ignored for now because it was drawn at an exaggerated height.

9. In the Match Photo dialog, click the Done button.

Setting Building Height

To accurately set the height of the building, follow these steps:

1. Orbit to a bird's-eye view. Activate the Push/Pull tool, and click once on the top of the building (Figure 16.17).

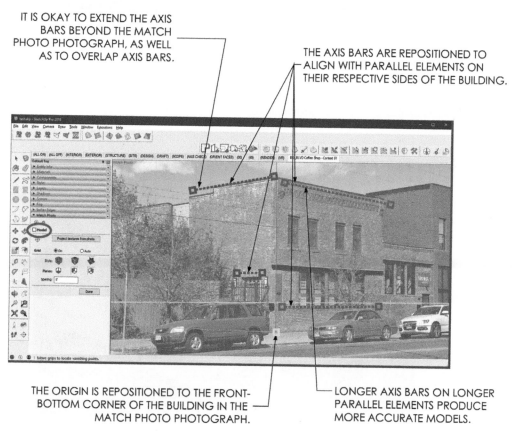

IT IS OKAY TO EXTEND THE AXIS BARS BEYOND THE MATCH PHOTO PHOTOGRAPH, AS WELL AS TO OVERLAP AXIS BARS.

THE AXIS BARS ARE REPOSITIONED TO ALIGN WITH PARALLEL ELEMENTS ON THEIR RESPECTIVE SIDES OF THE BUILDING.

THE ORIGIN IS REPOSITIONED TO THE FRONT-BOTTOM CORNER OF THE BUILDING IN THE MATCH PHOTO PHOTOGRAPH.

LONGER AXIS BARS ON LONGER PARALLEL ELEMENTS PRODUCE MORE ACCURATE MODELS.

Figure 16.15 The Match Photo axis bars and origin aligned with the Match Photo photograph.

CLICK AND DRAG ON ANY
AXIS TO ZOOM THE PHOTO.

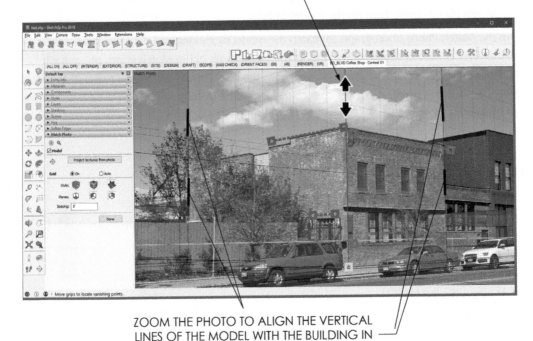

ZOOM THE PHOTO TO ALIGN THE VERTICAL
LINES OF THE MODEL WITH THE BUILDING IN
THE MATCH PHOTO PHOTOGRAPH.

Figure 16.16 Click and drag on any axis to zoom the photo.

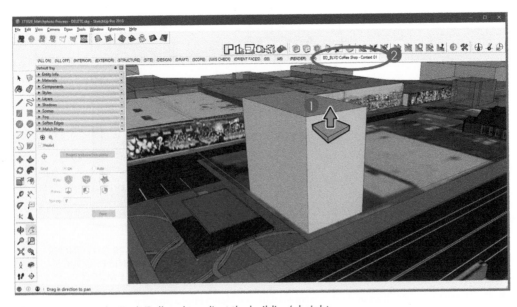

Figure 16.17 Use the Push/Pull tool to adjust the building's height.

Figure 16.18 Align the top of the model with the top of the building in the photograph.

2. Click on the Match Photo Scene tab to get back to Match Photo mode.

3. Move your cursor down until the top of the 3D building mass is aligned with the top of the building in the photograph (Figure 16.18). Click to finish the Push/Pull command.

4. Take a moment to orbit around and inspect the 3D mass model.

The building width and height are now accurately set. You know this because the building length and width are derived from the building footprint imported from Open Street Maps. The height of the building is accurately determined by reverse engineering a perspective photograph and aligning it with the known building footprint.

Adding 3D Detail

To add detail to your model, follow these steps:

1. Once again, click on the Match Photo scene tab at the top of your screen.

2. In the Match Photo dialog, click on Project Textures to apply the Match Photo photograph to the 3D surfaces. This is what makes a geo-model so "light." The detail is held in a photograph rather than represented by 3D geometry. There is no need to overwrite existing materials or trim partially visible faces.

3. Orbit to a 3D view, and then trace over the applied texture images using the SketchUp Drawing tools to create the major breaks in the facades.

4. Use the Modification tools to turn those breaks in the surfaces into further developed 3D details. Go back to the Match Photo scene to use the photograph as a guide for modeling. Draw from other photographs and your own experience when modeling.

Figure 16.19 Context model with added detail.

5. Using the Paint Bucket tool, hold the Alt key (Command on a Mac) to sample the Open Street Maps snapshot, then apply the Open Street Maps snapshot to the roof (Figure 16.19).

TIP For less important context buildings, this level of detail is completely acceptable. Usually, you will use the depth-of-field effect in Lumion to tune out the far-away context building's lack of detail.

Importing 2D Detail

Match Photo is best used to create the broad strokes of a model or the massing in general. Once a building mass is complete, you can use imported images to add high-resolution texture images where they are needed. Use the import image as material technique to replace low-resolution Match Photo materials with your high-resolution close-up photographs.

1. Zoom in on the front facade of the building.
2. Click on the File drop-down menu, and choose Import.
3. Verify that the Files of Type drop-down menu is set to All supported image types and the Texture radio button is on. Navigate to the class files folder for this chapter, and select BD_BLVD Coffee Shop - Context 02.jpg. Click the Import button.
4. Click once directly on the surface to place the image (Figure 16.20).
5. Move your cursor away from the start point to loosely scale the image; click again to finish the import. The image will repeat, or tile, across the surface.

Figure 16.20 Click directly on the surface. Avoid using edges and points when you initially place an image as a texture.

Tweaking a Texture

You can use the Texture Tweaker pins to fine-tune your texture images. Just follow these steps:

1. Right-click on the surface with the new image, and select Texture and then Position to modify the imported texture image.

2. Each of the Texture Tweaker fixed pins has a specific job for modifying the texture image. Click once on a pin to pick it up, and click again to put it down. Reposition the four pins on the four corners of the front facade in the photograph shown in Figure 16.21.

3. Click and drag the red pin to the bottom-left corner of the front facade in the model. This will move the entire texture image (Figure 16.22).

4. Click and drag the green pin to the bottom-right corner of the front facade in the model. This will properly scale and rotate the image to align with the model (Figure 16.22).

Figure 16.21 Click on the pins to reposition them as shown.

Figure 16.22 Click and drag the pins as shown to tweak the texture image.

5. Click and drag the blue pin to the top-left corner of the front facade in the model. This will properly scale and shear the image to further align with the model (Figure 16.22).

6. Click and drag the yellow pin to the top-right corner of the front facade in the model. This will properly distort the image so that it fits the entry wall perfectly (Figure 16.22).

7. Press the Enter key to finish the Texture Tweak and apply the changes (Figure 16.23).

Figure 16.23 The final texture tweaked image is clearer than the original Match Photo image.

TIP Another way to remove unwanted objects from a texture image is to use an external image editor. Right-click on a surface with a texture applied to it, and select Texture > Edit Texture Image. This will open the texture image in the assigned image editor.

Making Unique Materials

The Make Unique Material feature allows you to find a good chunk of one material and make another unique material from that. You can apply the new, optimized material to the rest of the model, eliminating trees, shadows, and low-resolution texture images (Figure 16.24).

1. Draw a rectangle around a piece of the brick with the least amount of trees, shadows, and objects. A projected texture image's quality will be best toward the foreground of the Match Photo image (Figure 16.25).

2. Right-click in the rectangle, and select Make Unique Texture. This will create a new material cropped to the extents of the rectangle.

3. Activate the Paint Bucket tool. Hold down the Alt key (Command on a Mac), and click on the new unique material to sample it, making it the current material.

4. To apply the new, optimized material, click on surfaces that have a lower-resolution texture image. At this point you can delete the rectangle.

UNDESIRABLE TREES

UNDESIRABLE SITE OBJECTS

Figure 16.24 Use the Make Unique Material function to clean up unwanted objects in the texture image.

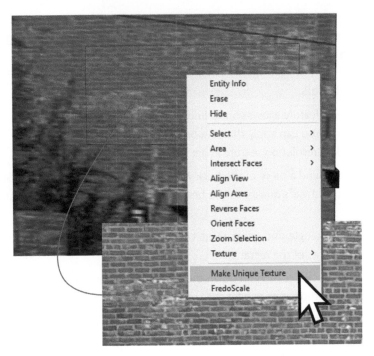

Figure 16.25 The "best" portion of the brick material is captured in a rectangle.

Another benefit to making a material unique is that you eliminate pieces of images that are not being used, resulting in smaller file sizes.

5. Right-click on the front-entry wall texture image, and select Make Unique Material. You won't see a difference in your model, but everything in the image that is not shown on the surface will be deleted.

TIP Right-click on a surface, and choose Texture > Edit Texture Image. Use the Clone Stamp tool in Adobe Photoshop to reduce the repetitious patterns and work out the final small details, such as tree branches and power lines.

Continue to use the import texture image and make unique texture strategies to further develop and add detail to the context model (Figure 16.26).

Model Organization

Now you need to put this context model in the proper ELEMENT_Context group. To properly organize the model, follow these steps:

1. Triple-click on the new model to select all connected geometry.

2. Right-click on the selection, and choose Make group.

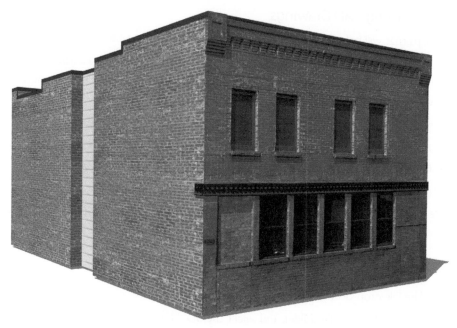

Figure 16.26 The final context model with optimized texture images applied.

3. Click on the Edit drop-down, and choose Cut. This removes the group from the model and temporarily stores it on the computer's clipboard.

4. Double-click into the ELEMENT_Context group to enter group edit mode.

5. Click on the Edit drop-down, and choose Paste in place (Figure 16.27). This places the model within the group with the same placement it had outside of the group.

Background Import

Now it's time to create the 3D model of the design. Maybe you started with a 2D sketch, moved into 2D CAD, and now it's time for 3D (this example assumes you have the CAD plans). This workflow is very common for visualization artists.

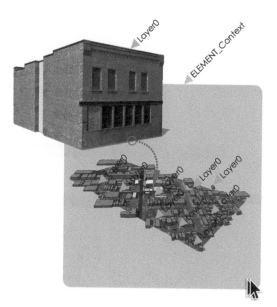

Figure 16.27 Putting the context building into the proper group.

The first step is to bring in the proposed CAD plan or sketch. Either way, this belongs on the ELEMENT_Background layer.

Working with Existing CAD Drawings

Here are a few tips that will help you when you're working with someone else's CAD drawings:

☑ Don't always trust someone else's CAD work. Use the CAD cleanup scripts (available at smustard.com) or ThomThom's CleanUp[3] in SketchUp. Better yet, open the DWGs in your CAD program, and run the Flatten, Overkill, and Purge commands.

☑ In CAD, use the LAYISO and wblock commands to separate out the drawing into usable pieces.

☑ In SketchUp, extrude the plan horizontally rather than trying to fill in the plan and extrude vertically. See Chapter 17, Renovation, for detailed instructions on this technique.

☑ When you use the File > Import dialog, be sure to set Files of type to **.dwg.**

☑ Group the CAD drawing, add to the ELEMENT – Background layer, and lock just the same as a sketch or field notes.

Import CAD Background

1. Click on the File drop-down menu, and choose Import.

2. Navigate to your Project Files folder, and select the BD_BLVD Coffee Shop - CAD Background.dwg. Make sure that the Files of type are set to AutoCAD Files (*.dwg, *.dxf).

3. Click on the Options button (Figure 16.28), check on Preserve drawing origin.

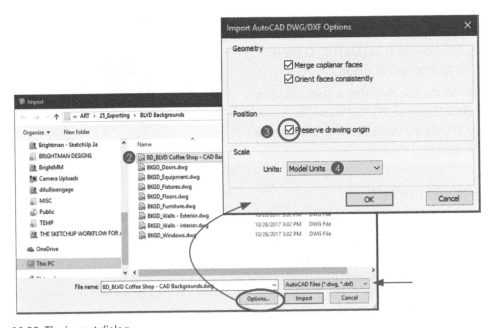

Figure 16.28 The import dialog.

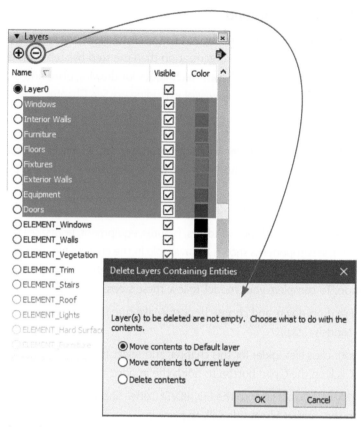

Figure 16.29 Delete layer dialog.

4. Verify that the units match the units set in your CAD program. For this file, the units are in inches so it's safe to use the Model Units setting. Click Okay to close the Options dialog, then click on Import to return to SketchUp.

5. Once the CAD drawing is imported, it is good to make sure you got the units right. Try measuring a door, and verify that it is close to 3' wide.

6. Next, check for any rogue layers that have found their way in, select them, then delete. Send the geometry to the default layer as shown in Figure 16.29, all edges and surfaces belong on Layer0.

TIP When selecting layers in the Layers dialog, hold the control key (Option on Mac) and click to add additional layers to the selection, click a selected layer again to deselect. Hold shift to select all layers between the first layer selected and the second click.

7. Finally, select the newly imported CAD drawing, and assign the ELEMENT_Background layer. Consider locking the CAD import by right clicking on it and choosing Lock. Now it can't be moved or deleted until it is unlocked.

Modeling from the CAD Background

At this point, you can use the SketchUp Drawing and Edit tools to create the walls, floors, and ceilings. For this exercise, we are focused more on model organization than the step-by-step tools needed to create geometry. In the renovation project, you will learn techniques for drawing plans and extruding horizontally, rather than the seemingly obviously easy way of extruding up. See Chapter 17, Renovation, for a more in-depth explanation of this technique.

TIP This book covers the overall, big-picture organization. Check out SketchUp for Professionals Advanced for step-by-step instructions on how to make this entire project, including the objects within.

Add Detail

Now you are ready to add the walls, doors, windows, fixtures, equipment, floors, ceilings, and roof, as shown in Figure 16.30. The components shown are available in the chapter files you downloaded earlier from **brightmandesigns.com/TSWFA**. Rather than walking you through every step of modeling, let's focus on model organization. To complete your model, follow these steps:

1. Click on the File drop-down, and choose Import. Make sure that the Files of type drop-down is set to SketchUp Models (*.skp).
2. Navigate to your class files folder for this chapter, and select the BD_BLVD Coffee Shop - Walls.skp component. Click on the Open button to finish the import.
3. Assign the ELEMENT_Walls layer to the BD_BLVD Coffee Shop - Walls.skp component. Click on the marker on the Larimer Street sidewalk to place it.
4. Continue to insert components with the insert point on the marker and apply the corresponding ELEMENT layer.

Nesting and Layering

The safe play is to always stick with LEVEL, ELEMENT, LOCATION, CONDITION. But in practice, we are always looking for shortcuts to get the same results. For a new construction project, there are no existing conditions to compare to. This means that we can eliminate the CONDITION groups and layers.

Also, because this is a one-story project with no basement or levels above, we can eliminate the LEVEL groups and layers. This will drastically simplify our model organization and ultimately speed up our process. Let's assign the next nested layer group:

1. Double-click into the ELEMENT_Walls group to enter group edit mode (Figure 16.31).
2. Select both of the exterior wall groups, then assign the LOCATION_Exterior layer.

TIP The exterior walls are separated into two groups so there can be two active section planes for the plan. One to cut the low windows, one to cut the high windows.

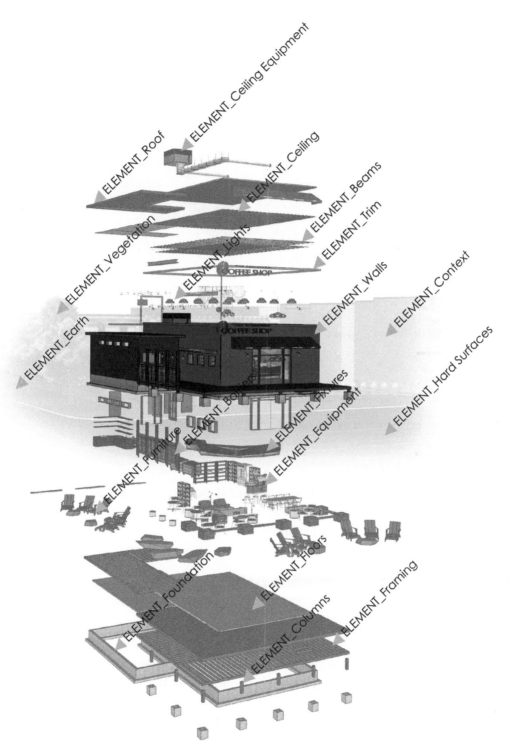

Figure 16.30 The final model with detail added (shown exploded for effect).

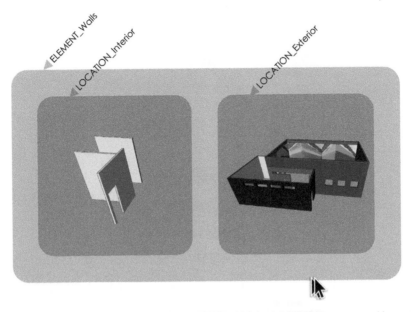

Figure 16.31 The ELEMENT model organization of walls. Next, add the LOCATION groups and layers for each ELEMENT group.

3. Select the interior wall group, then assign the LOCATION_Interior layer.

4. Apply the process to each of the appropriate imported ELEMENT groups (Figure 16.32).

Working with Objects

When you add objects to your model, you can either double-click into the proper container to place the object or you can place the object at the base level of the model and then cut and paste in place to the correct container. Follow these steps to add more objects:

1. Search for "BD coffee cup" in the 3D Warehouse.

2. Click the thumbnail of a result, and place it on a table in your model.

3. This decorative object is currently at the base level of SketchUp and should actually reside within the ELEMENT_Decorative Objects group.

4. Click the Edit drop-down, and choose Cut.

5. Double-click into the Decorative Objects group, then double-click into the Exterior group, then click on the Edit drop-down, and choose Paste in place (Figure 16.33).

TIP Purge your models to remove unused entities. Click on the Window drop-down menu, and choose Model Info. In the Statistics tab, click on Purge Unused to remove all unused layers, materials, styles, and components. Purging before saving often drastically reduces the size of the file.

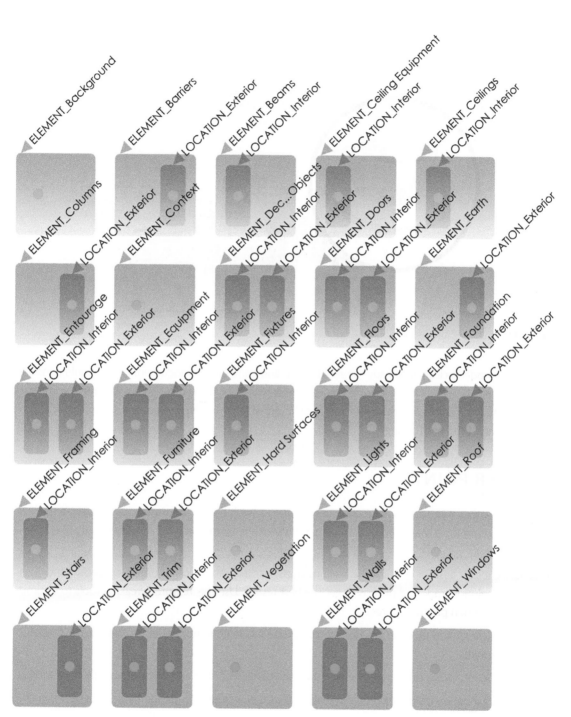

Figure 16.32 Final model organization. Note that some ELEMENTS do not require a LOCATION. This helps to further simplify the model organization.

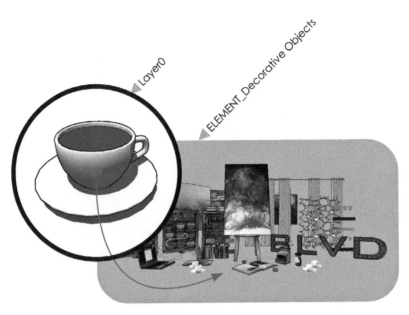

Layer0

ELEMENT_Decorative Objects

Figure 16.33 Model organization.

Now the model is clean. It is ready for visualization and construction documents. You should consider jumping ahead to Part VI, Drawings, to complete the drawings for the project. After you finish, come back to Chapter 17, Renovation, and finish out the book in order. Force yourself to go through it all twice. Congratulations and keep on trucking!

CHAPTER POINTS

☑ There are other, more advanced techniques for using Match Photo. View a tutorial that explains how to use multiple Match Photos to further advance the context model at **brightmandesigns.com/TSWFA/ch16**.

☑ Match Photo is best for creating the building mass. Use a combination of projected photos and higher-resolution imported photos to get the best results. Use the Texture Tweaking tools to optimize higher-resolution photo textures.

☑ Geo-modeling is not an exact science. Don't hesitate to sketch in minor details to make the model more complete.

☑ Model organization is simplified by eliminating the Level_01 group and layer for a single-story project.

☑ Model organization is simplified by eliminating the CONDITION groups and layers for a new construction project.

Chapter 17
Renovation

Sometimes you need to tear something down, then build it again. But if you are going to leave some of the existing structure and add on, a renovation scenario brings up tricky situations for defining new, existing, and demolished conditions. Don't worry—there is a concrete system for handling these projects, as well as some helpful features buried in the template that will help with making design decisions.

Renovations require two models: an existing conditions model and a proposed conditions model. It is best to build the existing conditions to completion, save it, then save another as proposed conditions.

RENOVATION PROCESS

A successful renovation project hinges on meticulous organization and adhering to the following warning: Finish the existing conditions model in its entirety before moving on to the proposed conditions model. This will save headaches and, most important, duplicated work. Check out the steps of a renovation project below:

- ☑ Prepare field note outlines as described later in this chapter.
- ☑ Record field notes using the clear system described later in this chapter.
- ☑ Return to the office and scan drawings, then save the scanned image to the appropriate folder: PROJECT/IMAGES/YYMMDD. As described in Chapter 4, File and Folder Management.
- ☑ Import field notes into SketchUp as described later in this chapter.
- ☑ Build the existing conditions model right on top of the field notes as described later in this chapter, eliminating the need to have big drawings at your desk. Remember: Finish this model in its entirety before moving on.

- ☑ Run ConDoc Plan Generator, or create scenes as described in Chapter 23, Drawings. This creates existing conditions drawing scenes, also called as-builts.

- ☑ Drag and drop ConDoc drawings or stack viewports as described in Chapter 23, Drawings, to create the actual existing conditions drawings.

- ☑ Save the existing conditions model to ensure it is all up to date, then save another as proposed conditions. This creates a duplicate file that you will be prompted to name.

- ☑ Add new walls in the New group. Remove portions of existing geometry/objects, and relocate them to the Demolished group. It is handy to use the Scope Diagram utility scene during this process.

- ☑ The proposed conditions drawings already exist because they were carried over from the existing conditions model. You will need to run the ConDoc Plan Generator again or create scenes as described in Chapter 23 for demolition scenes.

- ☑ Annotate drawings using text, dimensions, and labels, plus scrapbooks as described in Chapter 24, Annotations.

- ☑ Export as .pdf as described in Chapter 25, Exporting, print, present, stamp, and build.

THE MILWAUKEE STREET RENOVATION PROJECT

This renovation project gives an opportunity to make the old new again, transform the space from dated to modern. The client would like to remodel the main floor and add a new kitchen, bathroom configuration, and master bedroom suite upstairs. Removing the old roof, building a second floor on top of the existing lower level, and transforming it into a brand-new house is commonly called a *pop top* in Denver. Also adding an accessory dwelling unit in the back by the alley (ADU). The design will be updated with a modern flare (Figure 17.1).

TIP If you already have DWGs, you might not need to go out and take field notes at the site. You can simply import the .dwg files and trace over them, using the same techniques and model organization you would use to trace an image of your field notes. The only difference is that you have points to snap to rather than handwritten dimensions. See Chapter 16, New Construction, for more instructions on importing computer-aided design (CAD) drawings.

Preparing for a Site Visit

When you're making decisions about new construction, it is important to be well-informed about existing conditions. Creating accurate as-built drawings is a critical early step in the design process. For this exercise, you are preparing for a site visit, so you will record and document the existing conditions, using SketchUp and LayOut to expedite the process. The techniques in this section will give you an organized plan of attack for measuring and documenting any building.

Figure 17.1 Final, polished rendering of 3655 Milwaukee Street.

Often when visiting a site, you'll spend hours pacing the building, sketching the footprint, and trying to record everything on one landscape page—or even trickier, you might try to break things up on multiple pages. This is a difficult task! Fortunately, there is a way to create your initial field sketch in 5 minutes—before you even leave the office. Follow the steps in this section to trace the building footprint in SketchUp and print at an ideal scale from LayOut onto custom grid paper.

Adding the Location

To add the location, follow these steps:

1. Open SketchUp, and start a new model.

2. Click on the File drop-down menu, and select Geo-Location, then Add Location. In the search bar, type 3655 Milwaukee St, Denver, CO, then press Enter (Figure 17.2).

Figure 17.2 The Add Location dialog.

3. Once you track down the correct residence, click the Select Region button.

4. Use the pins to position the selection area over the entire property (Figure 17.3).

5. Click the Grab button to import the selected Google Earth snapshot and terrain (Figure 17.4).

Figure 17.3 Grab plenty of context around the site, just in case.

Figure 17.4 Shown on the left is the low resolution aerial imagery available for free from SketchUp. On the right, PlaceMaker accesses higher resolution imagery from OpenStreetMap and Nearmap. This feature alone makes PlaceMaker a must-have.

Creating the Building Footprint

To create the building footprint, follow these steps:

1. Trace the roof outline using the Rectangle tool. For this task, it is faster to use the Rectangle tool to trace over each portion of the roof rather than using the Line tool (Figure 17.5).

Figure 17.5 Use the Rectangle tool to trace the roof outline.

TIP Enable length snapping to make what seem to be loose sketches much cleaner with precise round measurements. Typically, when you're tracing a site, a 1" tolerance for length snapping is ideal. Click on the Window drop-down menu, and choose Model Info. Then click on the Units tab to adjust the length snapping features.

2. Reference Google Streetview (Figure 17.6) to fill in the details not shown in the aerial imagery.

3. Using the Offset tool, offset the roof outline as shown in Figure 17.7 to create the interior and exterior wall lines. Use the Eraser tool to delete any extra unwanted edges, and the line tool to patch in additional lines.

4. Save the model to your TEMP folder or appropriate project folder as **BD_3655** Milwaukee St – Existing Conditions.skp.

5. Using the Select tool, triple-click on the sketch of the building footprint to select all the connected geometry.

6. Right-click on the selection and choose Make Group.

7. Click on the Edit drop-down menu, and choose Copy.

Figure 17.6 Gather more information from Google Street View, Google Maps, and Bing Maps to supplement low-resolution aerial imagery.

Figure 17.7 Offset the outer lines to create an estimated building footprint.

Pasting into LayOut

Typically, graph paper lines are spaced apart at 1/10", 1/8", or 1/4", which can make field sketching difficult if the drawing scale is not suited to one of these scales. LayOut allows you to create a custom grid that matches any architectural scale, even a custom or irregular scale. Just follow these steps:

1. Start a new LayOut presentation using the BD_8.5 x 11 – Field Notes template included in the Chapter 17 resources, you should place this template in your RESOURCES/TEMPLATES folder.

2. Click on the Edit drop-down menu, and choose Paste. The SketchUp geometry will be inserted into LayOut as a generic SketchUp model linked to the LayOut presentation, displayed in a viewport (Figure 17.8).

3. Expand the viewport to cover the entire page.

4. Select the new generic viewport, and adjust the properties in the SketchUp Model inspector, as shown in Figure 17.9.

Creating an Optimized Scale

The as-built sketch does not fit perfectly on the page at 1/8" = 1' 0"; it is too small. At 1/4" = 1' 0", the drawing is too big. What you really need is an irregular scale that falls somewhere between these two.

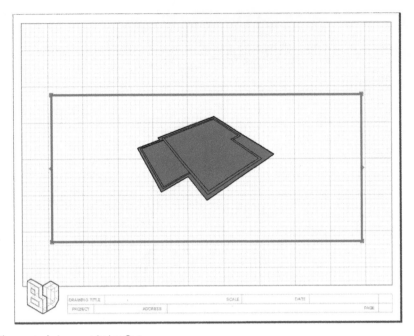

Figure 17.8 The pasted viewport in LayOut.

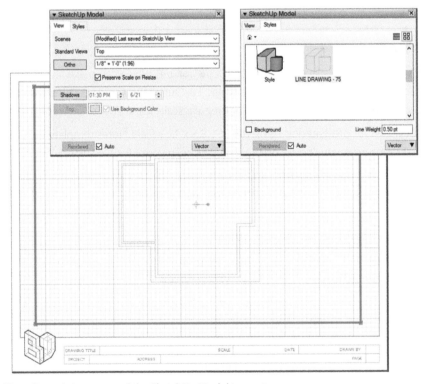

Figure 17.9 The adjusted viewport and the SketchUp Model inspector.

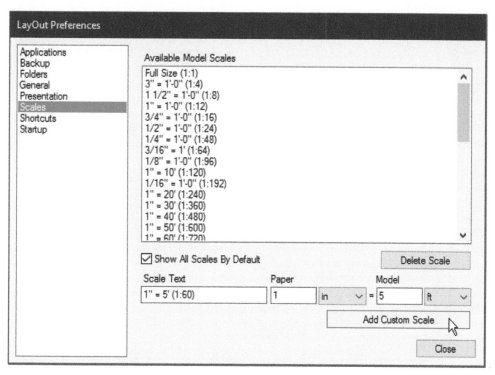

Figure 17.10 Add an irregular scale in the Preferences dialog.

In this section, you will create a custom scale in LayOut so that your as-built drawing is maximized on the page, giving you the most space to work with in the field.

1. Experiment with different standard scales in the SketchUp Model inspector. You'll see that a standard scale does not work well for this drawing.

2. At the bottom of the Scale drop-down menu, click the Add Custom Scale button.

3. This automatically launches the LayOut Preferences dialog box. Technically, 1/4" scale is equivalent to 1" = 4', so try to work one level up; 1" = 5' fits perfectly (Figure 17.10).

4. Assign the 1" = 5' scale to the viewport, then resize and reposition the viewport on the page as needed (Figure 17.11).

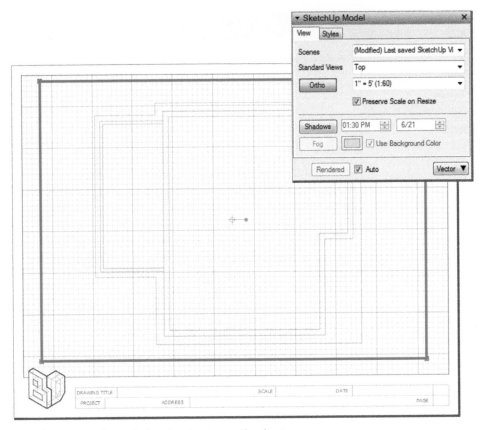

Figure 17.11 The 1" = 5' scale maximizes the drawing on the sheet.

Matching the Grid to Scale

Now that you have created an irregular scale to maximize your drawing size, you will want to match your grid to the irregular scale of 1" = 5' (Figure 17.12). This will make the task of field sketching faster, easier, and much more accurate. Follow these steps:

1. Click on the File drop-down menu, and choose Document Setup. Click on the Grid tab in the left column.

2. Click the Show Grid check box to toggle on the grid visibility.

3. Set the Major Grid spacing to 1".

4. Set the number of divisions to 5.

5. While you have this tab open, check on the Print Grid feature.

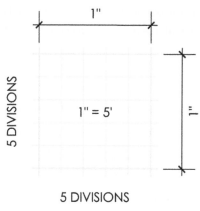

5 DIVISIONS

1"

1" = 5'

1"

5 DIVISIONS

Figure 17.12 A 1" grid with five divisions perfectly matches the scale, 1" = 5'.

Aligning the Drawing with the Grid

1. Right-click in the LayOut work area, and check on the Grid Snap feature. This will allow you to align the drawing with the grid.

2. Using the Select tool, select the viewport. Click and drag on the left side of the Precise Move grip to pick it up, then release to place it on the inside corner of the wall in your drawing.

3. Click and drag on the drawing within the viewport, and allow the Precise Move grip to snap to the grid (Figure 17.13).

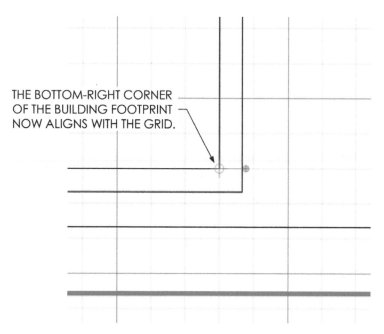

THE BOTTOM-RIGHT CORNER
OF THE BUILDING FOOTPRINT
NOW ALIGNS WITH THE GRID.

Figure 17.13 Align the bottom-right inside corner with the grid.

TIP At this point, you could explode the building outline plan and apply a more complex graphic style using the Shape Style inspector in LayOut. For instance, you could make the roof outline dashed and adjust line weights.

Exporting the PDF

Now that your building outline is ready for the field, you'll need to export to PDF, print, and head to the site.

1. Click on the File drop-down menu, and select Export, then PDF.

2. Save this file in your TEMP folder or in the EXPORTS folder in the appropriate project folder. Name the file BD_3655 Milwaukee – Field Notes.

3. The PDF Export Options dialog opens automatically. Adjust the settings as shown in Figure 17.14.

4. When the export finishes and the **.pdf** opens, click on the File drop-down menu and choose Print. Print a copy of the drawing for each floor that you intend to document, and make some extra copies just in case.

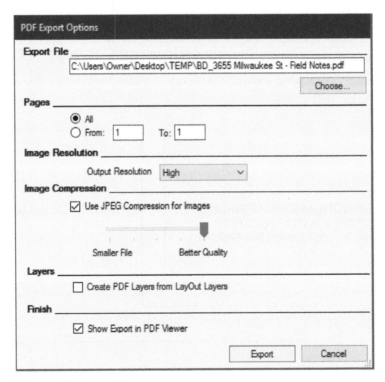

Figure 17.14 The PDF Export Options settings.

Recording Field Notes

Recording dimensions in the field can be a tricky task. The following tips will help you stay organized when you're taking notes in the field and ultimately prepare your field notes for importing and efficient three-dimensional (3D) modeling.

- ☑ Record the measurements only in decimal inches, rather than feet and inches (Figure 17.15). This will ultimately make modeling in SketchUp easier. For instance, write 87 rather than 7' 3". This will save you room on the page and keystrokes in SketchUp.

- ☑ Note the inside wall-to-wall dimensions instead of trying to draw wall thicknesses at a small scale. If there are several different wall types/ thicknesses, use a highlighter to call out the wall thicknesses from a wall type key. Alternatively, you can make a general note—for example, "all walls are 5" unless otherwise noted"—rather than dimensioning every wall's thickness (Figure 17.16).

- ☑ Give yourself plenty of room by always working at the largest scale possible. If the building is very large, it could make more sense to use a tabloid-size sheet or multiple letter-size sheets.

- ☑ Use general notes to minimize repetitive notes on the field notes drawing (Figure 17.17). Call out general ceiling heights, door heights, finishes, etc.

- ☑ Add the overall room dimensions in the center of the room in a drawing (Figure 17.18). Use the same X-distance and Y-distance format every time.

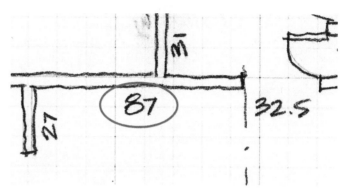

Figure 17.15 Record your measurements in decimal inches.

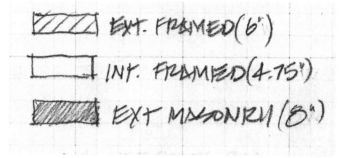

Figure 17.16 A wall key saves room on the drawings by eliminating dimensions.

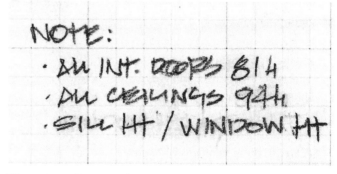

Figure 17.17 Use general notes to eliminate repetitive and ambiguous notes.

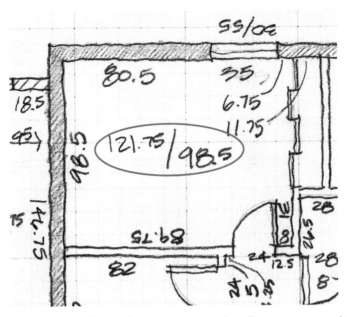

Figure 17.18 Overall room dimensions provide a reality check to ensure that all measurements add up correctly.

- ☑ Record the sill heights and window heights on the outer perimeter of the plan, with the text oriented to be read from the outside of the page (Figure 17.19). Use the format: sill height/head height.

- ☑ Avoid using dimension lines. Record wall, window, and door dimensions within the building drawing oriented in line with the dimensions they define (Figure 17.20).

- ☑ Record the wall locations only on the main plan. Bring letter-sized tracing paper to document additional layers, such as equipment (Figure 17.21), reflected ceiling plans, framing, etc.
  This will help you keep your drawing clean and organized. Be sure to mark where each drawing sits by tracing the corners of your plan.

Sticking to these standards will increase efficiency when measuring in the field, and also when modeling in the office. The final field measurements are shown in Figure 17.22.

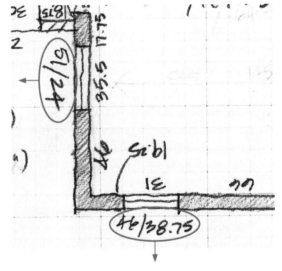

Figure 17.19 Sill heights and window heights should be oriented to be read from the outside of the plan; later in this chapter you will see how this makes creating the existing conditions model in SketchUp easier.

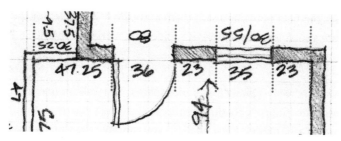

Figure 17.20 Dimensions running along the walls.

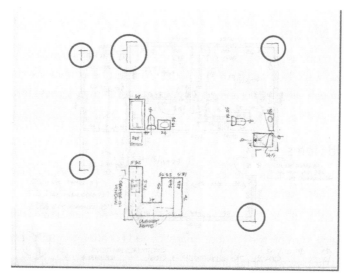

Figure 17.21 The equipment information and dimensions are recorded on a separate piece of trace paper.

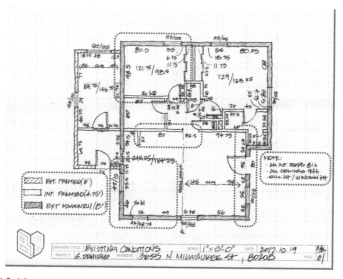

Figure 17.22 The final field measurements.

Scan all the pages of your field notes, and save them in the IMAGES folder for the project. To maintain your organization, create a subfolder in the IMAGES folder and name it YYMMDD_Field Measurements, using today's date.

TIP Canvas is a promising new 3D scanner for interior spaces. You walk around the space with an ipad that has a scanner attached to it. It collects all dimensions, even one's you never thought you would use and compiles them into a 3D model. For a small fee you can have the scan cleaned up into a perfect SketchUp model. This technology might make measuring obsolete! Check it out at canvas.io.

The As-Built 3D Model

Creating the as-built 3D model is possibly the most important step in the design process for a renovation project. All design decisions will be made from this model, so it must be extremely accurate. Any mistakes made here will carry through every model and drawing you create; ultimately, these mistakes will drastically affect the actual construction!

Importing the Field Notes

To complete this exercise, you will use the scanned field notes from the resource files folder. To import your field notes, follow these steps:

1. In SketchUp, open the `BD_3655 Milwaukee Street - Existing Conditions.skp` file.

2. In the Layers dialog, turn off the Location snapshot and Location terrain layers.

3. Click on the File drop-down menu, and select Import. Set the Files of type setting to All Supported Image Types. If you don't, you won't be able to see your scanned image files. Make sure the Image radio button is activated for the import type (Figure 17.23).

4. Navigate to the TSWFA folder, select the `BD_3655 Milwaukee Street - Field Notes.jpg` scan, and click the Open button.

5. Click once to place the image, then move your cursor away to scale the image. You don't need to be exact right now because you will scale precisely in the next step (Figure 17.24). Click again to finish placing the image.

6. Right-click on the image, and select Explode. Exploding an image converts it to a surface with a material applied to it. The material's texture image is the imported image.

7. Double-click the surface, then right-click, and choose Make Group.

8. Select the new group containing the field notes; in the Entity Info dialog, assign the ELEMENT_ Background layer.

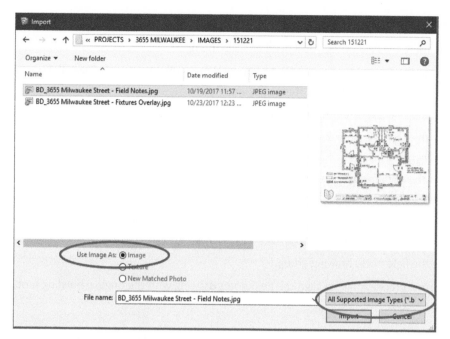

Figure 17.23 The Import settings.

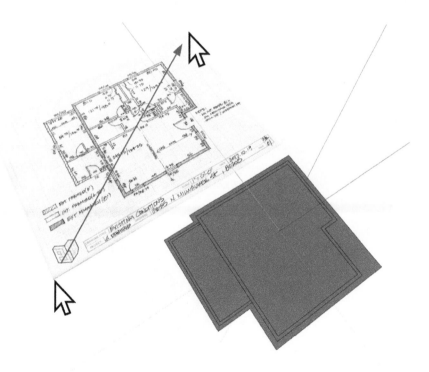

Figure 17.24 You don't need to be precise when you insert the image.

Scaling the Field Notes

After you insert the field notes, you'll need to scale them.

1. Activate the Tape Measure tool. Find a known dimension. Measure the overall distance of the building and remember that distance (Figure 17.25).

2. Using the Select tool, double-click into the field notes drawing group.

3. Using the Tape Measure tool, measure that same overall distance on the field notes (Figure 17.26).

4. Immediately after the second click, enter what the actual distance should be, then press Enter. This is the distance that you remembered from step 1—in this example, 21' 9 3/4", though on your model, this distance might be slightly different.

5. SketchUp asks if you would like to resize the active group or component. Choose Yes. This sets the measurement to be the same as what you just typed in.

6. Close the field notes drawing group.

7. Perform a precise move to align the field notes drawing with the original building footprint sketch (Figure 17.27).

TIP X-ray mode is helpful for this stage of modeling. Activate by clicking on the View drop-down, then Face Style, then X-ray. Keep in mind that Face Style is a property of the style, so X-ray mode will turn off if you go back to the original design style.

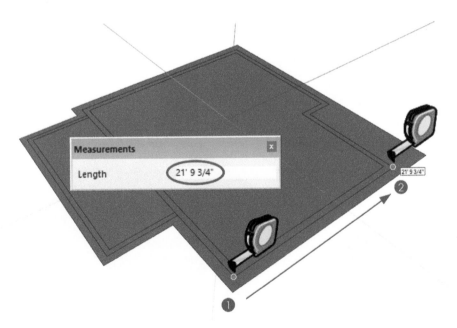

Figure 17.25 Measure the overall length of the building outline.

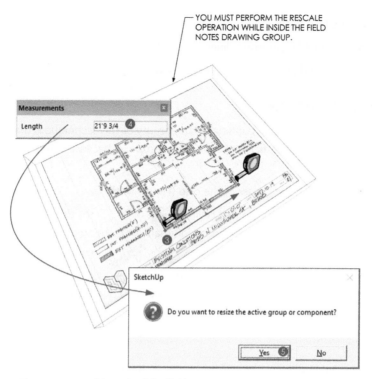

Figure 17.26 Measure the same overall length of the field notes image.

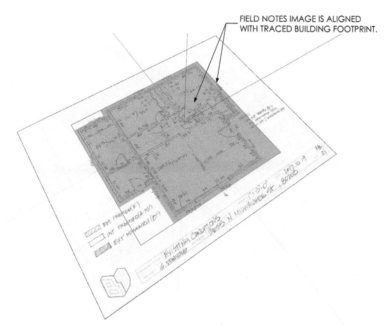

Figure 17.27 Align the properly scaled field notes drawing with the traced building outline.

8. Right-click on the field notes group, and select Lock.

9. Delete the original building footprint lines. You no longer need them.

10. Click on the File drop-down menu, and choose Save.

Modeling from the Field Notes

Now you are ready to draft the existing conditions. The beauty of this technique is that there is no need to look back and forth between your field notes and the computer because your notes are already in the model.

1. Draw an 8" x 8" square in the corner of the plan (Figure 17.28).

2. Push/pull the square up to the recorded ceiling height of 94". Since the template default units are in inches, there is no need to type the quotation mark for inches (Figure 17.29).

3. Using the Push/Pull tool, extrude the plan horizontally (Figure 17.30 and Figure 17.31). As you are pushing/pulling, tap the Ctrl key (Option key on a Mac) to toggle the Create New Starting Face command. This leaves a copy of the starting face and edges behind and allows you to mark horizontal breaks and openings. Leave a starting face at every major opening, such as walls, doors, and windows.

TIP Turn corners by extruding out by the wall thickness—in this model, 8". Then use the Push/Pull tool to extrude perpendicular to the wall.

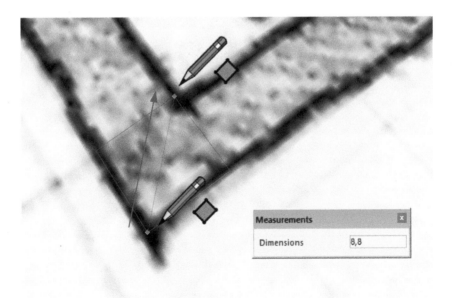

Figure 17.28 Square drawn in the southeast corner of the plan.

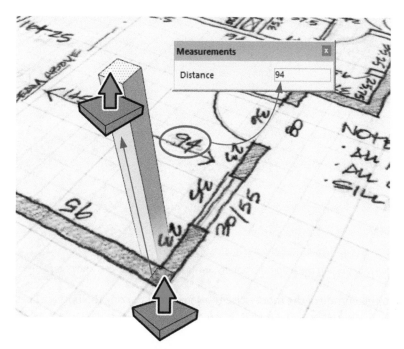

Figure 17.29 Pull the square up to the recorded ceiling height to begin to form the exterior walls.

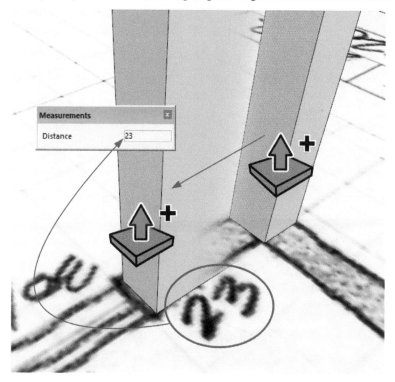

Figure 17.30 Extrude the plan horizontally using the Push/Pull tool. Read the dimensions of each section off the field notes drawing.

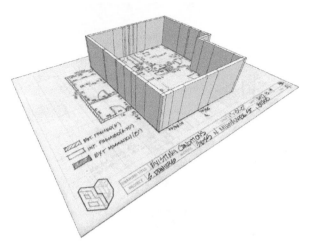

Figure 17.31 Continue extruding the plan horizontally around the entire house, and complete all the exterior walls.

4. Navigate to the outside of the model. Use the Move tool to copy the bottom lines of the door and window openings up to the noted sill heights, then again for the head heights (Figure 17.32, Figure 17.33, and Figure 17.34).

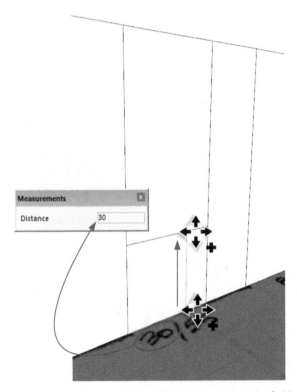

Figure 17.32 Use the Move tool to copy edges up to the sill heights noted on the field notes drawing (southeast corner of the plan is shown).

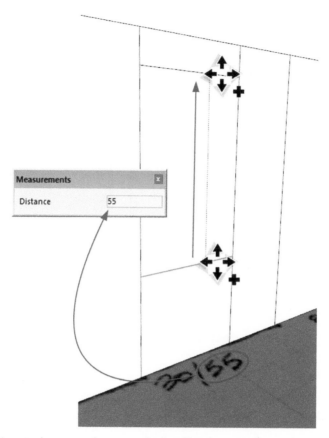

Figure 17.33 Use the Move tool to copy edges up to the head heights noted on the field notes drawing (southeast corner of the plan is shown).

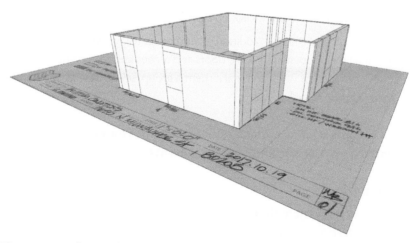

Figure 17.34 The exterior walls extruded with starting faces, sill lines, and head lines that define major openings.

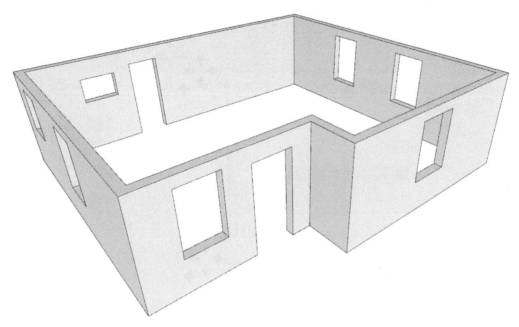

Figure 17.35 The final exterior walls with the ELEMENT_Background layer turned off.

5. Using the Eraser tool, delete all the extra edges on the inside walls of the model, as well as any unwanted geometry on the outside walls. Leave behind only the lines that define the openings.

6. Use the Push/Pull tool to create all major openings as shown in Figure 17.35. Push from the outside of the house in. After creating the first opening, you can double-click on the other openings and use the memory of the Push/Pull tool.

7. Select all the new exterior walls, right-click on the selection, and choose Make Group.

8. Draw the interior walls and the back addition exterior walls using the same techniques. Leave a starting face at all major openings for the doors and arches and to turn the corners. When you are finished, select all interior walls, and make them a group, select the back addition exterior walls, and make them a group as well.

TIP See video on the chapter page for a tutorial of the process. Then use this section as a reference once you learn from the video. Visit **brightmandesigns.com/ch17**.

Layering and Organizing

You need to organize your model from the moment you begin creating it and continue that organization throughout the process. Keep in mind that though we always organize LEVEL, ELEMENT, LOCATION,

CONDITION, we don't always complete the model organization process in that order. To start organizing the model, follow these steps:

1. Select the group containing the interior walls.

2. Right-click on the group, and choose Entity Info.

3. In the Entity Info dialog, assign the LOCATION_Interior layer to the group containing the walls (Figure 17.36).

4. Select the group containing the exterior walls.

5. In the Entity Info dialog, assign the LOCATION_Exterior layer to the group containing the exterior walls.

6. Select both groups of walls: interior and exterior.

7. Right-click on the selection, and choose Make Group.

8. In the Entity Info dialog, assign the ELEMENT_Walls layer to the group containing the walls (Figure 17.37).

9. Using the Select tool, double-click into the new group of walls, then double-click into the LOCATION_Interior group. Select all geometry within the group, right-click on the selection, and choose Make Group.

10. In the Entity Info dialog, assign the CONDITION_Existing layer to the new group containing the walls.

11. Repeat this process for the Exterior Walls within the CONDITION_Exterior group. The model organization should resemble Figure 17.38.

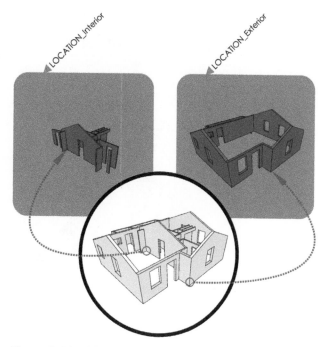

Figure 17.36 LOCATION layers assigned to the groups containing wall geometry.

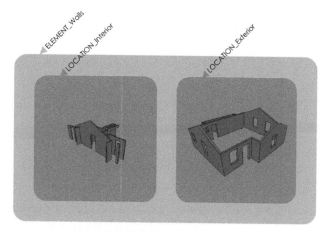

Figure 17.37 ELEMENT – Walls layer assigned to the group that holds the LOCATION groups.

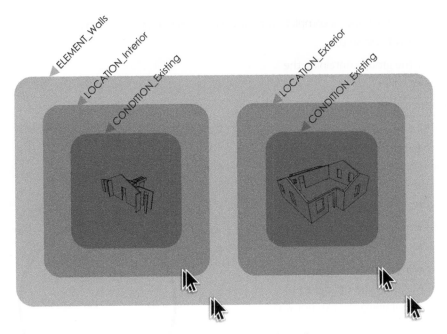

Figure 17.38 ELEMENT, LOCATION, and CONDITION layers applied to the wall geometry.

Adding Detail

Now you are ready to add the doors, windows, fixtures, equipment, floors, ceilings, and roof using the same organization techniques, as shown in Figure 17.39. The components shown are available in the chapter files you downloaded earlier from **brightmandesigns.com/TSWFA/ch17**. To complete your existing conditions model, follow these steps:

1. Click on the File drop-down, and choose Import. Make sure that the Files of type drop-down is set to SketchUp Models (*.skp).

2. Navigate to your class files folder for this chapter, and select the BD_3655 Milwaukee - Existing Doors.skp component. Click on the Import button to finish the import. Place the insert point at the front bottom corner of the walls as noted in Figure 17.39.

3. Assign the ELEMENT_Doors layer to the BD_3655 Milwaukee - Existing Doors.skp component.

4. Continue to insert components and apply the corresponding ELEMENT layer.

5. Next, double-click into each of the ELEMENT groups and create the necessary groups to assign the LOCATION and CONDITION layers as shown in Figure 17.39.

TIP An identical set of fully grouped and layered components is included, so you can import the pieces and see how they should be layered, then remove from the model and try for yourself.

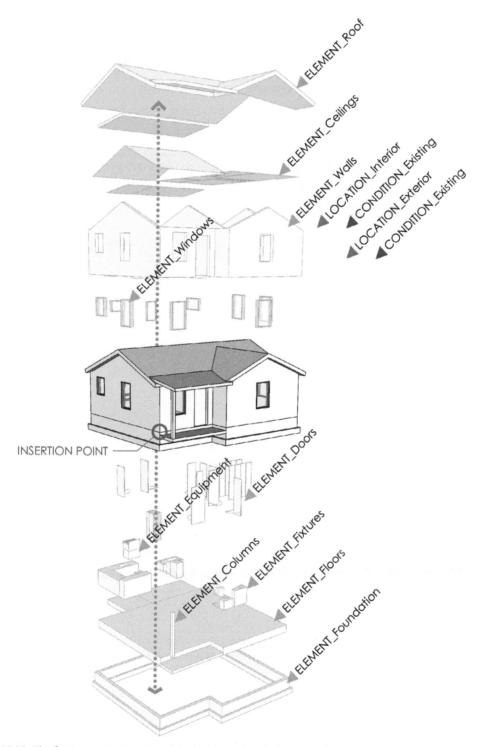

Figure 17.39 The final model with detail added (shown exploded for effect).

Now that all the ELEMENT, LOCATION, and CONDITION layers have been applied, it is time to pull everything together into one LEVEL group.

1. In the Layers dialog, click on the plus sign to add a layer. Name it LEVEL_01.

2. Select all the ELEMENT groups, right-click and choose Make Group.

3. While the new group is still selected, in the Entity Info dialog, assign the LEVEL_01 layer. The model organization is now complete and should resemble Figure 17.40.

TIP Completely finish the as-built 3D model before you move on to the design phases. To move forward immediately, you could use the completed model from your chapter files. A complete existing conditions model is included in the chapter resources.

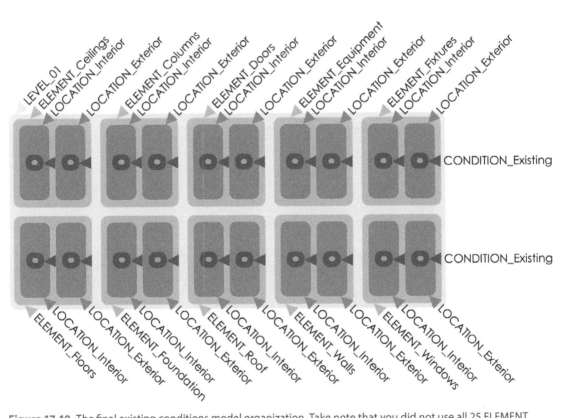

Figure 17.40 The final existing conditions model organization. Take note that you did not use all 25 ELEMENT layers; you used only the ones that were needed to represent the existing conditions accurately.

Proposed Conditions Model

The *proposed conditions model* is where you will demolish select existing conditions and add your new design. At this point, having a complete *existing conditions model* is imperative. In the future, any changes you make to the existing conditions model will need to be duplicated in your new proposed conditions model. So make sure you take the time to accurately finish the as-built model. When you are ready to transition your existing conditions model to a proposed conditions model, just follow these steps:

1. In SketchUp, open the `BD_3655 Milwaukee St - Existing Conditions.skp` model from the chapter resource files.

2. Click on the File drop-down menu, and select Save As.

3. Name the file BD_3655 Milwaukee St – Proposed Conditions.skp.

4. Navigate to your TEMP folder or the appropriate project folder, and click the Save button.

Demolition

Often, you will need to demolish portions of an existing building in order to complete your renovation. Within the proposed conditions model, simply move the geometry you want to demolish to the CONDITION_Demolished group (Figure 17.41). The Cut and paste in place commands are made for this task. Keep in mind that you might need to create the CONDITION_Demolished group as you go. You need to create this group only for the ELEMENTS that you are demolishing some or all of.

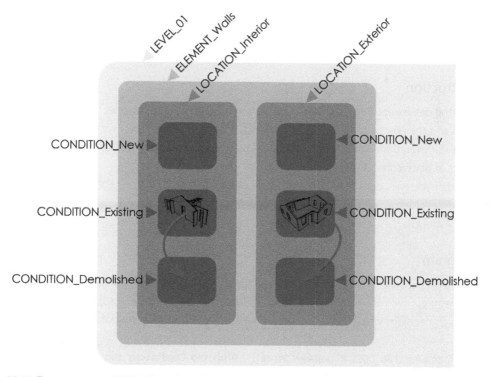

Figure 17.41 To represent an ELEMENT as demolished, move it from the existing group to the demolished group.

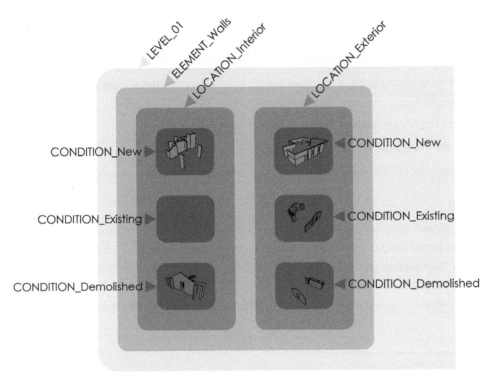

Figure 17.42 Add proposed construction elements in the CONDITION_New container.

New Construction

To complete the design, you'll need to add new walls and entities to your model. To do that, all you need to do is add the new proposed entities to the CONDITION_New group within each ELEMENT (Figure 17.42). Put everything in its correct container by either building within the container or using the Cut and paste in place commands.

It is likely that you will add a CONDITION_New container to each of the ELEMENT groups as you are adding the new entities. Once you do, insert the appropriate geometry, objects, and elements within their corresponding groups.

Scope Diagram

When you're working on a remodel design, you can view the model as a scope diagram to see which entities are existing, which are new, and which are to be demolished (Figure 17.43). This will help you make informed design decisions visually, without always having to check the layering of the groups in the Entity Info dialog.

Open the completed BD_3655 Milwaukee Street - Proposed Conditions.skp model from the chapter files. Click on the scope diagram's Scene tab and explore the model's organization strategies and layering.

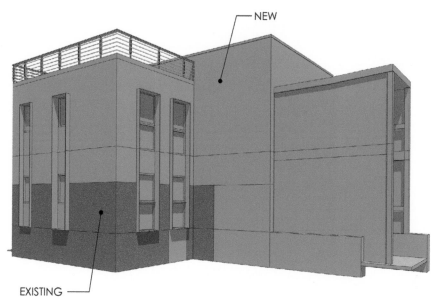

NEW

EXISTING

Figure 17.43 Existing entities are gray, new entities are green, and demolished entities are orange.

Use the ConDoc System heads-up display to navigate through the model and further understand how everything is put together.

CHAPTER POINTS

☑ Gather as much information as you can before visiting the site.

☑ When you're recording dimensions, develop a system and stick to it.

☑ It is critical that you complete the accurate and organized as-built 3D model before you move on to the proposed design model.

☑ Download the `BD_Field Note - Letter Landscape.layout` template at **brightmandesigns.com/TSWFA** and save to your RESOURCES/TEMPLATES folder. This template is set up with spaces for the critical information that you will typically record when you are completing as-built drawings.

☑ The Paste in Place command allows you to easily move geometry and objects between containers.

PART V

Visualization

SketchUp was the first program that could create acceptable outputs relatively quickly and easily. Now, photo-real rendering programs have come so far that they are easy and fast, too. These advancements in technology open up infinite possibilities for presentation graphics and visual styles. In the following chapters, we will look at preparing a model, SketchUp rendering, and photo-real rendering, and we will look into the future of visualization.

Chapter 18
Introduction to Visualization/Preparation

This book focuses more on model organization techniques that net a clean model that can be dissected into construction documents and rendered in SketchUp or, more likely, third-party plugins and software.

In this chapter, we will explore many types of visualization, but this book will not cover the intricacies of each of the plugins and programs. The list is rapidly changing, so it is up to you to stay in front of emerging technologies. It is better to be aware of the possibilities, know where to look, then track down the right solution for you.

In the past, rendering would get in the way. It was too difficult; it took too long. It stifled the design process. It used to be only for polished client presentations and marketing materials. Now it's so fast that it can be used for exploring design iterations, internal meetings, and client presentations (Figures 18.1–18.5).

The new constant in this arena is Lumion, a photorealistic rendering program that provides real-time feedback while preparing nonreal-time output such as stills, animations, and virtual reality (VR). It is fast, easy, and specifically designed for architects. Lumion cures all the pain points of the past—long render times, complex interface, render farms, complicated workflows. I have created extensive tutorials on Lumion and how it is seamlessly integrated into the SketchUp Workflow for Architecture.

If you want to extend the SketchUp Workflow for Architecture into the realm of visualization, buy Lumion and watch our tutorials. This topic changes too fast to even write about. At brightmandesigns.com, we stay up-to-date on the latest versions of Lumion, and we are always updating the workflow to fit the latest release.

Figure 18.1 Portfolio rendering. Sketchy styles are great for dressing up an incomplete model or presenting early ideas.

Figure 18.2 Portfolio renderings. Photo-real renderings are better for marketing images.

Figure 18.3 Portfolio renderings, Lumion interior.

Figure 18.4 Portfolio renderings, Lumion exterior.

Figure 18.5 Portfolio renderings. SketchFX plugin for SketchUp produces a more refined sketchy look than stock SketchUp.

PRESENTATIONS

There are several types of visualizations, or presentation types, that can be extracted from your well-organized three-dimensional (3D) model. Each presentation type has strengths and weaknesses that are best realized before you go into a board room to sell the idea. Know them so you can make a more effective presentation, speak more directly to your audience, and successfully sell your idea.

Stills

Still shots are the tried-and-true method of presenting. They are easily e-mailed or printed. They are versatile—everyone knows how to use a still image and write on it with a red marker. They are reliable, so no Internet is needed at the meeting to make them work. Keep these tips in mind when creating stills.

☑ Render at a resolution appropriate to print your presentation. Never go below 150 dpi. So if you need a 24" x 36" poster, render at Lumion's poster size of 7680 x 4320 (Figure 18.6). (7680 pixels/36" = 213 dpi.) Technically, you could print as much as 51.2" wide and your poster would still be acceptable for print.

☑ 300 dpi is the best, but it is also the point of diminishing returns where the human eye can't really notice a difference. So making a higher resolution than this is only costing you more render time and file size.

☑ Only model what you need to render. A major benefit of stills is that you can treat them like a Hollywood set, creating only what you will see in the view. Don't bother modeling what is behind you, or the wall in front of you, because you won't see it.

☑ Keep in mind that more geometry, effects, lights, and higher resolution will take longer to render.

| Email 1280x720 | Desktop 1920x1080 | Print 3840x2160 | Poster 7680x4320 |

Figure 18.6 Lumion's rendering settings are a good baseline for acceptable resolutions.

Animation

Animations have been around awhile, too, but only now are they much more attainable. They're great for a portfolio page on your website, building an audience on YouTube, and taking clients on an engaging, controlled, scripted journey through their future building. Keep these tips in mind when creating animations:

☑ Slower is always better. When the camera is flying around, or you are walking through a space, exaggerate how slow you can go.

☑ Be a director—make it cinematic. Tell the story of your project through moving pictures.

☑ Don't just use a helicopter path; patch in dynamic views and B-roll, and don't hesitate to leave the camera path subtle, or static, and let cars and people move through the scene. This can give those I-can't-look-at-this-without-getting-sick clients a break.

☑ Resolution should always match the screen you are presenting on. Most conference rooms these days will have a monitor that supports 1080p or possibly 4K. The best resolution for these screens is 1920 x 1080 pixels. Anything less will look pixelated; anything more will be past the point of diminishing returns and simply take longer to render with no net gain.

☑ 4K resolution is rapidly becoming the new standard in high-resolution monitors and televisions. Lumion now supports 4K output at 3840 x 2160.

☑ You will need to model everything you see along a camera path; nothing kills the magic of an animation like an empty horizon or incomplete area beyond. Use landscape elements, mountains, trees, and photo-textured buildings to block the horizon (Figure 18.7).

Figure 18.7 Seeing the horizon versus not seeing the horizon. When the horizon is visible, the animations loses authenticity. Consider filling it in with landscape elements or, more easily, lower the camera position.

Virtual Tours

Virtual tours are a great, lightweight 3D experience to share with your clients. Keep these tips in mind when creating them:

☑ Virtual tours are great for website portfolios and sharing designs with clients in a format that is easily accessible and navigable. They are lightweight enough to run on a phone or tablet, which increases the likelihood that they will be shared.

☑ You can create virtual tours using Lumion (Figure 18.8) and many SketchUp extensions. Just search the Extension Warehouse for the latest list; there are far too many to test and keep up with.

☑ Lumion offers additional functionality in that it renders and stores your virtual tours on myLumion. com. This makes it easy to manage and share your work.

☑ Once you render your virtual tour, compile and deliver more engaging 360 presentations with krpano. Check it out at **krpano.com**.

Virtual Reality

VR is new on the scene but only recently brought to the masses. Although there is still work to be done, it is finally impressive and easy to use. This new technology has not yet hit the mainstream, so keep these tips in mind when creating virtual reality presentations:

Figure 18.8 A virtual tour is created by wrapping a jpg around a cube, then distorting the image as the viewer pans through to create the illusion of 3D.

- ☑ Use real-time, navigable VR for design decisions rather than client presentations. These experiences are more engaging, but clients usually have a hard time getting over the coolness of being inside the model. Save real-time VR for yourself, and colleagues, who have had time to do all the demos, understand the navigation controls, and are ready to make some informed design decisions.

- ☑ Navigating in VR can bring on motion sickness. Avoid this by teleporting rather than flying to different views. If you think a client might get sick, don't put them in VR. Is there any worse outcome to a design presentation than the client getting physically ill? Don't risk it.

- ☑ Use static, higher polished, rendered 360 panos to present to clients. These take longer to render but are much better. There are fewer controls, which means less navigation and less motion sickness. Lumion creates beautiful 360 panos for use in many different VR goggles.

- ☑ 360 panos are lightweight and easy to share. Branded Google Cardboard is a great, inexpensive leave-behind that will keep your presentation, design, and firm at the top of a client's mind.

REAL OBJECTS

Approaching and modeling objects is a challenging task. Typically, everyday objects that make a convincing scene are "organic" in shape. Many beginner modelers approach these objects with the standard SketchUp modeling tools, which ultimately creates a hard-lined object that was obviously modeled in SketchUp (Figure 18.9). When you're modeling objects, keep the following tips in mind:

TIP Build this chair, and other real objects, in our SketchUp for Professionals Advanced online course.

- ☑ Examine the object to determine the details that make it unique and recognizable.

- ☑ Think about your approach. What basic forms can be modified to create the desired object? Is an additive approach best? Or would a subtractive approach be better?

- ☑ Use advanced modeling techniques learned in SketchUp for Professionals Advanced to create more realistic objects.

- ☑ Leverage extensions such as Shape Bender, Artisan, and FredoScale to expedite the creation of complex geometry.

- ☑ You will probably conclude that it is worth paying for professionally built models of objects at **FormFonts.com**.

Figure 18.9 A cartoonish chair (at right) conveys the form of a chair but not necessarily a real style. The stylized chair (at left) is a more accurate representation of a real chair.

POPULATING A SCENE

Any image you create will ultimately be used to sell an idea. Your design image should evoke excitement and the desire to be a participant in the image. You should put as much thought into populating your renderings as a realtor puts into staging a house for sale. Breathe life into the space by adding decorative objects, people, and action. Keep the following tips in mind when you're populating a scene:

☑ Address your audience. Who are you selling this design to, and what will get them excited about the space? Now is a good time to think back to your first meetings, when the client expressed their main desires.

☑ Add decorative objects within the ELEMENT_Decorative Objects group (Figure 18.10). Tables without food, magazines, or other details are boring. Including such details makes a scene realistic; however, you don't want them to render in the furniture plan, so it is important to separate them out on a different layer.

☑ Download professionally modeled and textured components at **FormFonts.com**.

☑ Use custom textures from Google Images searches, SketchUp Texture Club, or FormFonts. (See Chapter 8, SketchUp Collections.)

☑ To sell the experience, populate models with people participating in appropriate activities. Add them to the ELEMENT_Entourage container. For winter scenes, use people in jackets. At a restaurant, mix casually and professionally dressed people. For an office, add activity such as presentations and

Figure 18.10 Decorative objects such as magazines, plates, and pillows liven up a scene but are not necessary to render in plan. Such entities belong on the ELEMENT_Decorative Objects layer.

collaborative group discussions. Perform a Google search for "office," and investigate what a real office looks like. Take note of the clutter that can add realism to an image, then apply those subtle nuances when staging your scenes (see Figure 18.11 and Figure 18.12).

Figure 18.11 This scene lacks decorative objects and people. The space is accurately represented, but the viewer has no idea how the space will be used.

Figure 18.12 This scene is full of life and activity. Decorative objects and people give the viewer an idea of how the space will be used.

PREPARING A MODEL

Photorealistic rendering is possible with Lumion and many of the available extensions for SketchUp, but you should first optimize the model for rendering using the Orient Faces utility scene (Figure 18.13). This utility scene displays the geometry in your model based on which side of the surface is facing you. The fronts are pink, and the backs are yellow. Rendering the fronts of faces will produce more predictable results.

1. Click on the Orient Faces utility scene tab.

2. Double-click into Groups and Components, then right-click on a yellow face and choose Reverse Faces to change it to pink. You can select multiple faces—right-click on the selection and choose Reverse Faces to change more than one face at a time.

3. Click on the Design utility tab to verify that the correct material is applied to the surface. Usually, after reversing a face, you will need to apply a material to the front that was previously hidden.

4. Reverse the rest of the faces until all of them are pink.

5. Click on the Render tab, then Save. This is best place to save in and also to import into a photo-real rendering program such as Lumion.

TIP The left-click Reverse Faces plugin reverses the face with one click. It even works through groups and components. It is available as an .rb download at **smustard.com/script/ReverseFaces.**

PINK REPRESENTS THE FRONT OF A
FACE THAT IS FACING THE CAMERA.

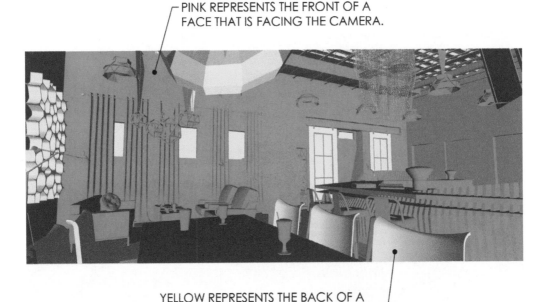

YELLOW REPRESENTS THE BACK OF A
FACE THAT IS FACING THE CAMERA.

Figure 18.13 The Orient Faces utility scene makes it easy to identify the fronts and backs of faces. Typically, your results will be more consistent when you render the fronts of surfaces.

CHAPTER POINTS

- ☑ Populate your scenes to sell your idea. Make the viewer want to participate in the image.

- ☑ To minimize cost and exports while maximizing efficiency and connectivity, pick a photorealistic renderer that works inside SketchUp.

- ☑ Use an image editor to fine-tune the final output.

- ☑ Lumion is an all-inclusive solution that creates each of the different presentation types. It is my renderer of choice.

- ☑ Make sure the fronts of all faces are directed out. See this clearly using the Orient Faces utility scene.

Chapter 19
Rendering

Your design is complete and fully modeled, but now you need to sell the idea before moving on to full construction documents. It's time to visualize! Use still images, animation, virtual tours, and immersive virtual reality (VR) experiences to tell the story of your design. In this chapter, we will explore the different programs needed to create the perfect presentation. Whether you are selling your design internally or to a client, or even fundraising, rendering your SketchUp model is critical to meeting your goals.

SKETCHUP STILLS

SketchUp renderings are traditionally "sketchy." Utilizing the loose lines and cartoonish materials available in SketchUp conveys design intent in a way that is much softer than a sharp, photorealistic rendering. These images are ideal for exploring designs at your desk or with colleagues at internal meetings (Figure 19.1).

Choosing an Appropriate Style

A style will drastically affect the way in which your audience receives your SketchUp rendering. If your design is still in a loose schematic state, present it with a sketchy style to remove some of the details you haven't thought out. If your design is fairly complete and advanced, use a hard-line style instead to ensure the details are clearly represented. See Figure 19.2, Figure 19.3, and Figure 19.4.

Figure 19.1 Stock SketchUp is best suited to internal presentations and design iterations.

Figure 19.2 A sketchy style rendered in hidden line mode leaves much of the detail to the viewer's imagination or presenter's explanation, which is great for designs that are still in schematics. If you haven't addressed the materials, don't show them.

Figure 19.3 A style with clean lines and textures is best for a design that has been well developed.

Figure 19.4 SketchFX renderings of the same house. SketchFX is available at fluidinteractive.com/products/sketchup-extensions/sketchfx/.

TIP SketchFX is an impressive extension that gives Adobe Photoshop-like filters and overlays right inside of SketchUp. It's great for taking the cartoonish look out of your renderings—and putting the sketch back in SketchUp.

Creating Scenes

After you determine the style you want to use, you can create the scene.

1. Navigate to a desired view, then select an appropriate style from the Style browser.

2. To add a new scene, click on the plus sign (+) at the top-left corner of the Scenes dialog.

3. Using the LO_ format, rename the scene LO_Perspective 01. Check on all the properties to save.

4. Repeat to create additional scenes.

TIP The ConDoc Perspective tool (Figure 19.5) is free and automates several complex operations with the click of a button. This tool adds a scene, names the scene with numbering, and assigns a beautiful presentation style. This tool is included in the free version of ConDoc. Download it at **condoctools.com**.

Figure 19.5 The ConDoc Perspective tool.

Exporting Images from SketchUp

The easiest way to produce an image is to use the Export 2D Graphic command in SketchUp. This creates a two-dimensional (2D) snapshot of the screen in several formats, including raster and vector.

1. Click on the Scene tab that you would like to export.

2. Click on the File drop-down, and select Export 2D Graphic.

3. Set the Export Type to **.jpg** if you plan to print or e-mail the rendering as is. This is one of the most common raster image formats. If you plan to perform a lot of postprocessing, consider exporting the scene as a **.tiff** file.

4. Click on the Options button to set the image resolution as shown in Figure 19.6.

5. Navigate to the appropriate project folder. Add a File name (typically match the scene name) and click on the export to finish.

Figure 19.6 Image export options.

SKETCHUP ANIMATIONS

SketchUp animations are easy to create, and they provide an excellent way to explore a three-dimensional (3D) space without having the model open and rendering in real time.

Creating an Animation Model

To create an animation file, follow these steps:

1. Within SketchUp, click on the File drop-down, and select New to start a new model.

2. Click on the File drop-down, and choose Import. Verify that the Files of type drop-down menu is set to SketchUp Files (*.skp). Inserting one SketchUp model into another creates a link between the instance and the referenced model. This technique will limit the number of scenes and Scene tabs in the proposed conditions model. When you make changes to the original BD_BLVD Coffee Shop. skp model, you can just right-click on the reference in the Animation file and select Reload to see the updated model.

3. Navigate to and select the BD_BLVD Coffee Shop.skp file. Click the Open button to import the model.

4. Save the file as BD_BLVD Coffee Shop – Animation.skp.

Adding Scenes

SketchUp animations are scene-based. This means that SketchUp will link together all the scenes in the animation into one movie. Be sure to check on all the properties to save and choose which scenes should be included in the animation (Figure 19.7). Typically, every scene you create in the animation file will be included.

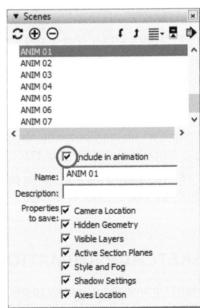

1. In the Scenes browser, click the Add New Scene button to create a new scene. Move it to the end of the list using the up and down arrows at the top of the Scenes dialog. Check on all Properties to save.

2. Name the scenes based on segments. For example, each scene in the first stream of animation should have the same prefix, try 01_ or INTRO_.

3. Click on the Window drop-down, and choose Model Info. Click on the Animations tab.

4. Check on the Scene Transitions, and adjust the amount of time between scenes based on personal preference. Typically, you should leave the Scene Delay set to 0 for a more fluid animation.

5. Add additional scenes in the sequence. To see them play back, right-click on any scene tab at the top of the screen and choose Play Animation.

Figure 19.7 In the SketchUp Scenes dialog, the Include in animation box is checked for each ANIM scene.

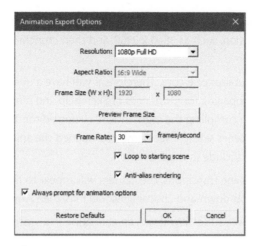

Figure 19.8 Animation export settings.

Exporting Animations

To export your animation, follow these steps:

1. Click on the File drop-down, and choose Export, then Animation, then video.

2. Click the Options button at the bottom-left corner of the Export Animation dialog. The settings shown in Figure 19.8 are ideal for most screen sizes without wasting rendering resources.

3. Navigate to your TEMP folder or an appropriate project folder, name the file, and select Export.

SketchUp Animation Tips

Keep the following tips in mind when you're creating animations in SketchUp.

☑ Add a skydome to the animation file to create a more realistic sky effect. Search the 3D Warehouse for skydome (Figure 19.9).

☑ Use Ruby Scripts to make your animations smoother. Visit finish.smustard.com/script/PresentationBundle2 to purchase and experiment with FlightPath, PageSmoother, and several other extensions included in the Presentation Bundle.

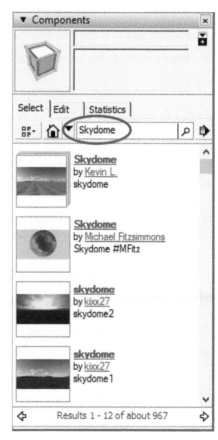

Figure 19.9 A skydome places a picture of a real sky behind an image, which looks better than a simple colored sky.

- ☑ The dimensions for high-definition 1080p are 1920 pixels wide by 1080 pixels high. Thin out lines by exporting at a higher resolution, such as 3840 x 2160, and then crunching the file down in a video editor.

- ☑ Each instance of SketchUp utilizes one core. Therefore, if you have a quad-core system, you could maximize your machine by opening four instances of SketchUp and rendering the animation in four separate segments and then compiling the segments in a video editor. To do this, you would need one animation file with all the scenes set up. Every time you opened the animation file, you would need to uncheck different scenes to include in the animation.

- ☑ With more time between scene transitions, the camera will appear to fly slower. Adjust this setting by clicking on the Window drop-down and choosing Model Info, then Animation settings.

- ☑ A higher frame rate will allow you to slow down an animation in a video editor without deteriorating the quality.

- ☑ By using simple video editing programs such as Windows Movie Maker or iMovie, you can add a lot to your animations. For example, you can add captions, fade effects, and chop out the "bouncing" effect often present in scene-based animations.

- ☑ Sketchy styles do not typically render well in animations.

PHOTOREALISTIC RENDERING

Once a design has reached a level of detail that resembles a real space, it is best to render it as a photo-realistic image. This will make typical "cartoony" SketchUp renderings look real by adding soft shadows, reflections, light sources, and other natural properties of light.

TIP If a design is incomplete and isn't populated, your photorealistic rendering will look amateurish.

In the not-so-distant past, photorealistic rendering was a huge task involving exporting to expensive software packages that only Hollywood studios could afford and only Hollywood special effects wizards knew how to use. Today, photorealistic rendering can be accomplished in SketchUp, or by connecting your SketchUp model to an external rendering program (see Figure 19.10, Figure 19.11, Figure 19.12, and Figure 19.13).

Photorealistic Rendering Software

Although SketchUp is acceptable for in-house presentations, it is often not refined enough for marketing and fundraising. You need something that mirrors life.

Figure 19.10 Photorealistic exterior rendering, rendered in Lumion.

Figure 19.11 The same view in SketchUp.

Figure 19.12 Photorealistic Interior rendering, rendered in Lumion.

Figure 19.13 The same view in SketchUp.

SketchUp Rendering Extensions

Most rendering plugins are extremely inexpensive, and they produce beautiful images that rival professional stand-alone rendering software. Listed below are several options for rendering inside SketchUp. Each program or plugin has its own unique features and benefits. They all create a photorealistic image from right inside SketchUp. These plugins are inexpensive but also limited on output options, features, object libraries, and quality. Rendering extensions are typically inexpensive, in the $100 range. I have personal experience with or have heard good things from colleagues regarding the following.

☑ Twilight Render: **twilightrender.com**

☑ Shaderlight: **artvps.com**

☑ SU Podium: **suplugins.com**

☑ V-Ray for SketchUp: **chaosgroup.com/en/2/vrayforsketchup.html**

Lumion

Lumion is installed on your desktop and opens in a similar fashion to SketchUp. You double-click on an icon, import your SketchUp model, then get to work using the application's set of tools. Lumion offers more functionality (Figure 19.14) and extensive tool sets, and is more powerful when compared to in-SketchUp rendering.

Lumion has been my renderer of choice for the past five years. Lumion solved all my rendering woes. It is fast, easy, and beautiful. Beyond its face-value simplicity, there is a depth of additional tweaks and tricks to make your visualization workflow even better. So why is Lumion the best?

Dynamic Link

Lumion allows for a direct .skp import (along with many other file types). Once you import and place your model in Lumion, you either apply Lumion properties to your SketchUp textures or swap the SketchUp textures with Lumion textures. Set up all your stills, animations, virtual tours, and VR. Export and present to your client.

Once it's time to make some design changes, revise the model in SketchUp, reload in Lumion, then re-export. As long as you don't change the names of your materials in SketchUp, everything stays linked, which makes revisions and creating design iterations a breeze. There is even a new Lumion Live Sync for SketchUp plugin that displays real-time updates from SketchUp in Lumion.

Preprocessing

In Lumion, you set up your presentation views then add effects. There are many different types of effects, weather, sun, etc. you can add before rendering (Figure 19.15). You can also add artistic effects that would normally

Figure 19.14 The Lumion logo.

be done in Photoshop—for example, noise, color correction, exposure, and lens flare. The ability to add these effects not only eliminates a step in your workflow, but it also eliminates the need for Photoshop altogether and drastically simplifies the rendering process.

TIP We always share our effects in tutorials and blog posts. Download a base package of Lumion Effects at **brightmandesigns.com/TSWFA/ch19.**

Figure 19.15 Lumion has a wide array of built-in styles and customizable effects.

Presentation Options

Lumion allows you to easily create stills, animations, virtual tours, and VR presentations. It is the entire package. It has everything you need to create any type of presentation all in one software.

Libraries

Lumion comes packed with a collection of objects, including vegetation, people, and furniture (Figure 19.16). The importance of libraries is so often overlooked. When comparing pricing, keep in mind that Lumion has several thousand objects included.

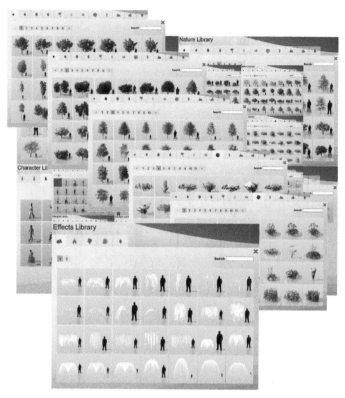

Figure 19.16 Lumion has an extensive library including more than 4,000 objects, most important of which is vegetation.

Postprocessing

It is always a good idea to run your final images through an image processor to fine-tune the brightness, contrast, color balance, etc. Photoshop and Lightroom are powerful image editors that you install locally on your computer. These programs come packaged together and are inexpensive and effective. Adobe is truly the industry standard for postprocessing graphics. These programs are designed for exactly what we need to do as a professional designer.

CHAPTER POINTS

☑ Stock SketchUp is not ideal for client presentations.

☑ Don't share SketchUp renderings. You can do better with extensions or Lumion.

☑ Choose the right style for your project's level of completion. A half-baked design can be advanced by using a sketchy style. A more complete model should be rendered a photo-real.

Chapter 20
Altered Reality

The future is now! In just a few years, virtual reality (VR) has stormed onto the scene and become the latest industry craze. Over the past two years, every booth at the major design trade shows has had to have a set of VR goggles. There's no disputing it's cool, but is it really a useful tool? Is this technology here to stay? Or is it likened to go the way of three-dimensional (3D) televisions, Google Glass, and QR codes? Based on my early and more recent experiences, I believe it is here to stay.

VIRTUAL REALITY

If you haven't tried a recent VR experience, do it. You will be amazed! The field of view areas have widened, the pixels are smaller, and the ease of use has drastically improved. Now, after you do the experience, do it again and again until the coolness wears off. It's only after you get past the coolness that you can really focus on the task at hand. Now let's talk about how to really use VR effectively.

Design Process

VR is great for placing yourself in a proposed design. The immersion into a space before it is built can answer so many questions that drawings can't. You can arrange furniture, move structures, and really feel the space. Is a ceiling too low? Analyze the sight lines. Basically, you can live in an environment momentarily before construction.

Real-time VR (Figure 20.1) is best for design. Put the goggles on, immerse yourself in the design, pull the goggles off, make a change, put the goggles on, and immerse yourself instantly in the new design. The graphics cards, hardware, and software are now at a place to make this look great.

When standing in the space, the right solution becomes much clearer and gives you confidence in your design decisions.

Client Presentations

VR presentations offer a challenge. Clients are often in awe, distracted by the technology, and unable to offer real feedback. If you do have a more informed, tech-savvy client who can handle the 3D environment, you are more likely to get useful feedback.

Static VR experiences are better for client presentations (Figure 20.2). These can be more casual—such as in a Google Cardboard. You can include everyone because they are cheap, rather than tethering one person to a high-priced rig.

Figure 20.1 Escape creates real-time room scale VR experiences to study space at a real scale.

Figure 20.2 Lumion exports image cubes and quadrilateral jpgs, which create more polished 3D presentations.

Hardware

Many clients don't want to mess up their hair, or they feel silly being the only one in the room with the goggles on. It can even make some people sick.

You need VR goggles to view your 3D VR output. There are several choices when it comes to hardware, each with their own strengths and weaknesses. It's worth knowing your options.

Google Cardboard

Cheapness is its superpower! Literally made of cardboard, the Google Cardboard (Figure 20.3) costs around $15, making it great for presentation deliverables. The experience is immersive, but the generic design does not fully enclose your viewing area. The pros are that it works with just about any phone, so clients can take it back to the office and show everyone else. It's best for quick and casual viewing. But because it doesn't strap to your head, it can be rather uncomfortable and cumbersome to use for more than a minute or two.

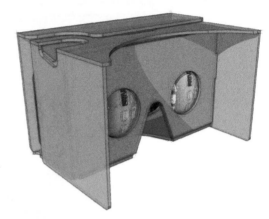

Gear VR

The Gear VR (Figure 20.4) is one step up, still requires an expensive phone, but costs only $100 for the setup. These goggles are very comfortable and are perfectly designed for the Samsung Galaxy line of phones. It is lacking in computing power, similar to Google Cardboard, because it runs on a phone. It is best used for static panorama viewing and is typically not powerful enough to fully navigate through a model and make it look good.

Figure 20.3 The Google Cardboard is inexpensive and easily branded, making it a great leave-behind at presentations.

Oculus Rift/HTC VIVE

The best quality of presentation and experience will come from a high-powered computer attached to a wired headset. The Oculus Rift and HTC VIVE (Figure 20.5) are still battling it out, and each has different advantages and limitations. They are both great solutions.

The Oculus Rift is inexpensive and portable, and it offers up a large community of games and VR experiences. The HTC VIVE has better resolution

Figure 20.4 The Gear VR is inexpensive and more comfortable, but it lacks computing and graphics horsepower.

but requires a larger area and more complex setup. Both of these goggles must run on a strong gaming computer, but they offer up the best graphics and full immersion in the virtual world. They both give the option for room-scale VR, the ability to physically walk around within the virtual world (just be sure to set up the boundaries).

Software

There are endless software options for VR.

Lumion allows for effects, complex lighting, and beautifully polished renders. At the current time, Lumion does not offer real-time VR, only stereo-scopic 3D panoramas (Figure 20.6).

Figure 20.5 High-end VR requires a high-end desktop rig.

There are loads of other software clawing to be the best. Some are designed to be beautiful, others to be utilitarian. The following real-time VR solutions are worth exploring.

- ☑ Iris: **irisvr.com**
- ☑ Insite: **insitevr.com**
- ☑ Kubity: **kubity.com**
- ☑ Symmetry: **symmetryvr.com**
- ☑ Modelo: **modelo.io**
- ☑ Enscape: **enscape3d.com**
- ☑ *See the latest list at* **brightmandesigns.com/TSWFA/ch20.**

Figure 20.6 Lumion can render high-quality, polished, 360 panoramic jpgs, perfect for VR presentations.

AUGMENTED REALITY

Augmented reality, sometimes called AR or mixed reality, is a technology that superimposes a computer-generated image on a user's view of the real world, providing a composite view.

Remember Pokémon Go? How cool was that—a bunch of people chasing digital animals in the real world? Now what if you could actually extract value out of this technology, rather than just distracting the world for a few weeks?

Imagine a Terminator-style heads-up display on glasses that could provide real-time feedback for first responders, coordinating GPS and voice information. Now let's refocus—how can this be used in the building industry? It could be used to show framing, wiring, and systems behind an existing wall without destroying any drywall. Imagine hard hats with heads-up displays, showing clashes in the actual building and isolated views of systems before they are actually placed. Or place a digital model on the conference table so everyone with goggles on sees the same thing.

A huge advantage of AR is that you are not cut off from the world; you can share the experience with others in the room. Although less immersive, it shows more promise for real-world applications.

TIP Google Glass was an early failed attempt at augmented reality, coining the phrase *glassholes*. If you have ever seen someone wearing these at a trade show, you know what I mean. A forward-pointing camera made anyone you looked at uncomfortable. Maybe a sleeker, camera-less version will be more popular.

Microsoft HoloLens

The leading AR headset is the Microsoft HoloLens (Figure 20.7). SketchUp is embracing this technology and already has an app available, which allows you to set the model on a table to walk around it or stand inside it and explore within. Check it out at **sketchup.com/products/sketchup-viewer**. Although promising, this technology still has a long way to go. The hardware is still very expensive, as is the app.

SightSpace Pro

SightSpace Pro has been in the AR game since before it was a thing. The app allows you to place a 3D model in the real world to be viewed through a phone or tablet. This gives you real context to analyze a design (Figure 20.8). This app is available now, is inexpensive, and provides a low barrier of entry into the world of AR. Check it out at sightspace.pro.

Figure 20.7 The SketchUp viewer for HoloLens app overlays a 3D model into the real world.

Figure 20.8 SightSpace Pro overlays a 3D design model on a live feed of the real world.

CHAPTER POINTS

☑ VR and AR are really cool. But what is even cooler than technology is using technology to solve problems, save time and money, and make better design decisions.

☑ At a bare minimum, get yourself a Google Cardboard to see if you catch the VR bug.

☑ Is VR here to stay? Only the market can decide. If you give it a chance and find that VR finds its way into your workflow, then the likely answer is yes.

☑ Use the right VR for your audience—real time for design in-house and more polished, static, 360 panoramas for presentations.

☑ Don't skimp on hardware; make sure you understand the headset specifications and requirements. A slow machine will provide an unimpressive VR experience.

☑ Stay tuned to our blog at **brightmandesigns.com/blog** for more up-to-date information on AR and VR.

PART VI

Construction Documents

During the Construction Documents (CD) phase, you will document all the final design decisions and compile them into a set of construction documents. These documents are the culmination of the SketchUp Workflow for Architecture, and they are where all your hard work and organization really pay off. In this section, you will see that you *can* create construction documents in LayOut and that the process is actually very efficient. Modeling is the hard part; documenting is easy.

Chapter 21

Crucial Concepts for Construction Documents

Creating construction documents doesn't have to be difficult. It's challenging enough to get drawings graphically and technically correct, so ideally you get the software out of your way. With the SketchUp Workflow for Architecture, you get all your ducks in a row in the model so that when it's crunch time, you can move quickly through documentation. You've created a design and organized it meticulously per the standards in Part IV; now let's lay out the entire process that follows.

1. Select a prebuilt title block. These show up on LayOut TITLE BLOCK layer (you will build a series of title blocks in Chapter 22, Title Blocks).

2. Insert the SketchUp model on the LayOut DRAWINGS layer. Several drawing "recipes" are provided in Chapter 23, Drawings.

3. Add annotations, dimensions, text, and schedules in LayOut. In Chapter 24, Annotations, you will create some prebuilt pieces of annotation called scrapbooks. These belong on the ANNOTATIONS layer.

4. Export your drawing set to .pdf to print and permit or to .dwg to share with consultants. Every possible export you will need is covered in Chapter 25, Exports.

Before you create the construction documents, you should understand some crucial SketchUp and LayOut concepts that will help you create your drawings quickly and efficiently. These are the strategies, techniques, and rules of thumb you will use to keep this train on the tracks. Then we will get to using what you learn in this chapter to build a title block, create drawings, annotate, and export.

ALWAYS OFF

Because of the way SketchUp works as a surface modeler, there will be times when you don't want to see an edge but you won't be able delete it because it is needed to complete a surface. This often happens when model organization groups meet—for example, at new and existing walls, between levels, and where exterior meets interior.

One option is to hide the edge, but hiding is more of a modeling utility than a permanent fix. If you never want to see a specific entity, assign it to the CONDOC_Always Off layer, which is always turned off in plan, section, elevation, and perspective.

Refer to the following images in Figure 21.1:

1. Notice that where the door was demolished and the new wall container meets the existing wall container, there are still lines. These lines need to remain in the model to make the surfaces, but they shouldn't be seen.

2. Double-click all the way into the existing wall's container, and select the edges as shown. Assign them to the CONDOC_Always Off layer. The edges are not gone yet because they also exist in the new wall's container.

3. Double-click all the way into the new wall's container, and select the edges as shown. Assign them to the CONDOC_Always Off layer.

4. The wall appears seamless now, as it should for perspective renderings and elevations.

5. Switch to the SCOPE utility scene, and note that both the new and existing functionality are maintained.

TIP Remember the all-edges-and-surfaces-are-drawn-on-Layer0 rule discussed in Chapter 5, SketchUp Basics? The CONDOC_Always Off layer is the one exception to that rule.

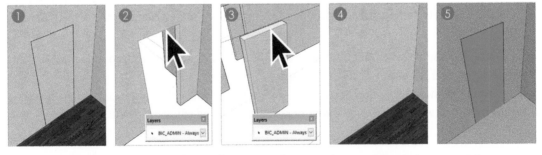

Figure 21.1 The CONDOC_Always Off layer allows you to show seamless transitions between containers.

LEVEL OF DETAIL

To conserve time and computing resources, include an appropriate level of detail in your models. If you are creating a building model to be used for design, presentation, and construction documents, you should think in terms of 1/8" plans. Typically, generic wall thicknesses provide plenty of detail, either to studs or including gypsum board. You don't need to model layers for drywall, studs, or plates in the main design model; you need to include only generic thicknesses and openings (Figure 21.2). Excessive detail is usually unnecessary, plus it will slow you down. You can describe any detail beyond that in a detail drawing, which is detached from the main proposed conditions design model.

Modeling studs, drywall, and sheathing (Figure 21.3) is not necessary for creating construction documents. Model more detail if you are using a plugin such as Estimator to calculate each part of the building or if you are creating three-dimensional (3D) details.

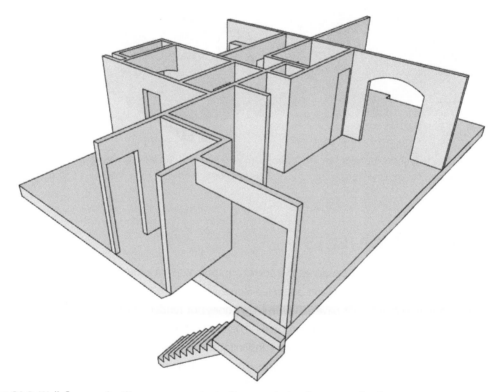

Figure 21.2 Wall, floor, and ceiling masses are typically enough detail to create the drawings needed to describe a design.

Figure 21.3 A detailed model representing the actual construction is helpful for estimating and detail vignettes, but it is not necessary for construction documents and visualization. Model by John Brock.

REPRESENTING OBJECTS

Many objects have a 3D form that produces the correct graphic when it is rendered in a plan—for example, toilets, tables, sinks, couches, and beds (see Figure 21.4).

There are also many objects that have a 3D form that does not render correctly in plan. For these, a graphic style can be forced with a two-dimensional (2D) graphic. Some examples are doors, upper cabinets, electrical outlets, and windows. To help you understand this concept, realize that a door shown in plan has a very graphical representation. Slicing through a three-dimensional door with a section plane will not produce the graphic you need for a plan. For any object like this, there will be a 3D object that

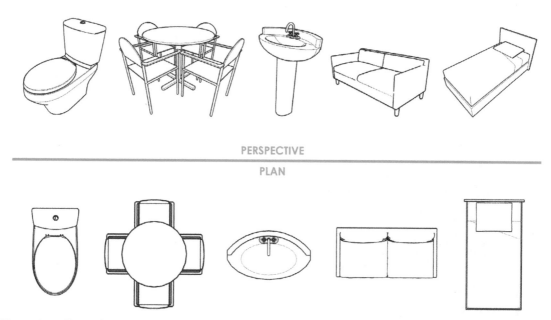

PERSPECTIVE

PLAN

Figure 21.4 These objects render properly in plan when looked at from above.

will be visible in perspective, section, and elevation views and a 2D graphic that will be visible in plan views (Figure 21.5).

The ConDoc Dynamic Door and Dynamic Window automatically reconfigure themselves when stretched to fit an opening. The 3D object and 2D graphic are compiled into one component that (Figure 21.6) resides within the CONDITION group. This object belongs on Layer0 as shown in Figure 21.7.

Figure 21.5 Utilizing a 2D graphic and a 3D object will allow the object to be represented properly in any drawing. These objects don't render properly in plan and require a 2D graphic.

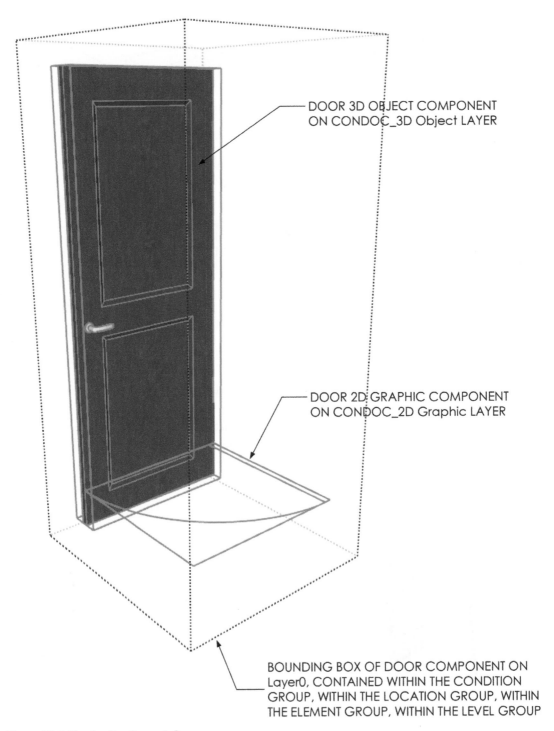

DOOR 3D OBJECT COMPONENT
ON CONDOC_3D Object LAYER

DOOR 2D GRAPHIC COMPONENT
ON CONDOC_2D Graphic LAYER

BOUNDING BOX OF DOOR COMPONENT ON
Layer0, CONTAINED WITHIN THE CONDITION
GROUP, WITHIN THE LOCATION GROUP, WITHIN
THE ELEMENT GROUP, WITHIN THE LEVEL GROUP

Figure 21.6 The ConDoc Dynamic Door.

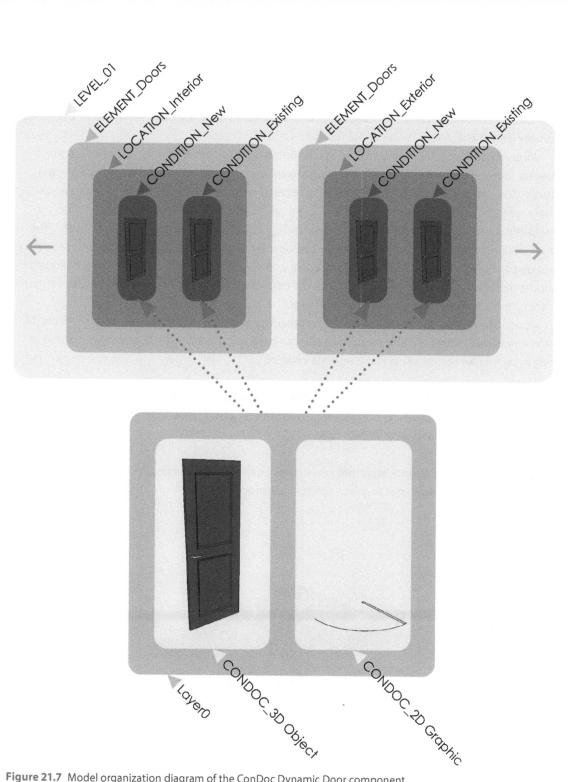

Figure 21.7 Model organization diagram of the ConDoc Dynamic Door component.

SECTION PLANES

Section planes are the key to describing 3D spaces in 2D diagrams. Most people think section planes are just used for building sections; but really, any plan is also created using a section plane, even if placed horizontally (Figure 21.8).

Horizontal section planes can be placed at the main level of the model or in an ELEMENT group if needed. One reason for placing it here is to cut different entities at different heights. Multiple section planes allow you to control which entities are being cut at what height (Figure 21.9). For instance, you might want the exterior walls to be cut at a different height than the interior walls. In such a case, you could add several section planes within the ELEMENT groups to cut everything exactly as needed. The main section plane should cut through the highest opening that needs to be represented. Use secondary section planes within the ELEMENT_Wall groups, or even further to the LOCATION groups, to accurately cut the model down further. The section cut at the base level of the model trumps all secondary cuts within groups, so each section is limited by the larger.

Section planes are separated by containers. In other words, a section plane within a group affects the geometry in that group only. This means that you can have multiple active section planes per scene, as long as each active section plane is in a separate container.

TIP It's okay to add multiple groups for any level of the nested groups with the layer applied to it, even if they are repeating the same layer. Overlayering is a common mistake, but in this case, it is being used for a purpose. This will allow more section cuts.

TIP You can use the same stacking techniques to make more descript building sections and detail vignettes. You can peel each layer back at a different distance.

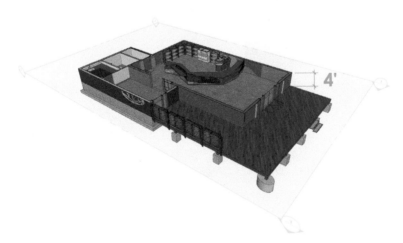

Figure 21.8 The horizontal section planes sit approximately 4' above the finished floor.

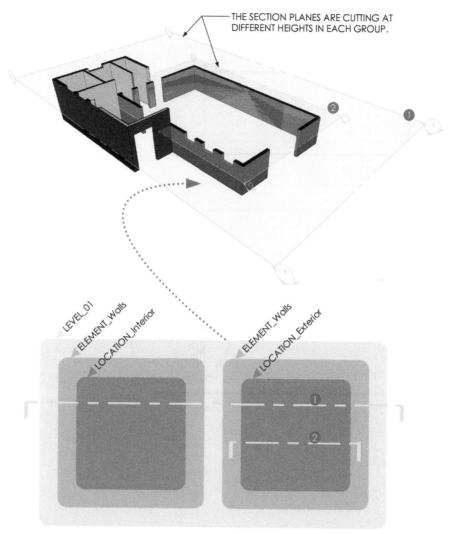

THE SECTION PLANES ARE CUTTING AT DIFFERENT HEIGHTS IN EACH GROUP.

LEVEL_01
ELEMENT_Walls
LOCATION_Interior

ELEMENT_Walls
LOCATION_Exterior

Figure 21.9 One active section plane per group. The larger section planes trump the smaller.

RENDERING SETTINGS THEORY

LayOut provides expanded rendering settings. You should set each viewport to render independently of the next as a vector, raster, or hybrid. Vector is ideal for large, high-resolution prints of fairly simple line drawings (Figure 21.10), and Raster is ideal for anything heavy with texture images (Figure 21.11). A hybrid combines both styles for a composite view with vector linework and raster texture images (Figure 21.12). Keep in mind that hybrid rendering can often take up to twice as long to complete.

TIP X-ray faces and back edges can be represented only by the raster rendering setting.

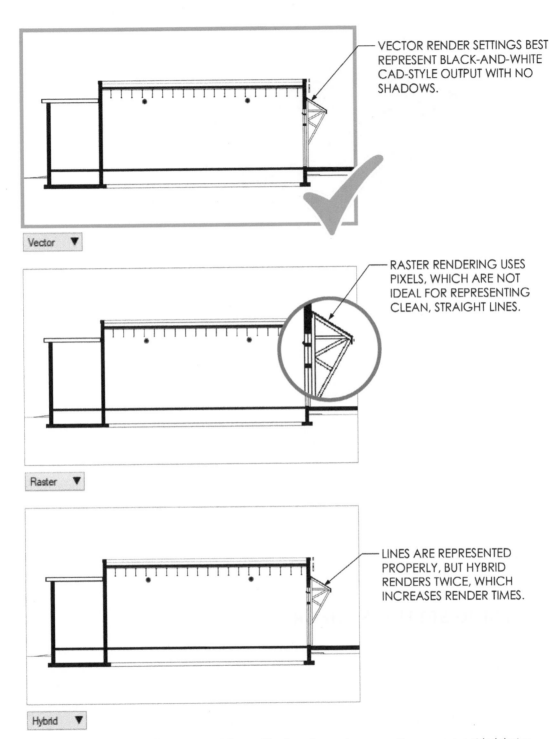

VECTOR RENDER SETTINGS BEST REPRESENT BLACK-AND-WHITE CAD-STYLE OUTPUT WITH NO SHADOWS.

Vector ▼

RASTER RENDERING USES PIXELS, WHICH ARE NOT IDEAL FOR REPRESENTING CLEAN, STRAIGHT LINES.

Raster ▼

LINES ARE REPRESENTED PROPERLY, BUT HYBRID RENDERS TWICE, WHICH INCREASES RENDER TIMES.

Hybrid ▼

Figure 21.10 The vector rendering setting is best utilized on viewports representing computer-aided design (CAD)-style black-and-white output without shadows.

SKY COLORS AND WATERMARKS CANNOT BE REPRESENTED.

RASTER-BASED TEXTURE IMAGES ARE REPRESENTED AS AVERAGED COLOR FILLS.

SHADOWS ARE RASTER-BASED AND NOT REPRESENTED IN VECTOR RENDERS.

Vector ▼

RASTER RENDER SETTINGS BEST REPRESENT COMPLEX STYLES, WATERMARKS, SKETCHY EDGES, BACK EDGES, X-RAY, AND SHADOWS.

Raster ▼

COMPLEX SKETCHY EDGES ARE REDUCED TO STRAIGHT VECTOR LINES.

Hybrid ▼

Figure 21.11 The raster rendering setting is best utilized on viewports with complex styles and texture images, typically perspective views and any scene with a complex style.

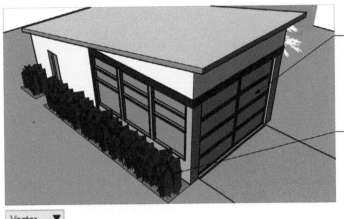

VECTOR RENDERING IS RARELY USED FOR A PERSPECTIVE BECAUSE IT DOES NOT SHOW TRANSPARENCIES.

TRANSPARENT .PNG TEXTURES ARE NOT REPRESENTED ACCURATELY.

Vector ▼

RASTER PIXELATION IS NOT IDEAL FOR LARGE-SCALE PRINT.

Raster ▼

HYBRID BEST REPRESENTS STRAIGHT EDGE STYLES AND SHADOWS.

Hybrid ▼

Figure 21.12 The hybrid setting is best utilized on viewports that have fairly simple styles with straight lines, combined with texture images and shadows.

LINE WEIGHT THEORY

There is no such thing as a line weight in SketchUp, only a multiplier that will be translated to a line thickness in LayOut. The number you enter into the Line Weight field in LayOut is the thinnest line that will be displayed in the viewport. Any profiles, section cuts, or depth cues will be multiplied by this number to thicken them up (Figure 21.13). For instance, if the section cuts are set to 3, the profiles are set to 2, and the viewport line weight is set to .4, then the thinnest lines will be .4, the profiles will be .8, and the section cuts will be 1.2.

You will need to adjust this number based on the detail in your drawing as well as the size and scale of your drawing. Don't worry: There are suggested line weights that will work for each popular scale, or you can use the ConDoc Tools to completely automate this task.

STACKING VIEWPORTS

The ability to completely control line weights in your drafting software is critical to any drafting workflow. To completely control this in LayOut—unlocking unlimited line weights—you will need to master the concept of stacking viewports.

Each plan drawing in your set of construction documents is composed of one or more viewports. Each viewport is linked to a plan scene within SketchUp. Each plan scene within SketchUp represents an array of line weights. This means that you will typically create one scene for "heavy" line weights (walls and floors) and one scene for "light" line weights (doors, windows, furniture, etc.).

To do this, you will need to stack the viewports in LayOut. Each viewport can have a line weight applied to it. Once you apply a line weight to the viewport, the style will translate that line weight into an array based on the profile and section cut settings. Figure 21.14 illustrates why it is best to assign line weights of .4 and 1.0. As you can see in the figure, these settings provide the largest array of line weights for a rather large architectural scale.

There is really no limit to the number of viewports you can stack; however, to keep your presentation and number of scenes manageable, two is usually enough (Figure 21.15); three or more are necessary only if you need several different hatches.

All viewports that comprise a drawing belong on the DRAWINGS layer in LayOut. You could use layers to control the stacking order, but then you would have a lot more layers to manage in LayOut. An easier way to manage the stacking order is to send the viewport backward and forward. Either use the Arrange toolbar or right-click on a viewport and select Arrange, then Send Backward or Send Forward to manage the stacking order or sublevels of the layer.

The suggested stacking order and rendering settings of viewports is as follows (Figure 21.16):

☑ Light viewport on top, rendered as a hybrid, no active section

☑ Heavy viewport below, rendered as a vector, active section

☑ Any hatching on the very bottom, rendered as a vector for fills and raster for patterns, active sections

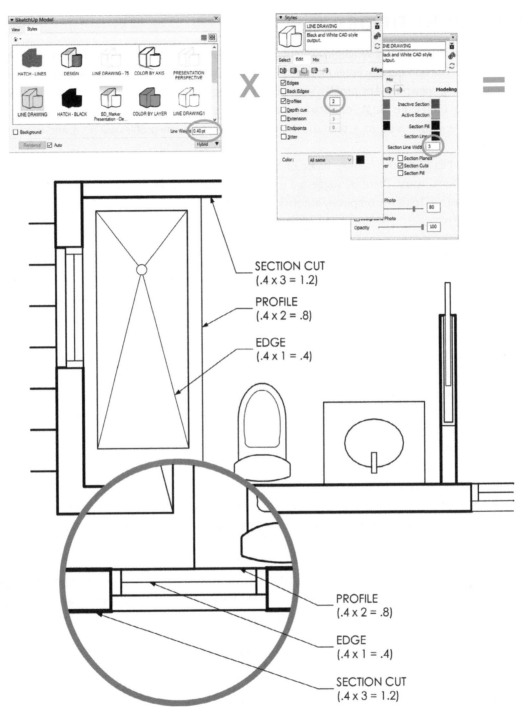

Figure 21.13 A line weight in LayOut is the product of the multipliers assigned to styles in SketchUp combined with the line weight assigned to the viewport in LayOut.

TIP There is no need to insert the SketchUp model multiple times to create multiple stacked viewports. You can copy and paste the viewport right on top of the copied viewport. You can also use the Duplicate command available in the Edit drop-down menu. Hold down the Shift key and use the arrow keys to nudge the new viewport four times up and four times to the left so that it is once again aligned.

HATCHING

Through the creative use of styles, or simply by drawing the hatch in LayOut, you can add hatching to your LayOut drawings. Each hatch method has its own limitations and requirements regarding efficiency and rendering settings. Before you incorporate hatching, explore all the options and then apply the best strategy for your particular design and set of drawings.

SketchUp Hatch

Using SketchUp to create the hatch provides a dynamically linked hatch in LayOut. This means that if you move a wall, the wall lines and hatch will update simultaneously in all the LayOut drawings. This method is ideal because it eliminates the need to redraw hatches as your design evolves.

If you are printing in black and white, you can create a nice array of fills with grays 10 to 25 percent apart. However, you need to be selective with the amount of hatching you use in this way because each hatch requires its own viewport, which further complicates the stacking of viewports.

The hatch styles made in Chapter 8, SketchUp Collections, makes all geometry filled in with a vector fill or a pattern fill. When shown in parallel projection, at the bottom of the viewport stack, the hatch viewport fills in the lines above properly. Walls must have a bottom face in order to see the hatch. 2D Graphics will block out the hatch below (Figure 21.17).

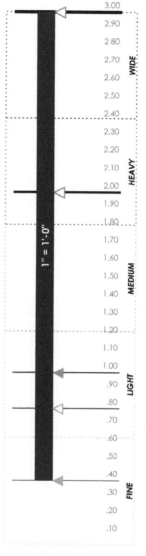

◀ LIGHT VIEWPORT
◀ HEAVY VIEWPORT
(FILL = LINE WEIGHT IS ASSIGNED IN LAYOUT)
(NO FILL = LINE WEIGHT IS A PRODUCT OF STYLE MULTIPLIER)

Figure 21.14 An array of line weights. This diagram is a good learning tool for interpreting the more complex line weight diagrams in Chapter 23, Drawings.

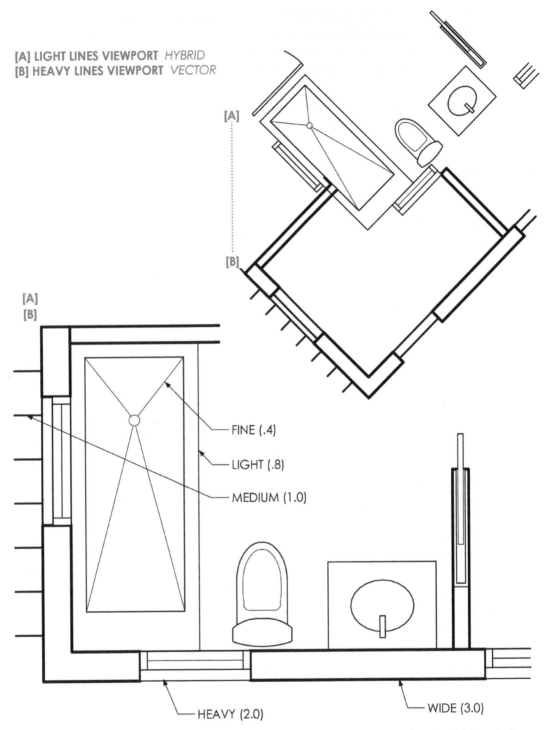

[A] LIGHT LINES VIEWPORT *HYBRID*
[B] HEAVY LINES VIEWPORT *VECTOR*

[A]

[B]

[A]
[B]

FINE (.4)

LIGHT (.8)

MEDIUM (1.0)

HEAVY (2.0)

WIDE (3.0)

Figure 21.15 When stacked together, the viewports provide five line weights in one drawing; this is typically plenty to develop a beautiful graphic drawing style.

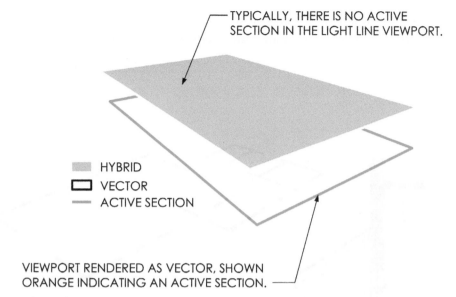

TYPICALLY, THERE IS NO ACTIVE
SECTION IN THE LIGHT LINE VIEWPORT.

HYBRID
VECTOR
ACTIVE SECTION

VIEWPORT RENDERED AS VECTOR, SHOWN
ORANGE INDICATING AN ACTIVE SECTION.

Figure 21.16 The render settings and stacking order are very important: Vectors render as a wireframe; hybrids render with a transparent background in the viewport.

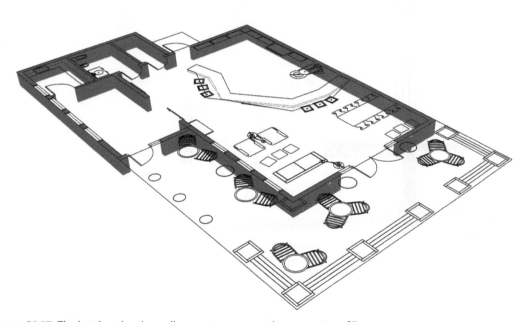

Figure 21.17 The hatch styles show all geometry as one color or a pattern fill.

You can also use the new section fill feature in SketchUp 2018 to hatch (Figure 21.18). The Section Fill property of a style helps tremendously with creating vertical building sections and plans with simple hatches.

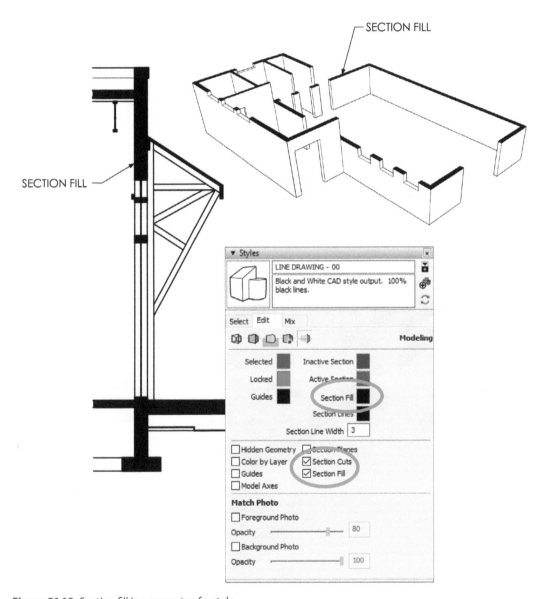

Figure 21.18 Section fill is a property of a style.

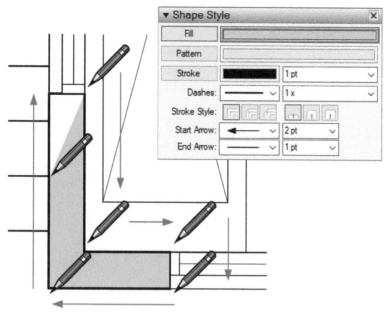

Figure 21.19 Use the Drawing tools in LayOut to create vector fills.

LayOut Hatch

Another hatching method is to use the Drafting tools in LayOut to create a solid vector fill or raster pattern (Figure 21.19). To do that, activate any of the Drawing tools, set the fill to the desired hatch color or hatch pattern, and turn off the stroke. Add LayOut shapes or lines with fills and patterns to define special hatched areas. Be sure to right-click on the fill and select Arrange > Send to Back so that the lines will be on top.

The major downside to creating hatches in LayOut is that there is no dynamic link between the hatch and the drawing. If you update the plan, you will need to be aware of any conflicts created with the hatching. The benefit of this method is that you will be able to add as much hatching as you like with any pattern you need. Typically, this technique is best utilized for smaller areas of hatching.

TIP Right-click on any hatch, and choose Send to Back. All hatches sit at the bottom of the stack on the DRAWINGS layer.

CHAPTER POINTS

☑ Leverage ConDoc layers to achieve a desired look and level of detail within your drawings.

☑ Choosing the right rendering setting will make your presentation look better and save you time.

☑ Line weights are achieved through multipliers assigned in SketchUp and applied to a viewport's line weight. The line weight array is further expanded by stacking multiple viewports.

☑ A 3D object is always present when a 2D graphic is used to force a visual style.

Chapter 22

Title Blocks

A title block gives a first impression of your company—whether you have your act together. A sloppy title block instills doubt in the drawings within, whereas a professional, clear title block will instill confidence. In this chapter, you will create a title block for presentation drawings and another for construction documents.

By effectively using LayOut collections, you will be able to open your own title block and already have your company's address and logo inserted so you won't have to keep changing it.

TEMPLATES

Templates can be quite useful. They can be hard-lined, traditional architectural title blocks, or they can be optimized for screen presentations. In this section, you will create a customized architectural title block and a go-to title block for presentations and for construction documents (Figure 22.1).

Creating a Presentation Title Block Template

Before you can use a title block template, you'll need to create it. You have already reviewed all the skills and tools you need to do just that. In this section you will create a presentation title block (Figure 22.2).

Getting Started

Follow these step-by-step instructions to create your own presentation title block:

1. Open LayOut, and start a new presentation using the BD_8.5x11 – Landscape template.
2. Click on the File drop-down menu, and choose Document Setup > Grid.

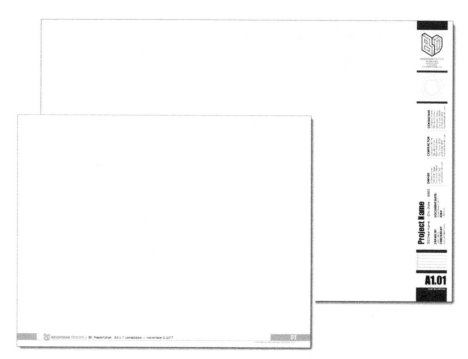

Figure 22.1 The presentation and architectural title blocks.

Figure 22.2 A presentation title block is perfect for quick presentations. It gives any diagram, image, or sketch a professional branded frame.

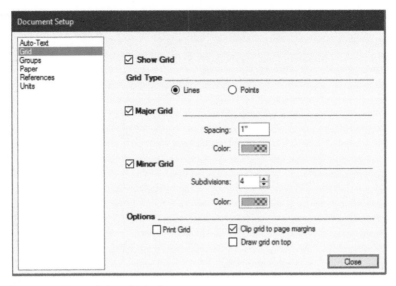

Figure 22.3 The Document Setup dialog, Grid tab.

3. On the Grid tab (Figure 22.3), turn on the grid and adjust it to 1" with four subdivisions.

4. Right-click in the gray background area, and check Grid snap.

5. Unlock and set the active layer to TITLE BLOCK.

Adding Lines and Shapes

To develop a unique graphic style, you'll need to add lines, as indicated here:

1. Activate the Line tool, turn on the Stroke, turn off the Fill and set the stroke color to a 75 percent gray and a thickness of 1 as shown in Figure 22.4.

2. Click once to start the line at the bottom-right corner of the margin, move your cursor straight across on the axis, then double-click to finish the segment (Figure 22.5).

3. Activate the Rectangle tool, turn off the Stroke, turn on the Fill, and set the fill color to a 75 percent gray (Figure 22.6).

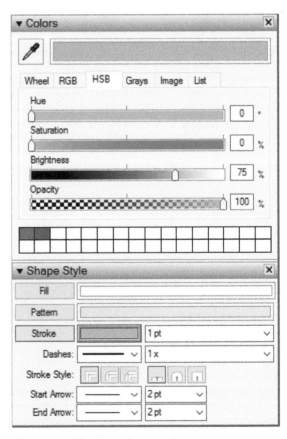

Figure 22.4 The Shape Style settings.

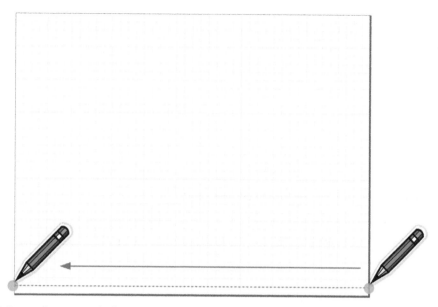

Figure 22.5 Draw a line across the bottom.

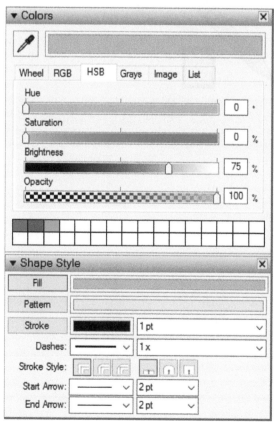

Figure 22.6 The Shape Style settings.

4. Click once to start the rectangle at the bottom-right corner of the margin (Figure 22.7). Draw a rectangle as shown.

5. Using the Select tool, hold Ctrl (Option on a Mac) to make a copy of the rectangle straight across to the other side of the title block (Figure 22.8).

6. Using the Select tool, scale the recently copied rectangle to half its size as shown in Figure 22.9.

Adding Images

By following these steps, you can add images to your presentation title block.

1. Click on the File drop-down menu, and choose Insert.

2. Navigate to the TSWFA files, and choose the `BD_Cubix Logo - Linear.jpg`.

3. Using the Select tool, resize and position the logo image on the title block as shown (Figure 22.10).

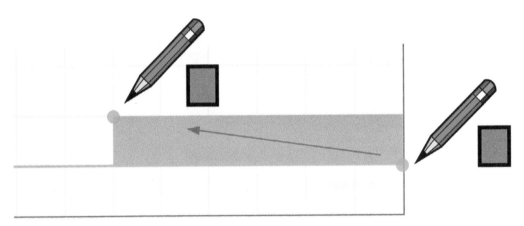

Figure 22.7 Draw the rectangle.

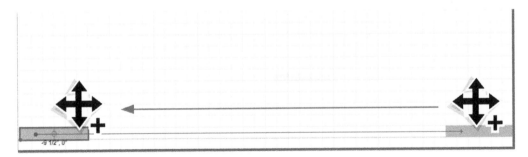

Figure 22.8 Make a copy of the rectangle.

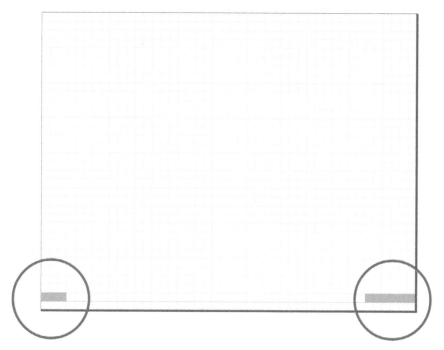

Figure 22.9 Arrange the rectangles as shown.

Figure 22.10 Image placed on the title block line.

Adding Text

Use the Text tool to add several informational text boxes to your title block (Figure 22.11).
Follow these steps:

1. Add a text box for your drawing name and the date created using the Text Style properties shown in Figure 22.12. These are default auto-text tags. Type ":: <FileName> :: <DateModified>" or insert them from the Text drop-down > Auto-text. Once you tap Esc to finish editing the text, the field will populate with the corresponding information.

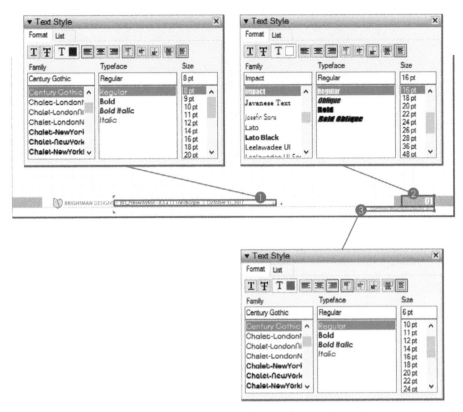

Figure 22.11 Place text boxes in your title block. Overall graphic numbering the text boxes.

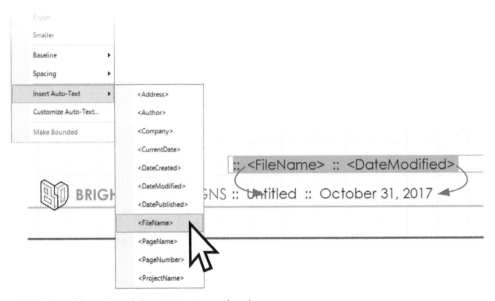

Figure 22.12 Text edit mode and the auto-text populated.

Figure 22.13 Text edit mode and the auto-text populated.

2. Add a generic text box for the sheet number using the Text Style properties shown in Figure 22.13. While in text edit mode, click on the Text drop-down and choose Insert Auto-Text, then select "PageNumber>."

3. Add a generic text box for the copyright information using the text style properties shown in Figure 22.13. Add your info here, such as Copyright Brightman Designs, 2017.

Saving as a Template

Now that you have created your own title block, you can optimize the settings and save it to your collection.

1. Click on the File drop-down menu, and choose Document Setup.

2. On the Grid tab, turn off the grid.

3. On the Paper tab, turn off the margins.

4. Click on the File drop-down menu, and choose Save As Template.

5. Select the RESOURCES/TEMPLATES folder and save it with the name BD_Presentation – 8.5 x 11 Landscape.

Now, every time you open LayOut or start a new presentation, this title block will be available in the Getting Started window.

Creating an Architectural Title Block Template

Before you can use an architectural title block template, you'll need to create one. You have already reviewed all the skills and tools you need to do just that. An architectural title block is better suited for construction documents (Figure 22.14). Built into the template are placeholders for client and team contact information.

Figure 22.14 An architectural title block is larger and has more information.

Getting Started

Follow these step-by-step instructions to create your own architectural title block:

1. Open LayOut, and start a new presentation using the BD_Blank - 8.5 x 11 Landscape template.

2. Click on the File drop-down menu, and choose Document Setup > Grid.

3. On the Grid tab (Figure 22.15), turn on the grid and adjust it to 1" with four subdivisions.

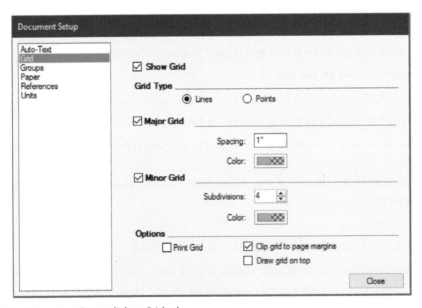

Figure 22.15 The Document Setup dialog, Grid tab.

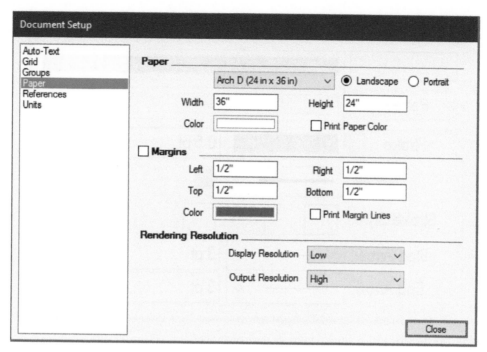

Figure 22.16 The Document Setup dialog, Paper tab.

4. On the Paper tab (Figure 22.16), change the paper size to Arch D (24 in x 36 in) and adjust the margins to 1/2".

5. Right-click in the gray background area, then check Grid snap.

6. Unlock and set the active layer to TITLE BLOCK.

Adding Lines and Shapes

To develop a unique graphic style, you'll need to add lines, as indicated here:

1. Activate the Rectangle tool, turn off the Stroke, turn on the Fill, and set the fill color to a 25 percent gray. Click once to start the line at the bottom-right corner of the margin (Figure 22.17).

2. Draw a rectangle as shown (Figure 22.18).

3. Using the Select tool, hold Ctrl (Option on a Mac) to make a copy of the rectangle straight up by 2 1/2".

4. Using the Select tool, scale the rectangle down, then once the command is finished, type 1/4" and press Enter. This dials in a precise dimension.

5. Add and arrange the rectangles as shown (Figure 22.19).

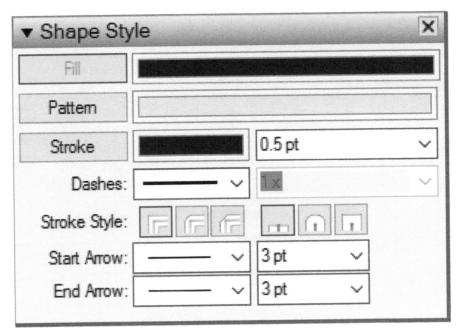

Figure 22.17 Use the Shape Style settings to create the margin lines.

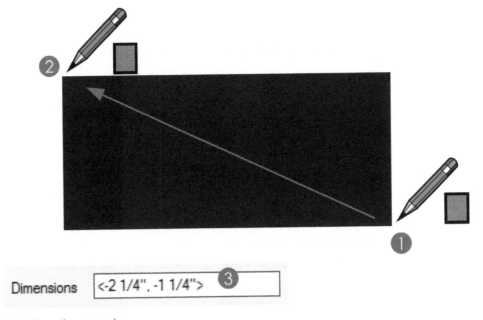

Figure 22.18 Draw the rectangle.

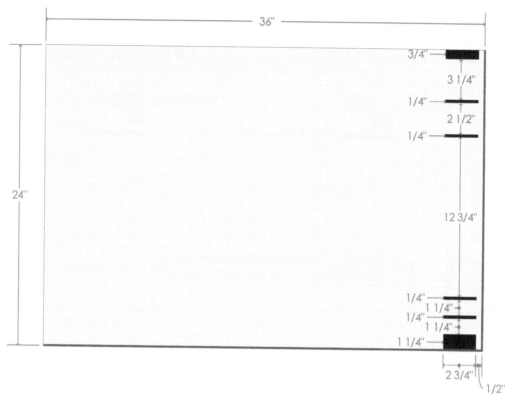

Figure 22.19 Arrange the rectangles as shown.

Adding Text

Use the Text tool to add several informational text boxes to your title block. Once a text box is created, use the Select tool to rotate and place the text as shown in Figure 22.20.

Follow these steps:

1. Add a text box for the sheet description.

2. Add a text box for the sheet number.

3. Add a text box for the project name.

4. Add a text box for the project address.

5. Add text boxes for the project details and team as shown in Figure 22.21.

TIP You can assign different properties to the text in a text box. Double-click in the text box, and select the top line of text. Within the Text Style inspector, change the selection to bold, independent of the rest of the text in the text window (Figure 22.22).

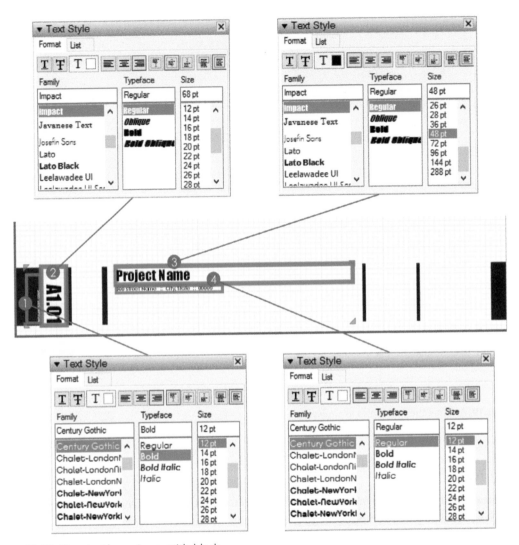

Figure 22.20 Place text boxes in your title block.

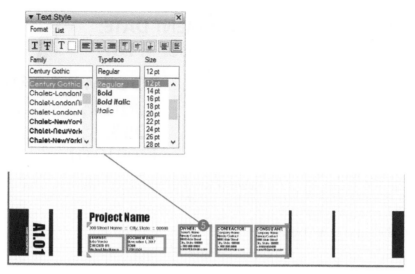

Figure 22.21 Place text boxes in your title block.

Assign Auto-text Attributes

Auto-text will save you time on repetitious pieces of text. Create one auto-text tag so you can easily insert linked text. This makes your title block more dynamic; it will actually start to fill itself out, too. Keep in mind that auto-text is case-sensitive.

Follow these steps to assign some default auto-text tags:

Figure 22.22 Two different text styles applied within the same text box.

1. Double-click into the Sheet Description text box, and replace the current text with <Page-Name>. The page name assigned within the Pages inspector will populate (Figure 22.23).

2. Double-click into the Page Number text box, and replace the current text with <PageNumber>. Notice that you can combine regular text with auto-text (Figure 22.24).

Figure 22.23 The Sheet Description auto-text box.

Figure 22.24 The sheet number auto-text populates with the LayOut page number.

3. Double-click into the project information text box, and replace the current text with <DateModified> (Figure 22.25). Follow these steps to assign some custom auto-text tags:

DOCUMENT DATE:
November 1, 2017
JOB#:
170910.01

DOCUMENT DATE:
<DateModified>
JOB#:
170910.01

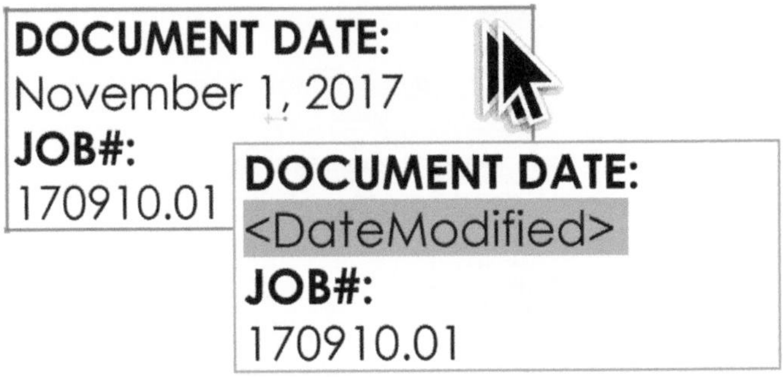

Figure 22.25 Document date is now linked to the date when the project is saved.

1. Double-click into the Project Name text box, and replace the current text with <Project-Name>. There is no auto-text information associated with this tag, so nothing special will happen yet.

2. Click on the File drop-down, and choose Document Setup > Auto-Text.

3. Click on the plus (+) sign to add a new custom text tag (Figure 22.26).

4. Type <ProjectName> in the new tag field. Press Enter to confirm the new tag.

5. In the Settings input below, type the Project Name as you would like it to show up on the empty title block template (Figure 22.27 and Figure 22.28).

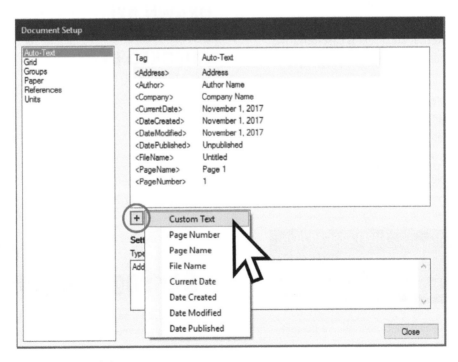

Figure 22.26 The Auto-Text dialog.

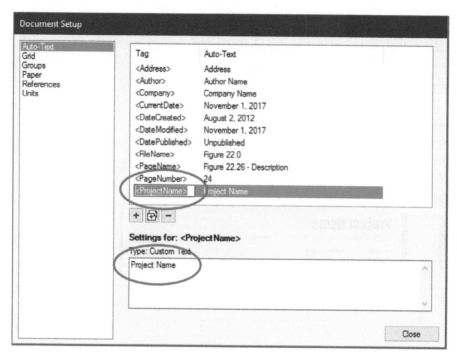

Figure 22.27 The Auto-Text dialog, adding custom text tag.

Figure 22.28 The <ProjectName> tag now properly displays as Project Name.

Consider adding custom auto-text tags for team information, project address, and any other repetitive text. This way, you can fill out the project information once within the auto-text tag settings, then it will update on all title blocks and cover pages.

Adding Accents and Details

By following these steps, you can add details and accents to your title block (Figure 22.29):

1. Using the Line tool and Polygon tool set to three sides, create the lines and triangles for the revision list. You could also add some preformatted, ready-to-fill text fields.

2. Add lines between the project team members as shown.

3. Add a series of dotted circles to create a subtle placeholder for an architectural stamp. The Offset tool helps with this task.

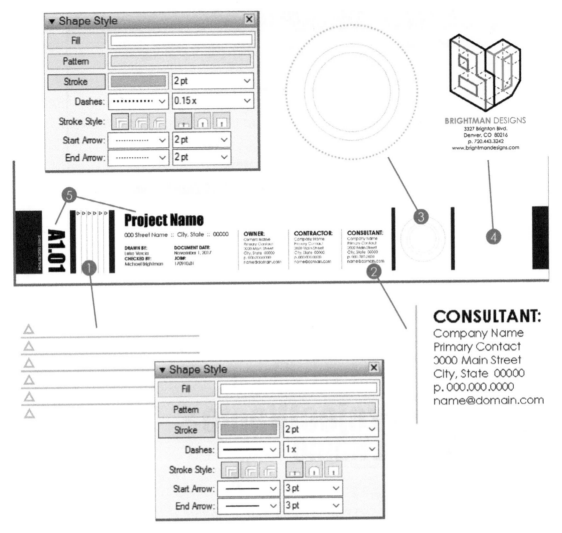

Figure 22.29 Add miscellaneous details and accents.

4. Click on the File drop-down menu, and choose Insert. Navigate to the TSWFA files, and choose the `BD_Cubix Logo - Square.jpg`. Using the Select tool, resize and position the logo image on the title block.

5. Duplicate the page number and project name text boxes. Change the color of the text to create a subtle drop shadow effect as shown in Figure 22.30.

Figure 22.30 A subtle drop shadow effect can give the title block more pop.

Saving as a Template

Now that you have created your own title block, you can optimize the settings and save it to your collection.

1. In the Layers inspector, lock the TITLE BLOCK layer.

2. Set the active layer to DRAWINGS.

3. Click on the File drop-down menu, and choose Document Setup.

4. On the Grid tab, turn off the grid.

5. On the Paper tab, turn off the margins.

6. Click on the File drop-down menu, and choose Save As Template.

7. Select the RESOURCES/TEMPLATES folder, and save it with the name BD_24x36 Landscape – Architectural.

Now, every time you open LayOut or start a new presentation, this title block will be available in the Getting Started window.

Custom Title Blocks

Now get creative and design your own. Use your logo, address, and pertinent information. If you are looking for inspiration on design ideas, try a Google Images search for "modern construction drawings." Pinterest has some nice inspiration boards, too.

If you find something you like, you can import it as an image, trace over it, then adjust it to make it your own.

You can even duplicate the title blocks you just made and mold them into different sizes and orientations, portrait or landscape (Figure 22.31).

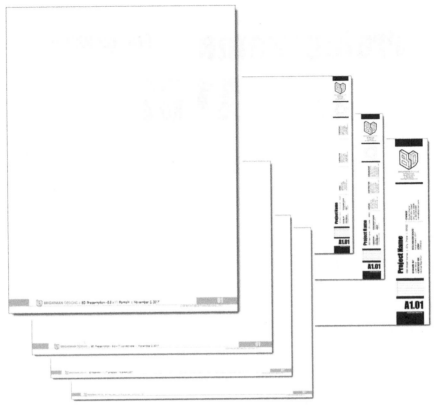

Figure 22.31 Modify the presentation and architectural title blocks into several sizes and layout orientations to fit any project.

CHAPTER POINTS

☑ You can download professionally built title blocks and scrapbooks at **brightmandesigns.com/TSWFA** and **condoctools.com**, as well as review extended content regarding the creation of construction documents with SketchUp Pro and LayOut.

☑ Create the templates now so you don't have to think about it when it's crunch time.

☑ Good sizes for presentations are letter, legal, and tabloid.

☑ Good sizes for construction documents are Arch C, Arch D, and Arch E.

Chapter 23

Drawings

I t's time to explain your design with clear and concise diagrams. Using the SketchUp Workflow for Architecture, you can create any type of drawing in any style—plans, sections, elevations, and details displayed in black and white or color. Combining the skills you already have with the recipes in this chapter, you will learn how to create your drawings quickly.

DRAWINGS

Every drawing is composed of a scene, or a combination of several scenes with varying styles, all combined and carefully stacked within LayOut. The instructions throughout this chapter explain how to make many common plans that are needed to describe a building. Keep these tips in mind:

TIP The ConDoc Tools completely automate everything described in this chapter relating to creating scenes and stacking viewports. If you value your time, use ConDoc.

- ☑ There are three different ways to control the visibility of geometry in scenes: hide, layer visibility, and sections planes.

- ☑ These are simply recipes that you can put together for success. Once you understand how they go together, riff on it—adjust styles, layers, hatches, and line weights. Make it your own. There are infinite possibilities.

- ☑ In new construction, we typically hatch the exterior walls different from the interior walls. In renovation, we hatch new walls different from existing walls.

- ☑ These drawings give you a good idea of what is possible. They will work for most projects, but you will need to mix, match, and blend these techniques based on your project and visual style.

TIP A crucial part of model organization is that all edges and surfaces are drawn on Layer0, so it is assumed Layer0 is always turned on in every scene to create the plans. This saves space in the scene organization diagrams.

☑ Some drawings can be reused to create new drawings. For instance, it might be easier to add electrical symbols to a construction plan, or a reflected ceiling plan, than create a separate drawing stack.

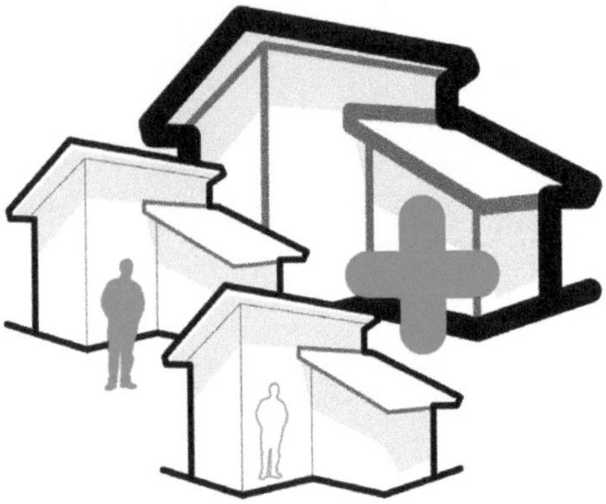

Perspectives

Perspective drawings are the easiest of all, requiring only one viewport; no section planes are necessary. Style is up to you; perspectives can be sketchy, hard-lined, color, or black-and-white. The ConDoc Perspective tool (Figure 23.1) automates interior and exterior perspective scenes by assigning a style, adjusting layers, optimizing shadows, and numbering the scenes (Figure 23.2).

Figure 23.1 The ConDoc Perspective tool is free and automates the creation of perspective scenes.

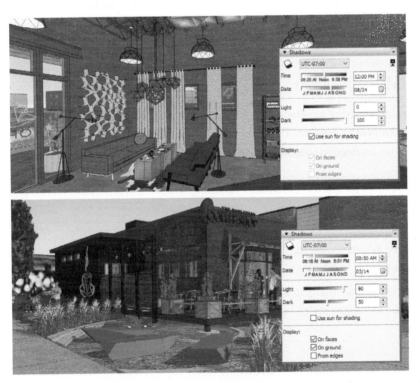

Figure 23.2 Exterior perspectives look great with a sketch style and hard shadows. To best represent interior perspectives, turn the shadows off, turn on Use sun for shading, then set the light slider to 0 and the dark slider to 100. This will brighten up the entire space, especially the ceiling.

Line weights depend on the size of the rendering and the style you choose. Perspectives do not have a scale, so you can't set it as one-size-fits-all. If you are using the LINE DRAWING - Presentation (Figure 23.2) style created in Chapter 8, SketchUp Collections, then a range of .25 to 1 is safe. Use the rule of thumb below:

- ☑ Letter size: .25 line weight
- ☑ Tabloid: .5 line weight
- ☑ 24" x 36": .75 line weight
- ☑ 36" x 48": 1 line weight

Adjust as necessary; some sketchy edge styles look better with nonconventional line weights. When in doubt, use the prescribed line weights, but don't hesitate to try a few options.

It is always best to set up the scene in SketchUp, then assign it to a viewport in LayOut. Create the Perspective scenes in SketchUp with the listed layers visible, and then stack the viewports in LayOut with the settings and order shown in Figure 23.3.

TIP The free ConDoc Perspective tool automates optimal shadow settings. Click to add an exterior perspective, hold Ctrl (Option on Mac), and click to add an interior perspective.

Elevations and Sections

To learn how to create sections and elevations, you will use a more complex and developed model, `BD_3655 Milwaukee St - Proposed.skp`, that includes multiple levels. Typically, a section or elevation section plane will exist at the base level of the model, outside of any container.

Multiple active section planes in different ELEMENT containers can help you control how different nested elements are represented. For instance, you could cut the site away from a section at a depth different than the one from the foundation.

Section drawings and elevation drawings only require one viewport. Figure 23.4 shows an array of suggested line weights for sections and elevations.

Perspective

Perspectives provide a visually attractive 3D snapshot.

Most of the ELEMENT layers are visible, but this is ultimately based on preference.

Render settings is dependent on the style, but raster is a safe default.

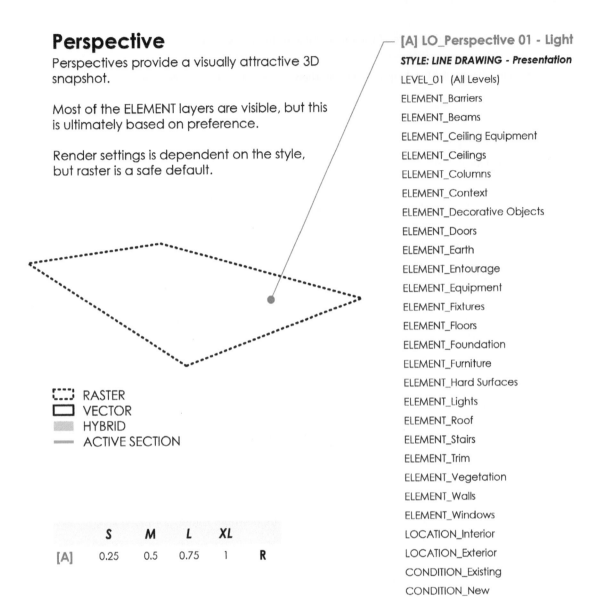

RASTER
VECTOR
HYBRID
ACTIVE SECTION

	S	M	L	XL	
[A]	0.25	0.5	0.75	1	R

[A] LO_Perspective 01 - Light

STYLE: LINE DRAWING - Presentation

LEVEL_01 (All Levels)
ELEMENT_Barriers
ELEMENT_Beams
ELEMENT_Ceiling Equipment
ELEMENT_Ceilings
ELEMENT_Columns
ELEMENT_Context
ELEMENT_Decorative Objects
ELEMENT_Doors
ELEMENT_Earth
ELEMENT_Entourage
ELEMENT_Equipment
ELEMENT_Fixtures
ELEMENT_Floors
ELEMENT_Foundation
ELEMENT_Furniture
ELEMENT_Hard Surfaces
ELEMENT_Lights
ELEMENT_Roof
ELEMENT_Stairs
ELEMENT_Trim
ELEMENT_Vegetation
ELEMENT_Walls
ELEMENT_Windows
LOCATION_Interior
LOCATION_Exterior
CONDITION_Existing
CONDITION_New
CONDOC_3D Object

Figure 23.3 Perspective scene organization diagram.

ELEVATION AND SECTION LINE WEIGHTS

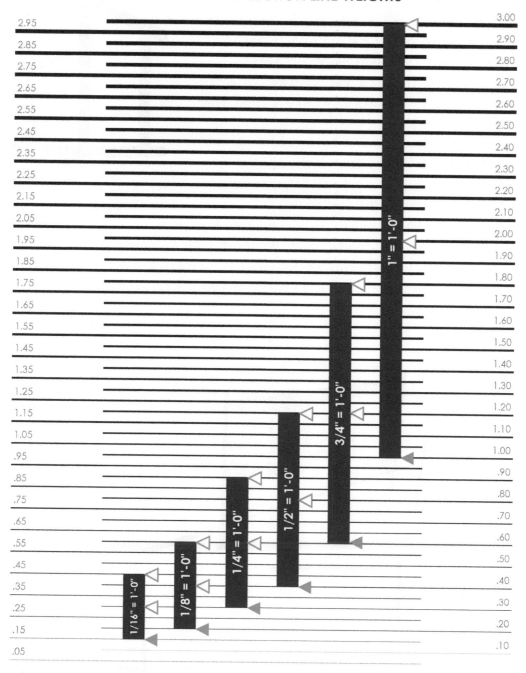

Figure 23.4 Line weight chart for section and elevation drawings.

Building Sections

Building sections describe the relationship between the levels of a structure, and they provide interior elevation information. Keep these other tips in mind when you create section drawings:

☑ The ConDoc Section tool automates section scenes by adding the active section plane, naming the scenes in sequence, and optimizing all other settings (Figure 23.5).

☑ Place the building section plane at the base level of the model so it cuts through all ELEMENTS (Figure 23.6).

☑ Right-click on a section plane, and choose Align View to set the camera view perpendicular to the section plane.

Figure 23.5 The ConDoc Section tool.

☑ Use the LINE DRAWING - 00 style to create a black-and-white drawing, or use the LINE DRAWING - Presentation style to create a color section.

☑ Use the Drawing tools in LayOut to create fills and accentuate the two-dimensional (2D) SketchUp drawings to give them more visual pop. In SketchUp 2018, you can add section fills to your style.

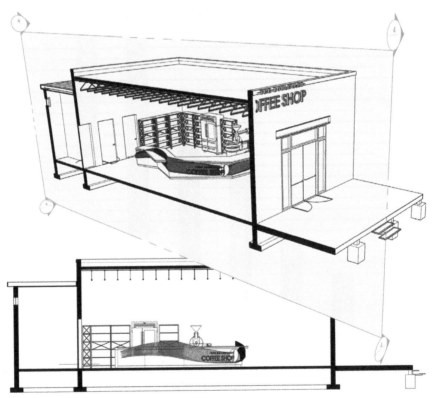

Figure 23.6 A building section plane is typically added at the base level of the model for a building section. Bury additional section planes inside ELEMENT groups to achieve the desired visual effect.

Create the Section scenes in SketchUp with the listed layers visible, and then add the viewport in Lay-Out with the settings shown in Figure 23.7.

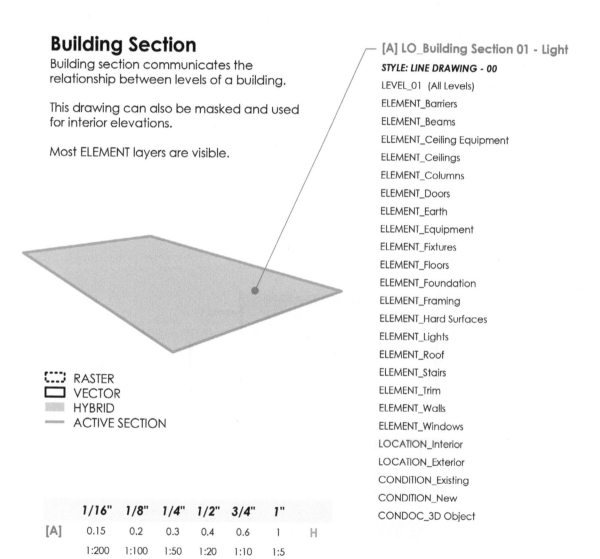

Building Section

Building section communicates the relationship between levels of a building.

This drawing can also be masked and used for interior elevations.

Most ELEMENT layers are visible.

⸺ RASTER
▭ VECTOR
▬ HYBRID
― ACTIVE SECTION

[A] LO_Building Section 01 - Light

STYLE: LINE DRAWING - 00

LEVEL_01 (All Levels)
ELEMENT_Barriers
ELEMENT_Beams
ELEMENT_Ceiling Equipment
ELEMENT_Ceilings
ELEMENT_Columns
ELEMENT_Doors
ELEMENT_Earth
ELEMENT_Equipment
ELEMENT_Fixtures
ELEMENT_Floors
ELEMENT_Foundation
ELEMENT_Framing
ELEMENT_Hard Surfaces
ELEMENT_Lights
ELEMENT_Roof
ELEMENT_Stairs
ELEMENT_Trim
ELEMENT_Walls
ELEMENT_Windows
LOCATION_Interior
LOCATION_Exterior
CONDITION_Existing
CONDITION_New
CONDOC_3D Object

	1/16"	1/8"	1/4"	1/2"	3/4"	1"	
[A]	0.15	0.2	0.3	0.4	0.6	1	H
	1:200	1:100	1:50	1:20	1:10	1:5	

Figure 23.7 Building Section scene organization diagram.

Interior Elevations

Interior elevations are typically drawn at a larger scale than building sections and elevations, and they describe vertical dimensions and finishes. Keep the following tips in mind when you're creating interior elevations:

☑ Start by using a building section scene in SketchUp, or even an existing building section scene. Or you can use one that was created with the ConDoc Section tool.

☑ Turn off layers, and hide as much geometry as possible in SketchUp. LayOut will process all the geometry that is turned on, even if it is not shown in your viewport.

☑ Apply a clipping mask in LayOut to isolate the desired portion of the drawing (Figure 23.8).

☑ Use the LINE DRAWING - 00 style to create a black-and-white drawing, or use the LINE DRAWING - Presentation style to create a color interior elevation.

☑ Use the Drawing tools in LayOut to create fills and accentuate lines. This will give your drawing more pop.

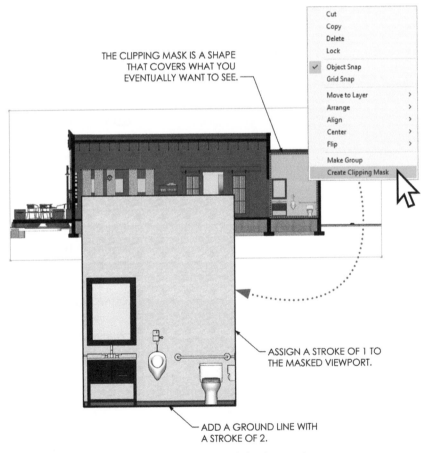

Figure 23.8 The interior elevation uses a building section and clipping mask.

Exterior Elevations

Exterior elevations convey materials and vertical heights. Keep the following tips in mind when you're creating exterior elevations:

- ☑ The ConDoc Elevation tool expedites this entire process (Figure 23.9).

- ☑ Right-click on a surface on the elevation that you are creating, and choose Align View to set the camera perpendicular to the selected face. This technique is especially helpful when aligning the camera view with an angled wall.

- ☑ In SketchUp, use section planes to peel away unwanted portions of the site.

- ☑ In SketchUp, use fog to provide a sense of depth.

- ☑ In LayOut, use a clipping mask to remove unwanted portions of the site (Figure 23.10).

- ☑ You can get trees from three-dimensional (3D) trees in SketchUp or from the preloaded 2D tree scrapbook collections in LayOut. Use the LINE DRAWING - 00 style to create a black-and-white drawing, or use the LINE DRAWING - Presentation style to create a color elevation.

Figure 23.9 The ConDoc Elevation tool.

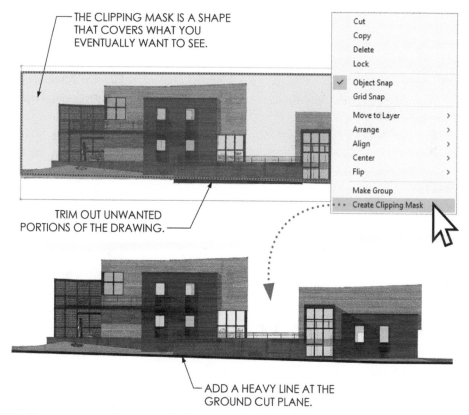

THE CLIPPING MASK IS A SHAPE THAT COVERS WHAT YOU EVENTUALLY WANT TO SEE.

TRIM OUT UNWANTED PORTIONS OF THE DRAWING.

Cut
Copy
Delete
Lock

✓ Object Snap
Grid Snap

Move to Layer
Arrange
Align
Center
Flip

Make Group
• • • Create Clipping Mask

ADD A HEAVY LINE AT THE GROUND CUT PLANE.

Figure 23.10 Remove unwanted portions of a building elevation by applying a clipping mask.

TIP Any LayOut entity that complements the drawing, such as a hatch or ground line, belongs on the DRAWINGS layer.

Create the Elevation scenes in SketchUp with the listed layers visible, and then add the viewport in LayOut with the settings shown in Figure 23.11.

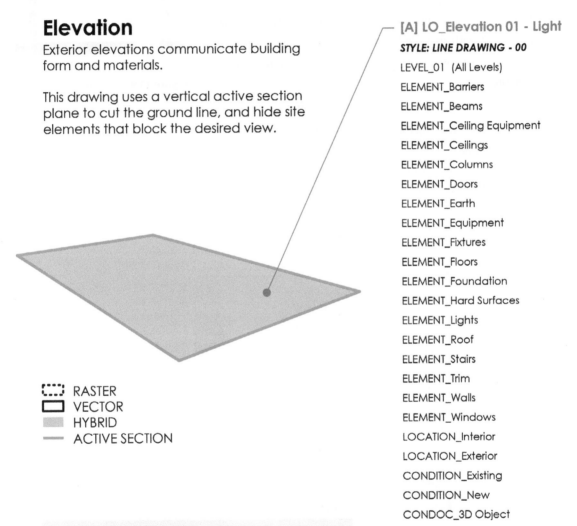

Elevation

Exterior elevations communicate building form and materials.

This drawing uses a vertical active section plane to cut the ground line, and hide site elements that block the desired view.

[...] RASTER
[ ] VECTOR
HYBRID
— ACTIVE SECTION

[A] LO_Elevation 01 - Light

STYLE: LINE DRAWING - 00

LEVEL_01 (All Levels)
ELEMENT_Barriers
ELEMENT_Beams
ELEMENT_Ceiling Equipment
ELEMENT_Ceilings
ELEMENT_Columns
ELEMENT_Doors
ELEMENT_Earth
ELEMENT_Equipment
ELEMENT_Fixtures
ELEMENT_Floors
ELEMENT_Foundation
ELEMENT_Hard Surfaces
ELEMENT_Lights
ELEMENT_Roof
ELEMENT_Stairs
ELEMENT_Trim
ELEMENT_Walls
ELEMENT_Windows
LOCATION_Interior
LOCATION_Exterior
CONDITION_Existing
CONDITION_New
CONDOC_3D Object

	1/16"	1/8"	1/4"	1/2"	3/4"	1"	
[A]	0.15	0.2	0.3	0.4	0.6	1	H
	1:200	1:100	1:50	1:20	1:10	1:5	

Figure 23.11 Elevation scene organization diagram.

Plans

Each *plan drawing* is created by stacking two or more viewports on top of one another. Use the scene organization diagrams (SODs) to create the necessary scenes in SketchUp. Next, assign the scenes to viewports in LayOut, and stack the plans as shown in the SODs to create each plan drawing. While you're building these plans, keep in mind the following:

☑ All the plans should share the same camera location with the top-down view set to parallel projection.

☑ It is okay for several floor plan scenes to share the same section plane.

☑ Color fill hatches render as a vector; pattern hatches must render as a raster. When in doubt, set hatches to render as hybrid to catch all.

☑ Typical stacking order is as follows: light lines on top, heavy lines under, vector hatch, then raster hatch must be on the bottom.

☑ Sometimes you need a bigger plan to further explain a complex space and make room for cramped annotations and dimensions. Create enlarged plans by increasing the drawing scale and clipping the plan viewports.

☑ Typically, the section plane for a plan should be approximately 4' off the finished floor.

TIP This is a complicated process with a lot of steps represented by the SODs and viewport stacking diagrams. Your first time through might be a little frustrating. Now would be a good time to visit **brightmandesigns.com/TSWFA/ch23** and watch the video tutorials on how to create these drawings, then use the book as a guide as you make the drawings yourself.

Figure 23.12 illustrates typical plan line weights when using two viewports. It is an excellent tool for determining the best line weight arrays at different scales. The settings shown are very close to the default line weights used by the ConDoc Drawings.

Existing Conditions Plan

The *existing conditions plan* represents the structure as it stands, before you make any changes. This is the simplest plan drawing to create because it only has two stacked viewports. The existing conditions plan is derived from the `BD_3655 Milwaukee St - Existing Conditions.skp` model (Figure 23.13).

Use the SODs to create the necessary scenes in SketchUp. Next, assign the scenes and properties to viewports in LayOut, and stack the plans as shown in the SODs to create the existing conditions plan (Figure 23.14).

Foundation Plan

The *foundation plan* describes what the new structure is to be built on. New walls are delineated through the use of a hatch fill, and below-grade footings are shown dashed. The foundation plan is derived from the `BD_BLVD Coffee Shop.skp` model (Figure 23.15).

Use the scene SODs to create the necessary scenes in SketchUp. Next, assign the scenes and properties to viewports in LayOut, and stack the plans as shown in the SODs to create the foundation plan (Figure 23.16).

Construction Plan

The *construction plan* describes what is to be built. New walls are delineated through the use of a hatch fill. The new construction plan is derived from the `BD_BLVD Coffee Shop.skp` model (Figure 23.17).

Use the scene SODs to create the necessary scenes in SketchUp. Next, assign the scenes and properties to viewports in LayOut, and stack the plans as shown in the SODs to create the construction plan (Figure 23.18).

TIP The construction plan is a great base for many other plans. Turn on the ELEMENT_Furniture layer to make a furniture plan. Turn on the ELEMENT_Equipment layer to make an equipment plan. Turn on ELEMENT_Lights for a lighting/electrical plan.

Roof Plan

The *roof plan* describes what is to be built. A roof plan can also be used as a site plan if the ELEMENT_Earth, ELEMENT_Hard Surface, and ELEMENT_Vegetation layers are visible. The roof plan is derived from the `BD_BLVD Coffee Shop.skp` model (Figure 23.19).

Use the scene SODs to create the necessary scenes in SketchUp. Next, assign the scenes and properties to viewports in LayOut, and stack the plans as shown in the SODs to create the roof plan (Figure 23.20).

Floor Framing Plan

The *floor framing plan* describes what is to be built, and how it will be held up. This drawing relies heavily on the 2D graphics applied to the columns, beams, and framing members. The floor framing plan is derived from the `BD_BLVD Coffee Shop.skp` model (Figure 23.21).

Use the scene SODs to create the necessary scenes in SketchUp. Next, assign the scenes and properties to viewports in LayOut, and stack the plans as shown in the SODs to create the floor framing plan (Figure 23.22).

Roof Framing Plan

The *roof framing plan* describes what is to be built, and how it will be held up. This drawing relies heavily on the 2D graphics applied to the columns, beams, and framing members. The roof framing plan is derived from the `BD_BLVD Coffee Shop.skp` model (Figure 23.23).

Use the scene SODs to create the necessary scenes in SketchUp. Next, assign the scenes and properties to viewports in LayOut, and stack the plans as shown in the SODs to create the roof framing plan (Figure 23.24).

TYPICAL PLAN LINE WEIGHTS

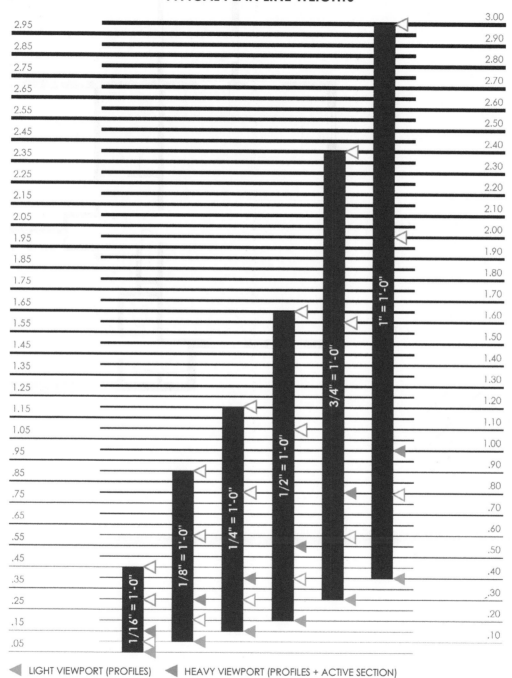

Figure 23.12 Line weight chart for a typical plan.

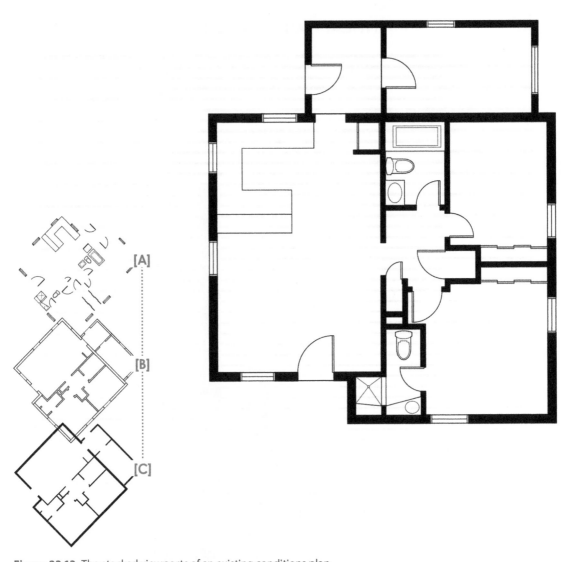

Figure 23.13 The stacked viewports of an existing conditions plan.

Existing Conditions Plan

The existing conditions plan represents a structure as it stands at the beginning of a project.

All walls are hatched black to give a simple representation of the space plan.

This drawing is ideal for sketching on top of to generate design ideas.

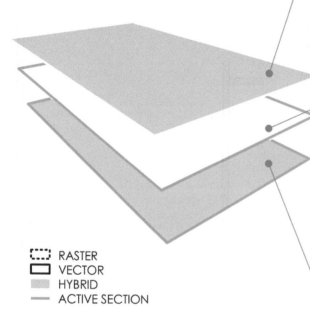

RASTER
VECTOR
HYBRID
ACTIVE SECTION

[A] LO_Existing Conditions Plan 01 - Light

STYLE: LINE DRAWING - 00

LEVEL_01
ELEMENT_Barriers
ELEMENT_Doors
ELEMENT_Equipment
ELEMENT_Fixtures
ELEMENT_Windows
LOCATION_Exterior
LOCATION_Interior
CONDITION_Demolished
CONDITION_Existing
CONDOC_2D Graphic

[B] LO_Existing Conditions Plan 01 - Heavy

STYLE: LINE DRAWING - 00

LEVEL_01
ELEMENT_Columns
ELEMENT_Floors
ELEMENT_Roof
ELEMENT_Stairs
ELEMENT_Walls
LOCATION_Exterior
LOCATION_Interior
CONDITION_Demolished
CONDITION_Existing
CONDOC_2D Graphic

[C] LO_Existing Conditions Plan 01 - Hatch A

STYLE: HATCH - 00

LEVEL_01
ELEMENT_Walls
LOCATION_Exterior
LOCATION_Interior
CONDITION_Demolished
CONDITION_Existing
CONDOC_2D Graphic
CONDOC_Always Off

	1/16"	1/8"	1/4"	1/2"	3/4"	1"	
[A]	0.05	0.1	0.15	0.2	0.3	0.4	H
[B]	0.15	0.3	0.4	0.55	0.8	1	V
[C]	NA	NA	NA	NA	NA	NA	H
	1:200	1:100	1:50	1:20	1:10	1:5	

Figure 23.14 The SOD for the existing conditions plan.

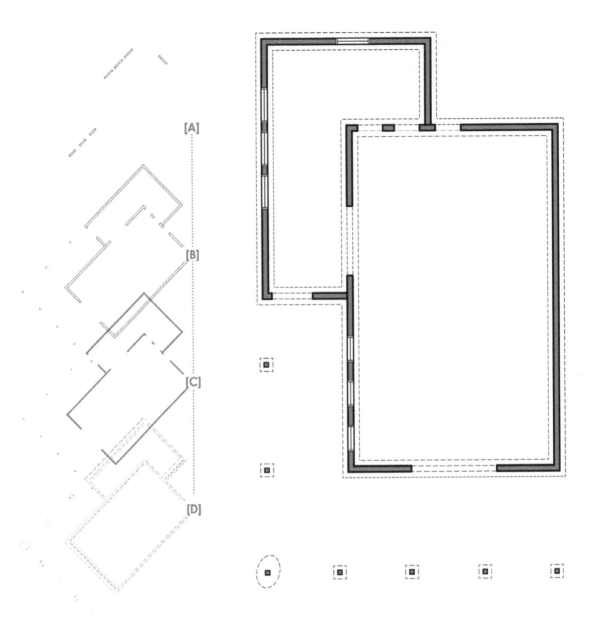

Figure 23.15 The stacked viewports of a foundation plan.

Foundation Plan

The foundation plan communicates where to pour the foundation walls.

Dashed lines represent the foundation of the building.

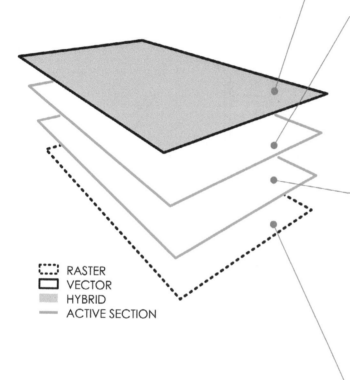

[A] LO_Foundation Plan 01 - Light
STYLE: LINE DRAWING - 00
LEVEL_01
ELEMENT_Windows
LOCATION_Exterior
CONDITION_Existing
CONDITION_New
CONDOC_2D Graphic

[B] LO_Foundation Plan 01 - Heavy
STYLE: LINE DRAWING - 00
LEVEL_01
ELEMENT_Columns
ELEMENT_Walls
LOCATION_Exterior
CONDITION_Existing
CONDITION_New
CONDOC_2D Graphic

[C] LO_Foundation Plan 01 - Hatch A
STYLE: HATCH - 50
LEVEL_01
ELEMENT_Columns
ELEMENT_Walls
LOCATION_Exterior
CONDITION_Existing
CONDITION_New
CONDOC_2D Graphic
CONDOC_Always Off

[D] LO_Foundation Plan 01 - Dashed
STYLE: LINE DRAWING - Dashed
LEVEL_01
ELEMENT_Foundation
LOCATION_Exterior
LOCATION_Interior
CONDITION_Existing
CONDITION_New
CONDOC_2D Graphic

RASTER
VECTOR
HYBRID
ACTIVE SECTION

	1/16"	1/8"	1/4"	1/2"	3/4"	1"	
[A]	0.05	0.1	0.15	0.2	0.3	0.4	H
[B]	0.15	0.3	0.4	0.55	0.8	1	V
[C]	NA	NA	NA	NA	NA	NA	V
[D]	0.25	0.35	0.5	0.6	0.9	1.2	R
	1:200	1:100	1:50	1:20	1:10	1:5	

Figure 23.16 The SOD for the foundation plan.

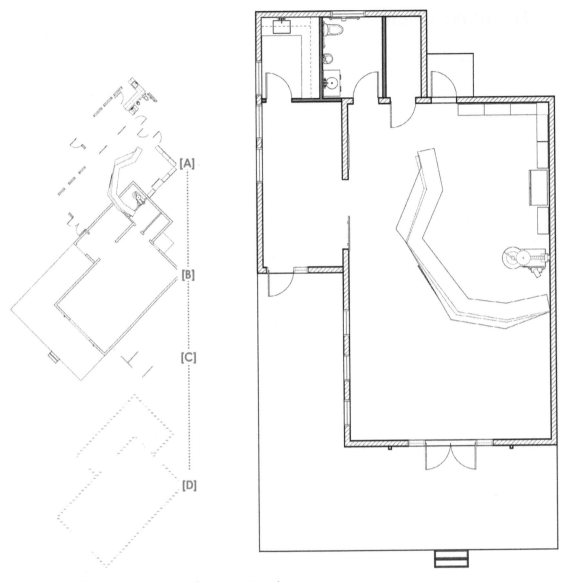

Figure 23.17 The stacked viewports of a construction plan.

Construction Plan

Construction plan represents what is to be built from scratch.

Walls are hatched by interior and exterior.

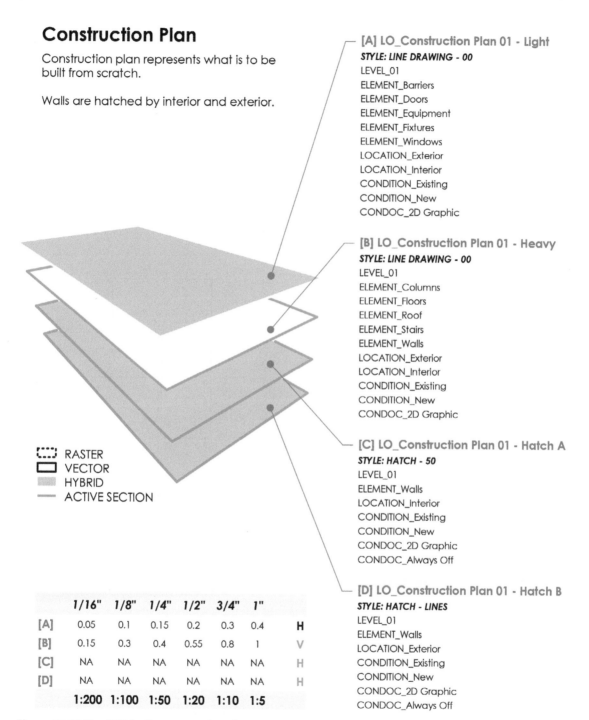

RASTER
VECTOR
HYBRID
ACTIVE SECTION

[A] LO_Construction Plan 01 - Light
STYLE: LINE DRAWING - 00
LEVEL_01
ELEMENT_Barriers
ELEMENT_Doors
ELEMENT_Equipment
ELEMENT_Fixtures
ELEMENT_Windows
LOCATION_Exterior
LOCATION_Interior
CONDITION_Existing
CONDITION_New
CONDOC_2D Graphic

[B] LO_Construction Plan 01 - Heavy
STYLE: LINE DRAWING - 00
LEVEL_01
ELEMENT_Columns
ELEMENT_Floors
ELEMENT_Roof
ELEMENT_Stairs
ELEMENT_Walls
LOCATION_Exterior
LOCATION_Interior
CONDITION_Existing
CONDITION_New
CONDOC_2D Graphic

[C] LO_Construction Plan 01 - Hatch A
STYLE: HATCH - 50
LEVEL_01
ELEMENT_Walls
LOCATION_Interior
CONDITION_Existing
CONDITION_New
CONDOC_2D Graphic
CONDOC_Always Off

[D] LO_Construction Plan 01 - Hatch B
STYLE: HATCH - LINES
LEVEL_01
ELEMENT_Walls
LOCATION_Exterior
CONDITION_Existing
CONDITION_New
CONDOC_2D Graphic
CONDOC_Always Off

	1/16"	1/8"	1/4"	1/2"	3/4"	1"	
[A]	0.05	0.1	0.15	0.2	0.3	0.4	H
[B]	0.15	0.3	0.4	0.55	0.8	1	V
[C]	NA	NA	NA	NA	NA	NA	H
[D]	NA	NA	NA	NA	NA	NA	H
	1:200	1:100	1:50	1:20	1:10	1:5	

Figure 23.18 The SOD for the construction plan.

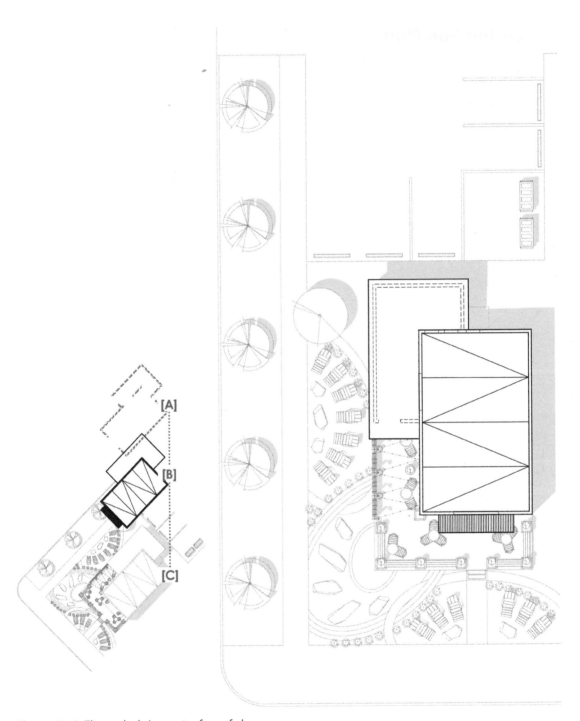

Figure 23.19 The stacked viewports of a roof plan.

Roof Plan

The roof plan drawing does not use levels.

It uses only three viewports, which are stacked out of the usual order - heavy is on top.

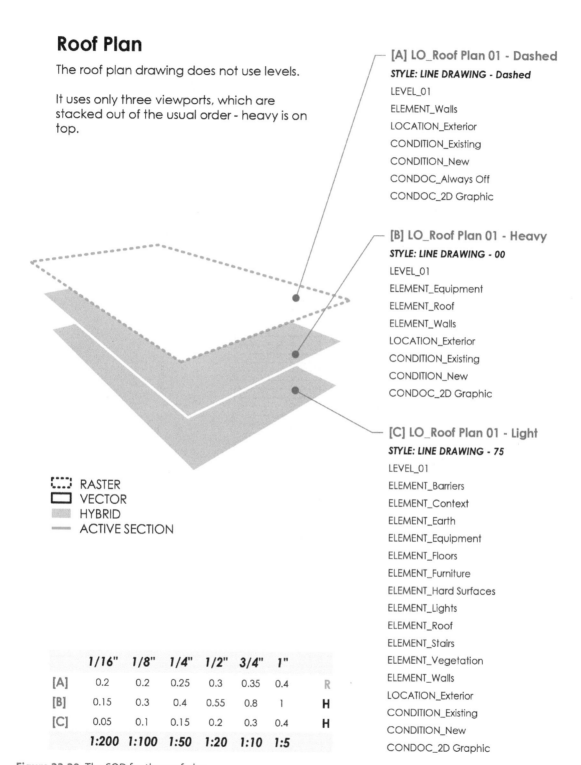

RASTER
VECTOR
HYBRID
ACTIVE SECTION

[A] LO_Roof Plan 01 - Dashed
STYLE: LINE DRAWING - Dashed
LEVEL_01
ELEMENT_Walls
LOCATION_Exterior
CONDITION_Existing
CONDITION_New
CONDOC_Always Off
CONDOC_2D Graphic

[B] LO_Roof Plan 01 - Heavy
STYLE: LINE DRAWING - 00
LEVEL_01
ELEMENT_Equipment
ELEMENT_Roof
ELEMENT_Walls
LOCATION_Exterior
CONDITION_Existing
CONDITION_New
CONDOC_2D Graphic

[C] LO_Roof Plan 01 - Light
STYLE: LINE DRAWING - 75
LEVEL_01
ELEMENT_Barriers
ELEMENT_Context
ELEMENT_Earth
ELEMENT_Equipment
ELEMENT_Floors
ELEMENT_Furniture
ELEMENT_Hard Surfaces
ELEMENT_Lights
ELEMENT_Roof
ELEMENT_Stairs
ELEMENT_Vegetation
ELEMENT_Walls
LOCATION_Exterior
CONDITION_Existing
CONDITION_New
CONDOC_2D Graphic

	1/16"	1/8"	1/4"	1/2"	3/4"	1"	
[A]	0.2	0.2	0.25	0.3	0.35	0.4	R
[B]	0.15	0.3	0.4	0.55	0.8	1	H
[C]	0.05	0.1	0.15	0.2	0.3	0.4	H
	1:200	1:100	1:50	1:20	1:10	1:5	

Figure 23.20 The SOD for the roof plan.

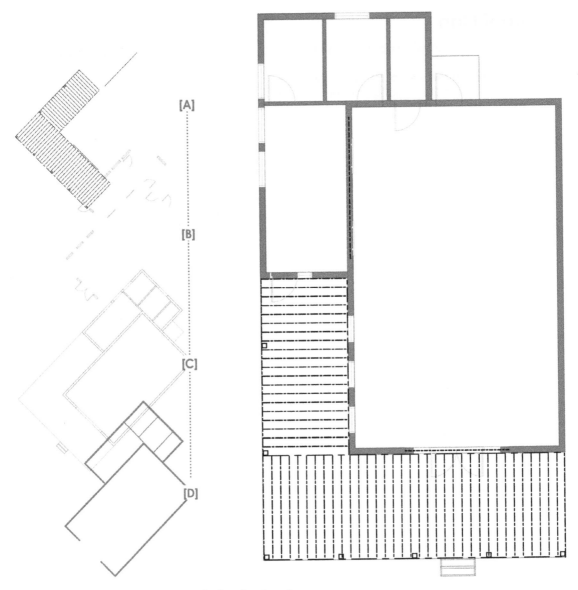

Figure 23.21 The stacked viewports of a floor framing plan.

Floor Framing Plan

The floor framing plan represents the structure that holds up the building.

It is composed of a faded base plan with heavier black 2D graphics of framing members laid on top.

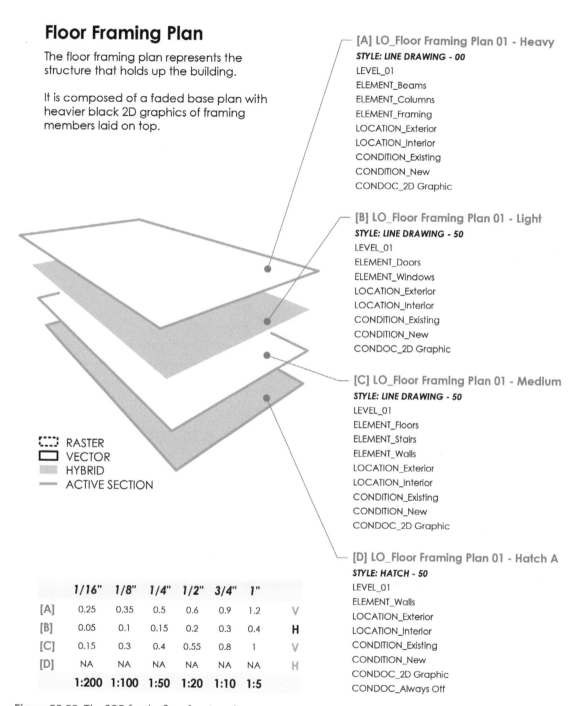

[A] LO_Floor Framing Plan 01 - Heavy
STYLE: LINE DRAWING - 00
LEVEL_01
ELEMENT_Beams
ELEMENT_Columns
ELEMENT_Framing
LOCATION_Exterior
LOCATION_Interior
CONDITION_Existing
CONDITION_New
CONDOC_2D Graphic

[B] LO_Floor Framing Plan 01 - Light
STYLE: LINE DRAWING - 50
LEVEL_01
ELEMENT_Doors
ELEMENT_Windows
LOCATION_Exterior
LOCATION_Interior
CONDITION_Existing
CONDITION_New
CONDOC_2D Graphic

[C] LO_Floor Framing Plan 01 - Medium
STYLE: LINE DRAWING - 50
LEVEL_01
ELEMENT_Floors
ELEMENT_Stairs
ELEMENT_Walls
LOCATION_Exterior
LOCATION_Interior
CONDITION_Existing
CONDITION_New
CONDOC_2D Graphic

[D] LO_Floor Framing Plan 01 - Hatch A
STYLE: HATCH - 50
LEVEL_01
ELEMENT_Walls
LOCATION_Exterior
LOCATION_Interior
CONDITION_Existing
CONDITION_New
CONDOC_2D Graphic
CONDOC_Always Off

RASTER
VECTOR
HYBRID
ACTIVE SECTION

	1/16"	1/8"	1/4"	1/2"	3/4"	1"	
[A]	0.25	0.35	0.5	0.6	0.9	1.2	V
[B]	0.05	0.1	0.15	0.2	0.3	0.4	H
[C]	0.15	0.3	0.4	0.55	0.8	1	V
[D]	NA	NA	NA	NA	NA	NA	H
	1:200	1:100	1:50	1:20	1:10	1:5	

Figure 23.22 The SOD for the floor framing plan.

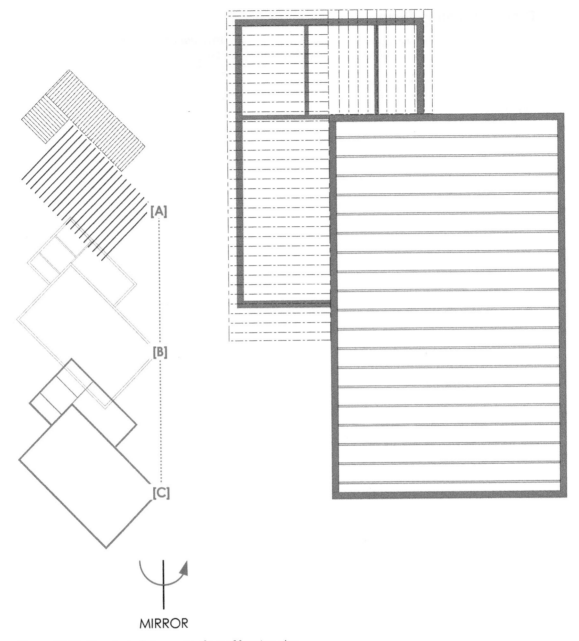

MIRROR

Figure 23.23 The stacked viewports of a roof framing plan.

Roof Framing Plan

The roof framing plan represents the structure that holds up the roof.

It is composed of a faded base plan with heavier black 2D graphics of framing members laid on top.

All section cuts are at 8' above the finished floor looking up at ceiling.

Viewports need to be mirrored in LayOut to show correctly as a plan.

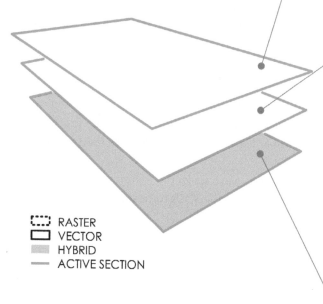

RASTER
VECTOR
HYBRID
ACTIVE SECTION

[A] LO_Roof Framing Plan 01 - Heavy

STYLE: LINE DRAWING - 00

LEVEL_01
ELEMENT_Beams
ELEMENT_Columns
ELEMENT_Framing
LOCATION_Exterior
LOCATION_Interior
CONDITION_Existing
CONDITION_New
CONDOC_2D Graphic

[B] LO_Roof Framing Plan 01 - Medium

STYLE: LINE DRAWING - 50

LEVEL_01
ELEMENT_Floors
ELEMENT_Stairs
ELEMENT_Walls
LOCATION_Exterior
LOCATION_Interior
CONDITION_Existing
CONDITION_New
CONDOC_2D Graphic

[C] LO_Roof Framing Plan 01 - Hatch A

STYLE: HATCH - 50

LEVEL_01
ELEMENT_Walls
LOCATION_Exterior
LOCATION_Interior
CONDITION_Existing
CONDITION_New
CONDOC_2D Graphic
CONDOC_Always Off

	1/16"	1/8"	1/4"	1/2"	3/4"	1"	
[A]	0.25	0.35	0.5	0.6	0.9	1.2	V
[B]	0.15	0.3	0.4	0.55	0.8	1	V
[C]	NA	NA	NA	NA	NA	NA	H
	1:200	1:100	1:50	1:20	1:10	1:5	

Figure 23.24 The SOD for the roof framing plan.

Furniture Plan

The *furniture plan* describes what is to be built. New walls are delineated through the use of a hatch fill. The furniture plan is derived from the `BD_BLVD Coffee Shop.skp` model (Figure 23.25).

Use the SODs to create the necessary scenes in SketchUp. Next, assign the scenes and properties to viewports in LayOut, and stack the plans as shown in the SODs to create the furniture plan (Figure 23.26).

Presentation Plan

The *presentation plan* visually describes the materials that will be used to finish the space. You can use the LINE DRAWING – Presentation style that also shows colors and textures. The presentation plan is derived from the `BD_BLVD Coffee Shop.skp` model (Figure 23.27).

Use the SODs to create the necessary scenes in SketchUp. Next, assign the scenes and properties to viewports in LayOut, and stack the plans as shown in the SODs to create the presentation plan (Figure 23.28).

Reflected Ceiling Plan

The *reflected ceiling plan* represents the design of the ceiling, illustrating lights, soffits, and exposed structure (Figure 23.29). The active section plane is placed at 8' above finished floor, and faces up to accurately create a reflected ceiling plan. The reflected ceiling plan is derived from the `BD_BLVD Coffee Shop.skp` model.

Use the SODs to create the necessary scenes in SketchUp. Next, assign the scenes and properties to viewports in LayOut, and stack and mirror the plans as shown in the SODs to create the reflected ceiling plan (Figure 23.30 and 23.31).

Demolition Plan

The *demolition plan* represents the pieces of the structure that will remain, as well as the pieces that will be removed. Walls and entities to be removed are represented by dashed lines in this plan. The demolition plan is derived from the `BD_3655 Milwaukee St - Proposed.skp` model (Figure 23.32).

Use the SODs to create the necessary scenes in SketchUp. Next, assign the scenes and properties to viewports in LayOut, and stack the plans as shown in the SODs to create the demolition plan (Figure 23.33).

Demolition Reflected Ceiling Plan

The *demolition reflected ceiling plan* represents the pieces of the structure that will remain, as well as the pieces that will be removed, specifically the ceiling. Walls and entities to be removed are represented by dashed lines in this plan. The active section plane is placed at 8' above finished floor, and faces up to accurately create a demolition reflected ceiling plan. The demolition reflected ceiling plan is derived from the `BD_3655 Milwaukee St - Proposed.skp` model (Figure 23.34).

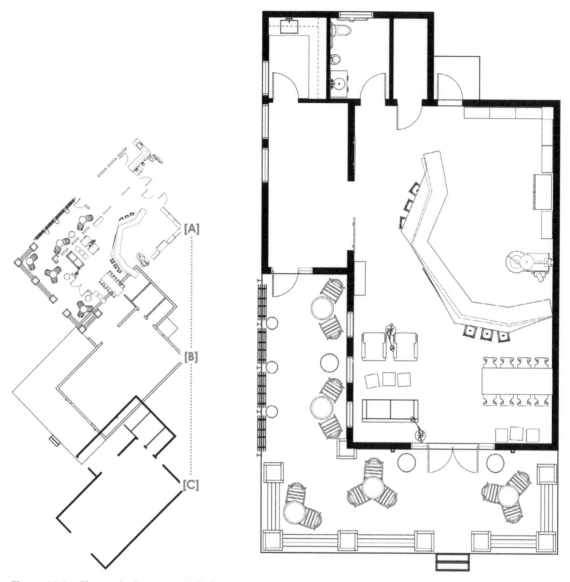

Figure 23.25 The stacked viewports of a furniture plan.

Furniture Plan

The furniture plan represents the space plan and furniture layouts.

Walls are hatched solid black to focus on the space plan with furniture, rather than what is new or existing.

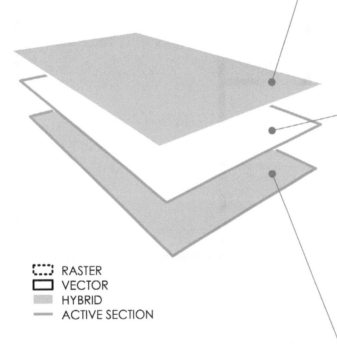

RASTER
VECTOR
HYBRID
— **ACTIVE SECTION**

[A] LO_Furniture Plan 01 - Light
STYLE: LINE DRAWING - 00
LEVEL_01
ELEMENT_Barriers
ELEMENT_Doors
ELEMENT_Equipment
ELEMENT_Fixtures
ELEMENT_Furniture
ELEMENT_Windows
LOCATION_Exterior
LOCATION_Interior
CONDITION_Existing
CONDITION_New
CONDOC_2D Graphic

[B] LO_Furniture Plan 01 - Heavy
STYLE: LINE DRAWING - 00
LEVEL_01
ELEMENT_Columns
ELEMENT_Floors
ELEMENT_Roof
ELEMENT_Stairs
ELEMENT_Walls
LOCATION_Exterior
LOCATION_Interior
CONDITION_Existing
CONDITION_New
CONDOC_2D Graphic

[C] LO_Furniture Plan 01 - Hatch A
STYLE: HATCH - 00
LEVEL_01
ELEMENT_Walls
LOCATION_Exterior
LOCATION_Interior
CONDITION_Existing
CONDITION_New
CONDOC_2D Graphic
CONDOC_Always Off

	1/16"	1/8"	1/4"	1/2"	3/4"	1"	
[A]	0.05	0.1	0.15	0.2	0.3	0.4	H
[B]	0.15	0.3	0.4	0.55	0.8	1	V
[C]	NA	NA	NA	NA	NA	NA	H
	1:200	1:100	1:50	1:20	1:10	1:5	

Figure 23.26 The SOD for the furniture plan.

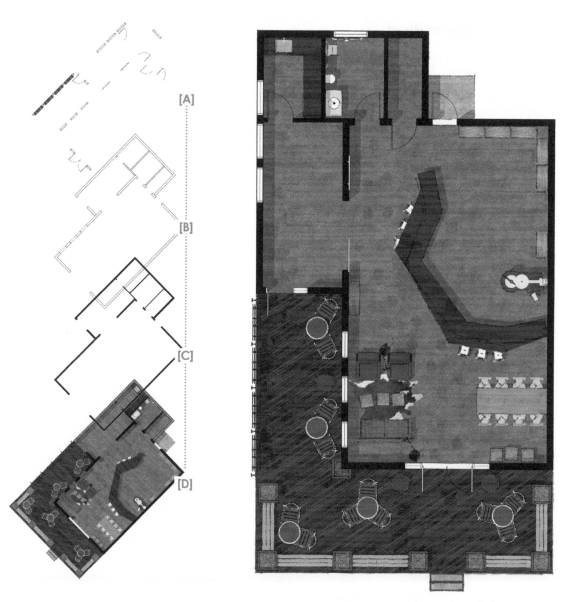

[A]

[B]

[C]

[D]

Figure 23.27 The stacked viewports of a presentation plan.

Presentation Plan

The presentation plan visually represents the finishes in plan.

This drawing does not use the conventional hatch scenes; Hatch B is more of an overall base plan.

Consider turning decorative objects on to add more detail to this drawing.

[A] LO_Presentation Plan 01 - Light
STYLE: LINE DRAWING - 00
LEVEL_01
ELEMENT_Barriers
ELEMENT_Doors
ELEMENT_Windows
LOCATION_Exterior
LOCATION_Interior
CONDITION_Existing
CONDITION_New
CONDOC_2D Graphic

[B] LO_Presentation Plan 01 - Heavy
STYLE: LINE DRAWING - 00
LEVEL_01
ELEMENT_Roof
ELEMENT_Walls
LOCATION_Exterior
LOCATION_Interior
CONDITION_Existing
CONDITION_New
CONDOC_2D Graphic

[C] LO_Presentation Plan 01 - Hatch A
STYLE: HATCH - 00
LEVEL_01
ELEMENT_Walls
LOCATION_Exterior
LOCATION_Interior
CONDITION_Existing
CONDITION_New
CONDOC_2D Graphic
CONDOC_Always Off

[D] LO_Presentation Plan 01 - Hatch B
STYLE: LINE DRAWING - Presentation
LEVEL_01
ELEMENT_Barriers
ELEMENT_Equipment
ELEMENT_Fixtures
ELEMENT_Floors
ELEMENT_Furniture
ELEMENT_Roof
ELEMENT_Stairs
ELEMENT_Walls
LOCATION_Exterior
LOCATION_Interior
CONDITION_Existing
CONDITION_New
CONDOC_2D Graphic
CONDOC_Always Off

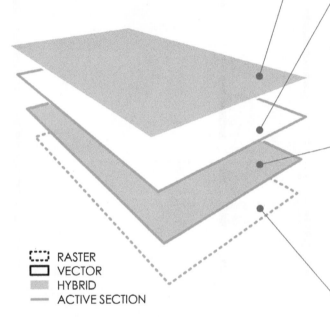

- ⬚ RASTER
- ▭ VECTOR
- ▨ HYBRID
- — ACTIVE SECTION

	1/16"	1/8"	1/4"	1/2"	3/4"	1"	
[A]	0.05	0.1	0.15	0.2	0.3	0.4	H
[B]	0.15	0.3	0.4	0.55	0.8	1	V
[C]	NA	NA	NA	NA	NA	NA	H
[D]	0.35	0.40	0.60	0.80	1.00	1.50	R
	1:200	1:100	1:50	1:20	1:10	1:5	

Figure 23.28 The SOD for the presentation plan.

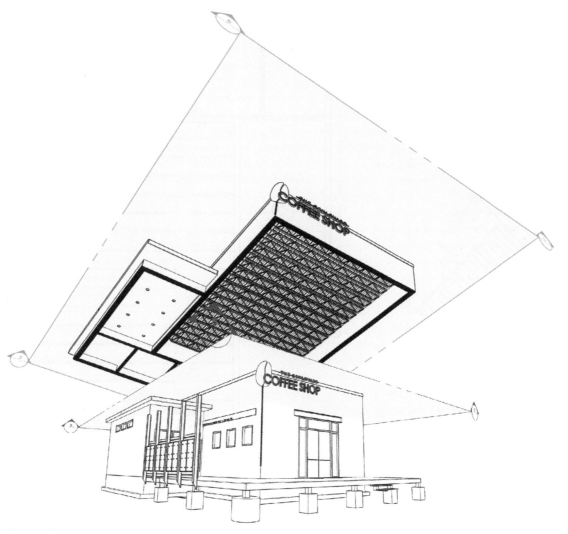

Figure 23.29

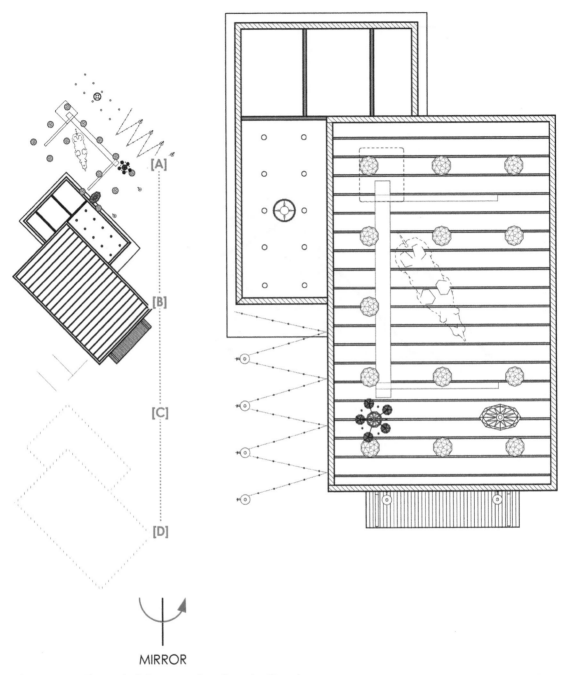

[A]

[B]

[C]

[D]

MIRROR

Figure 23.30 The stacked viewports of a reflected ceiling plan.

Reflected Ceiling Plan

The reflected ceiling plan represents the ceilings, soffits, equipment, and lighting.

It is used for both existing conditions models and proposed conditions models.

All existing walls are hatched black; all new walls are hatched with lines.

All section cuts are at 8' above the finished floor looking up at ceiling.

Viewports need to be mirrored in LayOut to show correctly as a plan.

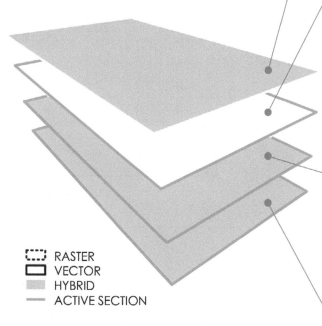

RASTER
VECTOR
HYBRID
ACTIVE SECTION

[A] LO_Reflected Ceiling Plan 01 - Light
STYLE: LINE DRAWING - 00
LEVEL_01
ELEMENT_Ceiling Equipment
ELEMENT_Lights
LOCATION_Exterior
LOCATION_Interior
CONDITION_Existing
CONDITION_New
CONDOC_2D Graphic

[B] LO_Reflected Ceiling Plan 01 - Heavy
STYLE: LINE DRAWING - 00
LEVEL_01
ELEMENT_Beams
ELEMENT_Ceilings
ELEMENT_Columns
ELEMENT_Roof
ELEMENT_Walls
LOCATION_Exterior
LOCATION_Interior
CONDITION_Existing
CONDITION_New
CONDOC_2D Graphic

[C] LO_Reflected Ceiling Plan 01 - Hatch A
STYLE: HATCH - 50
LEVEL_01
ELEMENT_Walls
LOCATION_Interior
CONDITION_Existing
CONDITION_New
CONDOC_2D Graphic
CONDOC_Always Off

[D] LO_Reflected Ceiling Plan 01 - Hatch B
STYLE: HATCH - LINES
LEVEL_01
ELEMENT_Walls
LOCATION_Exterior
CONDITION_Existing
CONDITION_New
CONDOC_2D Graphic
CONDOC_Always Off

	1/16"	1/8"	1/4"	1/2"	3/4"	1"	
[A]	0.05	0.1	0.15	0.2	0.3	0.4	H
[B]	0.15	0.3	0.4	0.55	0.8	1	V
[C]	NA	NA	NA	NA	NA	NA	H
[D]	NA	NA	NA	NA	NA	NA	H
	1:200	1:100	1:50	1:20	1:10	1:5	

Figure 23.31 The SOD for the reflected ceiling plan.

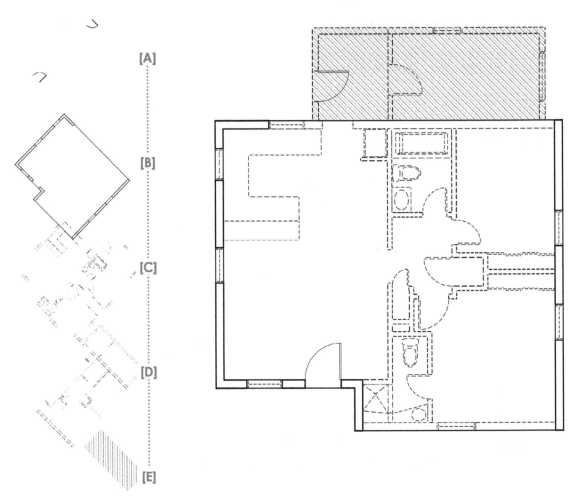

[A]

[B]

[C]

[D]

[E]

Figure 23.32 The stacked viewports of a demolition plan.

Demolition Plan

The demolition plan represents existing entities to remain with a solid line and existing entities to be demolished with a dashed line.

This requires the Demolition layer to be turned on, and the New layer turned off.

Hatch is optional, but it does make the drawing pop.

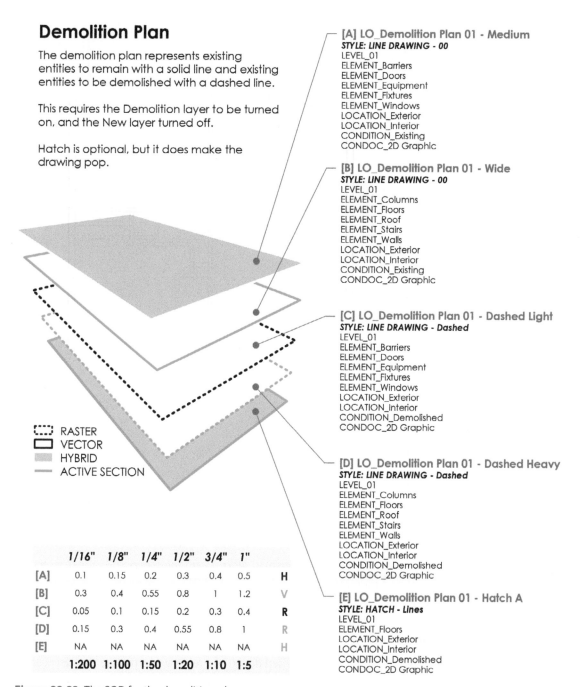

[A] LO_Demolition Plan 01 - Medium
STYLE: LINE DRAWING - 00
LEVEL_01
ELEMENT_Barriers
ELEMENT_Doors
ELEMENT_Equipment
ELEMENT_Fixtures
ELEMENT_Windows
LOCATION_Exterior
LOCATION_Interior
CONDITION_Existing
CONDOC_2D Graphic

[B] LO_Demolition Plan 01 - Wide
STYLE: LINE DRAWING - 00
LEVEL_01
ELEMENT_Columns
ELEMENT_Floors
ELEMENT_Roof
ELEMENT_Stairs
ELEMENT_Walls
LOCATION_Exterior
LOCATION_Interior
CONDITION_Existing
CONDOC_2D Graphic

[C] LO_Demolition Plan 01 - Dashed Light
STYLE: LINE DRAWING - Dashed
LEVEL_01
ELEMENT_Barriers
ELEMENT_Doors
ELEMENT_Equipment
ELEMENT_Fixtures
ELEMENT_Windows
LOCATION_Exterior
LOCATION_Interior
CONDITION_Demolished
CONDOC_2D Graphic

[D] LO_Demolition Plan 01 - Dashed Heavy
STYLE: LINE DRAWING - Dashed
LEVEL_01
ELEMENT_Columns
ELEMENT_Floors
ELEMENT_Roof
ELEMENT_Stairs
ELEMENT_Walls
LOCATION_Exterior
LOCATION_Interior
CONDITION_Demolished
CONDOC_2D Graphic

[E] LO_Demolition Plan 01 - Hatch A
STYLE: HATCH - Lines
LEVEL_01
ELEMENT_Floors
LOCATION_Exterior
LOCATION_Interior
CONDITION_Demolished
CONDOC_2D Graphic

Legend:
- ⬚ RASTER
- ▭ VECTOR
- ▬ HYBRID
- — ACTIVE SECTION

	1/16"	1/8"	1/4"	1/2"	3/4"	1"	
[A]	0.1	0.15	0.2	0.3	0.4	0.5	H
[B]	0.3	0.4	0.55	0.8	1	1.2	V
[C]	0.05	0.1	0.15	0.2	0.3	0.4	R
[D]	0.15	0.3	0.4	0.55	0.8	1	R
[E]	NA	NA	NA	NA	NA	NA	H
	1:200	1:100	1:50	1:20	1:10	1:5	

Figure 23.33 The SOD for the demolition plan.

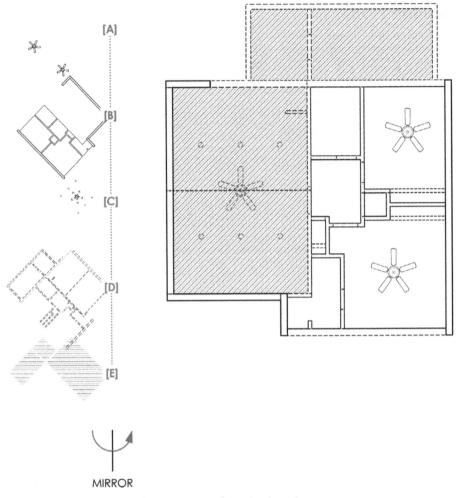

MIRROR

Figure 23.34 The stacked viewports of a demolition reflected ceiling plan.

Use the SODs to create the necessary scenes in SketchUp. Next, assign the scenes and properties to viewports in LayOut, and stack and mirror the plans as shown in the SODs to create the demolition reflected ceiling plan (Figure 23.35).

Renovation Construction Plan

The *renovation construction plan* represents the proposed design of a renovated structure that delineates new and existing walls. The renovation construction plan is derived from the BD_3655 Milwaukee St - Proposed.skp model (Figure 23.36).

Use the SODs to create the necessary scenes in SketchUp. Next, assign the scenes and properties to viewports in LayOut, and stack the plans as shown in the SODs to create the renovation construction plan (Figure 23.37).

Demolition Reflected Ceiling Plan

The demolition reflected ceiling plan represents existing entities to remain with a solid line and existing entities to be demolished with a dashed line.

This requires the Demolition layer to be turned on, and the New layer to be turned off.

All section cuts are at 8' above the finished floor looking up at ceiling.

Viewports need to be flipped in LayOut to show as plan.

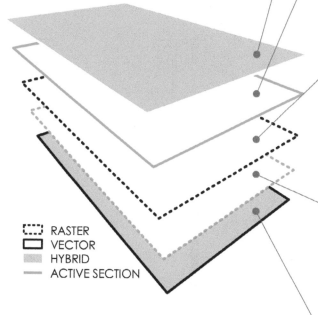

[A] LO_Demolition Reflected Ceiling Plan 01 - Medium
STYLE: LINE DRAWING - 00
LEVEL_01
ELEMENT_Ceiling Equipment
ELEMENT_Lights
LOCATION_Exterior
LOCATION_Interior
CONDITION_Existing
CONDOC_2D Graphic

[B] LO_Demolition Reflected Ceiling Plan 01 - Wide
STYLE: LINE DRAWING - 00
LEVEL_01
ELEMENT_Ceilings
ELEMENT_Columns
ELEMENT_Walls
LOCATION_Exterior
LOCATION_Interior
CONDITION_Existing
CONDOC_2D Graphic

[C] LO_Demolition Reflected Ceiling Plan 01 - Dashed Light
STYLE: LINE DRAWING - Dashed
LEVEL_01
ELEMENT_Ceiling Equipment
ELEMENT_Lights
LOCATION_Exterior
LOCATION_Interior
CONDITION_Demolished
CONDOC_2D Graphic

[D] LO_Demolition Reflected Ceiling Plan 01 - Dashed Heavy
STYLE: LINE DRAWING - Dashed
LEVEL_01
ELEMENT_Ceilings
ELEMENT_Walls
LOCATION_Exterior
LOCATION_Interior
CONDITION_Demolished
CONDOC_2D Graphic

[E] LO_Demolition Reflected Ceiling Plan 01 - Hatch A
STYLE: HATCH - Lines
LEVEL_01
ELEMENT_Ceilings
LOCATION_Exterior
LOCATION_Interior
CONDITION_Demolished
CONDOC_2D Graphic

:::: RASTER
□ VECTOR
▨ HYBRID
— ACTIVE SECTION

	1/16"	1/8"	1/4"	1/2"	3/4"	1"	
[A]	0.1	0.15	0.2	0.3	0.4	0.5	H
[B]	0.3	0.4	0.55	0.8	1	1.2	V
[C]	0.05	0.1	0.15	0.2	0.3	0.4	R
[D]	0.15	0.3	0.4	0.55	0.8	1	R
[E]	NA	NA	NA	NA	NA	NA	H
	1:200	1:100	1:50	1:20	1:10	1:5	

Figure 23.35 The SOD for the demolition reflected ceiling plan.

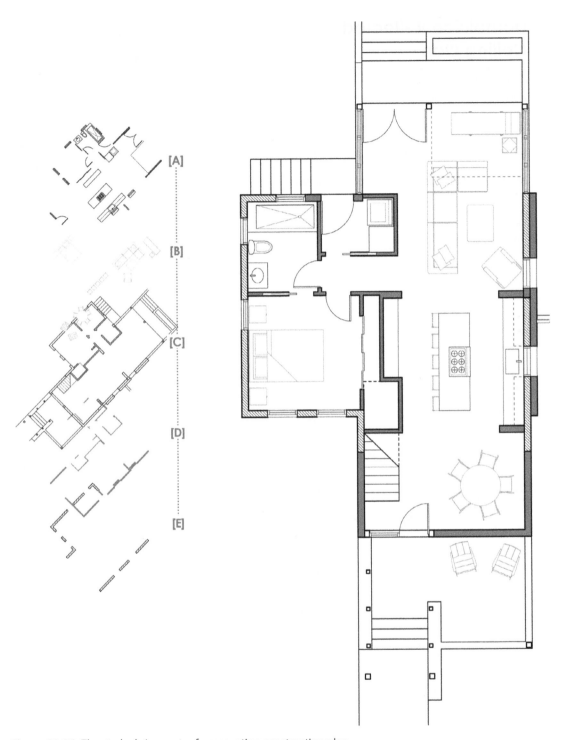

[A]

[B]

[C]

[D]

[E]

Figure 23.36 The stacked viewports of a renovation construction plan.

Renovation Construction Plan

The renovation construction plan represents what is to be built in addition to the existing building elements to remain.

Existing walls are hatched black. New walls are hatched with lines.

Wall Type A represents retaining walls.

Furniture is shown as light gray in a separate stacked viewport (optional).

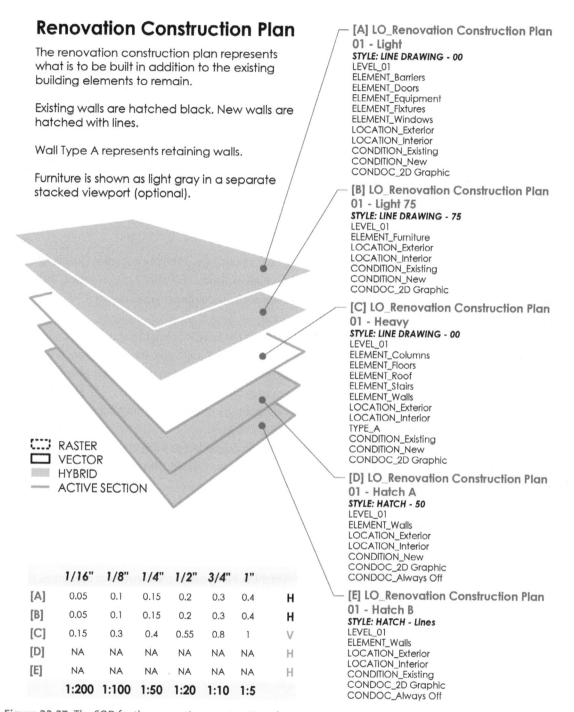

[A] LO_Renovation Construction Plan 01 - Light
STYLE: LINE DRAWING - 00
LEVEL_01
ELEMENT_Barriers
ELEMENT_Doors
ELEMENT_Equipment
ELEMENT_Fixtures
ELEMENT_Windows
LOCATION_Exterior
LOCATION_Interior
CONDITION_Existing
CONDITION_New
CONDOC_2D Graphic

[B] LO_Renovation Construction Plan 01 - Light 75
STYLE: LINE DRAWING - 75
LEVEL_01
ELEMENT_Furniture
LOCATION_Exterior
LOCATION_Interior
CONDITION_Existing
CONDITION_New
CONDOC_2D Graphic

[C] LO_Renovation Construction Plan 01 - Heavy
STYLE: LINE DRAWING - 00
LEVEL_01
ELEMENT_Columns
ELEMENT_Floors
ELEMENT_Roof
ELEMENT_Stairs
ELEMENT_Walls
LOCATION_Exterior
LOCATION_Interior
TYPE_A
CONDITION_Existing
CONDITION_New
CONDOC_2D Graphic

[D] LO_Renovation Construction Plan 01 - Hatch A
STYLE: HATCH - 50
LEVEL_01
ELEMENT_Walls
LOCATION_Exterior
LOCATION_Interior
CONDITION_New
CONDOC_2D Graphic
CONDOC_Always Off

[E] LO_Renovation Construction Plan 01 - Hatch B
STYLE: HATCH - Lines
LEVEL_01
ELEMENT_Walls
LOCATION_Exterior
LOCATION_Interior
CONDITION_Existing
CONDOC_2D Graphic
CONDOC_Always Off

RASTER
VECTOR
HYBRID
ACTIVE SECTION

	1/16"	1/8"	1/4"	1/2"	3/4"	1"	
[A]	0.05	0.1	0.15	0.2	0.3	0.4	H
[B]	0.05	0.1	0.15	0.2	0.3	0.4	H
[C]	0.15	0.3	0.4	0.55	0.8	1	V
[D]	NA	NA	NA	NA	NA	NA	H
[E]	NA	NA	NA	NA	NA	NA	H
	1:200	1:100	1:50	1:20	1:10	1:5	

Figure 23.37 The SOD for the renovation construction plan.

Details

Details Can be built in 3D as vignettes, or as 2D diagrams using ConDoc DRAFT Mode. A *detail* explains the finite construction of a specific building condition. When you're creating details in any drafting program, there is a disconnect between the dynamically linked design model and the detail drawings. It would be nearly impossible to build a model with the level of detail and organization necessary to show all levels of detail at any architectural scale. Because of this, it is okay to "detach" your details from the design model.

Figure 23.38 illustrates typical detail line weights. It is an excellent tool for determining the best line weight arrays at different scales. The settings shown are very close to the default line weights used by the ConDoc Drawings.

2D Details

2D details are the industry standard for diagramming how a building is to be put together. Line weights and annotations make a balanced visual that is clear and self-explanatory (Figure 23.39). ConDoc DRAFT Mode aids in the creation of 2D details. If you are familiar with 2D computer-aided design (CAD), you will love ConDoc DRAFT Mode.

ConDoc DRAFT Mode (Figure 23.40) is accessed through the ConDoc System panel. DRAFT Mode locks you in a top-down 2D view and limits navigation to a 2D CAD-type operation. Layers are displayed by colors that correspond to line weights. Toggle through line weights within the ConDoc System panel.

The ConDoc Match Properties tool allows you to quickly sample and apply one line's layer to another. This is much faster than selecting a line and then assigning a layer through the Entity Info dialog. The Match Properties tool is reminiscent of the AutoCAD Express Tools.

The Detail tool automates the process of creating the scenes needed to stack in LayOut (Figure 23.41), similar to the other ConDoc tools. Click once, and all six scenes are created. This saves a lot of time.

TIP Go to a building section scene, right-click on the active section plane, and choose Create group from slice. Cut the resulting group, then paste into DRAFT Mode. You can use this as a starting point for your 2D details.

Use the SODs to create the necessary scenes in SketchUp. Next, assign the scenes and properties to viewports in LayOut, and stack the plans as shown in the SODs to create the 2D Details (Figure 23.42).

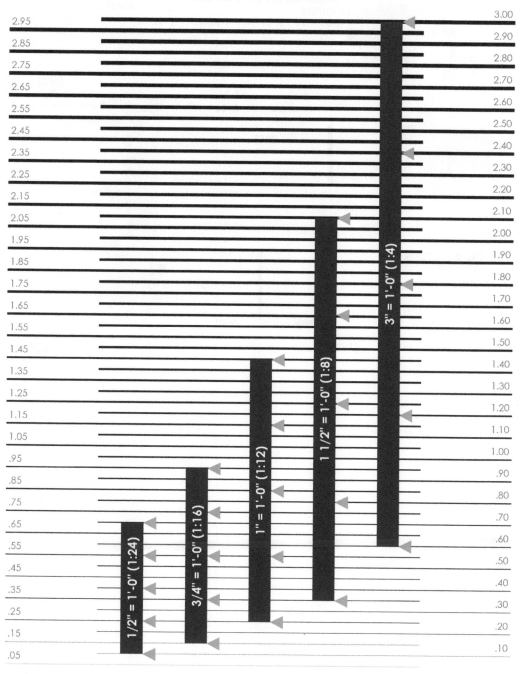

DETAIL LINE WEIGHTS

◄ LIGHT VIEWPORT (PROFILES)   ◄ HEAVY VIEWPORT (PROFILES + ACTIVE SECTION)

(FILL = LINE WEIGHT IS ASSIGNED IN LAYOUT)   (NO FILL = LINE WEIGHT IS A PRODUCT OF STYLE MULTIPLIER)

Figure 23.38 Line weight chart for 2D detail drawings created in DRAFT mode.

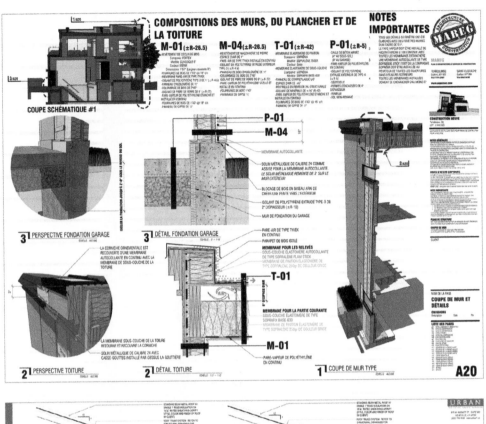

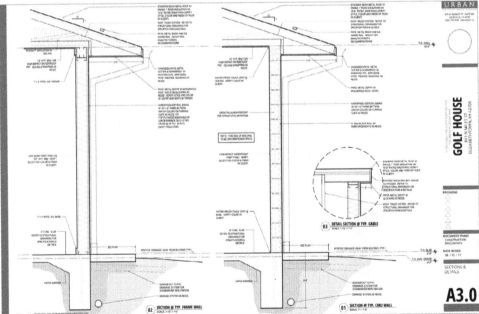

Figure 23.39 Wall sections and details created using the ConDoc Tools DRAFT Mode. House design and drawings by MABEG Architecture and Construction. Golf House design and drawings by Eric Whitmore, Urban 1 Architecture.

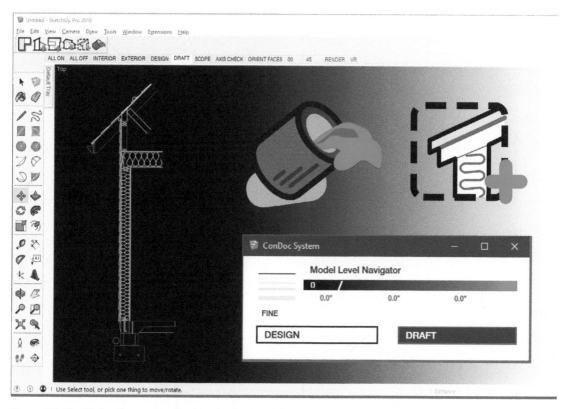

Figure 23.40 2D details are expedited by the ConDoc DRAFT Mode, Detail tool, and Match Properties tool. This provides a very capable 2D drafting solution right inside of SketchUp.

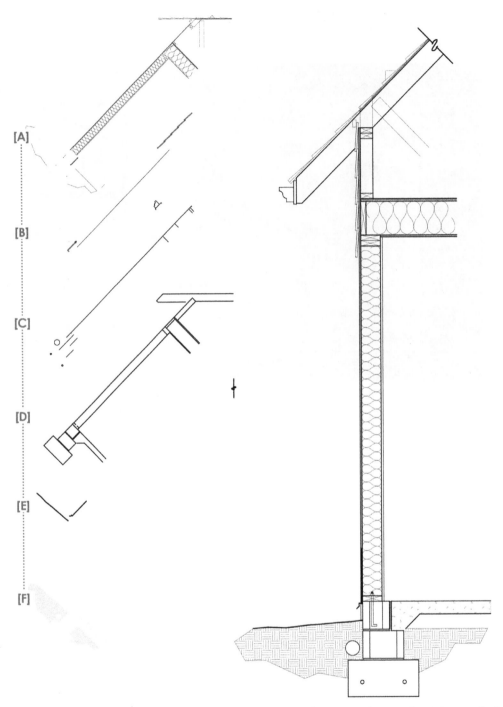

Figure 23.41 A 2D detail is composed of six separate viewports with five varying line weights. When stacked together, they create a complete drawing.

2D Detail

2D details are larger-scale diagrams that explain how the building will be constructed.

Only DRAFT layers are visible.

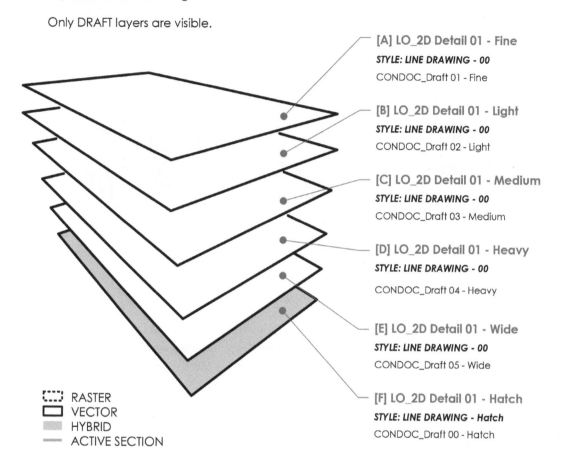

[A] LO_2D Detail 01 - Fine
STYLE: LINE DRAWING - 00
CONDOC_Draft 01 - Fine

[B] LO_2D Detail 01 - Light
STYLE: LINE DRAWING - 00
CONDOC_Draft 02 - Light

[C] LO_2D Detail 01 - Medium
STYLE: LINE DRAWING - 00
CONDOC_Draft 03 - Medium

[D] LO_2D Detail 01 - Heavy
STYLE: LINE DRAWING - 00
CONDOC_Draft 04 - Heavy

[E] LO_2D Detail 01 - Wide
STYLE: LINE DRAWING - 00
CONDOC_Draft 05 - Wide

[F] LO_2D Detail 01 - Hatch
STYLE: LINE DRAWING - Hatch
CONDOC_Draft 00 - Hatch

RASTER
VECTOR
HYBRID
ACTIVE SECTION

	1/2"	3/4"	1"	1 1/2"	3"	
[A]	0.1	0.1	0.25	0.35	0.6	V
[B]	0.25	0.35	0.55	0.8	1.2	V
[C]	0.4	0.55	0.85	1.25	1.8	V
[D]	0.55	0.75	1.15	1.65	2.4	V
[E]	0.7	0.95	1.45	2.1	3	V
[F]	NA	NA	NA	NA	NA	H
	1:200	1:100	1:50	1:20	1:10	

Figure 23.42 The SOD for the 2D detail.

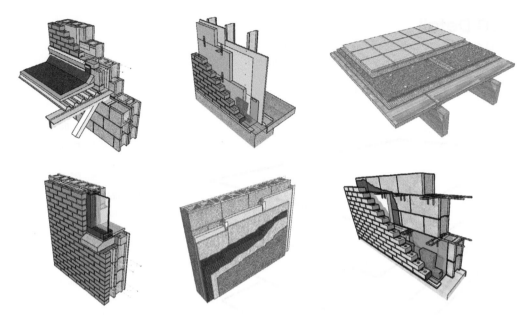

Figure 23.43 3D details are available in the 3D Warehouse.

3D Details

SketchUp is a 3D program, so there is no reason you shouldn't branch out and create 3D details. Often, 3D details can do a better job explaining conditions than 2D can, but they are not the industry standard and usually take much more effort to create. It is best to model in SketchUp and then annotate in LayOut. Don't use text in SketchUp; it is hard to control in LayOut viewports. As a starting point, try searching the 3D Warehouse for construction details (Figure 23.43).

TIP Save all of your 2D and 3D details in the scrapbooks library so you can use them on other projects. Frequently, a typical project type uses standardized details, and you can save a significant amount of time by building a collection of details.

CHAPTER POINTS

☑ The ConDoc Tools drastically expedite all the tedious tasks. It is a fully automated process.

☑ Many drawings can be created by starting with what you already have.

☑ Use these recipes to make your own creations.

☑ DRAFT Mode is 2D CAD embedded right into SketchUp.

Chapter 24
Annotations

Your office's graphic standards can be available at the click of a button and shared on a network drive where everyone can contribute to it. All of this and more is possible with LayOut collections.

ANNOTATIONS

Annotations are the extra layer of information that further describe the drawings. Annotations complement the graphic with accurate dimensions and precise descriptions. Keep these tips in mind when you annotate your drawings:

☑ Because it is difficult to draw accurate column lines in LayOut, draw them in SketchUp. Treat column lines as two-dimensional (2D) graphics that complement a three-dimensional (3D) object of a beam and framing.

☑ Door and window center lines are drawn in LayOut. Draw end to end for windows, or inside to inside for openings, then conveniently rotate the line about center.

☑ Be sure to switch to the ANNOTATIONS layer, which should be active most of the time you are drafting in LayOut.

☑ It is okay to link your model to several different layout files to break up the set. This will reduce rendering time and allow you to distribute work among the team.

☑ When you're dimensioning, typically it is best to turn off Auto Scale and set the Dimension Scale manually in the drop-down menu. This will eliminate potential errors from snapping to a point outside of a viewport.

☑ If you find yourself using the same annotation, take the time to add it to your scrapbooks.

☑ Use scrapbooks as a palette to quickly access line weights, fonts, styles, and fills.

☑ See Chapter 13, LayOut Tools, for instructions on using the Text, Label, Dimension, and Table tools.

SCRAPBOOKS

Scrapbooks are prebuilt pieces of annotation, composed of LayOut geometry and entities. Scrapbooks are not a special file format; they are simply LayOut presentations containing LayOut entities grouped in useful ways. Although scrapbooks serve a functional purpose of further explaining a design, they also contribute to the overall graphic style of the drawings. Lines, shapes, fills, and fonts all contribute to your own personal graphic standards.

Creating a Scrapbook

You have already reviewed all the skills and tools that you need to create your own scrapbook. Follow these step-by-step instructions to create a custom scrapbook collection to complement the presentation and construction document title blocks.

Getting Started

To get started, simply follow these steps:

1. Click on the File drop-down menu, and choose New. Select the BD_8.5 x 11 - Landscape template, and choose Open.

2. Click on the File drop-down menu, and choose Document Setup. In the Paper tab, change the paper size to 5" x 5".

3. In the Pages inspector, double-click on the only page and rename it SYMBOLS. Click on the plus sign (+) to add two more pages. Name the pages CALLOUTS and PALETTES (Figure 24.1).

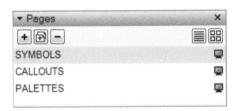

Figure 24.1 Typical scrapbook presentation pages.

4. In the Layers inspector, delete the TITLE BLOCK layer because you don't need it in a scrapbook collection. Rename the DRAWINGS layer to BACKGROUND. Rename the ANNOTATIONS layer to SCRAPBOOKS and leave it as the current layer (Figure 24.2).

TIP A scrapbook's layers are not inserted with the scrapbook. When you insert a scrapbook, all its entities are assigned to the active layer in the current presentation. This is why it is pointless to have several different layers in a scrapbook.

Figure 24.2 Typical scrapbook presentation layers.

Symbols

Symbols are used to add graphic and text information to a drawing. They can be used to count doors and windows, as well as define north and the graphic scale of a drawing. In this section, you will create several commonly used symbols for creating a set of construction documents.

Door Tag

Door tags are used to count new doors and reference them to the additional information provided in the door schedule. Follow these steps to create a simple door tag:

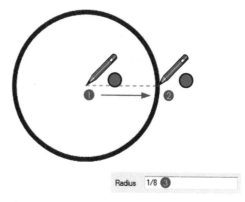

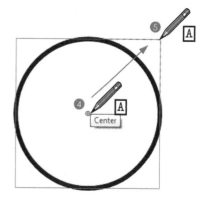

Figure 24.3 Create a precise circle for the door tag.

1. Activate the Circle tool, set the stroke width to .5, and turn off the Fill. Click once to define the center point of the circle (Figure 24.3).

2. Move your cursor away from the center point, and click to loosely define the radius.

3. Immediately type a precise radius of 1/8, then press Enter.

4. Activate the Text tool. While you hold down the Ctrl key (Option on a Mac), click and hold on the center point of the circle (Figure 24.4).

5. Move your cursor away from the center point to create the text box, and release the mouse button to finish. Add generic text to the text box, such as 01, and press Esc to finish.

Figure 24.4 Add text to the door tag.

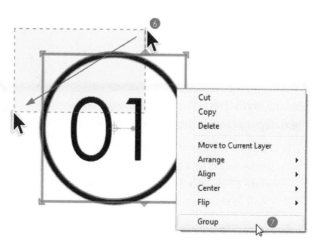

6. Activate the Select tool, and click and drag from right to left to select both the circle and the text entities as shown in Figure 24.5.

7. Right-click on the selection, and choose Make Group.

TIP If a piece of annotation in a scrapbook contains more than one entity, those entities must be grouped for the entire symbol to come in as one.

Figure 24.5 Group the door tag so that it functions properly as a scrapbook.

Window Tag

Window tags are used to count new windows and reference them to the additional information provided in the window schedule. Follow these steps to create a simple window tag:

1. Activate the Polygon tool, set the stroke width to .5, and turn off the Fill. Assign the number of sides by entering 6s, then press Enter (Figure 24.6).

2. Click once to define the center point of the hexagon.

3. Move your cursor away from the center point, and click to loosely define the radius.

4. Type a precise radius of 1/8, then press Enter.

5. Activate the Text tool. Hover on the top and side center points to encourage an inference. While holding the Ctrl key (Option on a Mac), click and hold on the inferenced center point of the hexagon (Figure 24.7).

6. Move your cursor away from the center point to create the text box. Release the mouse button to finish. Add generic text to the text box, such as A, and press Esc to finish.

7. Activate the Select tool. Click and drag from right to left to select both the circle and the text entities.

8. Right-click on the selection, and choose Make Group so it functions properly as a scrapbook (Figure 24.8).

North Arrow

A north arrow graphic shows the viewer an accurate north direction on the drawing. Follow these steps to create a simple north arrow:

1. Activate the Circle tool, and set the stroke width to 1 and the Fill color to white. Click once to define the center point of the circle (Figure 24.9).

2. Move your cursor away from the center point, and click to loosely define the radius.

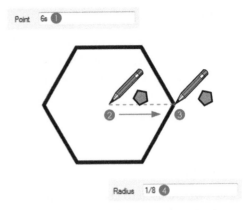

Figure 24.6 Create a precise polygon for the window tag.

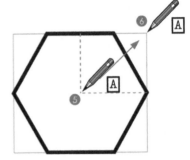

Figure 24.7 Add text to the window tag.

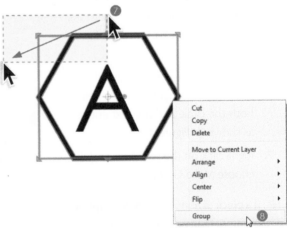

Figure 24.8 Group the window tag so it functions properly as a scrapbook.

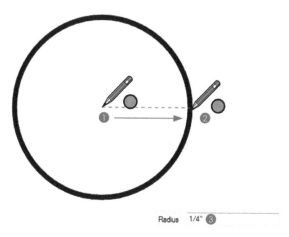

Radius 1/4" ③

Figure 24.9 Add a precise circle as the base of the north arrow.

On Point

Center

Figure 24.10 Add a line to define the north direction.

3. Immediately type a precise radius of 1/4", then press Enter.

4. Activate the Line tool, and set the stroke width to 3. Click once on the center point of the circle to start the line (Figure 24.10).

5. Move your cursor away from the start point of the line, and double-click on the top point of the circle to finish.

6. Select both entities, then right-click and choose Make Group so that it functions properly as a scrapbook.

Graphic Scale

A graphic scale gives the viewer of the drawing a visual reference for the architectural scale applied to the drawing. Follow these steps to create a simple graphic scale:

1. Activate the Rectangle tool, set the Fill to black, and turn off the Stroke. Click once to start the rectangle (Figure 24.11).

2. Move your cursor away from the start point, and click again to loosely define the dimensions of the rectangle.

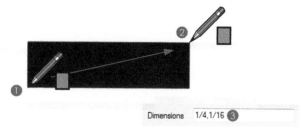

Dimensions 1/4,1/16 ③

Figure 24.11 Draw a precise rectangle to start the graphic scale.

3. Type the precise dimensions for the rectangle as 1/4, 1/16, then press Enter.

4. While holding down the Ctrl key (Option on a Mac), click and drag on the rectangle to make a copy (Figure 24.12).

5. Snap the bottom-left corner of the copy to the top-right corner of the original.

6. While holding down the Ctrl key (Option on a Mac), click and drag on the second rectangle to make another copy.

7. Snap the top-left corner of the copy to the bottom-right corner of the original.

8. While the rectangle is still selected, click and drag the right Scale grip to the right of your screen (Figure 24.13).

9. Release the grip to finish loosely scaling, and immediately type a precise scale factor of 2, then press Enter.

10. Repeat the copying and scaling steps to produce the image shown in Figure 24.14.

11. Add generic text to each division of the scale as shown in Figure 24.15. This text will need to be edited depending on the scale of the drawing it represents.

12. Select all graphic scale entities, right-click on the selection, and choose Make Group so it functions properly as a scrapbook.

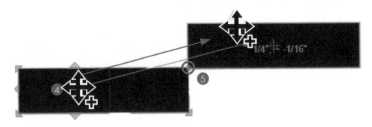

Figure 24.12 Copy the rectangle.

Figure 24.13 Scale the rectangle.

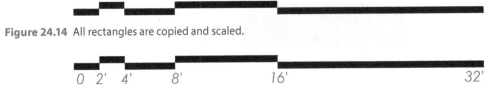

Figure 24.14 All rectangles are copied and scaled.

0   2'   4'   8'   16'   32'

Figure 24.15 Add text to the graphic scale.

Drawing Title

A drawing title calls out what a drawing is and also provides a number for coordinating drawings. Follow these steps to create a simple drawing title:

1. Activate the Line tool, set the stroke width to 1, and turn off the Fill. Click once to start the line (Figure 24.16).

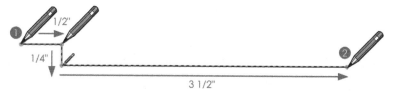

Figure 24.16 Draw the main line for the drawing title.

2. Draw a line 1/2" to the right, 1/4" down, and then 3 1/2" to the right.

3. Change the stroke width to .5. Click on the existing line to start another line (Figure 24.17).

4. Move your cursor down on the green axis. At this point, type a precise dimension of 1/8, then press Enter, then press Esc to finish the line.

5. Activate the Rectangle tool, set the stroke width to 1, and turn on the Fill and color it black. Click once to start the rectangle.

6. Move your cursor away from the start point, and click again to finish.

7. Add text to the drawing's title as shown in Figure 24.18.

8. Select the entire drawing title, right-click on the selection, and choose Make Group so it functions properly as a scrapbook.

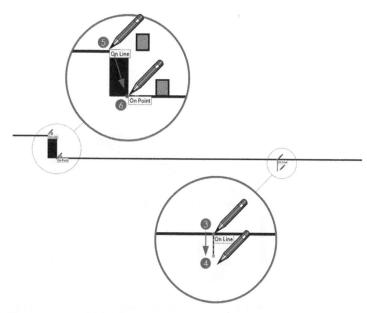

Figure 24.17 Add the detail.

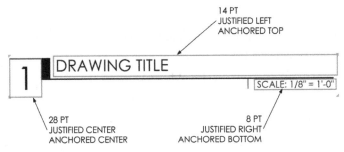

Figure 24.18 Add and arrange text on the drawing's title.

Callouts

Callouts are used to link and coordinate drawings. A callout is text that references another drawing on another page. Use the Pages inspector to advance to the Callouts page of your scrapbook presentation. Separating the scrapbooks into pages keeps them organized and makes them easier to use.

Interior Elevation

An interior elevation callout points at an interior wall and references the actual interior elevation with a drawing and sheet number.

1. Activate the Text tool. Set the stroke width to 1, the Fill to white, and the font size to 10.

2. While holding the Ctrl key (Option on Mac), click and drag to create a text box.

3. Add the text 0/A.000, and press Esc to finish.

4. Right-click on the text, and choose Size to Fit to optimize the vertical size of the text box. Resize the text box horizontally as needed.

5. Activate the Line tool, turn the Stroke on and set to 1. Also, turn off the Fill. Click on the top-left corner of the text box to start the line (Figure 24.19).

6. Hover on the text box's midpoint to encourage an inference.

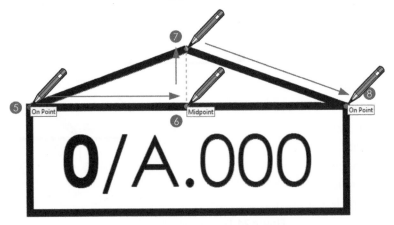

Figure 24.19 Use the Line tool to draw the arrow indicating elevation direction. (Fill is turned off for effect.)

7. Move your cursor up, and click to end the line segment.

8. Double-click on the top-right corner of the text box to finish.

9. Select the entire elevation callout, right-click on the selection, and choose Make Group so it functions properly as a scrapbook.

Section

A building section callout defines where a building section is cut through the plan and references the actual building section drawing with a drawing and sheet number.

1. Activate the Line tool, set the stroke width to 1, and turn off Fill. Click once to start the line.

2. Draw a line as shown in Figure 24.20. Double-click on the last inferred point to finish the line.

3. Activate the Split tool, and click on the two endpoints as shown (Figure 24.21).

4. Select the two ends, and assign a stroke width of 2.

5. Select the middle line, and assign a dash pattern to represent the section cut line.

6. Activate the Text tool, and add a text box on the long end of the section callout baseline. Enter the generic text 0/A.000. Reposition and resize the text box as needed (Figure 24.22).

7. Select the entire section callout, right-click on the selection, and choose Make Group so it functions properly as a scrapbook.

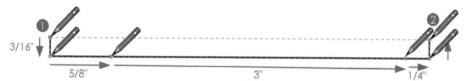

Figure 24.20 The baseline of the section callout.

Figure 24.21 The Split tool breaks lines into separate segments, which can have different Shape Style properties.

Figure 24.22 Add text to the section callout.

Detail

A detail callout defines the portion of a building condition to be further explained and enlarged and references the actual detail drawing with a drawing and sheet number.

1. Activate the Rectangle tool, set the stroke width to 1, and turn off the Fill. Press the up arrow key to switch to a rounded-corner rectangle, and immediately type a precise radius of .25, then press Enter (Figure 24.23).

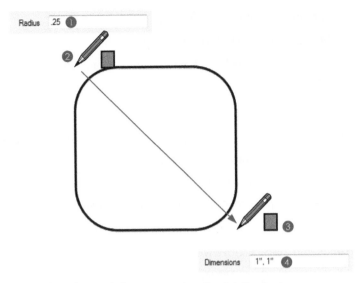

Figure 24.23 Draw a rectangle with rounded corners to start the detail callout.

2. Click once to define the start point of the rectangle.

3. Move your cursor away from the start point, and click to loosely define the dimensions.

4. Immediately type the precise dimensions 1", 1", then press Enter.

5. Use the Line tool to draw a leader line as shown in Figure 24.24.

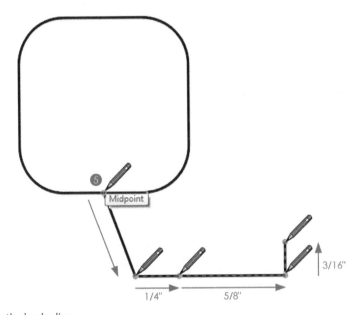

Figure 24.24 Draw the leader line.

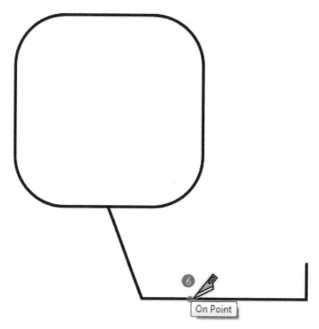

Figure 24.25 Use the Split tool to break the leader line into two segments.

6. Use the Split tool to break the leader line as shown in Figure 24.25.

7. Select the rectangle, and assign a dash pattern. Adjust the pattern scale as needed. Keep in mind that any entity can be modified after it is created.

8. Select the leader line, and assign a stroke width of .5.

9. Select the end of the leader line, and assign a stroke width of 2.

10. Activate the Text tool, and add a text box on the long end of the leader line. Enter the generic text 0/A.000. Reposition and resize the text box as needed (Figure 24.26).

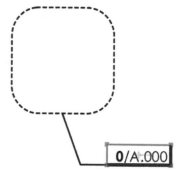

Figure 24.26 Add text to the detail callout.

11. Select the entire detail callout, right-click on the selection, and choose Make Group so it functions properly as a scrapbook.

Palette

You can use a palette scrapbook as a quick way to assign default settings. With most tools, you can hover in the Scrapbooks inspector and match the default properties of the active tool to a specific scrapbook. Add these entities to your palette so you can draw much more efficiently in LayOut.

TIP Entities that will never be sampled or inserted into a drawing can be placed on a locked layer. For example, the text that describes the scrapbook won't be imported—assign it to the BACKGROUND layer, then lock the BACKGROUND layer.

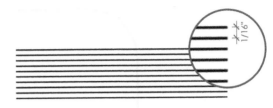

Figure 24.27 If you place several lines close together instead of placing just one, clicking on a line will be easy even when the palette is condensed into the smaller Scrapbooks inspector.

To create a palette scrapbook, follow these steps:

1. In the Pages Inspector, advance to the PALETTES page.
2. Draw a line approximately 2" long.
3. Using the Select tool, hold down the Ctrl key to make a copy, and then hold down the Shift key to lock the axis. Click and drag the line down by 1/16". immediately type "10x" to copy the line 10 times as shown in Figure 24.27.
4. Select all the lines, right-click on the selection, and choose Make Group.
5. Add a text box to the right of the group, and enter the generic text description on the first line and 0.00 pts on the second line (Figure 24.28).
6. Copy the group and the generic description down the page seven times.
7. Select the top group of lines, and change the stroke width to 0.18 pts in the Shape Style inspector. Also change the text description to Fine on the first line and 0.18 pts on the second line.
8. Change all stroke widths and corresponding descriptions as shown in Figure 24.29.
9. Select all the text descriptions, right-click on the selection, and choose Move to Layer > Background.
10. Lock the BACKGROUND layer. Entities on a locked layer cannot be sampled or inserted as a scrapbook.

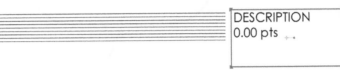

Figure 24.28 The beginning of a palette.

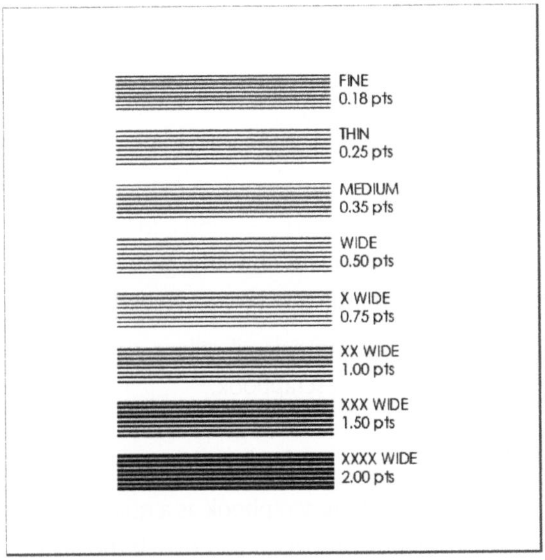

Figure 24.29 The final palette.

Schedules

Schedules are used to convey the quantities you'll need of products, such as doors, windows, and

finishes. A *schedule* in LayOut is actually very simple, created using the Table tool (Figure 20.30). Keep the following tips in mind when you're creating schedules in LayOut:

☑ There is no dynamic link to the entities you are scheduling, so make sure you count carefully. It is usually easier to catch schedule mistakes when the schedule and drawings are printed.

☑ Once you build a schedule, add it to a scrapbook collection for use on other projects.

☑ Use the Drawing tools in LayOut to complement complex schedules.

☑ It is easier to build schedules in Excel or Google Sheets. Then insert, format, etc. Use the same spreadsheet to start each schedule; this way, you can format all schedules the same way.

☑ When importing an Excel file, it is better to format using LayOut rather than import the formatting from Excel.

☑ Using the Style tool, you can sample a schedule, or LayOut table, and apply its formatting to another. This will apply the formatting by cell, so if you use the same rows for headings, everything will line up.

Saving Scrapbooks

Now that you have created a custom scrapbook, add it to your collections. Just follow these steps:

1. Click on the File drop-down menu, and choose Save as Scrapbook.

2. Select the RESOURCES/SCRAPBOOKS folder, and save it as BD_Annotations.

Now this scrapbook will always be available in the Scrapbooks inspector collections drop-down.

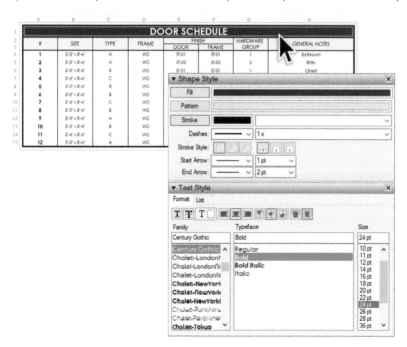

Figure 20.30 Use the Text Style inspector and Shape Style inspector to create numerous schedule options.

USING COLLECTIONS

Take a few minutes to experiment with your new creations.

1. Click on the File drop-down menu, and choose New.

2. Select the BD_Presentation - 8.5 x 11 Landscape template that you just created, and click Open.

3. In the Scrapbooks inspector, click on the Collections drop-down menu, and choose the BD_Annotations scrapbook.

Practice adding scrapbooks to your presentation and using scrapbooks as palettes. While you're practicing, keep the following tips in mind:

☑ Activate a tool, then hover over a scrapbook and click to absorb the scrapbook's properties as the tool's default settings.

☑ Tools can pull default settings from any scrapbook entity. For example, the Text tool can absorb default settings from lines, and the Line tool can absorb default settings from a piece of text within a scrapbook.

☑ With the Select tool active, click on a scrapbook in the Scrapbooks inspector, and then click in your presentation to place it.

☑ Scrapbooks are simply grouped LayOut entities. Use the Select tool to double-click into a scrapbook and modify it once it is inserted into your presentation. This operation is similar to navigating containers in SketchUp.

☑ When you insert a schedule (table), you can use the Document Setup/References window to relink to a different schedule. Or just use the scrapbook schedule as a palette to apply to new imports.

CHAPTER POINTS

☑ Download scrapbooks at **brightmandesigns.com/TSWFA**.

☑ Multiple entities must be grouped together to function as a single scrapbook.

☑ Be creative and develop your own scrapbooks and drawing style. There are no rules, so the possibilities are endless!

☑ A scrapbook can be one entity or a mixture of any entities available in LayOut, including images, SketchUp models, text, dimensions, and geometry.

☑ Anything that you use over and over should be made readily available as a scrapbook. Consider creating a Detail Library scrapbook full of 2D and 3D SketchUp details.

☑ Use the linear graphic style to add additional symbols, callouts, and palettes to expand your linear style scrapbooks.

Chapter 25

Exporting

I t's done! Time to export, print, stamp, permit, and start swinging hammers. In this
chapter, we will explore all the best practices on exporting.

To get the most out of your model, extract the most valuable information from it so you can share the
right information with clients and consultants.

EXPORTING TO PDF

The most likely export you'll need is a PDF. You can do this directly from LayOut; there's no need for
Adobe Acrobat. A PDF is optimized for sharing and printing—ideal to send to the print shop. Follow these
guidelines when exporting your final drawing set as a PDF.

1. Click on the File drop-down, and choose Export, then PDF.
2. Turn off Create PDF layers from LayOut layers.
3. Check on Show Export in PDF Viewer.
4. Click on Export. The PDF will open in your viewer so you can give it a once-over as a last check for
   errors, and make sure everything looks right.

TIP If the export files are too large, consider using jpg image compression, but keep the quality high.

EXPORTING TO CAD

At some point, you may want to move your SketchUp design into your favorite computer-aided design
(CAD) program. The model organization tools in this book make it simple to export your design as a
two-dimensional (2D) or three-dimensional (3D) model—and share your design with consultants so that

engineering drawings can be completed. Typically, consultants do not work with SketchUp, so you will need to either export to a 3D format they can work with or to a 2D format that is easily adapted to their layering system.

Exporting 3D

Exporting your SketchUp model to another 3D model format is the easiest way to communicate with other 3D programs. Depending on your needs, this method does not always provide the flexibility needed to utilize the model. If you do want to export to another 3D format, follow these steps:

1. Within SketchUp, click on the File drop-down menu and select Export > 3D Model (Figure 25.1).

2. Click on the Export type drop-down menu, and select the desired format. You can export to several formats, including **.dae, .kmz, .3ds, .dwg, .dxf, .fbx, .obj, .wrl,** and **.xsi.**

3. Click the Options button to adjust specific settings relating to the file type you are exporting. They will be different for each export file type. Figure 25.1 shows the .dwg settings.

4. Navigate to the TEMP folder (or the appropriate EXPORTS folder), add a YYMMDD folder, and then click the Export button to finish. A 3D model export typically maintains all layering and grouping; component instances are turned to blocks and maintain their connectivity.

TIP Working between SketchUp and Revit or any other 3D program? Check out SimLab's huge library of import and export extensions to get a clean transfer at **simlab-soft.com/3d-plugins/sketchup_plugins.aspx.**

Figure 25.1 The AutoCAD Export Options dialog box.

Exporting 2D

Typically, you export to 2D CAD to move into another CAD program, or you might just need to share 2D CAD backgrounds with other consultants. A major benefit of 2D CAD is that it is fairly fast and easy to use, and almost everyone in the design field knows how to use it. Sometimes you just need to get the job done. It is okay to think and design in SketchUp 3D and then refine and document your design in a familiar 2D CAD program. The SketchUp Workflow for Architecture is extremely flexible, so don't hesitate to abandon ship at this point and use another program if that is what works for you.

Exporting to a 2D CAD that everyone can use has different challenges. The main one is that the layers in most CAD programs are not set up the way they are in SketchUp. You can get around this by exporting 2D .dwg's from SketchUp to CAD by layers or line weights. You will export once for the existing doors, windows, walls, fixtures, etc., and then export another set for new entities (Figure 25.2).

Creating Scenes

Now it's time to set up the scenes that represent each piece of the .dwg backgrounds. You can visualize the scenes using a scene organization diagram (SOD) for the level 01, new, exterior walls (Figure 25.3). The 3D view shown in the figures are in perspective for effect; they will actually be top-down parallel projection views.

1. Adjust the layer visibility, style, and shadow settings to reflect the desired background export.

2. In the Scenes dialog, click on the plus sign (+) to add a new scene.

3. Repeat this process for each desired background export (Figure 25.4).

TIP Every scene you create must have the same camera view. To ensure that they are all the same, set the camera view to top, select all the BKGD scenes in the Scenes dialog, then click the Scene Update button; update only the camera view and uncheck all other properties. Click Update. Now all the scenes have the same camera view.

Exporting 2D Graphic

Now that you have scenes created, export them to a .dwg for use in other CAD programs.

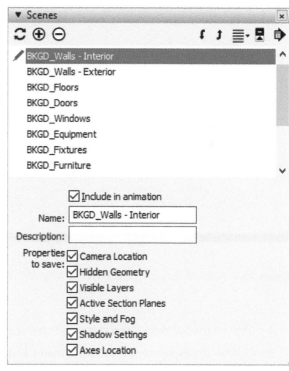

Figure 25.2 Each scene will be its own .dwg export and ultimately its own external reference to the consultant's background drawings.

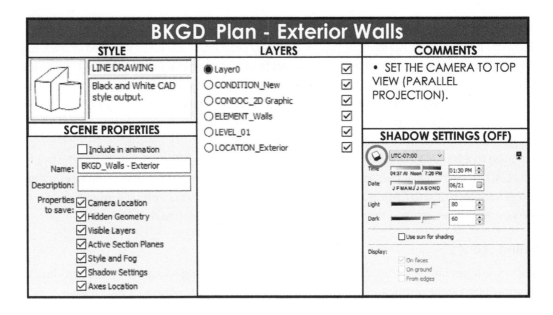

BKGD_Plan - Exterior Walls

STYLE	LAYERS	COMMENTS
LINE DRAWING Black and White CAD style output.	◉ Layer0 ☑ ○ CONDITION_New ☑ ○ CONDOC_2D Graphic ☑ ○ ELEMENT_Walls ☑ ○ LEVEL_01 ☑ ○ LOCATION_Exterior ☑	• SET THE CAMERA TO TOP VIEW (PARALLEL PROJECTION).

SCENE PROPERTIES

☐ Include in animation

Name: BKGD_Walls - Exterior

Description:

Properties to save:
☑ Camera Location
☑ Hidden Geometry
☑ Visible Layers
☑ Active Section Planes
☑ Style and Fog
☑ Shadow Settings
☑ Axes Location

SHADOW SETTINGS (OFF)

UTC-07:00

Time 04:37 AI Noon 7:26 PM 01:30 PM

Date JFMAMJJASOND 06/21

Light — 80

Dark — 60

☐ Use sun for shading

Display:
☑ On faces
☐ On ground
☐ From edges

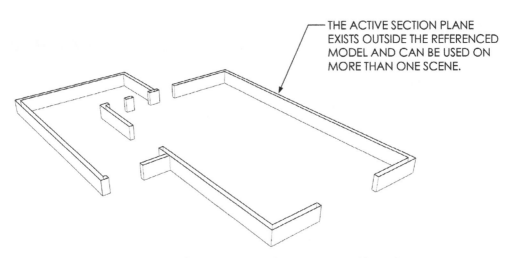

THE ACTIVE SECTION PLANE EXISTS OUTSIDE THE REFERENCED MODEL AND CAN BE USED ON MORE THAN ONE SCENE.

Figure 25.3 Swap the ELEMENT_Walls layer for other ELEMENT layers to create additional existing export scenes.

1. Click on the File drop-down menu and choose Export, then 2D Graphic (Figure 25.5).

2. Click on the Export type drop-down menu, and choose .dwg.

3. Click on the Options button to open the Export Options dialog. Set the format to AutoCAD 2000. (The year 2000 is a pretty good year for compatibility between software packages and AutoCAD versions. If you know the exact version you need, choose it instead.)

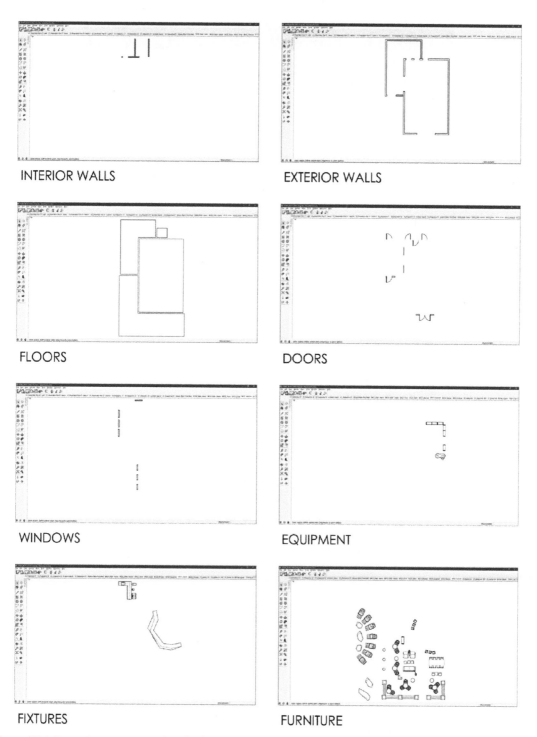

Figure 25.4 Exporting a separate .dwg file for each layer used in CAD gives consultants the flexibility to build any plan they need.

Figure 25.5 The 2D Export dialog.

4. Navigate to the appropriate EXPORTS folder, and add a folder with today's date in the YYMMDD format to keep things organized.

5. Click the Export button to finish.

Using the DWG Exports

Once all the exports are completed, they can be compiled into a single CAD drawing to create any type of plan needed (Figure 25.6). Ideally, you will e-mail all these background .dwg files to consultants or host them for download on a server. Then the consultants can insert the drawings into their CAD program

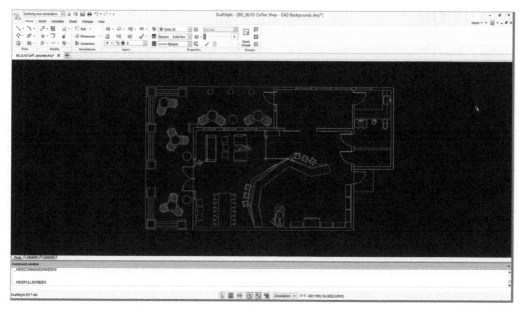

Figure 25.6 This proposed plan was created by referencing several .dwg exports from SketchUp into a 2D CAD program. Each .dwg reference is on a different colored layer; each color represents the possibility for varying line weights.

however they like. When you update the design, re-export the backgrounds and then just send a message to the consultants so they know to download and overwrite their files. This method is by far the most efficient way to keep everyone on the same page, but it requires all consultants to be proficient in 2D CAD.

For consultants who don't really know how to use CAD this way, you might find it easier to just do it for them. Simply reference the DWG exports into your favorite CAD program to create a series of drawings for them. Be sure to maintain the drawing origin for each reference to ensure that all drawings stack right into place. At this point, assign line weights to each of the external references as a whole.

TIP If you don't have a CAD program to compile the drawings, you can import all the drawings into SketchUp as .dwg files and then export the entire file as a 3D .dwg.

You can also use the 2D export to abandon ship and then finish the documentation in your favorite 2D CAD program. Reference the files in the same way, and then you can explode, redraw, and modify your file at will. Keep in mind that when you export 2D CAD snapshots, there is no connectivity between the components—they do not become blocks. These DWGs are basically exploded, simple line work that might require some rebuilding and redrawing.

CONCLUSION

Well, you made it! This is the end, and if I could send you off with some parting advice, it would be this:

☑ Watch the tutorials! Print is great for a quick reference; video tutorials are great for learning new concepts by following along step by step.

☑ Buy ConDoc! If you are fully invested in the SketchUp Workflow for Architecture and you are a professional who charges fixed fees and looks for ways to shave hours, ConDoc will make you money. It also includes a professional forum and monthly office hours so you can connect with others who are using this system to produce professional work.

☑ If you are in a pinch, we have a paid 3D helpline service to coach you through difficult tasks, clean up a model, and get you back on track.

☑ If you realize you just need it done, we have a team of professionals to model, render, or draft your project. We offer design, drafting, visualization, and workflow training services. So if you need it done fast, or if you need to expand your business by leveraging my team, don't hesitate to call.

☑ I could work on this book forever. Technology is changing so fast, and new products and programs are being launched every day. Stay up-to-date on the latest products, tutorials, and revelations on our blog at **brightmandesigns.com/blog**.

CHAPTER POINTS

☑ Export to PDF before printing; make sure you uncheck Create PDF layers from LayOut layers.

☑ Most consultants will know exactly what to do with 2D CAD background exports. AutoCAD 2000 is a format that just about anyone can open.

☑ 3D exports are typically used to migrate to a different program.

☑ Stay in touch and up-to-date at **brightmandesigns.com**.

Index